Border Encounters

Border Encounters

Asymmetry and Proximity at Europe's Frontiers

Edited by
Jutta Lauth Bacas and William Kavanagh

berghahn
NEW YORK · OXFORD
www.berghahnbooks.com

Published in 2013 by

Berghahn Books

www.berghahnbooks.com

© 2013, 2016 Jutta Lauth Bacas and William Kavanagh
First paperback edition published in 2016

Library of Congress Cataloging-in-Publication Data

Border encounters : asymmetry and proximity at Europe's frontiers / edited by
Jutta Lauth Bacas and William Kavanagh.
    pages cm
  Includes bibliographical references and index.
  ISBN 978-1-84545-396-1 (hardback) — ISBN 978-1-78533-219-7 (paperback) —
  ISBN 978-1-78238-138-9 (ebook)
  1. Borderlands—Europe—Case studies. 2. Europe—Ethnic relations—Case
studies. 3. Regionalism—Europe—Case studies. I. Lauth Bacas, Jutta, 1956–
author, editor of compilation. II. Kavanagh, William.
  JN34.5.B66 2013
  303.48′24—dc23

                                                                    2013014952

British Library Cataloguing in Publication Data

A catalogue record for this book is available from the British Library

ISBN 978-1-84545-396-1 hardback
ISBN 978-1-78533-219-7 paperback
ISBN 978-1-78238-138-9 ebook

To the memory of Daphne Berdahl
1964–2007

Contents

Illustrations

Introduction

Border Encounters
Asymmetry and Proximity at Europe's Frontiers

Jutta Lauth Bacas and William Kavanagh

Europe has experienced tremendous changes over the past two decades, and some of the most significant are those affecting its borders. The era of political and socio-economic transformation after 1989 reconfigured the European landscape to an extent not seen since the Second World War. The dissolution of the Soviet Union, the dismemberment of Yugoslavia and the enlargement of the European Union – particularly the accession of twelve countries to the European Union (EU) in 2004 and a further two in 2007 – entailed complex processes affecting many state borders. Borders that had been closed were opened (the fall of the Berlin Wall being the most prominent example), but borders were also redefined, radically reshaping the 'inside' and 'outside' of the EU. Previously open borders were strengthened, and in some cases of former political coalitions (the Soviet Union, Yugoslavia, Czechoslovakia) falling apart, borders now exist where there once were none.

These complex processes of borders being opened in some parts of Europe and redefined or reinforced in others have also fundamentally changed the social relationships of those living in borderland regions. The aim of the present volume is to investigate ongoing developments at some of these changing borders from the ground up, taking a local perspective. The primary focus is on border encounters in Europe (though not necessarily limited to EU countries), that is, face-to-face interactions and relations of compliance and confrontation as people bargain and exchange goods and information while manoeuvring at, and most importantly be-

---

Notes for this chapter begin on page 21.

yond, state borders. The second aim is to analyse social hierarchies that are questioned, contested or confirmed in these border encounters. Since frontiers bring people together in spatial proximity (though clearly such physical proximity does not necessarily entail social proximity), the present anthropological case studies from a number of European borderlands wish to shed light on the question of how, and to what extent, the border context 'colours' and shapes the changing interactions and social relationships between people at the frontier. Of great interest are the hierarchical relations between the people who meet at international borders: permanent residents on one or another side of an international frontier, as well as travellers, tourists, petty traders and pensioners in interaction with border guards, police officers or security personnel with the power to grant or to delay passage beyond the physical limit of the frontier. In the changing Europe of recent decades, a new and multifaceted reality – far from the metaphorical figure of the omnipotent guard in front of Kafka's 'Castle' – has developed in the border encounters the present volume aims to investigate in more detail.

Border Studies in Anthropological Discourse

Anthropological interest in borders did not begin with the political and socio-economic transformations in Europe in the years following the collapse of the Soviet Union, but those events certainly helped to make the 'anthropology of borders' one of the 'growth industries' of the discipline today. The changes in the geopolitical landscape of Europe were paralleled by social scientists' increasing interest in understanding and analysing social processes concerning and occurring at borders.

In many ways it was Norwegian anthropologist Fredrik Barth's introduction to the collection of essays he edited in 1969 under the title *Ethnic Groups and Boundaries: The Social Organization of Cultural Difference* that prompted anthropologists to question the structural-functionalist assumptions of bounded tribes and communities, and the view of culture focused on shared patterns of meaning that left little room for change. For Barth (1969: 10), 'ethnic groups are categories of ascription and identification by the actors themselves'. He argues that

> the critical focus of investigation from this point of view becomes the ethnic boundary that defines the group, not the cultural stuff that it encloses.... Ethnic groups are not merely or necessarily based on the occupation of exclusive territories; and the different ways in which they are maintained, not only by a once-and-for-all recruitment but by continual expression and validation, need to be analysed. (Barth 1969: 15)

Later, in 1974, a pair of North American anthropologists, John Cole and Eric Wolf, published *The Hidden Frontier: Ecology and Ethnicity in an Alpine Valley*, a study of two neighbouring villages on the provincial border between the Romance-speaking Trentino and the German-speaking South Tyrol in Italy. Although the villages are only a mile apart, Cole and Wolf (1974: 281) conclude that the two communities 'differ not only in internal structure and in their external relations to larger polities. They are also engaged in essentially distinct symbolic games.' They point out that the theoretical approach of their study

> supports the statements made recently by Fredrik Barth in an introduction to a book on ethnic groups and boundaries, where he emphasizes that boundaries are created and persist despite a flow of personnel and social relations across them (Barth 1969: 10–11). We are sympathetic to his view that since it is the ethnic boundary and the conceptualizations of a people themselves about the boundary that define interaction between two ethnic groups, one must direct attention to understanding the ethnic boundary. (1974: 281)

And while admitting that they have followed an approach essentially similar to Barth's in their own study, Cole and Wolf (1974: 281) go on to state: 'Yet we have found that the actions of people at the local level – particularly with regard to interlocal contact across the ethnic boundary – do not respond only to local influence, but are affected by actions and ideals of a much wider area.' All of this ties in with their emphatic claim in the preface to the book (Cole and Wolf 1974: xi): 'We strongly believe that the study of small populations which form components of complex societies must take account of that complexity before the interpretation of what happens "on the ground" can become meaningful.'

The social anthropologists Hastings Donnan and Thomas M. Wilson, authors of a number of fine scholarly publications on the anthropology of borders, in which they also evaluate Cole and Wolf's (1974) scientific approach and contribution to border studies, point out in their book *Borders: Frontiers of Identity, Nation and State* (Donnan and Wilson 1999: 33):

> Cole and Wolf could be said to represent the coming together of a symbolic boundary focus with a political economy perspective which attempts to situate local boundary making within wider historical and political processes.... By introducing a political economy perspective to Barth's emphasis on symbolic boundaries, Cole and Wolf effectively marked an important transition in the anthropological study of boundaries and heralded the beginning of a new form of inquiry.

Bringing the anthropological interest in what is happening 'on the ground' together with an awareness of the importance of the wider social context that deeply influences the events and interaction in the local arena is also an important starting point for the present volume, where both the physical and social proximity of the actors involved in face-to-face interaction on the border, as well as the hierarchical setting in which they might interact due to asymmetric economic factors and complex state regulations, are taken into account in the following chapters.

Since the pioneering works of Barth and Cole and Wolf, anthropologists have used their research at international borders to examine the often subtle interrelations between local communities and their nation states and neighbouring nation states, showing in more detail how proximity to a border may influence local culture. Starting from the realization, noted by Donnan and Wilson (1999: 40), that since all borders are arbitrary constructions based on cultural convention, in a sense all borders are metaphors (although the boundaries of nation states are always more than metaphorical), other authors have extended the terms 'border' and 'borderlands' to literary theory, cultural studies and debates about ethnic, class and gendered identities. Dissatisfied with anthropological theorizing about 'community' that focused mainly on structure, British anthropologist Anthony Cohen (1985: 12) took up a number of Barth's ideas and developed a new definition of the concept of community, stating that the term 'community':

> expresses a relational idea: the opposition of one community to others or to other social entities. Indeed, it will be argued that the use of the word is only occasioned by the desire or need to express such a distinction. It seems appropriate, therefore, to focus our examination of the nature of community on the element which embodies this sense of discrimination, namely, the boundary. By definition, the boundary marks the beginning and end of a community. But why is such marking necessary? The simple answer is that the boundary encapsulates the identity of the community.... Boundaries are marked because communities interact in some way or other with entities from which they are, or wish to be, distinguished.

Cohen went on to say that while the marking of the boundary may be physically expressed, 'not all the components of any boundary are so objectively apparent. They may be thought of, rather, as existing in the minds of the beholders. This being so, the boundary may be perceived in rather different terms, not only by people on opposite sides of it, but also by people on the same side' (Cohen 1985: 12).

An important characteristic of the boundary is its openness to multiple interpretations or meanings, to 'multivalency' or 'polysemy'. In his writing, Cohen (1985: 13) concluded that 'consciousness of community is, then, encapsulated in perception of its boundaries'. Thus, both the term community and the term boundary imply the idea of a relation to an Other. All identity, therefore, is constructed in the double sense of similarity and difference with respect to Others. Self-definition depends on antithesis, identity on counter-identity. As he said in another book, Cohen (1982: 2) was intent on advancing the view that community difference and identity rest not on structures, but in the minds of those who perceive and live them, a view of social organization 'as a means through which people order, value and express their knowledge of their worlds of experience, rather than as a structural determination of such knowledge and experience'. This epistemological approach to boundary studies, which is well aware that borders do not exist 'per se' but have to be understood also as perceived boundaries that become relevant and meaningful to social actors in relation to an (imagined or present) Other, is essential for the anthropological contribution in the present volume.

However, both Cohen and Barth have had their critics. Donnan and Wilson (1999: 25) pointed out that Cohen's recognition that it is not enough to focus on the relations within a local boundary and that any local collectivity must be viewed in the wider context of which it forms a part, 'often comes down to … an argument about the ways in which external forces can be manipulated to symbolic advantage at the local level', with the result that 'one side of the boundary between localities and the structures beyond has tended to receive rather more attention than the other'. They went on to note that 'similar criticisms have been leveled at Barth … he too tends to focus on one side rather than the other, emphasizing internal identification rather than external constraint and the shaping influence of wider structures, such as those of class and the state' (Donnan and Wilson 1999: 25). Their comment is another hint at the relevance of hierarchies *between* social actors and the asymmetries of their power relations that might gain special importance in border encounters, where social actors are not only engaged in cross-cultural communication but frequently have to deal also with the constraints of a hierarchical setting as well. The present volume aims to present more empirical evidence of these complex processes and to investigate in more detail how social actors deal with asymmetry occurring in cross-border encounters.

In 1989, historian Peter Sahlins published *Boundaries: The Making of France and Spain in the Pyrenees,* a study of a Catalan valley divided by the border between France and Spain, which has influenced anthropologists' as well as historians' understanding of nationalism and state formation. Sahlins's (1989: 8–9) basic thesis was that

> States did not simply impose their values and boundaries on local society. Rather, local society was a motive force in the formation and consolidation of

nationhood and the territorial state. The political boundary appeared in the borderland as the outcome of national political events, as a function of the different strengths, interests, and (ultimately) histories of France and Spain. But the shape and significance of the boundary line was constructed out of local social relations in the borderland.

Citing Benedict Anderson's (1983: 15) description of nations as 'imagined communities', in the sense that they are created and invented, 'because the members of even the smallest nations will never know most of their fellow-members, meet them, or even hear of them, yet in the minds of each lives the image of their communion', Sahlins (1989: 9) commented that this definition 'usefully corrects the positivist conception of national identity as a product of "nation building", focusing our attention instead on the symbolic construction of national and political identities'. Pointing out that other authors have emphasized the importance of differentiation in the development of ethnic, communal and national identity, Sahlins (1989: 9) stated: 'In the French-Spanish borderland, it is this sense of difference – of "us" and "them" – which was so crucial in defining an identity. Imagining oneself a member of a community or a nation meant perceiving a significant difference between oneself and the other across the boundary.'

It is important to note that according to Sahlins (1989), the proximity of the Other across the boundary contributed to the construction of national identity long before the local society was assimilated to a dominant centre. By introducing the aspect of proximity as a crucial element in the process of constructing and structuring national identity, he moved borderland communities from the margins into the focus of attention of social anthropologists as well as historians studying the appearance of national identity in various contexts. Sahlins's study also showed, as Donnan and Wilson (1999: 52) stated in their review, 'that there is no intrinsic, inherent, nor necessary relationship between territory, identity and sovereignty. Borderlands are places where these converge in ways which must be interrogated, in order to discover the role which culture plays in wider processes of state and national politics, economics and society'.

An important development in the anthropology of borderlands was Wilson and Donnan's work on the role of the state and relations of power as they are experienced and contested at the local level of national borders. In the edited volume *Border Identities: Nation and State at International Frontiers* (1998), Wilson and Donnan and their contributors scrutinized the influence of state power on cultural identities and everyday life at the periphery of the state. They wrote: 'Borders are always domains of contested power, in which local, national and international groups negotiate relations of subordination and control' (Wilson and Donnan 1998: 10). They went on to refer to the negotiation of identity in places where the border might simultaneously bind people together or separate and divide them:

> In terms of their ethnic identities, at least three main types of border population can be identified: (i) those who share ethnic ties across the border as well as with those residing at their own state's geographical core; (ii) those who are differentiated by cross-border ethnic bonds from other residents of their state; and (iii) those who are members of the national majority in their state, and have no ethnic ties across the state's borders. (Wilson and Donnan 1998: 14)

One could, however, point out that there is certainly a fourth type: those who do not share (or do not wish to recognize that they may share) ethnic ties with those at their own state's geographical core and, at the same time, have no ethnic ties (or do not recognize that they have ethnic ties) across the state's borders.

Donnan and Wilson further pursued their interest in comparative consideration of state borders' importance to the construction of identity and culture in *Borders: Frontiers of Identity, Nation and the State* (1999). Extending their analysis of borders as domains of contested power and drawing on comparative ethnographic material concerning highly conflictive borders (for example, that of Northern Ireland with the Republic of Ireland), they elaborated their argument on the role of border regions in the processes of negotiating, strengthening or weakening of state power. Their analytical approach took as a starting point the cultural aspect of international borders and the role that culture as everyday practice plays in the social construction and negotiation of these borders. Wilson and Donnan (2005a: 3) later commented: 'The ethnography of everyday life in border communities is simultaneously the study of the daily life of the state', admitting that 'state power is always unstable and in continuous need of being re-established' (Wilson and Donnan 2005a: 4) by meaning-making and meaning-carrying cultural practices. Donnan and Wilson (1999: 62) concluded that 'borders are simultaneously structures and processes, things and relationships, histories and events'. Inspired by Donnan and Wilson' emphasis on a dynamic approach to border studies, the editors of this present volume decided to investigate one aspect of social interaction at state boundaries, namely, the dynamic interrelation of proximity and asymmetry in face-to-face encounters at changing (be they opening or closing) European borders.

In the growing field of border studies, an international research network, called EastBordNet, aims to explore the ongoing transformations of 'Eastern' European borders, drawing together researchers focusing both on the north-east (the Baltic area) and on the south-east (the Balkan area) of Europe.[1] Under the title 'Remaking Eastern Borders in Europe', the processes of redefining borders at the eastern periphery of Europe are studied from an anthropological perspective. In the framework of this EastBord-Net programme, anthropologist Sarah Green (2009) introduces a new conceptual perspective to border studies by discussing the differentiation between borderlines, traces and tidemarks. She reviews the anthropological critique of conceptualizing the border as a geographical line by stressing that 'lines are obviously insufficient, in themselves, as an understanding of border' (Green 2009: 10), since thinking of the border as a line tends not to take into consideration how people actually experience this borderline in their everyday lives. She avoids introducing the term 'borderlands', as used by Alvarez (1995), or the term 'frontier', as per Donnan and Wilson (1999), but suggests the metaphor of 'tidemark' to mix the notion of a particular place with the sense of time passing: 'tidemark combines space and historical time, and envisages both space and time as being lively and contingent' (Green 2009: 18). Green (2012: 125) sees borders not simply as located somewhere *here* (italics in the original), but as multiply qualified places, related to other historical, political or economic entities and also located in past and future/imagined experiences of people living there. With her understanding of transforming borders as 'tidemarks', Green argues for a multidisciplinary approach to the study of borders, which 'appear, disappear and change shape, location and meaning in line with activities, relations, conflicts, ideas, and regulations that come together, leaving their particular mark as borders until something else comes along'.[2]

In discussing border studies and its related concepts, Robert Alvarez (2012) also reflects on some methodological implications of recent scholarly investigations on borders. Especially in studies investigating the Mexican-U.S. border (to which he mainly refers), Alvarez considers the unchanging presence of the geopolitical borderline to also have shaped the anthropology of borderlands, reproducing a rather state-centric approach. However, in the quest for a better understanding of the reality of the border, more recent studies have focused on connections and crossings along the Mexican-U.S. border (Alvarez 2012: 27) and on the forms and types of connectivity that the border zone creates. This concept of connectivity and the newly growing interest in networks of social, cultural and economic exchange across lines of strong geopolitical separation (Alvarez 2012: 28) echo the reasoning of European social scientists who have investigated 'connectivity' as a key feature of social interactions and multiple exchanges between the physically separated shores of the Mediterranean (Horden and Purcell 2000; Kavanagh and Lauth Bacas 2011).

To summarize the above presentation and discussion, we would like to stress that border studies has turned out to be one of the fastest growing and fruitful branches of the discipline of anthropology, as well as of other social and political sciences. As the review of the relevant literature shows, two main features appear to characterize the anthropological focus on international borders. One definitive common feature of anthropological studies of borderlands is an emphasis on the cultural aspects of international borders, where the social meaning attributed to borders is accented to provide a better understanding of the role culture might play in processes of boundary construction or border maintenance. Another important characteristic of the anthropology of borders is the emphasis on first-hand information gathered through fieldwork and participant observation in border areas themselves. As already noted, anthropological border studies take as their main premise that 'some things can only occur at borders' (Donnan and Wilson 1999: 4). Though of various sorts, these social 'things' have in common that they happen at a meeting place between two states and different national cultures. Since life at the border is thus structured very specifically by the presence or proximity of the Other, the present volume looks at various forms and features of 'proximity' as a main point of interest in all the contributions presented here. Because international borders are simultaneously shaped by wider processes of state and national politics, they are also places where institutionalized hierarchies and asymmetries between social actors exist and might be negotiated, processes that all the contributors to this volume have also taken into consideration.

Proximity and Asymmetry in Border Encounters

This summary will discuss three basic features of the underlying theoretical assumptions of the present volume, and the following chapters will further develop them in one way or another. First, border areas that mark off one state from another frequently turn out to be, unsurprisingly, areas of ethnic tension or cross-national conflict. In many cases the geopolitical borderline itself may be the result of international conflicts. Precisely because of their contested geographical position, border regions often become battlegrounds for conflicting parties with opposed claims, either international or intra-national. Second, and despite the sword of Damocles of territorial disputes and conflicts, border regions are also most likely to be social settings for cross-national encounters. Numerous anthropological case studies from various border regions have shown that hardly any border control system, even one with a fierce security apparatus, can ever completely suppress social contacts across borders, although it may severely curtail them. Third, whereas border areas are important fields for defining the state's territory and sovereignty, they are, as anthropological evidence shows, mainly peripheral to the national centres of power and decision-making. Border denizens' relation to the state of which they are supposed to be an integral part may itself turn out to be a source of conflict. State agents may treat members of their own nation state differently from members of the nation state across the border and from third-country nationals, especially in cases where the latter arrive without visa documents and thus are considered to have crossed the border illegally. In this regard borders can offer special insight into how social actors relate to 'their' nation state. According to Donnan and Haller (2000: 8), social anthropologists at borders can explore how those who cross and live alongside them manage competing loyalties and multiple identities.

It is important to keep in mind that no two borders are identical in all respects, as Wilson and Donnan (1998: 12) recognized when they said that '*a priori* assumptions about the nature of "the border" are likely to founder when confronted with empirical data; far from being a self-evident, analytical given which can be applied regardless of context, the "border" must be interrogated for its subtle and sometimes not so subtle shifts in meaning and form according to setting.'

Features of locality have to be understood as strong elements in the process of constructing social identity at the border, as Sarah Green underlined (Green 2005: 5). Since most border regions are set apart from other areas of the national territory by the features mentioned above, border-landers' sense of identity and belonging may differ from that of residents of more central, more developed or more powerful areas of the state. In this respect we can speak of the emergence of a 'border identity' that takes into account the specific locality and proximity to the Other present in the region under investigation. Acknowledging the danger of reifying a highly contested category, we can use the term 'border culture' to refer to the ensemble of locality, social practices and border identity, stressing the specificity of 'what happens on borders'. In this anthropological understanding, the notion of border culture is closely linked to the physical existence of international borders and the reality of state control, which may result in a frontier that is either 'soft' or 'hard', meaning that the border may be more or less 'porous'.

International borders are social fields for defining difference and distances, and at the same time are places conducive to cross-cultural encounters and proximity. As has been pointed out, borders 'are where the "space of flows" meet (or collide?) with the "space of places"' (Anderson, O'Dowd and Wilson 2003: 10). Face-to-face interaction at the border brings people with different ethnic and national backgrounds into close social contact and physical proximity at the same time. But the underlying institutionalization and hierarchy of the border setting often goes hand in hand with 'backstage' activities where actors seek to reach personal goals by manipulating the Other. Or as M. Anderson (1996: 7) noted: 'Frontiers are the limits of permissible behaviour, but these limits are necessarily perceived in very different ways by different people.' In the fluidity of the face-to-face encounter at the border, social actors sometimes try to create mutual understanding and intimacy in order to arrange a personal deal. The point to reflect on is the interconnection of antagonism and asymmetries involved in face-to-face border interaction, which will be the main interest of the following ethnographic case studies.

The present volume presents new anthropological contributions on various forms of face-to-face relations at international borders, including case studies on conflictive interaction with state agents, case studies on smuggling and bribery at the border and studies on the reception of 'clandestine' migrants arriving in Europe. The contributions presented here are unique in their investigation and exploration of precisely this interrelation between physical proximity and social asymmetry, whereby they focus on aspects that until now have been under-researched in other borderland studies. The central dimension of the analysis is the interaction of social actors, often in an antagonistic, conflictive relationship, establishing proximity through face-to-face contacts in a specific border context.

In analysing these diverse, often conflicting processes, physical proximity is understood as a key category characterizing the spatial closeness of social actors involved in cross-border interactions. The interesting point about proximity occurring in border encounters is that the border situation brings the actors involved into social and physical contact, whereupon they are able to build some sort of social relationship in the framework of nation states bordering each other, although they are often strangers. These social encounters in borderlands may include physical closeness quite different from that experienced in other places and forms of social interaction. For example, common consensus holds that a meticulous body check of passengers boarding a plane is but a standard routine, even though very private zones of the body are touched in public with many viewers present. Neither are travellers' personal belongings any longer 'private matters'. Who, if not a security officer or a border guard, would want or be allowed to rummage through someone's personal luggage or handbag? In other words, the border brings security officers and travellers into both physical closeness and rather intimate interactions in a very particular way. The present volume will present various such cases that explore and discuss in detail who the actors involved are and how they get into relations of proximity.

However, not all the chapters in this book discuss the often fleeting, nearly anonymous types of proximity such as that between travellers and border police, or immigrants and immigration control officers. Some focus instead on long-term relations of social proximity that permanent residents of villages and towns near a borderline maintain with their neighbours living on the other side of the frontier.

A second category central to the following case studies is the concept of social asymmetry. According to Bourdieu (1984), asymmetry occurs whenever one actor occupies a higher position than another in the social hierarchy of the different types of capital they have access to. These asymmetries, as they relate to economic, social, cultural and symbolic capital, are not fixed but produced and reproduced over time in historically changing forms of social interaction. Based on this assumption, asymmetry in border encounters can be understood as social relations that bring actors into a hierarchical relationship involving asymmetry especially with regard to the nation state of which they are or are not members. Membership (or not) of the state one wishes to enter – one of the most relevant symbolic resources in borderland encounters – largely defines and structures the interactions of both strangers and neighbours meeting at a border. As Wilson and Donnan (2005a) have argued elsewhere, state power is always present at the edge of the state, investing its representatives with authority and means of coercion in the borderland. The contributors to the present volume analyse and elaborate this subtle relationship between asymmetry and its recognition or subversion based on solid ethnographic fieldwork, showing how social asymmetry becomes highly relevant in some of the border settings under investigation, whereas it may be less important in others. This understanding of social behaviour on redefined European borders, informed by long-term ethnography, permits the examination of processes related to border crossings from the ground up, in a local perspective. All the authors engaged here in investigating European border encounters are interested in the question of the circumstances and ways in which partners in hierarchical relationships interact and react to the underlying asymmetry at the very moment of the border encounter. Since borderlands are also transitional spheres of negotiating and challenging state power, some contributions present more explicit examples of how social actors in specific fields handled or manipulated asymmetry in power relations.

The contributions to this volume help expand this theoretical discussion and further contextualize the key terms 'proximity' and 'asymmetry' with regard to European border encounters. This contextualization becomes even more interesting when their focus turns to the present EU enlargement and the actual processes of opening and redefining borders of the European Union. As borders in Europe are constantly made and remade by the social constructions of those who live and work on them, the relations of actors engaged in borderland encounters are similarly defined and redefined in an ongoing process. Finally, the essays presented in this volume encourage reflection on some of the political determinants of social interactions at both the internal and external borders of the European Union, with special reference to the Schengen Agreement and the European Policy of Migration and Asylum.

Changing Border Encounters in Today's Europe

The following chapters especially emphasize investigation of changing forms of interactions and changing dynamics of asymmetry and hierarchy that have recently become observable in numerous border encounters. Fine-tuned anthropological case studies from EU countries such as Spain, Italy and Greece, and from non-EU countries like Ukraine, Georgia and Turkey, explore how cultural differences are perceived and negotiated in personal encounters at the border, where the social setting often gives rise to antagonistic and hostile positioning of the cultural Other. The cases are grouped and presented according to three main themes that are central to characterizing major trends and developments in borderland regions in various European countries.

Border encounters on Europe's eastern frontiers are framed and structured by a basic divide between EU countries and non-EU countries, as well as the divide between the Schengen Area and the non-Schengen world. The European Commision Home Affairs office defines the Schengen Area as an 'area without internal borders' based on a treaty that came into effect in 1985 and led to the removal of systematic border controls between the participating countries and the simultaneous enhancement of border controls at entry points to the Schengen Area.[3] By 2012 the area encompassed most EU states (except the United Kingdom, Ireland, Cyprus, Bulgaria and Romania) and included a few associated non-EU countries (Iceland, Norway, Switzerland and Lichtenstein).[4]

Although member countries of 'Schengenland' have abolished regular police controls at their internal frontiers and tightened controls at their external borders, national borders as the geopolitical boundaries of the member states certainly continue to exist. EU states whose land or sea borders became external borders of the Schengen zone are obliged to maintain strict border surveillance and perform obligatory checks on travellers exiting or entering the area. The European Commission is entitled to address any failure on the part of a Schengen state to fulfil its obligation to patrol its section of the external border.[5] Enhanced efforts to control entry into the Schengen Area have become particularly relevant in terms of preventing and fighting the trafficking of human beings and controlling and managing irregular migration to Europe.[6] Fears of 'waves' of irregular migrants clandestinely entering the EU via land and sea routes[7] were widely discussed in the European press after the Arab Spring and led to political reactions by some member states. In July 2012, following an initiative made by France and Germany, the EU accepted a 'reform' of the Schengen Treaty that allowed Schengen countries to again carry out passport checks for incoming travellers at national borders 'for a limited period'.[8] These dynamics of the shifting politics of border control and border regimes in Europe will be further discussed below.

The Collection

The first common theme to be investigated by the contributors to this volume is the theme of Opening Borders, which concerns new forms of social interaction and cross-border contact that were made feasible by the reduction of on-the-spot border controls between most EU countries following the signing of the Schengen Agreement in 1985. Although 'limited' passport controls of travellers arriving at ports or airports were reintroduced in 2012 by some EU countries that saw themselves as affected by irregular migration, the overall architecture of the 2009 Stockholm Programme (a five-year plan with guidelines for justice and home affairs of EU member states for the years 2010–2014), with its stated intention of creating 'an open and secure Europe serving and protecting citizens', is still in effect.[9] Therefore the chapters in the section Opening Borders will address altered processes along European borders and review the social consequences of the Schengen Treaty before the partial reform of July 2012.

The chapters in the second part of the collection investigate the theme of Strengthening Borders, addressing recent developments at the frontiers of a number of central and eastern European nations. The third and last section of the book centres on the theme of Crossing Forbidden Borders, examining, amongst other forms of crossing 'forbidden' borders, the irregular entry of undocumented migrants to the territory of the European Union. All the contributions emphasize processes of connectivity in border encounters, which are framed or shaped by contrasts in the social standing or hierarchies of the actors involved.

Opening Borders

The cases presented in the first part of the collection, referring to the 'opening' borders between member states of the European Union, examine changes occurring on the inter-German border (before and after reunification), the German-Polish border, the Czech-Austrian border and the Portuguese-Spanish border.

The first chapter, 'Consumer Rites: The Politics of Consumption in a Re-unified Germany', by Daphne Berdahl, explores transformations that occurred at the former East German borderland village of Kella in the immediate post-reunification period. When the Berlin Wall fell, people who lived along the recently dismantled inter-German border found their lives drastically altered. Berdahl concentrates especially on how these changes have affected daily life, including social organization, gender roles and consumer patterns, at a place where the border was until recently a very powerful presence.

In his chapter 'Cross-Border Relations and Regional Identity on the Polish-German Border', Robert Parkin investigates the dramatic changes at an international border that formerly divided 'Eastern Europe' from 'Western Europe' but is now an internal European Union border. Poland's entry into the EU on 1 May 2004 was the culmination of a long-term goal after the collapse of the communist system in 1989. The largest of the 2004 accession states, it has already made its presence felt in the new Europe by exporting hundreds of thousands of citizens seeking work elsewhere in Europe. Such population movements may extend to long-term sojourns in Spain or the UK, or may be limited to day trips to Germany, just over the border from western Poland. The chapter describes attempts by local officials and some local people to reduce the significance of the Polish-German border even further, even as the eastern border – now an external EU border – is subject to ever greater control.

The chapter 'The Skeleton versus the Little Grey Men: Conflicting Cultures of Anti-nuclear Protest at the Czech-Austrian Border' looks at a case where the international border was reopened after the fall of the Iron Curtain but was blocked again temporarily by anti-nuclear activists as part of an act of political protest. Birgit Müller investigates the circumstances of this 'border blockade' and the political conflicts between Czech and Austrian political activists in the border region of Temelin. The construction and, in 2001, the start-up of the Czech nuclear power station at Temelin brought Austrian NGOs, citizens and regional politicians to block all the border crossings between the Czech Republic and Austria for two weeks in 2001. Although Austrian activists took pains to explain that the action was not directed against the Czech people but at the Czech and Austrian governments' unresponsiveness to their worries, it led Czechs to increasingly identify Temelin as a solely national issue and to reject Austrian interference. The chapter examines the forms of interaction and interdependence between Czech and Austrian anti-nuclear NGOs close to the border, as well as the different forms of political action directed towards their own governments and towards that of the other state.

The following chapter, 'Powerful Documents: Passports, Passages and Dilemmas of Identification on the Georgian-Turkish Border', looks at a non-EU border before and after the fall of the Soviet Union. Mathijs Pelkmans analyses conflicts in the interaction between border crossers and state officials at the border between Georgia and Turkey, especially during the immediate post-socialist period. His analytical interest focuses on passports, which, as official documents of identification, are useful tools for studying the linkages between border drawing, categorization and the formation of collective identities. Discussing the role of passports in the delimitation, solidification and partial demise of the Iron Curtain between (Soviet) Georgia and Turkey, Pelkmans argues that passports have different meanings and values depending on the 'identity' of the holder of the document and his or her relation to a specific border. It is particularly revealing to study those shifts in meaning in relation to changes in the nature of the border, as the focus on different stages of border regulations between Georgia and Turkey illustrates. In the 1990s, after the border between Georgia and Turkey was reopened, border dwellers found themselves at a moment of opportunity. Living in the border zone, they were among the first to hold international passports and thus could capitalize on new opportunities for trade. Moreover, by altering the data in these passports they put themselves in a favourable position due to the greater permeability of the borders between the neighbouring states.

William Kavanagh, in his chapter 'Proximity and Asymmetry on the Portuguese-Spanish Border', investigates what has or has not changed, not only in identities but in the social interaction and cross-border contacts between inhabitants of villages on either side of an 'old' EU border from which barriers and border guards completely disappeared after the Schengen Agreement came into force. Although the 'meaning' of the border appears to have changed after 1992, the ideal of the internal EU borders as 'open borders' is contrasted with anthropological evidence suggesting that on this northern section of the Portuguese-Spanish frontier, the removal of border controls has not erased the 'border in the mind'. As one of Kavanagh's informants told him: 'You may remove the door, but the doorframe remains.'

Strengthening Borders

The chapters in the second part of the collection investigate the theme of Strengthening Borders, which concerns recent developments at the frontiers of several central, eastern and south-eastern European nations. Very dramatic changes have occurred between countries that used to cooperate under the umbrella of the Soviet Union. The EU enlargement agreed upon in 2004 led to completely new arrangements at state borders that had formerly been permeable. Thus the opening up of borders inside the EU corresponds now to the 'hardening' of borders and the stressing of border surveillance between EU and non-EU countries. An equivalent process of 'hardening' can be observed between neighbouring regions that once formed part of the Soviet Union and are today independent nation states. The following essays illuminate those changes in border control and cross-border contacts as borderlanders experience them in daily life. The anthropological view 'from below' intends to shed light on the practical consequences of decisions taken in faraway centres of power and their 'side effects' and impact on the lives of those bordering the Other.

The chapter by Laura Assmuth, 'Asymmetries of Gender and Generation in a Post-Soviet Borderland', is based on a larger research project on 'Transnational Lives: A Comparative Ethnography of Communities at the Estonian-Russian and Latvian-Russian Borders'. In the framework of this project, cross-border interaction and movement in two cases of newly established borders in the former Soviet Union are studied. The borders in question, the easternmost borders of the European Union facing Russia, have enormous importance in the lives of many local people. Not all borderland residents are necessarily affected by the borders and border regimes, but those who, for various reasons, need and want to cross the border most definitely are. Who are these border crossers? How and why do they go to the other side? What kinds of ties do they maintain or develop? Assmuth explores these questions by focusing on actual border crossings and individual and family visits to the adjacent region in the neighbouring country or countries.

In the chapter '"We Are All Tourists": Enduring Social Relations on the Romanian-Serbian Border in Different Mobility Regimes', Cosmin Radu examines patterns of economic interaction and cross-border migration before and after the break-up of Yugoslavia. The on-site research for this contribution took place in the Romanian village of Gogosu and various Serbian communities on the other side of the border. After 1990 the villagers of Gogosu began crossing the border to look for informal jobs in construction, agriculture, housekeeping and forestry. Villagers from the once Yugoslav, now Serbian side of the border have been migrating since 1966, leaving many Yugoslav households incomplete as most of their young people are working in Austria and Germany. The Yugoslav/Serbian rural settlements thus came to constitute an informal labour market for

Romanians living on the border. The chapter looks at the implications of this short-term labour migration for household organization in Romania and at the significance of marriage and economic alliances between Romanians and Serbians at the local level.

In the chapter '"We Used to Be One Country": Rural Transformations, Economic Asymmetries and National Identities in the Ukrainian-Russian Borderlands', Tatiana Zhurzhenko investigates changes in two regions of the former Soviet Union where newly created nation states meet. The research, conducted at three border villages in the 'controlled near border area' of Ukraine's Kharkiv oblast, focuses on the role of the new border in the everyday lives of people on the Ukrainian-Russian borderland, and their perceptions of and attitudes to this new reality. The new border interrupts or reshapes family ties and social and economic contacts, and creates new advantages and disadvantages. At the same time, by integrating the new border into their everyday lives and adopting informal, often illegal, practices of dealing with the fact of the border, the local population challenges and changes the formal border regime and its symbolic meaning. For the people of Kharkiv oblast, the experience of 'becoming a borderland' has been part of another fundamental experience, that of 'becoming Ukrainians' through the Ukrainization of the administration, education system and media. The new national identity – a feeling of belonging to the 'Ukrainian people' and loyalty to the Ukrainian state – is not a function of their near-border location, but rather of social and economic changes in the region. But permanent contacts with Russian citizens and visits to Russian territory allow local inhabitants to compare changes on both sides of the border, and in some cases the border becomes a symbol of 'post-Soviet nostalgia'.

Crossing Forbidden Borders

The third and last section of the book concentrates on the theme of Crossing Forbidden Borders. The chapter 'Under One Roof: The Changing Social Geography of the Border in Cyprus' by Lisa Dikomitis examines the realities surrounding the crossing of a contested and officially unrecognized border in the Mediterranean area. In the case of Cyprus, which entered the European Union in 2003, formal and informal barricades known as the Green Line divide the island into two different political entities, the Greek-speaking Republic of Cyprus and the Turkish-speaking part of the island known as the Turkish Republic of Northern Cyprus, which is recognized only by Turkey. Guarded by UN peacekeepers and marked by omnipresent 'forbidden zone' signs, the Green Line has functioned as a de facto border since 1974 and cuts the island's capital, Nicosia, in two. Dikomitis investigates what happened when this partition line was partially opened in 2003, allowing Greek and Turkish Cypriots to cross from one side of their divided island to the other after twenty-nine years of separation. Based on participant observation on both sides of the border, the author explores Greek and Turkish Cypriots' experience of passing through the forbidden zone, actors' perceptions of the problems involved in border crossing and the differing social meanings given to those journeys by Greek and Turkish Cypriots. Dikomitis reveals in detail the different manner in which the two ethnic groups on Cyprus handle and evaluate the possibility of visiting the opposite part of the island. Her anthropological analysis concludes that although border crossing has became a routine ritual in recent years, the ethnic stereotypes that Greeks Cypriots and Turkish Cypriots hold about each other are still very much alive, and both sides express a strong feeling of a lack of understanding by their counterparts on the other side of the Green Line.

The final two chapters in the book deal with undocumented migration to the territory of the European Union, specifically to the southern European countries of Italy and Greece. The chapters have in common a focus on undocumented migrants' ability to cross the border at places where the borderline seems most difficult to control, that is, not on land but on the Mediterranean Sea. The Strait of Otranto and the Aegean Sea are maritime frontiers where the sea serves as both a barrier and a bridge, allowing small boats to enter national waters clandestinely. Based on an analysis of the specific reception structure of undocumented migrants in the two distinct national contexts, the essays discuss different national concepts of managing the encounter with the Other and strategies of coping with asymmetry and proximity in border encounters.

Maurizio Albahari's chapter, 'The Birth of a Border: Policing by Charity on the Italian Maritime Edge', is based on fieldwork in the south-eastern Italian border region of Apulia. It investigates border enforcement practices and discourses of the Italian state's surveillance and classification of mainly Muslim undocumented migrants, as well as discourses of assistance to these migrants by Italy and by the Roman Catholic church. Those who maintain, cross and debate the sociopolitical site of the border do not merely locally implement but also co-produce practices and discourses of secularism, citizenship and migration management. Meanwhile, this borderland has historically been subject to a disparaging moral geography. The national discourse of the underdeveloped Otherness of the Italian 'South' finds supranational analogies: how and where the 'North' secures its distinction vis-à-vis the 'South' is arguably integral to the New Europe's institutional and popular quest for distinctiveness.

The final chapter, 'Managing Proximity and Asymmetry in Border Encounters: The Reception of Undocumented Migrants on a Greek Border
Island', by Jutta Lauth Bacas, examines the reception of undocumented
boat migrants on the Greek island of Lesbos (also known as Mytilene,
after the name of the island's capital). When undocumented migrants enter Greek national territory by boat, face-to-face interaction between local
state agents and newcomers in the border zone takes place with limited
means of communication and in a hierarchically structured atmosphere.
By analysing the reception structure on the island of Lesbos, the chapter
draws attention to images of the Other established in these interactions
and seeks to shed light on different forms of managing proximity and
hierarchy in the process of receiving undocumented migrants. In more
general terms, the case study explores how cultural differences are perceived and negotiated at the border, where the basic social setting fosters
opposed and hostile positioning of cultural conceptualizations.

Conclusion

International borders are social fields where people with different ethnic
and national backgrounds come into close physical and social contact, at
the same time defining and stressing asymmetry by mechanisms of control and surveillance, and establishing social hierarchy. Inspired by the
tremendous changes at Europe's borders over the past two decades, the
present volume aims to dissect the complex processes occurring at the
redefined state borders, and more specifically the dialectic relationship
between proximity and asymmetry in cross-cultural encounters at European borders after 1989. The central dimension of the chapters in this volume is the focus on social interaction in often antagonistic and sometimes
conflictive contexts where social relations and proximity are established
through face-to-face contacts in specific border settings. The collection,
which offers new evidence to the growing body of anthropological work
on changing borders in Europe by focusing on proximity and asymmetry,
presents first-hand ethnographic accounts of borders between EU member countries as well as borders between EU states and non-EU countries.
Its co-editors have chosen, as a common starting point, to focus on face-
to-face encounters and connectivity across the border, delving into the
ambiguities, contradictions and conflicts occurring there. In contrast to
border studies in political science, the anthropological approach allows
the researcher to concentrate on the micro-context of the field site and
thus illuminate details of interaction with the Other across the border and
the formation and re-formation of social and cultural identities of actors

involved in Europe's contemporary transformations. In other words, the specific methodological approach of the co-authors of this volume is to investigate the 'face-to-face' experience of these border encounters, which in many cases, as the empirical contributions here show, are experiences of conflict and confrontation at Europe's frontiers. It is this turn to the micro-level that fills the often used theoretical concepts of European unification and post-socialist transformation with specific empirical meaning, tracing how the people involved 'on the ground' themselves make sense of the changes and asymmetries they experience in their everyday lives on the border. The present volume hopes to contribute to this deeper understanding of the complexity of geopolitical changes across European frontiers.

Notes

1. Further information on the European research programme 'Remaking Eastern Borders in Europe: A Network Exploring Social, Moral and Material Relocations of Europe's Eastern Peripheries' (COST Action IS0803) is provided on the website http://www.east bordnet.org.
2. Quote from the 'Remaking Borders' conference web page (Catania, Sicily, 20–22 January 2011), organized by the scientific network EastBordNet (COST Action IS0803). See http://www.eastbordnet.org/conferences/2011/index.htm. Retrieved 15 August 2012.
3. European Commission. 'Schengen area'. Europa web portal. URL: http://ec.europa.eu/dgs/home-affairs/what-we-do/policies/borders-and-visas/index_en.htm . Retrieved 15 August 2012.
4. A map of the Schengen Area can be found at: http://ec.europa.eu/dgs/home-affairs/what-we-do/policies/borders-and-visas/schengen/index_en.htm.
5. See http://ec.europa.eu/dgs/home-affairs/what-we-do/policies/immigration/irregular-immigration/index_en.htm Retrieved 15 August 2012.
6. EU priorities in the fight against organized crime and irregular migration have been defined on the basis of the Stockholm Programme of 2009 and the Pact on Asylum and Migration of 2008. For more information see the EU Home Affairs web portal: http://ec.europa.eu/dgs/home-affairs/what-we-do/policies/asylum/index_en.htm. Retrieved 15 August 2012.
7. For a short overview of EU positions and policy decisions relevant to fighting irregular migration, see http://ec.europa.eu/dgs/home-affairs/what-we-do/policies/immigration/irregular-immigration/index_en.htm. Retrieved 15 August 2012.
8. Various European newspapers, but not the EU Home Affairs' website, reported on the reform. The German edition of the *Financial Times* headlined its report of 7 June 2012 'This Schengen Reform Is a Defeat for Europe'. See: http://www.ftd.de/politik/europa/:mehr-grenzkontrollen-die-schengen-reform-ist-eine-niederlage-fuer-europa/70047589.html. Retrieved 15 August 2012.
9. In 2009 the EU adopted the Stockholm Programme with the title 'An Open and Secure Europe Serving and Protecting Citizens'. See: http://eur-lex.europa.eu/LexUriServ/LexUriServ.do?uri=OJ:C:2010:115:0001:0038:EN:PDF. Retrieved 15 August 2012.

References

Alvarez, R.R. 1995. 'The Mexican-US Border: The Making of an Anthropology of Border-lands', *Annual Review of Anthropology* 24: 447–70.

Alvarez, R. 2012. 'Borders and Bridges: Exploring a New Conceptual Architecture for (U.S.-Mexico) Border Studies', *Journal of Latin American and Caribbean Anthropology* 17(1): 24–40.

Anderson, B. 1983. *Imagined Communities: Reflections on the Origin and Spread of Nationalism.* London: Verso.

Anderson, J., L. O'Dowd and T.M. Wilson (eds). 2003. *New Borders for a Changing Europe: Cross-border Cooperation and Governance.* London: Frank Cass.

Anderson, M. 1996. *Frontiers: Territory and State Formation in the Modern World.* Oxford: Polity.

Barth, F. (ed.). 1969. *Ethnic Groups and Boundaries: The Social Organization of Culture Difference.* London: George Allen and Unwin.

Bourdieu, P. 1984. *Distinction: A Social Critique of the Judgement of Taste.* London: Routledge.

Cohen, A.P. 1982. *Belonging: Identity and Social Organisation in British Rural Cultures.* Manchester: Manchester University Press.

———. 1985. *The Symbolic Construction of Community.* London: Tavistock.

Cole, J.W. and E.R. Wolf. 1974. *The Hidden Frontier: Ecology and Ethnicity in an Alpine Valley.* New York: Academic Press.

Donnan, H. and D. Haller. 2000. 'Liminal No More: The Relevance of Borderland Studies', *Ethnologia Europaea* 30(2): 7–22.

Donnan, H. and T.M. Wilson (eds). 1994. *Border Approaches: Anthropological Perspectives on Frontiers.* Lanham, MD: University Press of America.

——— (eds). 1999. *Borders: Frontiers of Identity, Nation and State.* Oxford: Berg.

Green, S. 2005. *Notes from the Balkans: Locating Marginality and Ambiguity on the Greek-Albanian Border.* Princeton, NJ: Princeton University Press.

———. 2009. *Lines, Traces and Tidemarks: Reflections on Forms of Borderli-ness.* COST Action ISO803, Working Paper No. 1. URL: http://www.eastbordnet.org/wiki/Documents/Lines _Traces_Tidemarks_Nicosia_2009_090416.pdf . Retrieved 30 August 2013.

———. 2012. 'Reciting the Future: Border Relocations and Everyday Speculations in Two Greek Border Regions', *HAU: Journal of Ethnographic Theory* 2(1): 111–29.

Horden, P. and N. Purcell. 2000. *The Corrupting Sea: A Study of Mediterranean History.* Oxford: Blackwell.

Kavanagh, W. and J. Lauth Bacas. 2011. 'Editors' Introduction', *Journal of Mediterranean Studies* 20(1): v–xvi. Special Issue: Unfolding Perspectives in Mediterranean Anthropology. Malta: Mediterranean Institute.

Sahlins, P. 1989. *Boundaries: The Making of France and Spain in the Pyrenees.* Berkeley: University of California Press.

Wilson, T.M. and H. Donnan (eds). 1998. *Border Identities: Nation and State at International Frontiers.* Cambridge: Cambridge University Press.

———. 2005a. 'Territory, Identity and the Places In-between: Culture and Power in European Borderlands', in T.M. Wilson and H. Donnan (eds), *Culture and Power at the Edges of the State: National Support and Subversion in European Border Regions.* Münster: Lit 1–29.

——— (eds). 2005b. *Culture and Power at the Edges of the State: National Support and Subversion in European Border Regions.* Münster: Lit Verlag.

Part I

Opening Borders

Chapter 1

Consumer Rites
The Politics of Consumption in Re-unified Germany

Daphne Berdahl

A year after the Berlin Wall fell, residents of a former East German border village were treated to a sort of collective initiation ceremony into
West German society. One of many such encounters between East and
West in the early days of German re-unification,[1] this particular meeting
entailed a 'product promotion show' (*Werbeveranstaltung*) sponsored by a
West German health products company. For three hours, the 150 villagers assembled in the community hall learned about health, nutrition and
the spirit of capitalism. According to a 'renowned' nutritional society, the
company's sales representative explained, one would have to drink over
thirteen litres of milk each day to receive the necessary allowance of cal-
cium, eat two kilos of beef for the requisite daily amounts of iron, and consume a jar of honey a day to build up one's immune system through bee
pollen. 'Our health and our bodies are also forms of capital', she informed
her listeners, 'in fact they may be the only form of capital we possess. We
need to invest in them, like money in the bank.'

To eliminate the need for such huge quantities of food, she was offering
a 'course of treatment' (*Kur*) of tablets, powders and vitamins that would
clear arteries and reduce cholesterol within thirty days. Although the
'treatment' usually sold for DM 964, she announced, the first ten buyers
would receive it at half price. For those villagers who were unemployed or
retired, the full price of the 'treatment' nearly equalled a month's income.

Throughout the evening, this saleswoman used a variety of strategies
to promote her products. Alluding to the mounting tensions and suspi-

---

Notes for this chapter begin on page 41.

cions between East and West Germans throughout the country (ironically through people and practices like hers), she said: 'Today I want to restore trust.' Her tone was both paternalistic and patronizing as she presented herself as an educator, invested with authority as a self-proclaimed nutritionist and as a westerner. 'Invest in yourself', she urged members of the audience, invoking the languages of production and consumption while privileging the values of western individualism. Her frequent references to the body as 'capital' were a central aspect of her presentation's 'educational' function. Like many other advertisers, she was selling belonging.[2] But by linking her products' purported benefits to certain rules and values of western capitalism and consumption, she was also selling access to, or entry into, the new society: her actions entailed the work of making citizen-subjects. By the end of the evening, she had sold ten 'treatments' as well as numerous other products ranging from rugs and pillows to garlic pills.

I begin with this 'promotional show' for it provides much food for thought: it not only reflects the construction of Otherness in East and West through particular discourses about the body, but also illustrates how consumption became a realm in which and through which many of the dynamics between East and West were experienced, expressed, negotiated and contested. The acquisition of a certain 'cultural competence' (Bourdieu 1977) in consumption, I argue, became a central initiation rite for eastern Germans into West German society. Although my focus is on re-unified Germany, the complex dynamic of consumption I examine here is part of a much larger dynamic present in the globalization of consumption-oriented market economies, particularly in post-socialist societies.[3] Indeed, in the context of post-socialist transitions in eastern Europe, we should be reminded of the degree to which eastern-bloc political economies' inability to either shield their populations from the consumption 'triumphs' of the West or to in any way match them was one main cause of their collapse (Bauman 1992; Borneman 1991; Drakulic 1991).

As anthropological approaches to the study of consumption have shown (Berdahl 1999a; Friedman 1994; Liechty 2003; McCracken 1988; Miller 1994, 1995a, 1995b; Orlove and Rutz 1989), cultural practices of consumption are far more complex than the simple competition involved in buying and selling. The consumption I examine here, for example, was deeply embedded in the asymmetrical power relations between East and West, demonstrating that consumption has important political and symbolic dimensions (Appadurai 1986; Ferguson 1988). It is a gendered and gendering activity (De Grazia 1996; Mills 1997). It became, and to some extent remains, a form of resistance or oppositional practice.[4] In the former GDR, it has entailed the construction and negotiation of memories and nostalgia for former life ways that are in contest with emerging 'all-German' life ways. And, drawing from Arjun Appadurai's insight that 'from a theoretical point of view human actors encode things with significance, [while] from a methodological point of view it is the things-in-motion that illuminate their social context' (Appadurai 1986: 5), it involves what people actually do with things. In sum, I view consumption here not as a distinct sphere of cultural or economic life, but as something that permeates, and is permeated by, complex negotiations of identity, gender and memory within changing political and economic structures.

My aim in this chapter is to explore transformations in cultural meanings and practices of consumption since the fall of the Berlin Wall. By focusing on both productive consumption and the consumption of production, I attempt to destabilize traditional binaries of consumption and production that have characterized many consumption studies both within and outside of anthropology. Studies of consumption have similarly emphasized polarities of resistance and domination (Löfgren n.d.; Miller 1995b); in this essay I also attempt to offer a more nuanced notion of resistance (see also Abu-Lughod 1990; Ortner 1995), particularly in the realm of consumption. Further, my discussion of the politics of consumption both during and after socialist rule highlights certain continuities between socialism and post-socialism, thereby challenging, like other recent ethnographic studies of post-socialist transitions (Berdahl 1999a; Caldwell 2004; Dunn 2004; Hann 1993; Lampland 1995; Nagengast 1991; Verdery 1996), notions of total rupture (the 'big bang' scenario; see Verdery 1996) present in many popular representations of socialism's collapse.

My study derives from a borderland situation where the politics of consumption have been articulated in a variety of social spaces. Kella, the village where I conducted fieldwork between 1990 and 1992, is located directly on and is halfway encircled by the former border between East and West Germany. It was, and to some extent remains, a true borderland both literally and metaphorically – a place where identities are especially articulated as well as a transitional zone, a place betwixt and between cultures.[5] At the time of my fieldwork, Kella was, as Gloria Anzaldúa wrote of her borderland, 'a vague and undetermined place created by the emotional residue of an unnatural boundary. It is in a constant state of transition' (Anzaldúa 1987: 3).

Following the *Wende* in 1989 (the 'transition' or 'turn', the term used to refer to the fall of the Wall and collapse of socialist rule), much of the daily interaction between Kella's 600 residents and its neighbours to the west occurred while shopping. It is thus no accident, perhaps, that consumption became a central metaphor for East-West distinctions, a space where differences were most marked before and after the Wall fell.

Consuming Passions

Long before the fall of the Wall, of course, power and wealth imbalances between East and West were reflected most visibly in the realm of consumption. The eastern bloc 'economies of shortage' (Kornai 1992) contrasted sharply with the affluence and abundance of consumer goods in the West, and nowhere was this disparity more evident than in divided Germany. Anyone who visited Berlin before 1989 will recall the contrast between the Ku'damm and Unter den Linden. Local- and state-level practices, including the exchange of people for western currency, West German state loans to the GDR, images on western television (whose airwaves easily crossed the otherwise impermeable border) and the coveted *Westpakete* (western packages) full of chocolates, coffee and hand-me-down clothing for eastern relatives reflected this imbalance and confirmed an image of the 'golden West' as a world where 'everything shines' (*alles glänzt*), a paradise that, if attained, could solve most every problem.[6] As the Yugoslavian writer Slavenka Drakulič noted: 'Sometimes I think that the real Iron Curtain is made up of silky, shiny images.… These images that cross the borders in magazines, movies, or videos are … more dangerous than any secret weapon, because they make one desire that "otherness" badly enough to risk one's life by trying to escape. Many did' (Drakulič 1991: 27–28).

This observation also reflects why consumption under socialism was deeply politicized. The socialist 'ideology of rational distribution' (Konrad and Szelenyi 1979), which defined the centralized appropriation and distribution of surplus as being in the common interest of all citizens, depicted consumption in terms of the collective good rather than individual entitlement. The fact that the promise of redistribution was rarely met was a key factor in the 'politicization of consumption' under socialism (Verdery 1996: 28). In Kella, for example, dust-free displays of rare crystal and the wearing of western jeans were not only markers of distinction (see Berdahl 1999a); they were also intensely political acts. A blue Aral Gasoline bumper sticker posted on the inside of a cupboard, or red and green adhesive packaging peeled from a West German Wurst and stuck underneath the kitchen table, similarly entailed what Verdery has described as the forging of 'resistant political identities' through consumption (1996: 29). Further, the communist (SED) party in the GDR (as elsewhere in socialist eastern Europe) frequently measured the regime's success in material terms, reflected especially in its well-known slogan referring to West German postwar progress and abundance: 'outdistance without catching up.'[7] Such measurements of success and frequent assurances of imminent improvements in the standard of living, combined with constant deprivations in daily life (especially during the last decades of socialist rule), not only politicized consumption but also stimulated consumer desire (Borneman 1991; Verdery 1996). As John Borneman has argued, this combination of deprivation and stimulation structured much of East Germans' behaviour as consumers after the collapse of socialist rule: 'Socialism had trained them to desire. Capitalism stepped in to let them buy' (Borneman 1991: 81).

Immediately after the fall of the Wall, one of the most pervasive images was that of East Germans on a frenetic, collective shopping spree. Although, as noted above, these consumption practices were largely the product of a cultural order formed under an economy of scarcity, West German discourses hailed the triumph of capitalism and democracy as reflected and confirmed in the *Konsumrausch* ('consuming frenzy') of the Ossis (East Germans). Local and national newspapers carried numerous photos of East Germans gawking at western products; a typical newspaper headline, for example, read 'Waiting, Marvelling, Buying'. The DM 100 *Begrüßungsgeld* ('welcome money') that the West German state handed to all first-time visitors from the GDR and spontaneous gifts of cash from individual West Germans not only helped finance the easterners' spending spree, but also accentuated the discrepancies between East and West by placing westerners in the dominant position of gift-giver. As one villager recalled: 'I found the "welcome money" embarrassing. It made me feel like a beggar. And when a *Westler* tried to hand me twenty marks, telling me to buy something nice with it, I tried to give it back. I was so ashamed.'

Consumption became an important symbolic marker of this historical moment (represented most tangibly in what people chose to purchase with their 'welcome money') but was also constitutive of the meaning of the transition (*Wende*) itself: state socialism collapsed not merely because of a political failure, but because of its failure, quite literally, 'to deliver the goods' (Borneman 1991: 252). The drab and clumsy East German products that embodied this failure were quickly collected as 'camp'[8] by West Germans while the easterners who had made them resoundingly rejected them. Museum displays of GDR products similarly affirmed and constructed an image of socialist backwardness as reflected in and constituted by its quaint and outdated products. As one catalogue from a museum exhibit in Frankfurt shortly after the *Wende* read: 'East Germany has unwittingly preserved fossils of articles which, twenty to thirty years ago, were near and dear to us ... [It is] high time then to embark upon a lightning archeological excursion into the world of consumer goods before this distinctive quality is submerged beneath the tide of Western goods' (Bertsch 1990: 7).[9]

More than any other product, the East German Trabant (Trabi) quickly became a key symbol not only of the GDR, but of socialist inefficiency, backwardness and inferiority. A small, boxy car made of fibreglass and pressed cotton, the Trabi with its two-stroke engine contrasted sharply with the fast West German Mercedes, Porsches, and BMWs. Indeed, as Robert Darnton observed, this contrast in cars could not help but embody 'the two Germanys: one super-modern, hard-driving, serious, and fast; the other archaic, inefficient, absurd, and slow, but with a lot of heart' (Darnton 1991: 155). In the GDR, East Germans often waited fifteen years and paid the equivalent of two annual salaries to obtain one. With the fall of the Wall, the Trabi was not only rendered valueless in monetary terms, but was at first affectionately, and then as relations between East and West Germans grew increasingly hostile, antagonistically ridiculed in West German jokes as well as in everyday interactions.[10]

This consumption metaphor became increasingly prevalent as the hopes for a 'third way' of the 1989 protest movements were lost in the rush to German unity. Leftist critics in the GDR lamented their country's 'sell-out' to capitalism, for example, while West Germans derided the consumerism of their Ossi neighbours. East Germans themselves described being 'bought' by the West, as the following lines from a letter written just days after the fall of the Wall by a young man from Kella reflects: 'Maybe [the West Germans] will destroy the GDR this way [through the 'welcome money']. It's like an investment. They buy the GDR citizens ... and then they won't want to remain GDR citizens anymore.' Indeed, 'Deutschmark nationalism,' a term Jürgen Habermas coined to describe what he saw (and feared) as a rise in nationalist sentiment based on the promise of a consumer-oriented market economy supported by the almighty Deutschmark,[11] is widely viewed as having been the driving force behind the landslide victory of the coalition parties associated with Helmut Kohl's Christian Democratic Party in the East German elections of March 1990.[12]

Consumer Rites

Consumption was not only a metaphor for East-West distinctions before and immediately following the fall of the Wall, however. It was also a means of preserving and reconstructing them. Indeed, consumption was part of a process through which the once political boundary that divided East and West Germany was replaced by the maintenance, indeed invention, of a cultural one. In the taxonomies of classification – of identifying who was an Ossi and who was a Wessi – that became part of the construction of Otherness on both sides of the former border after the Wall fell

(Korff 1990), the lack of a certain cultural fluency in consumption quickly emerged as a key marker of an Ossi. In the first years after the *Wende*, for example, the stereotypical insecure Ossi walked with her head down and asked the store clerk not 'where' a specific item was, but 'do you have it?'[13] Whereas West Germans referred to certain products by their brand names – such as 'Tempo' for a tissue or 'Uhu' for glue – East Germans described their function. When people described differences between East and West Germans, they frequently pointed only to consumption practices. 'Ossis compare prices', I was often told. 'Wessis always know what they want to buy.' It was usually during shopping trips in an adjacent western town that people would recriminate themselves for behaving like an 'Ossi'. 'Now she probably knows I'm an Ossi', one woman whispered to me about the bakery clerk. 'I didn't know what that bread was called.'

The perceived backwardness of East German products was often projected onto the bodies of East Germans themselves. In the first years after the fall of the Wall, clothing, grooming, make-up, even smell were identifying markers of Ossis. According to a discourse of Otherness in the West, Ossis could be identified by their pale faces, oily hair, washed-out shapeless jeans, generic grey shoes and acrylic shopping bags. They smelled of body odour, cheap perfume or 'that peculiar disinfectant'. Wessis, on the other hand, were recognizable by their stylish outfits, chic haircuts, Gucci shoes, tan complexions and ecologically correct burlap shopping bags. They smelled of Estée Lauder or Polo for men. In describing eastern German women, for example, a a West German friend of mine commented: 'You can recognize Ossis because they like things that have been out of fashion here for a long time.' Similarly, a young woman from Kella explained: 'Women are most easily recognized [as Ossis]. You see the differences immediately. Especially with older and middle-aged women. Women in the West still wear make-up. Their hair is stylish. But here, women aren't confident enough of themselves to even speak over there. They have these unstylish, frizzy perms and no make-up.' Although different in content, these comments reflect how the inability to read complex and 'ever-shifting fashion messages' (Appadurai 1996: 82) was perceived as a marker of an Ossi. They also illustrate how distinctions between East and West were often structured in gendered terms: in the reading of bodies[14] that became part of the construction of Otherness on both sides of the former border, it was women's bodies that were especially read.

As tensions between East and West mounted on both sides of the former border, insults and complaints directed at easterners frequently focused on a stereotype of the materialistic Ossi ignorant of western consumption practices: 'Stupid Ossis! They don't know how to shop!'; 'See the packs of Zonis that are shopping again today?'; or 'Look at them! They're shopping again! Don't they have anything better to do?' After the currency union in July 1990, when easterners overwhelmingly opted to buy western products with their newly acquired Deutschmarks, West German discourses projected Ossis as ignorant and foolish for being seduced by the fancy packaging of western goods. East Germans were eagerly and naively buying western milk, many westerners explained, while farmers in the East were forced to dump out the milk they were unable to sell.

Easterners' ignorance of western consumption practices was not only ridiculed and berated; it was also exploited. Numerous villagers in Kella, as throughout the former GDR, were the targets and occasionally victims of various mail-order gimmicks, door-to-door charlatans and company-sponsored shows and trips (similar to the health products 'show' described earlier). Some villagers sent in money after receiving notice in the mail they had 'won' a house; others purchased items from door-to-door salesmen that were never delivered.

Just as unfamiliarity with western consumption practices was a key marker of an Ossi, then, learning how to consume became a central initiation rite into the new society. Eastern Germans not only had to learn how to navigate their way through new structures of consumer credit, domestic finance and money management, they also simply had to learn where and how to shop after having experienced only an economy of scarcity with standardized products and prices. If, as Arjun Appadurai has suggested, we view consumption as the 'principal work of late industrial society' (Appadurai 1996: 82), Ossis, it could be said, had a lot of work to do.

Through personal experience, collective negotiation and even through more formal instruction, easterners soon became well versed in product names, prices, advertising strategies and fashion messages. Women at a dinner party would talk for hours about the quality and prices of everything from coffee to mattresses. Children could recite the price of a loaf of bread from three different bakeries. Even the new grade school textbooks, read by children and parents alike, contained lessons on the aims and functions of advertising. 'Advertisements lie,' a ten-year old child told me, 'we've now learned that.' These lessons, discussions and collective negotiations of new consumption practices also became part of a new discourse of solidarity that often replaced the 'them' of the state with the foreignness of a market economy, a notion that 'we' need to be savvy about this new power just as we had to be savvy about the power of the socialist regime.[15]

People thus came to understand why the same margarine was cheaper at the discount store Aldi than at the more expensive Edeka market; they discovered the fine print in mail-order gimmicks; and they learned to ask 'where' a certain product was located rather than 'whether' the store had it. And as Ossis learned to differentiate Nikes from Reeboks,[16] they also began to uncover the cultural meanings of certain consumption practices. Several villagers with well-paid jobs in the West abandoned Aldi for the more prestigious grocery stores frequented primarily by western Germans. Others began paying careful attention to brand names of electronics, appliances and clothing. Taste, an important manner in which consumption expresses distinction (Bourdieu 1984), thus began to enter into the construction, experience and expression of difference in Kella.[17]

Designing Women

In the early years after the fall of the Wall, the realm of consumption and the effort to acquire cultural fluency in it were not merely a new source of activity, entertainment and labour. Consumption also became a site for the negotiation of gender, indeed a central means through which certain gender ideologies were conveyed and contested. As feminist scholars of eastern Europe pointed out, the transitions or 'revolutions' of 1989 were deeply gendered (e.g., DeSoto 1994; Einhorn 1993; Funk and Mueller 1993; Gal 1994; Rosenberg 1991; Verdery 1996). In the GDR, for example, state policies and ideology aimed to involve women directly in the process of socialist nation-building through participation in the labour force, required norms for women's involvement in local politics, and pro-natalist policies like state-sponsored child care and generous maternity benefits. After German re-unification, however, women were disproportionately affected by rising unemployment, the abolition of socialist gender quotas for political involvement, and the replacement of the socialist state welfare policies with the Federal Republic's social policies, which direct women towards the family, motherhood and part-time work (De Soto 1994; Rosenberg 1991). As throughout eastern Europe, the disappearance of an active second economy, informal networks and alternative groups after the collapse of state socialism resulted in a 'newly valorized' public that, as Susan Gal has pointed out, is often conceptually defined as male while the private is defined as naturally female (Gal 1996). In the former GDR (as elsewhere), these changes were accompanied by a rapid influx of western images and ideologies of womanhood that challenged forty years of East German women's experience under socialism as workers and mothers, or worker-mothers. Like many aspects of the *Wende*, the implications of these changes for women were reflected and, to a large extent, constituted in the realm of consumption. Anthropologists have widely recognized that commodities can carry with them particular cultural doctrines. Frequently, I would add, these doctrines can be highly gendered.

To illustrate, I turn to a Tupperware party held in Kella around the same time as the health products presentation. Keeping to its decades-old tradition of home marketing, Tupperware apparently saw a market niche in the former GDR. The enthusiastic salesperson at the gathering I attended, Sabine Schneider, was a native villager (in contrast to the health products representative from West Germany). She combined marketing skills, acquired at a training seminar for Tupperware representatives, with her own creative asides, providing a story for nearly every plastic container she presented: 'this one is perfect for keeping dinners warm while the men are away at *Frühschoppen*,'[18] or 'I always send this one to school with the kids.' Her audience of seven women marvelled at the range of offerings and possibilities: 'An onion would fit in here'; 'This would be good for leftover ground pork'; and 'This is just right for milk,' Sabine informed them.

Not only was consumption presented as a social and gendered activity, but the products themselves were laden with explicit and implicit gender ideologies. Above all, the plastic containers conveyed a certain cult of domesticity, something that resonated with the unemployment of women and upgrading of motherhood and femininity after re-unification (Nickel 1993). A woman's domain, as the marketing's setting itself indicated (we were seated around the kitchen table), was naturally in the private sphere of the family home, caring for her husband while he partakes in traditionally male activities, or for her children as they enter the outside world. The large offering and diversity of plastic Tupperware containers seemed to represent the triumph of capitalist abundance and the new possibilities it offered for women to be better nurturers and homemakers. By the end of the evening, her audience had apparently been converted: Sabine sold Tupperware products worth over DM 500.

The transformation from a communist to a kind of consumption regime was perhaps best exemplified by the seminar offerings of the regional office for women's affairs, or *Gleichstellungsstelle* ('women's equality office'). Introduced after re-unification to address the unique needs and interests of women in the 'New Federal States', this office provided financial support to women's groups and funded educational programmes throughout the former GDR.[19] Its lecture and seminar topics conveyed a message about what women had to learn in the new system. Often co-sponsored by the prominent West German Sparkasse bank, seminar topics included 'Wishing, Planning, Buying'; 'Fashioning One's Life and Consumption Behaviour'; and 'Shopping to your Advantage.'

Shopping, then, which for women under socialism had meant standing hours in long lines, bartering or dealing with tensions among shoppers competing for scarce consumer goods, became a form of recreation. 'I feel freer now', one woman told me, citing the liberating effects of frozen dinners and the availability of a range of consumer goods. 'I can do what *I* want. I go shopping, not necessarily to buy things, but to look.' In addition to the Tupperware parties, village women gathered in each other's homes to learn about the latest line in Avon cosmetics or to peruse the most recent catalogues from Otto or Quelle. For women in Kella, as elsewhere in the former GDR, acquiring cultural fluency in consumption not only entailed a lot of work, it was also highly gendered and gendering activity.

'Ostalgia' for the Present

Much of what I have just described would seem to support a thesis that eastern Germans passively accepted and internalized the hegemony of the West – a prevalent image in both eastern and western German discourses in the first years after the fall of the Wall. Easterners striving to imitate the West, however, also resisted it at the same time. This paradox is not inconsistent; rather, it reflects the complex and contradictory aspects of identity in the borderland (Rosaldo 1989). Like the construction, experience and expression of East-West distinctions, this dynamic of imitation and resistance frequently occurred in the realm of consumption.

In the effort to 'catch up' and blend in' with the Wessis, for example, many villagers discarded their East German clothes, abandoned their Trabis for second-hand West German cars, changed their hairstyles, and undertook extensive home renovation projects. On the other hand, however, they also began using East German products as a means of asserting an emerging consciousness or counter-identity as eastern Germans, or Ossis. As Steven Sampson has noted, 'Unification wiped out East Germany, but created an East German consciousness' (Sampson 1991: 19).

A conversation in 1991 with two women in their late twenties, Ingrid and Anna, about their smocks (*Kittel*) first brought this to my attention. The common attire of female factory workers under socialism, the smock had been a symbol of working women in the GDR both before and especially after 1989. At a church gathering where middle-aged women were wearing their smocks while serving tables, Ingrid remarked to me: 'You know, I never wear my smock any more. I used to run around the house all day in one, but not anymore since the *Wende*. It's because of them [women] over there (*drüben*). Nobody there wears a smock anymore. It's not modern.' During the course of her comment I noticed Ingrid becoming more interested in this topic, which she then pursued with a mutual friend, Anna, when she joined our conversation not having heard Ingrid's first remark:

Ingrid: 'Anna, do you still wear a smock?'
Anna: 'No.'

Ingrid: 'Since when?'
Anna: 'Since the *Wende*.'
Several weeks later, I ran into both women independently wearing their
smocks again. Because I saw both women almost daily, I knew this was a
practice they had only recently renewed. When I commented about this
to Ingrid, she grinned and said, 'I guess after we talked I realized I could
wear it again.' When I asked Anna, she explained: 'The wearing of smocks
subsided in the first years after the *Wende*, but somewhere it's a part of us.'

The smock incident was similar to other assertions of identity as East
Germans I witnessed during the course of my fieldwork. In another instance, a family chose to drive the Trabi instead of their western Opel
to a dinner with West German relatives, thus consciously highlighting,
indeed magnifying, the distinctions between them. 'We took the Trabi,'
they proudly told me, 'and parked it next to their 68,000 DM Mercedes.'
Similarly, a group of men decided to drink East German beer after it had
been nearly taboo to serve it socially; women resumed buying the eastern
German laundry detergent Spee.

During the mid 1990s, however, such subtle tactics of symbolic resistance became widespread cultural practices throughout eastern Germany.
Often referred to as the 'renaissance of a GDR *Heimatgefühl*' (feeling of
belonging or GDR identity), these practices were part of a discourse of
nostalgia and mourning – a 'hazy beautification of the past' (Huyssen
1995: 47) – that has contested a general (and often systematic) devaluation
of the East German past by dominant West German legal and discursive
practices. Such practices included the selling of East German factories to
western companies by the *Treuhand*, the agency headed by West Germans
that was charged with privatizing the former GDR economy, occasionally for next to nothing; the discrediting of the GDR educational system,
particularly the *Abwicklung*[20] of the universities; the renaming of schools,
streets and other public buildings; the trial of Berlin border guards that for
many eastern Germans represented a sort of victors' justice; debates over
what to do with and about East Germany's Stasi (state security police) heritage that often compared the GDR to the Third Reich; and to return to the
Trabi again, discourses that ridiculed the backwardness of East Germany
while ignoring the social and historical contexts that may have produced
it. As the eastern German psychotherapist Hans Joachim Maaz remarked:
'People here saved for half a lifetime for a spluttering Trabant. Then along
comes the smooth Mercedes society and makes our whole existence, our
dreams and our identity, laughable' (in McElvoy 1992: 219).

As a challenge to this undermining of some of the very foundations
of easterners' identity and personhood, a number of cultural practices
emerged that recalled GDR times (also referred to as 'our time'): P..., a

disco in East Berlin, for example, seeking to reconstruct the GDR period with East German drinks, music and the old cover charge; a cinema or regional television station showing old GDR films that were watched by more people than during the socialist period; a self-described 'nostalgia cafe' called the Wallflower (*Mauerblümchen*) decorated with artefacts from the socialist period and serving 'traditional' GDR fare; several supermarkets specializing in or at least carrying East German products, including one in eastern Berlin whose name seems to reflect a now common sentiment, typical of 'nostalgia's stubborn implications of loss and desire' (Ivy 1995: 56): 'Back to the Future'.[21]

In this business of 'Ostalgia' (*Ostalgie*), East German products have taken on new symbolic meaning when used the second time around. These recuperations are both defiant gestures towards, and ironic play with, images and stereotypes of Ossis. And they entail the manipulation of culturally provided forms of resistance (Abu-Lughod 1990) within the context of a market economy: consumer choice. Contrary to one of Kella's initial lessons in western consumption, then, Ossis' investment in themselves or their 'bodies as capital' has not entailed consuming pills, powders and vitamins; it has involved the acquisition of a certain amount of cultural competence in knowing how to consume.

However, now stripped of their original historical context of an economy of scarcity or oppressive regime, these products also recall an East Germany that never existed. Thus while there may be nothing new in the strategic use of consumption as oppositional practice, what is unique in this context is the way in which memory shapes, and is being shaped by, the consumption and re-appropriation of things. These products have, in a sense, become mnemonics, signifiers of a period of time that differentiates Ossis. They illustrate not only the way in which memory is an interactive, malleable and highly contested phenomenon, but also the process through which things become informed with a remembering – and forgetting – capacity. Here is not merely a tension but a dynamic interplay between nostalgia and memory, and one of the key links is consumption.

This dynamic of remembering and forgetting also represents a different twist in the important but, in many studies of consumption, often overlooked relation between consumption and production.[22] Ostalgic and similar practices do not merely reflect a form of 'structural nostalgia' (Herzfeld 1997)[23] or a longing for a glorified past; they also reveal a certain mourning for production. However counterproductive socialist production rituals may have been in generating workers' loyalty to the state (Buroway and Lukács 1992; Verdery 1996), they appear to have inculcated, to some extent at least, an identification with production.[24] People in Kella often recalled with pride, for example, the products of their labour in the local toy factory. Similarly, during a village parade in honour of German re-unification in October 1990, women replicated a sign that once hung on the walls of their workplace: 'My hand for my product.' In a society where productive labour was a key aspect of state ideology and the workplace was a central site for social life, the high incidence of unemployment throughout eastern Germany has profoundly undermined many peoples' sense of self and identity. The resurgence of eastern German products must thus be viewed in the larger context of the shift in the balance between production and consumption in the former GDR that has occurred through rapid deindustrialization.[25] Consuming products of 'Ostalgia' may not merely be an assertion of identity as eastern Germans, then; it also may recall an identity as producers that was lost in this transition.

Finally, this re-memorization of trivialities has also been part of a process through which consumption practices and the meaning of things have contributed to the creation and reification of a temporal and spatial boundary. 'Ostalgic' practices are not only part of a dynamic of boundary maintenance and invention between East and West, they have also helped to create a division between before and after 'the Fall.' The items purchased with the 'welcome money' connect personal biographies to a nationally (indeed, internationally) shared historical moment (the fall of the Wall). Yet they are also what Susan Stewart has called 'souvenirs of individual experience' (Stewart 1984) in connection to a rite of passage. The inexpensive cassette recorders that broke within months after their purchase or the gold jewellery that turned one's skin green became, in a sense, material signs of many easterners' first lesson in western consumption. They came to represent not only easterners' transformation into more knowledgeable consumers, but also symbolized the loss of an illusion of the 'golden West.' And the loss of this illusion has been one of the most devastating aspects of re-unification.

Conclusion: Ingrid's Collar

In a 1993 news magazine article identifying the emergence of such oppositional practices throughout the former GDR, the former East German writer Monika Maron is quoted as ridiculing the notion that anyone who buys 'Bautzener mustard or Thüringer wurst is a resistance fighter'.[26] Indeed, the marketing and consumption of 'Ostalgia' represents a certain commodification of resistance, particularly when several of the supposedly eastern German products are now produced and distributed by western firms. This framing of resistance to western German dominance in terms of product choices and mass merchandising entails a sort of 'Ostalgia' for the present[27] – practices that both contest and affirm the new order of a market economy.

Yet these practices also reflect an ongoing politicization of consumption, different in context but similar in form to that in the socialist period. Rather than using coveted western goods to construct and express resistant political identities, as under socialism, eastern Germans turned to old GDR products – an inversion of what John Borneman termed the 'mirror imaging process' that contributed to the construction of two German states and identities during the Cold War (1992). These consumption practices thus not only highlighted continuities between socialism and post-socialism, but underlined the dynamic of agency in consumption as well (Orlove and Rutz 1989). Above all, they both reflected and constituted important identity transformations and negotiations in a period of intense social discord. They also point to the complexities, ambiguities and contradictions of resistance (Ortner 1995: 184).

To illustrate, I turn to a final story involving Ingrid, who asked me one day how women in America wear their shirt collars. I told her I didn't really know. Somewhat taken aback and almost irritated by my ignorance, she said: 'Well, now it's modern to wear your collar up. That's how women do it in the West. Here [in the former GDR] women wear their collars down.' Ingrid seemed not only to be struggling to figure out current fashion etiquette on shirt collars, but also where she, as an Ossi who both mimicked and resisted what she perceived to be Wessi standards, fit in. For weeks after our conversation, I couldn't help noticing that on some days she was wearing her collar up, on other days down. Then, one night at a dinner party, I looked across the table and saw that her collar was askew – a rare occurrence for someone as concerned with her appearance as Ingrid: one corner of her collar was up; the other was down.

To me, this probably fortuitous position of Ingrid's collar was loaded with meaning, symbolizing the interstitiality of the borderland, the way in which its residents are somehow betwixt and between East and West, and the constructed and gendered nature of these distinctions as well as the role of consumption in this dynamic. I imagine the uneven collar was most likely the result of Ingrid's indecision over how to dress for the dinner party; she probably had spent some time in front of a mirror switching the collar back and forth until she had to leave, when she apparently was unable to check it one last time. As in the preceding weeks, her tampering with the collar entailed a gendered negotiation of and play with identity – a metaphor for identity in the borderland, indeed, for identity itself.

Thus the Trabi's move from the jokebooks of 1989 to the 'cult automobile' (*Kultauto*) of the 1990's and beyond,[28] the resurrection of the women's smocks (*Kittel*) and the simple craving for a glass of East German Rotkäpp-

chen champagne are products of complex and often contradictory processes of identity formation, re-evaluation and negotiation in the former
GDR. These processes are part of an on-going dialectic of remembering
and forgetting as well as a dynamic and often subtle interplay of imitation
and resistance, both of which are closely linked to the power, and social
life, of things (Appadurai 1986).

Epilogue

In the years since my initial fieldwork, I have visited Kella many times; my
most recent visit was in 2003.[29] Although there have been many changes
in the village – home renovations, freshly painted facades, new construction, furniture and clothing – the invisible boundary between East and
West remains. Indeed, even the generation too young to have any memory
of the GDR still identify themselves as 'Ossis.' Many young people have
either remained in the village or returned to Kella after living in the West.
According to church records through 2003, all marriages except one were
between easterners, and the one exception was to a descendant of a family
from Kella who fled in 1952. During a brief visit in 2002, Kai Niemann's
widely popular (among eastern Germans) song, *Im 'Osten* (in the East), often hailed throughout the former GDR as 'our national anthem',[30] boomed
loudly from young residents' cars. Despite the radical decline in tensions
and antagonisms between people on both sides of the former border, there
continues to be a strong identification as 'Ossis' among most villagers.
Indeed, I would still argue that Kella remains a borderland in the metaphorical sense of the term: although the literal border of the fence has long
disappeared, there is still a heightened consciousness of being betwixt and
between East and West.

   In terms of consumption practices, the rituals of initiation are a distant
memory; Kellans, like other eastern Germans, are very 'competent' consumers. Taste and style – in clothing, home décor, automobiles, vacation
travel – while determined by economic opportunities, have also increasingly become a means of social distinction and expressions of identity. And
now that Kella has been absorbed into a consumer market economy, many
villagers who experienced socialism offer clear and articulate critiques of
global capitalism. In discussing proposed reforms to the German welfare
state, for example, one man in his mid forties, recalling the benefits of full
employment and healthcare under socialism, angrily exclaimed, 'Now it's
all about money. Jobs go to people who will work for the least amount of
money, especially in eastern Europe. We have to pay so much for healthcare now that it's unbelievable. But that's capitalism.' This comment does

not reflect a desire to return to socialist rule, but like other forms of the post-socialist nostalgia prevalent in most central and eastern European societies, it represents not only a critique of capitalism but also, perhaps, a longing for an alternative moral order.

Notes

Editors' note: This is the last manuscript anthropologist Daphne Berdahl worked on before her untimely death in 2007. An earlier version with the same title appeared in the volume *On the Social Life of Postsocialism: Memory, Consumption, Germany*, edited by Matti Bunzl (2010). The final version, presented here with stylistic adjustments, has been approved by the co-editors of the volume *Border Encounters*.

1. I have chosen the hyphenated terms 're-unification' and 're-unified' to refer to the union of the FRG and GDR on 3 October 1990. Although I am aware of the arguments pointing to the teleological and ideological implications of the term 'reunification' as well as the fact that the territories united in 1990 do not represent Germany in an earlier state, I am also concerned that the omission of any term reflecting a previous union of this region as one country silences critical elements of Germany's past as well: the fact, for example, that Germany was divided in 1945 for a reason. Further, the area that I discuss in this book has experienced a resumption of earlier economic and social ties across regional, religious and former national borders. My use of the hyphen is thus a sort of compromise, an effort to avoid the naturalizing connotations of 'reunification' while reflecting an awareness of certain histories of divisions and recent restorations. At times I do use the word unity, however, as a literal translation of the official German term *Einheit*.
2. Advertisers targeting 'Ossis' were particularly focused on this theme, best exemplified by the slogan on billboards pushing the cigarette brand West throughout the GDR in the years after the *Wende*: 'Test the West'.
3. The emergence of consumption as an important topic for study in the context of post-socialist transitions is highlighted, among others, by Berdahl, Bunzl and Lampland (2000); Berdahl (1999b, 2005); Creed (2002); Humphrey (2002); Konstantinov (1996); Mandel and Humphrey (2002); Patico and Caldwell (2002); and Verdery (1996).
4. On consumption and resistance see, e.g., Fiske (1989); Hebdidge (1988); McRobbie (1989); Willis (1990).
5. My understanding of the borderland concept owes much to Gupta and Ferguson (1992) and Rosaldo (1989), among others.
6. See Borneman (1991: 130–49) for a discussion of East Germans' need for the 'fantasy-land' of the West.
7. In German: Überholen ohne einzuholen.
8. 'Camp' has been a topic for American cultural critics and anthropologists alike (cf. Ivy 1995; Ross 1980; Stewart 1984). Most relevant to my understanding here is Ross's observation that camp parodies 'the thing on its way out' (in Ivy 1995:56).
9. See Wilk (1994) for a discussion of temporal meanings of goods in a colonial context.
10. Stein (1993) and Brednich (1990) discuss in detail Trabi jokes and their identification of East Germans with 'the inferior product of their state' (Stein 1993: 40).
11. Stein (1993) points out that DM-nationalism was not a new phenomenon in the West and argues that Trabi jokes were an expression of a perceived threat to this West German identity.

12. As one popular saying described the election results: Nur Kohl bringt die Kohle (Only Kohl will bring us the money/cabbage), in Borneman (1991: 231).

13. This practice stems from a socialist economy of scarcity, when the issue was not where a product might be, but whether a store even had it.

14. William Kelleher (n.d.) similarly points out how boundary maintenance in Northern Ireland is sustained through the reading of bodies.

15. Numerous writings on the politics of everyday life in socialist societies have highlighted as well as nuanced an 'us versus them' opposition between citizens and the state. A very limited sampling includes Drakulic (1991); Kideckel (1993); Lampland (1995); Milosz (1991 [1951]); Nagengast (1991); Verdery (1996); Watson (1994).

16. See 'Das Ost-Gefühl - Heimweh nach der alten Ordnung', *Der Spiegel* 27(1995): 95.

17. This field of play is largely new here: under socialism, when commodities and clothing were either uniform or scarce, people took what they could get. Most villagers' taste in clothing, for example, was determined by the hand-me-downs sent by western relatives. 'I used to wear that dress every day', one woman recalled, pointing to an old photograph of herself, 'just because it was from the West. Now of course I know they just sent us the things they didn't want any more.' While people creatively used their limited resources to shape different styles and expressions of distinction under socialism, the range of possibilities – and the meanings of those possibilities – have changed.

18. Frühschoppen is the name of the Sunday morning festivities during Kirmes (the annual celebration in honor of the church's dedication) when, traditionally, lots of alcohol gets consumed by the male participants.

19. For a brief history of *Gleichstellungsstellen*, with its origins in 1980's West Germany, and an analysis of differences and conceptualizations of these offices after re-unification as reflective of differences among feminist concerns in the old and new federal states, see Ferree (1991).

20. Abwicklung, meaning 'to unwind' as well as 'to liquidate,' entailed the restructuring of East German universities through the dissolution departments and institutes, dismissal of east German faculty members (20 percent of professors and 60 percent of Mittelbau or intermediate ranks [Maier 1997: 305]), the recruitment of West German academics and concomitant influx of West German research agendas.

21. The Berlin examples stem from an article in *Der Spiegel* 27(1995). In the last ten years, this cultural phenomenon of 'Ostalgie' has expanded enormously, resulting in trivia games, books, mail-order catalogues, exhibits and television programmes, among many other products. The commodification of 'Ostalgie' arguably reached its peak in 2004 with the release of the widely popular and critically acclaimed film *Goodbye Lenin*. For more on the shifting meanings and practices of 'Ostalgie,' see Berdahl (1999b, 2001, 2005).

22. For a notable exception see, e.g., Mintz (1985).

23. Defined by Herzfeld as a 'collective representation of an Edenic order – a time before time – in which the balanced perfection of social relations has not yet suffered the decay that affects everything human' (1997: 109).

24. For a sensitive and incisive account of the history and complexities of production ideologies in relation to actual labour practices in the GDR, see Lüdtke (1994).

25. For discussions of the causes and consequences of East Germany's deindustrialization, see De Soto (forthcoming) and Geyer (1994).

26. 'Wehre dich täglich', *Der Spiegel* 52(1993): 46–48.

27. To transform a concept suggested by Frederic Jameson (1989).

28. The cult of the Trabi continues to this day, although most commonly in the form of parody and camp. Several eastern German cities offer 'Trabi Tours' or 'Trabi Safaris'; the 'two stroke' is exhibited in many museum displays. There are websites and clubs for Trabi fans, who meet to exchange memories and auto parts. For more on the Trabi see Berdahl (2001).

29. Editors' note: the ethnographic present of this chapter is retained despite the fact that Daphne Berdahl's last visit to Kella took place in 2003.
30. Indeed, there was much grumbling in eastern Germany about the fact that the western German music video station refused to play Niemann's song.

References

Abu-Lughod, L. 1990. 'The Romance of Resistance: Tracing Transformations of Power through Bedouin Women', *American Ethnologist* 17(1): 41–55.

Anzaldúa, G. 1987. *Borderlands/La Frontera: The New Mestiza*. San Francisco: Spinsters/Aunt Lute Books.

Appadurai, A. 1986. 'Introduction: Commodities and the Politics of Value', in *The Social Life of Things: Commodities in Cultural Perspective*. Cambridge: Cambridge University Press, 3–63.

———. 1996. *Modernity at Large: Cultural Dimensions of Globalization*. Minneapolis: University of Minnesota Press.

Bauman, Z. 1992. *Intimations of Postmodernity*. New York: Routledge.

Berdahl, D. 1999a. *Where the World Ended: Re-Unification and Identity in the German Borderland*. Berkeley and Los Angeles: University of California Press.

———. 1999b. '"(N)Ostalgie" for the Present: Memory, Longing, and East German Things', *Ethnos* 64(2): 192–211.

———. 2001. '"Go, Trabi, Go!": Reflections on a Car and Its Symbolization over Time.' *Anthropology and Humanism* 25(2): 131–41.

———. 2005. 'Expressions of Experience and Experiences of Expressions: Museum Re-Presentations of GDR History', *Anthropology and Humanism* 30(2): 235–51.

Berdahl, D., M. Bunzl, and M. Lampland (eds). 2000. *Altering States: Ethnographies of Transition in Eastern Europe and the Former Soviet Union*. Ann Arbor: University of Michigan Press.

Bertsch, G. 1990. 'The Galapagos Islands of the Design World?' In G. Bertsch, E. Hedler and M. Dietz (eds), *SED: Stunning Eastern Design SED: Stunning Eastern Design*. Cologne: Taschen.

Borneman, J. 1991. *After the Wall: East Meets West in the New Berlin*. New York: Basic Books.

———. 1992. *Belonging in the Two Berlins: Kin, State, Nation*. Cambridge: Cambridge University Press.

Bourdieu, P. 1977. *Outline of a Theory of Practice*. Cambridge: Cambridge University Press.

———. 1984. *Distinction: A Social Critique of the Judgement of Taste*. Cambridge, MA: Harvard University Press.

Brednich, R. 1990. 'Trabi-Witze: Ein populäres Erzählgenre der Gegenwart.' *Volkskunde in Niedersachsen* 7(1): 18–35.

Bunzl, M. (ed.). 2010. *On the Social Life of Postsocialism: Memory, Consumption, Germany*. Bloomington and Indianapolis: Indiana University Press.

Buroway, M. and J. Lukács. 1992. *The Radiant Past: Ideology and Reality in Hungary's Road to Capitalism*. Chicago: University of Chicago Press.

Caldwell, M. 2004. *Not by Bread Alone: Social Support in the New Russia*. Berkeley: University of California Press.

Creed, G.W. 2002. '(Consumer) Paradise Lost: Capitalist Dynamics and Disenchantment in Rural Bulgaria', *Anthropology of East Europe Review* 20(2), 119–25. *Retrieved 15 April 2013* from https://www.scholarworks.iu.edu/journals/index.php/aeer/.

Darnton, R. 1991. *Berlin Journal*. New York: W. W. Norton & Company.

De Grazia, V. (ed.). 1996. *The Sex of Things: Gender and Consumption in Historical Perspective*. Berkeley: University of California Press.

De Soto, H. 1994. ''In the Name of the Folk': Women and Nation in the New Germany', *UCLA Women's Law Journal* 5(1): 83–102.
———. 2000. 'Contested Landscapes: Reconstructing Environment and Memory in Post-Socialist Saxony-Anhalt.' In Berdahl, D., M. Bunzl, and M. Lampland (eds), *Altering States: Ethnographies of Transition in Eastern Europe and the Former Soviet Union.* Ann Arbor: University of Michigan Press.
Drakulič, S. 1991. *How We Survived Communism and Even Laughed.* New York: Norton.
Dunn, E. 2004. *Privatizing Poland : Baby Food, Big Business, and the Remaking of Labor.* Ithaca, NY, and London: Cornell University Press.
Einhorn, B. 1993. *Cinderella Goes to Market: Citizenship, Gender and Women's Movements in East Central Europe.* London: Verso.
Ferguson, J. 1988. 'Cultural Exchange: New Developments in the Anthropology of Commodities', *Cultural Anthropology* 3(4): 488–513.
Ferree, M.M. 1991. 'Institutionalizing Gender Equality: Feminist Politics and Equality Offices', *German Politics and Society* 24–25: 55–65.
Fiske, J. 1989. *Reading the Popular.* Boston Unwin Human.
Friedman, J. (ed.). 1994. *Consumption and Identity.* London: Harwood Press.
Funk, N. and M. Mueller (eds). 1993. *Gender Politics and Post-Communism.* New York: Routledge.
Gal, S. 1994. 'Gender in the Post-Socialist Transition: The Abortion Debate in Hungary', *East European Politics and Societies* 8(2): 256–86.
Geyer, M. 1994. 'Industriepolitik in der DDR. Von der großindustriellen Nostalgie zum Zusammenbruch.' In J. Kocka and M. Sabrow (eds), *Die DDR als Geschichte: Fragen-Hypothesen-Perspektiven.* Berlin: Akademie.
Gupta, A. and J. Ferguson. 1992. 'Beyond "Culture": Space, Identity and the Politics of Difference', *Cultural Anthropology* 7(1): 6–23.
Hann, C. (ed.). 1993. *Socialism: Ideals, Ideologies, and Local Practice.* Oxford: Routledge.
Hebdidge, D. 1988. 'Object as Image: The Italian Scooter Cycle', in *Hiding in the Light: On Images and Things.* London: Routledge, 11–115.
Herzfeld, M. 1997. *Cultural Intimacy: Social Poetics in the Nation State.* New York: Routledge.
Humphrey, C. 2002. *The Unmaking of Soviet Life: Everyday Economies After Socialism.* Ithaca, NY: Cornell University Press.
Huyssen, A. 1995. *Twilight Memories: Marking Time in a Culture of Amnesia.* New York: Routledge.
Ivy, M. 1995. *Discourses of the Vanishing: Modernity, Phantasm, Japan.* Chicago: University of Chicago Press.
Jameson, F. 1989. 'Nostalgia for the Present', *South Atlantic Quarterly* 88(2): 517–37.
Kelleher, W. 2003. *The Troubles in Ballybogoin: Memory and Identity in Northern Ireland.* Ann Arbor: University of Michigan Press.
Kideckel, D. 1993. *The Solitude of Collectivism.* Ithaca, NY: Cornell University Press.
Konrad, G. and I. Szelenyi. 1979. *The Intellectuals on the Road to Class Power.* New York: Harcourt Brace Jovanovich.
Konstantinov, Y. 1996. 'Patterns of Interpretation: Trader-Tourism in the Balkans (Bulgaria) as a Picaresque Metaphorical Enactment of Post-Totalitarianism', *American Ethnologist* 23(4): 762–82.
Korff, G. 1990. 'S-Bahn Ethnologie', *Österreichische Zeitschrift für Volkskunde* 44: 5–26.
Kornai, J. 1992. *The Socialist System: The Political Economy of Communism.* Princeton, NJ: Princeton University Press.
Lampland, M. 1995. *The Object of Labor: Commodification in Socialist Hungary.* Chicago: University of Chicago Press.
Liechty, M. 2003. *Suitably Modern: Making Middle-Class Culture in a New Consumer Society.* Princeton, NJ: Princeton University Press.

Löfgren, O. n.d. 'Creativity and Consumption: Some Reflections on the Pairing of Two Concepts'. Unpublished manuscript.

Lüdkte, A. 1994. 'Helden der Arbeit' — Mühen beim Arbeiten. Zur mißmutigen Loyalität von Industrialarbeitern in der DDR', in H. Kaelble, J. Kocka and H. Zwahr (eds), *Sozialgeschichte der DDR*. Stuttgart: Klett-Cotta.

Maier, C. 1997. *Dissolution: The Crisis of Communism and the End of East Germany*. Princeton, NJ: Princeton University Press.

Mandel, R. and C. Humphrey (eds). 2002. *Markets and Moralities: Ethnographies of Postsocialism*. Oxford, Berg.

McCracken, G. 1988. *Culture and Consumption*. Bloomington: Indiana University Press.

McElvoy, A. 1992. *The Saddled Cow*. London: Faber & Faber.

McRobbie, A. 1989. 'Second-Hand Dresses and the Role of the Ragmarket', in A. McRobbie (ed.), *Zoot-Suits and Second-Hand Dresses*. London: MacMillan.

Miller, D. 1994. *Modernity – An Ethnographic Approach: Dualism and Mass Consumption in Trinidad*. Oxford: Berg.

———. 1995a. 'Consumption Studies as the Transformation of Anthropology', in D. Miller (ed.), *Acknowledging Consumption*. London: Routledge, 263–92.

———. 1995b. 'Consumption and Commodities', *Annual Review of Anthropology* 24: 141–61.

Mills, M.B. 1997. 'Contesting the Margins of Modernity: Women, Migration, and Consumption in Thailand', *American Ethnologist* 24(1): 37–61.

Milosz, C. 1991 [1951]. 'Ketman', in Gale Sokes (ed.), *From Stalinism to Pluralism*. New York: Oxford University Press, 51–56.

Mintz, S. 1985. *Sweetness and Power: The Place of Sugar in Modern History*. New York: Penguin Books.

Nagengast, C. 1991. *Reluctant Socialists, Rural Entrepreneurs: Class, Culture, and the Polish State*. Boulder, CO: Westview Press.

Nickel, H.M. 1993. 'Women in the German Democratic Republic and in the New Federal States: Looking Backward and Forward (Five Theses)', in N. Funk and M. Mueller (eds), *Gender Politics and Post-Communism*. New York: Routledge.

Orlove, B. and H. Rutz (eds). 1989. *The Social Economy of Consumption*. Lanham, MD: University Press of America.

Ortner, S.B. 1995. 'Resistance and the Problem of Ethnographic Refusal', *Comparative Studies in Society and History* 37(1): 173–93.

Patico, J. and M. Caldwell. 2002. 'Consumers Exiting Socialism: Ethnographic Perspectives on Daily Life in Post-Communist Europe', *Ethnos* 67(3): 285–94.

Rosaldo, R. 1989. *Culture and Truth: The Remaking of Social Analysis*. Boston: Beacon Press.

Rosenberg, D. 1991. 'Shock Therapy: GDR Women in Transition from a Socialist Welfare State to a Social Market Economy', *Signs* 17(1): 129–51.

Ross, A. 1980. *No Respect: Intellectuals and Popular Culture*. New York: Routledge.

Sampson, S. 1991. 'Is There an Anthropology of Socialism?' *Anthropology Today* 7(5): 16–19.

Stein, M.B. 1993. 'The Present Is a Foreign Country: Germany after Unification', *Journal of Folklore Research* 30(1): 29–43.

Stewart, S. 1984. *On Longing: Narratives of the Miniature, the Gigantic, the Souvenir, the Collection*. Durham, NC: Duke University Press.

Verdery, K. 1996. *What Was Socialism, and What Comes Next?* Princeton, NJ: Princeton University Press.

Watson, R. (ed). 1994. *Memory, History and Opposition under State Socialism*. Santa Fe, NM: School of American Research Press.

Wilk, R. 1994. 'Consumer Goods as Dialogue about Development', in J. Friedman (ed.), *Consumption and Identity*. London: Harwood Press: 97–118.

Willis, P. 1990. *Common Culture*. London: Open University Press.

Chapter 2

Cross-Border Relations and Regional Identity on the Polish-German Border

Robert Parkin

Introduction

Poland's entry into the European Union on 1 May 2004 represented the culmination of a long-term goal for the post-communist political class.[1] Coming after entry into NATO in 1999, EU accession consolidated Poland's international status as a member of the Western military, diplomatic, commercial and political order. The largest and most populous of the 2004 accession states, it has already been making its presence felt in the new Europe, both diplomatically and in its export of hundreds of thousands of its citizens to seek work elsewhere in Europe.

Such population movements may include long-term sojourns in Spain or the UK, or be limited to day trips to Germany, just over the border from western Poland, which is fast losing its significance as a border. Indeed, much of this chapter describes attempts by local officials and some local people to reduce the significance of this border still further, even as the eastern border – now an external EU border – is subjected to greater control, a situation connected with recent administrative reforms within Poland itself (dating from 1 January 1999) coupled with the growing focus on stimulating regional units and identities across Europe generally (see Parkin 1999 and references therein, but especially Harvie 1994). Alongside this is a consideration of how local authorities themselves contribute to such identities, both internally and through their alliances with other authorities within and outside their own nation states. In doing so they supplement their supposedly rational administration by using ideas and concepts in symbolic ways in the service of particular ideologies of identity. As Cris Shore has said of 'Eurocrats' in Brussels (1993), bureaucrats generate symbolic meanings as well as design and implement policy: indeed, the former may support the latter. At the same time, these activities do not always have popular approval. Such tensions exist in the present case and are clearly of great interest to anthropologists.

Since one focus of the chapter is cross-border relations, something ought to be said too about borders as a topic of anthropological research (cf., e.g., Donnan and Wilson 1999, 1994; Wilson and Donnan 1998; O'Dowd 2001). Virtually all commentators on borders make the unexceptional observations that they bring people together as much as divide them and that any attempt to make a border more permeable reduces its significance. Much work, of course, has been directed at activities that are seen as challenging the integrity and significance of particular borders, such as cross-border trading, especially smuggling, migration and even tourism, as well as how border communities themselves are constituted (see Donnan and Wilson 1999 for a thorough discussion). At the same time, O'Dowd sees borders as also fundamentally undemocratic institutions even in an otherwise democratic Europe, since they owe their existence and exact configurations mostly to past wars, not democratic approval; yet even liberal democracy needs them to know whom to distribute rights and duties to as national citizens. With their extensive apparatuses of control, they are also, for Donnan and Wilson, both symbols of the state's power and sites of perhaps the most intense degree of official scrutiny that the law-abiding citizen is ever likely to encounter.

Nonetheless, local officials too may try to reduce the significance of particular national borders, in which case they may come into conflict with border guards and other police officials representing the state as a whole. In Europe, they do this particularly through the creation of cross-border regions. This goes far beyond the shortening of queues at the barriers or sending rescue services across the border to help with an emergency. O'Dowd neatly sums up their significance:

> Although most trans-frontier regions are created for pragmatic or instrumental reasons to access EU funding as a means of addressing shared environmental, planning or economic development problems, it may be argued that their real significance lies elsewhere [as] cross-national policy communities, advocacy and discourse coalitions, epistemic communities where the logic of communicative action, discourse and consensus creation may be just as important as the logic of instrumental action. (2001: 103)

Certainly all cross-border links between Poland and Germany seem to exist at least in part to celebrate themselves as well as to pursue practical concerns in the narrow sense, and they may even have a higher 'enjoyment' quotient for the officials involved than any real instrumentality.

As O'Dowd also points out (ibid.), the significance of cross-border regions and other links is frequently exaggerated by their supporters, whose core often consists of a local and rather unrepresentative elite of businessmen and officials, and regions are generally woefully under-resourced. One might also add that, given the paucity of 'hard policy' areas that national governments permit cross-border regions to act in, there is a distinct tendency to promote an innocuous and generally made-up cross-border 'culture' as an alternative, through festivals and the like. As we shall see, most of these observations apply to the present ethnographic situation too. First, however, I shall outline the 1999 administrative reforms in Poland that underpin these cross-border ties and give a brief account of my main research site, the new but also old province of Lubuskie, a border province roughly opposite Frankfurt an der Oder, the main German city and crossing point on this border.

Administrative Reform in Poland

Since 1 January 1999, Poland has had a new administrative structure with two main aspects.[2]

One is the establishment of an intermediate tier of administration, the *powiat*, usually translated as 'county' in English. This comes between the *województwa* or provinces – which have themselves been made larger but reduced in number – and the communes (*gminy*) and towns (*miasta*), which should be treated as one level for most purposes. The other aspect is a measure of decentralization, with each *województwo* being given its own *sejm* or parliament, under a speaker or *marszałek*, who is effectively also the political head of the provincial administration. This creation of new provinces, with their varying degrees of historical precedent and popular legitimacy, provides new opportunities for the development and possibly creation of new local and regional identities, both officially and unofficially, including those that cross national borders.

Decentralization suited Poland's policy of EU entry, being a response to the insistence of Brussels that all member states create some sort of regional structure, with or without local democratic institutions, as a means of disbursing development funds (the so-called structural funds). In Poland, decentralization had anyway been a long-standing policy of the Solidarity movement, which after 1989 saw it as a way of destroying the lingering power of the communist *nomenklatura* and the excessive central-ization socialist governments had exercised as a means of political control. But although most of the major political parties generally acknowledged that the 1999 reform was necessary, its actual implementation was highly controversial, and only the mediation of President Kwasniewski finally resolved the issue.

The Province of Lubuskie

Lubuskie was not one of the originally planned twelve provinces, but lo-cal people and officials exerted themselves to achieve separate recogni-tion through newspaper campaigns and petitions to parliament in War-saw. This was due less to a strong identification with any idea of Lubuskie than to a general disinclination to identify with any of the surrounding provinces whose merger with the area was otherwise impending, namely, Pomerania, Greater Poland or Lower Silesia. Nonetheless the idea of Lu-buskie is not in fact new, and the new province is in part a revival of an earlier province that existed in this area from 1945 to 1975. The name was chosen after the Second World War to link this area, until 1945 part of Germany, with an old Polish name and with Polish rule over it in the early Middle Ages: in other words, the adoption of the name was part of Po-land's irredentist agenda with regard to these territories, which it had now 'won back' after centuries of German rule.

The name and the territory it refers to appear to have a low profile on the German side of the border too. This is remarkable, given that the whole of Lubuskie in the historical sense (i.e., the territory extending more or less directly east and west of Frankfurt) was in German hands from at the latest 1249 to 1945, longer than Pomerania or East Prussia, where German settlement mostly dates from about 1350 to 1400, and much lon-ger than Silesia, which, although Germanized early on, became politically Prussian only in the 1740s. Yet it is precisely these latter regions that attract most German interest today, whether in the form of nostalgia as in the case of Pomerania and East Prussia, or outright irredentism as is frequently the case for Silesia. Since Germany retained most of Brandenburg proper, Lebuser Land, a truncated segment in Poland with few major towns or other resources, seems to have been largely forgotten by Germans who do not themselves have roots there.

Despite its takeover of other territory, Lubuskie is among the smaller new provinces and is relatively weak politically and economically. There tends to be a generational difference in ideas about identity here. The older generation that actually moved to Lubuskie from the *kresy*, the eastern territories lost to the Soviet Union in 1945, now mostly in their seventies and eighties, and to some extent their children, in their forties and fifties, still tend to identify with the *kresy*, regarding Lubuskie as their physical but not spiritual home. As for younger generations, many tend to think in terms of a purely national identity, insofar as they are not focused on absorbing a globalized, English-language culture through the Internet and other international media. Even after nearly sixty years of living in this part of the new territories, therefore, residents still have weak or non-existent regional identity, except in the negative sense mentioned earlier (i.e., of not being Silesians, Pomeranians, etc.).

Attempts to develop a sense of local identity are nonetheless being made at several official levels. Lubuskie has its own regional television news programme. One of the local newspapers had referred to 'Ziemia Lubuska' (Land of Lubuskie) even before the reforms, and others have been launched with the same focus or have shifted towards it; there are now newspapers for many of the new *powiaty* too. Another source of identity creation is local festivals.

Cross-border Identities

There are also, however, conscious attempts to establish cross-border identities along more or less the whole border, some official, some not, some somewhere in between. In the first place, this involves re-establishing continuity with a history that is long past and forgetting the break in that history represented by 1945. In the late 1940s, this was sometimes connected with Polish historians' and other apologists' claims that Poland was merely returning to territory it had previously ruled about a thousand years earlier. In the twenty-first century, it has at least as much to do with attempts to ignore the border that runs along the Oder/Odra and upper Neisse/Nysa rivers, and to re-create the territory on both sides of it as a single entity. This is especially visible in tourist literature, which often sets out to attract Germans in particular by re-creating a past when this whole area was not only German, but a playground for Berliners above all. This itself demands that the different ethnic and national histories of the area be glossed over.

Cross-border Cooperation

As mentioned earlier, cross-border cooperation between regional and local government bodies is a big issue in the context of European integration at present, at least among officials, if not always and everywhere the ordinary people they administer. These remarks apply equally to Poland, where they have an added interest, given EU membership. Cooperation also has narrower, more practical incentives for border communities in Poland: namely, it allows access to some EU funding under certain conditions, and local authorities on both sides of the EU border need international partners to qualify for it. Thus, for example, the construction of sewerage systems in Polish villages may be funded with EU money, so long as there is a cross-border dimension to them – not difficult to argue in this case, given that the border is a river system. However, not all cross-border links involve towns that are actually located right on the border, nor are local authorities themselves necessarily involved.

One example of cross-border cooperation is the twin town of Guben/ Gubin. It is actually one of a number of divided towns along the border that, having been single units within Germany before 1945, are sometimes compared with divided cities such as 'Mostar, Jerusalem and Berlin' (in Jahnke 2001: 18). They are thus not formerly separate cities that have linked up for purposes of greater cooperation (as happened in many cases along the Rhine between Germany and the Netherlands), but once-united towns and cities that have become divided through conflict. In the 1990s

Figure 2.1. Signboard in a Polish town celebrating its partnership with a German twin. Note that no indication is given of where the latter actually is. (Photo: Robert Parkin)

there were numerous attempts, with varying degrees of success, to reunite these towns, regardless of the border. Thus Zgorzelec/Görlitz now boasts cross-border bus services and special quick queues for taxis, whereas in Frankfurt/Słubice – site of the two most used crossings – there is still a lot of antagonism over border crossings and smuggling, despite the presence in both towns of the cross-border Viadrina University, a self-designated 'European University'.[3]

Along the scale of cooperation, Gubin and its German twin Guben lie somewhere in between these examples, in part because the two towns are more or less equal in size, unlike in other cases; therefore, people say, they only need one theatre, one technical school, etc., taken as a whole. A Polish island in the middle of the river, known as 'Theatre Island' after a former building on it, has been re-landscaped and opened to direct access to the German side. One German publication reporting on a conference on cooperation held in 2000 saw the landscaping itself as a symbol of cooperation, not only for the two towns but also for the whole of the cross-border region. What are needed here, the brochure suggests, are 'concrete building projects with symbolic significance' and 'a symbolic development policy containing a message for the population' (Jahnke 2001: 68–69, also 59).

The central border crossing is now restricted to pedestrians; vehicles must go south of the joint town to a new crossing at Gubinek (ibid.: 59). The greatest achievement of this cooperation to date is the construction of a new sewerage plant to serve both towns (see Figure 2.1). Yet the national dimension is never very far away. The plant, located on the Polish side, has to be a Polish company for legal reasons – it is not a joint venture – and it employs mainly Polish staff, apart from some German technicians who cross the border to work there every day. Indeed, it is accepted that the two towns will retain their national identities for the foreseeable future: one should think rather in terms of a 'German-Polish city' or a 'European site' (ibid.: 61).

Guben is obviously the most important partner for Gubin, given the possibilities for infrastructural cooperation, but the latter has other partners. One is Laatzen, a small town near Hanover that received refugees from Gubin in 1945. Their link dates back only some fifteen years or so and is cultural in kind rather than managerial or commercial. Another is Páks in Hungary, a link that is currently dormant but could be revived at any time – if, for example, a partner is needed for a future application. Generally, about 15–20 per cent of the mayor's time in Gubin went towards cross-border activities in 2002.

Another 'double city' is Frankfurt an der Oder / Słubice (formerly Ost-Frankfurt), which, despite the relative inactivity of the Euroregion that is also based around it (see below), is trying to develop cooperation directly across the busiest border crossing area (Figure 2.2). This dates back to 1993, when the declared goals were to improve cooperation regarding the economy, society and culture, and to remove mutual prejudices between Poles and Germans. One aspect of this cooperation was the creation of a cross-border university between Viadrina University in Frankfurt and the Collegium Polonicum in Słubice.

Figure 2.2. Bobrowice, Poland: plaque thanking the Foundation for German-Polish Cooperation for funding a new sewerage works in the town. (Photo: Robert Parkin)

Though it is an international university, teaching is mostly in German, not in Polish. One alleged result of this is that whereas it attracts high-quality German-speaking students from all over Poland, the German students there are basically local and less well-qualified, since the abler ones go elsewhere in Germany. Another aspect of cooperation was the restructuring of the motorway border crossing south of the city, at Świecko, a plan dating from 1994 and the first venture in cross-border planning between the two countries. More symbolic was the Europa Garden project, created to coincide with Frankfurt's 700th anniversary as a city in 2003, which laid out gardens on both sides of the Oder/Odra (Jahnke 2001: 34–35). The budget for this cooperation from 1999 to 2003 was DM 670.3 million.

Some of the intra-Polish tensions that can arise from such agreements are illustrated by recent events in Brody. This Polish village is dominated by a small castle, or what in England would probably count as a modest stately home, originally built and owned in the German period by the von Bruhl family, whose descendants still live near Kustrin, the next border town in Germany going north from Frankfurt. The castle fell into disrepair in the socialist period, though it was used intermittently as a store, hostel and so on. In the 1990s, restoration was attempted by two expatriate Poles. The first try, involving a South African Pole, never got off the ground at all. The second was made by a Canadian Pole who managed to restore one wing of the building before being arrested in Germany, leaving the village itself to recover from a deep sense of shock. The German-Polish friendship association he altruistically founded during the restoration work is now assumed in the village to have been a scam at least to reduce his debts, if not actually to fund his allegedly criminal activities. He was eventually released without charge, but the notices on the castle gates proclaiming European cooperation were still replaced with simple advertisements for the restaurant there. At one point the question arose as to whether the von Bruhl family themselves might become involved in completing the restoration of their old castle. It never came to anything, but it very publicly raised the possibility of a German takeover of what has become Polish property.

This is perhaps the most sensitive issue in this part of Poland, and it is aggravated by the realization that as an EU member Poland will have to allow foreigners to acquire land in the country without the irksome restrictions that apply at present. But much depends on one's attitude to Polishness. In Jędrzychowice, near Szlichtingowa, another palace is being restored by a member of the German branch of the original owning family, the Szlichtings, founders of Szlichtingowa itself about 350 years ago, who hailed from Latvia before moving to Lower Silesia. This lady, a German citizen, acquired the old palace through Polish frontmen but then married a Pole and is currently applying for Polish citizenship. This 'opting for Poland' is considered more acceptable.[4]

Another issue that has arisen in Brody concerns the renaming of the local gymnasium, whose pupils themselves were presented, as part of the decision-making process, with a list of six suggested names, five Polish but the sixth that of Alois von Bruhl, the German who actually built the castle and developed the village in the late eighteenth century. Perversely (from one point of view) they opted for Alois von Bruhl, since they knew their local history and were impressed by his significance in it. The school governors supported them in this, except for the director, who disallowed it on a technicality, and the commune council. Their counterargument was that this was a school in Poland and there were plenty of perfectly respectable Poles after whom it might be named, so why choose a German? In 2002 the matter fell into abeyance, pending the first local elections under the new system that autumn. Ultimately these changed nothing on the council, and after a further vote the school was finally named after the Polish nationalist poet Adam Mickiewicz (supported even by a majority of pupils). Some see the issues surrounding both the castle restoration and school renaming as reflecting a creeping Germanization that EU entry is only bound to increase, despite official denials that Germans are unwelcome.

One other aspect of cross-border cooperation is the occasional tensions that arise within particular bureaucracies. Among older officials in one town, I encountered some resentment of the bright, bilingual young things who had been brought in to run cross-border cooperation and were able to go on expenses-paid junkets to Germany to visit partner towns. This was aggravated by the fact that some of the older staff, but not their younger colleagues, had been left unpaid for months (not uncommon in itself) due to a delay in the town being reimbursed for some public expenditure by the provincial authorities in the administrative capital of Lubuskie, Gorzów Wielkipolska. Although the two budgets are ring-fenced from one another and money cannot be transferred between them, it still exacerbated the bad feeling.

The extent to which personalities are involved in these links is shown by the case of Szlichtingowa, in Wschowa *powiat*. Ties it had previously developed with Heel, in the Netherlands, fell into disuse because one of the key supporters of the link died and another became pregnant. The distance was not seen as an obstacle, and some hoped to revive the connection more formally for sporting and cultural exchanges with EU funding that had already been obtained, though it was unclear whether it would continue. In 2002, one German official in Forst proposed to continue his activities with Lubsko and Brody across the border after his imminent retirement precisely because of his perception that Poles in particular saw the relationships involved as personal, not just professional, and therefore expected to be dealing with the same opposite numbers all the time.

Euroregions

The German-Polish border is divided into four Euroregions, and Guben and Gubin are the joint headquarters of one, namely, Spree-Neisse-Bober / Sprewa-Nysa-Bóbr (henceforward SBN; named after local rivers). It covers most of the pre-reform province of Zielona Góra in Poland and the *Landkreis* of Spree-Neisse (Guben, Cottbus and Forst) in Germany, as well as Głogów in Lower Silesia. The other Euroregions along the border are focused on Szczecin (including certain parts of southern Sweden), Frankfurt an der Oder / Słubice, and Görlitz/Zgorzelec (Irek 2001).

Indeed, the whole Polish border now partakes in Euroregions together with the border districts of neighbouring states, and there is an annual conference of those involved on the Polish side of these organizations. Euroregions, which are basically unofficial associations of local authorities across borders, frequently describe themselves as NGOs. They were originally created in the early to mid 1990s to compensate for the continued centralization of administration in Poland in the years after the collapse of socialism but before the devolution of power after 1999. From the German point of view in particular, they were also seen as a way of combating unemployment by boosting cross-border trade. Once devolution arrived, some local politicians – especially the *marszałek* of the provincial *sejm* or parliament, who combines the post of speaker with that of head of policy for the province and effectively claims to be the head of its devolved government – argue that the Euroregions are now redundant, especially given their lack of formal power. Indeed, many Euroregion activities seem to consist of meetings containing little but exhortations to better cooperation, overcoming the legacy of the past and countering mutual stereotypes (Poles as smugglers, Germans as land-grabbers, etc.). Nonetheless, Euroregions have promoted cross-border cooperation in everything from trade to culture, tourism to school links, infrastructure to the easing of border restrictions. A more widespread view is that they will continue to have a role, despite their limitations.

Although there are plenty of precedents for them in western Europe, especially along the Rhine, the term 'Euroregion' appears to be particularly popular in eastern Europe as a way of affirming the European identity of new accession states like Poland. Euroregion logos are prominently displayed, especially at entrances to major towns in the area, but also on tour-

ist and other publicity material. As NGOs, Euroregions can only implement decisions that their member local authorities have passed separately
as part of routine local decision-making in their respective nation states.
Thus, despite all the rhetoric of cross-border cooperation overcoming national prejudices, there is necessarily a national dimension to their work.
For example, one of SBN's major achievements is that its residents can
now cross the border using identity cards only, without having to show
passports – yet this decision depended on the prior agreement of the respective national governments in Berlin and Warsaw. Euroregion officials
are rarely if ever salaried as such and almost invariably have other duties,
though they may have their own offices and even buildings in some cases
(e.g., in Gubin).

Dating from 1993, that is, prior to the 1999 reforms in Poland, the SBN
Euroregion originally consisted of just six communes on the Polish side
plus Forst and Cottbus in Germany, though it soon expanded to its current
limits. In Poland it is largely associated with the enthusiasm of one particular individual, a local civil servant in Zielona Góra and a former MP, but
a native of Gubin. Nonetheless, some of his German colleagues claimed
that the initiative in setting up the Euroregion actually came from their
side – a fairly typical conflict of claims. A more open conflict concerned
a German plan, never implemented, to shift the German headquarters of
the Euroregion from Guben to Forst, capital of the Spree-Neisse *Landkreis,*
which excited protests from precisely the same native of Gubin just mentioned, who saw this plan as a challenge to the unity of the Euroregion.
This could be interpreted as a local example of what seems to be a quite
common aspect of processes of devolution generally, namely, that their
advocates frequently want to halt the process once it reaches them.

Aims and Outcomes

At least in Lubuskie, money – especially the possibility of obtaining EU
money – is popularly seen as the main reason for entering into cross-border
relations of the sort described above. In practice this is only partly true.
For one thing, and quite simply, money is typically not sought for itself,
but for what it makes possible in terms of improving infrastructure and
services, especially education, and with them the quality of life for local
residents (cf. Irek 2001). This may also apply to what we might loosely call
'cultural' or 'symbolic' notions that support the idea of a particular cross-
border region having a common identity. Secondly, money is not always
emphasized by officials themselves. Both the leading Polish and German
figures in the SBN Euroregion, despite their enthusiasm for cross-border

cooperation, felt that it was more a matter of management than finance. In general, both thought the significance of the EU link exaggerated, applications being more trouble than they were worth – an accusation frequently also directed at the Euroregion itself by area communes trying to raise money through it.[5] The Polish representative in particular had no interest in developing contacts with Brussels directly (e.g., through the Committee of Regions) and did not even favour Poland's joining the EU.

Nonetheless, money is a factor in the minds of other officials, though they are not always in a position to take advantage of it. Application requirements like matching funds, a computer disc, or a version in English are tall orders for impoverished communes. For example, funding by the PHARE programme ('Poland and Hungary: Assistance for Restructuring their Economies'), through which the Euroregions frequently make applications or validate ones from member communes or *powiaty,* requires 25 per cent matching funds from applicants (mostly local administrations and NGOs) for projects of between €100,000 and €300,000. Even the €25,000 minimum needed is clearly out of reach for many, if not most, local authorities in Poland for what are essentially classed as small projects. However, Euroregion publicity stresses other advantages of membership, such as the systematic upgrading of administrative skills that involvement in its activities allegedly provides, and the fact that citizens of both countries in border areas can now cross the border using just identity cards. Other advantages include cooperation in providing emergency services and tourist facilities (especially cycle tracks and bridleways) and encouraging tourism more generally. For instance, the village of Bronków near Bobrowice received PHARE funds to develop agro-tourism through the Euroregion, though facilities appear modest at best (often the 'agro-tourism' or 'ecotourism' promoted in tourist literature in the area hardly seems to qualify as such in western European terms). Bobrowice itself secured PHARE funding to install sewerage systems.

Many officials reported difficulties, not only in applying for funds through the Euroregion, as already indicated, but also in obtaining basic information on what was on offer and how to go about applying for it. Seminars to explain this were inadequately advertised and thus may be missed. An application might be rejected due to a minor omission or mistake. The Frankfurt/Słubice Euroregion was considered especially difficult to work with, being generally uncooperative and inactive. Finding partners in Germany could also be difficult: they were often considered passive and unenthusiastic, accepting invitations to come to Poland but not reciprocating, and so on. One official told me it was often easier to cooperate with Germans away from the border, where there was less to 'cooperate' over.

Outcomes, in the areas of trade links and tourism in particular, have mostly proved disappointing. Businessmen are put off by their lack of knowledge of legal regimes in the other country, as well as by a perception of enhanced risks to investments, and so on. One Polish businessman said he had indeed obtained fresh contacts and business from his membership of the Euroregion – but only on the Polish side of the border. Tourism is held back by a lack of facilities, even at potentially major sites, and planned cycle routes and horse trails do not always join up because some communes are less enthusiastic than others in creating them. Cultural projects are often only short-term, even when they are talked up tremendously, because the money runs out. Thus a cultural Eurocentre that was set up in Łagów, a Polish resort village about thirty miles from the border, in the mid 1990s – widely trumpeted at the time as a great success for cross-border cooperation and cultural understanding – is now completely forgotten in the village itself, even in the administration and the converted castle, now a hotel and restaurant, that had accommodated it.

Nonetheless, cooperation in sporting and school exchanges, and in mutual support in emergencies, is valued in many cases, even on occasion where applications for funding have not yet succeeded. While the *powiat* is a source of policy initiatives but a drain on the funds of the *gmina,* the Euroregion can accept projects directly from the *gmina* and fund them. In the commune of Dąbie this proved especially fruitful for waste treatment and the environmental protection of local rivers. In effect, therefore, the *powiat* and the Euroregion represented parallel but different supra-commune bodies performing different roles.

Cross-border ties often suffer a publicity deficit. Some officials pointed to specific attempts to publicize Euroregion activities they had been involved in, not least by displaying the European logo on notices and publicity material, and at cultural and sports events involving cross-border ties. On the other hand, although the various Euroregions have newsletters that are provided free of charge to the general public, most town-twinning arrangements are scarcely publicized at all. One town in Poland displays a placard with a photograph of a tree-planting ceremony celebrating the town's twinning with a town in Germany, but it does not say where the partner town is (not even the partner country), let alone that the ceremony was actually held there (Figure 2.1). One official's response to this lacuna was that it was such a small town that everyone knew what was going on there anyway.

The actual location of partner towns is frequently uncertain. In one case, a partner town I was told was in Holland turned out to be in Denmark, and I had to tell the deputy mayor that another of his partner towns, this time in Germany, was not actually a member of the same, or indeed

Figure 2.3. Słubice, Poland: signboard announcing the nearby border with Germany as a 'Border of Tolerance' in German and Polish. (Photo: Robert Parkin)

any other, Euroregion. In general, the hope of developing a specific Euroregion identity beyond official circles seems wishful thinking at the moment, even among such circles.

The German Perspective

As already noted, German officials claim the credit for setting up the SNB Euroregion, though they admit they found a ready response in Poland. One of the original reasons, an official told me in Forst, was to try and do something about unemployment in the region. At least on the German side, membership could allow voting rights, or only speaking rights, as for firms (which tended to be sceptical of the venture anyway). In 2002 members were paying €255.64 for membership. There was existing funding until 2006, which would then have to be renewed if the venture was to keep going. My informant confirmed what I had been told in Guben (Poland), namely, that the link with Brussels was difficult and insignificant, though the Brandenburg office in Brussels had made space for a Euroregion display on one occasion. He also repeated that money was less important than human contact – central government had the last word about money anyway. Although 25–30 per cent of his work concerned cross-border relations, he was not paid as a Euroregion official.

This official also felt that the media and public were generally negative about cross-border ties in Forst. The Euroregion undertook to counter negative reporting by the media. Opposition had arisen in Guben at one point because cross-border shopping was being connected with local bankruptcies, but this is less true today. As far as Forst was concerned, however, most Poles only passed through it to somewhere else, and the newly introduced rail service from Żagan was little used as yet (as was a similar service from Guben to Zielona Góra). However, there may well have been more economic cooperation and trade than the authorities realized. Also, recent floods had encouraged partnership and practical cooperation. Fire brigades and all schools now had contacts across the border, and the sewerage plant in Gubin had promoted personal friendships.

Cross-border Meetings

Attending cross-border meetings brings out the similarities and, more noticeably on the whole, the differences between the two sides. I was able to attend one of a series of meetings to discuss cross-border cooperation in one twin town up to 2030. The meetings were arranged by the German side and funded with EU money from a budget that could only be used within the EU, of which Poland was not yet a member at this stage. This meant that the Polish officials who were expected to take part in these meetings could not, at that time, benefit from it financially as their German partners could. Officials in Poland frequently felt they were only junior partners in cross-border cooperation, as German partners sometimes pursued quite different agendas, not to mention their lukewarm attitude to Polish concerns.

Generally, in my experience, there was a slight but noticeable tendency for Germans to dominate the discussions. One concern was certainly cross-border prejudices and how to eliminate them, as well as how to create a sense of identity that would straddle the border. Sometimes the word 'mentality' was used here, especially by Germans, who tended to be more concerned with overcoming the prejudices and hostilities of the past and saw this as a psychological problem, though also one that could be overcome through education and individual goodwill. At this same meeting, identity and mentality were topics ascribed the same importance as the development of tourism, education or transport links. This is not to say that there was much agreement. While the German moderator stressed the 'identity of the double city', at least some Polish officials stressed national identity as the only meaningful option in the area. The Germans saw a strong local identity as a way of keeping people in the area to look for work – a particular problem in many towns in eastern Germany, given the torrent of people going westwards in search of employment.[6] Other Polish officials, on the other hand, said only jobs would keep people in the area; without them, there would be no identity anyway. Questions of identity were therefore discussed officially, but views of their significance, if any, varied.

Another, more general meeting brought together representatives of the Euroregion, local authorities and the (German only) police. The Polish representative of the Euroregion, who seemed to regard the meeting as largely a waste of time, saw the main problem as a lack of coordination between planners on either side of the border, suggesting that a joint planning committee was needed and highlighting a tendency for putting forward projects that were on the border but did not actually cross it. He also noted that Poland was ceasing to be attractive to German investment because wage rates were rising. His German counterpart, meanwhile, bemoaned the lack of bilingual menus on the border and reckoned that the main problems were economic: otherwise, everything was fine. Other German officials backed him up, highlighting the problems of Polish firms operating in Germany, including costs; restrictions on employment (often circumvented by using German frontmen); language; differences in wages, laws and tax regimes; and transport systems. Nonetheless, Polish firms generally showed flexibility in getting round such problems. Conversely, German businessmen were made uneasy by their ignorance of Polish law and fears over the safety of their investments in Poland. To facilitate such cooperation, it was said, psychological barriers needed to be removed (much applause at this), and both sides' interests and requirements taken into account in planning any aspect of cooperation. However, cross-border cooperation also raised unresolved constitutional issues for Germany, given that the semi-autonomous *Länder* were also involved.

Unofficial Links

This uncertainty and lack of publicity should not lead one to overlook certain popular initiatives in creating cross-border links. Most unusual in this respect is the story of Wellmitz, a village just north of Guben in Germany, and its relationship with Wełmice, a Polish village near Bobrowice. Struck by the similarity of names,[7] both sides decided to investigate further as soon as the border opened up and to develop the contacts thus made into a regular relationship. The key here was the partnership between a Polish woman (discussed more below) in Wełmice and a local historian in Wellmitz, but the latter died suddenly in 2001 at the age of thirty-one. Nonetheless the relationship continued, characterized by regular mutual visits to local festivals, sports events (especially football[8]) and so on. Also, the German village collected and sent clothing, toys and other goods to the visibly poorer Polish village. These contacts were pursued by local people in each village with little or no input from local officials, apart from their often turning up at festivals; indeed, those who set up this relationship liked to see themselves as cultivating 'human' contacts and not just an image, as official ties so often seemed to.

However, this informality had potential to change. The mainstay of the arrangement in the Polish village wanted to get herself elected *sołtys* (village mayor) in the 2002 elections, so as to be able to take things further. This plan failed because she was not registered as resident in the village but in Berlin, where she had been a long-term resident. Although she herself was born near Szczecin, her father and other relatives came from the village (one relative was on the *gmina* council), and after retiring from her job in Berlin she had decided to return there to buy a 'good old German house' and fix it up. Certainly her house, on the edge of the village, was in conspicuously good condition in what was otherwise obviously a very poor village. In many ways, she was a typical 'incomer', wishing to 'do things' in and for the village in the face of increasing hostility from the other inhabitants, not least because of her association with Germany and with her considerable numbers of paying German guests – many with pre-1945 links to the village – whom she invited on a regular basis.

By the summer of 2003, therefore, she had become somewhat isolated from the rest of the village and was cooperating instead with her cousin, who was a Bobrowice *gmina* council member, and the mayor of Bobrowice, a right-winger from Warsaw who by 2002 had held the post for ten years, was politically well connected (*mocny,* or 'strong') and knew how to get things done, as well as with her German friends in Wellmitz, whom she frequently visited. The former village mayor of Wełmice had been re-elected against a single weak opponent and was allegedly encouraging villagers to boycott the woman's efforts to develop links with Wellmitz further. For this reason she now felt disillusioned and closer to Germans than to her own countrymen, who were polite to her face but accused her behind her back of pursuing cross-border ties for her own financial benefit through applications for funding. Having largely withdrawn from contact with them, she was now placing her faith in her own allies to take things further, which in effect meant bringing in officialdom. Given the disparity in population between Wellmitz (nearly 1,000 people) and Wełmice (300 plus), and the fact that Wellmitz itself was the centre of a commune of 2,000 people, cooperation was now in any case better pursued at the inter-commune level (Wellmitz-Bobrowice), that is, officially. One project here involved Herta AC, the Berlin football club, which was interested in renovating the football ground in Wełmice as part of its long-term search for new talent – but this would go through the commune, not the village. Thus, in the course of a single year, the cross-border relationship between these two villages had failed to bring the villagers together on their own terms and instead become a vehicle for Germans to visit 'their' old village without having to take much notice of the Poles who had replaced them. It was also in the process of being taken out of the hands of even the willing villagers by local officialdom.

In another example of individual initiative, one elderly German I met, who had been born in Lubsko in Poland and was now a frequent visitor to what he still called 'Sommerfeld' (its pre-1945 name), was well known to the local administration and had plans to publish a book of old postcards of the town – a common publishing project in the area generally at the time.[9] He was particularly anxious to demonstrate his goodwill towards Poland and the Poles who had taken over his birthplace, and to overcome the past, being concerned to distance himself from those Germans who turned their backs on cross-border links of this sort. Such demonstrations of goodwill were frequent (especially, perhaps, on the German side; Poles tended to refer to them only when things went wrong) and may seem heartening, but the very stress on them indicates an underlying tension in these relationships that was absent from other examples elsewhere in Europe. Quite simply, they were not yet taken for granted.

Some General Conclusions

In conclusion, therefore, officials often see themselves as cultivating an identity for the province or for the whole cross-border area – provided, of course, that they recognize the word 'identity' to begin with, which is not always the case.

Secondly, national politics may also have an impact on these activities. While national centres, that is, Berlin and Warsaw, want to keep key decisions in their own hands – especially those on funding, which, whatever its source or destination, still goes through them – they are not above exploiting local cross-border ties for their own ends. In the forums of the Euroregions especially, local officials and politicians are able to say things that Berlin or Warsaw might like to say but cannot, for either domestic or diplomatic reasons. The principal such reason is probably that the respective national populations as wholes are more sceptical of cooperation with the other state than are those along the border. At the same time, complaints about the nature of cross-border cooperation might create a diplomatic incident at the international level but can be made more innocuously at the local level. Local contacts thus provide national governments with a way of sending both positive and negative messages about cooperation to one another without doing so themselves.

Another aspect of relationships between national capitals and border areas is the potential to reverse the polarity of centre-periphery relations by developing not just cross-border cooperation, but strong and fairly autonomous cross-border regions. For example, both Guben and Gubin, located on fairly remote parts of the border, complain of neglect by their respective national governments. However, by combining their hinterlands as a Euroregion and placing its headquarters in the double town, they have themselves become regional centres.

Thirdly, at the risk of romanticizing the situation somewhat, it is worth stressing the large amount of goodwill underlying these activities. There is still no shortage of either Poles or Germans who have little time for, or even continue to hate, one another. The activities even of advocates of increasing cross-border cooperation do not always run smoothly, sometimes creating resentment on the other side, though rarely threatening a complete breakdown. This reflects an inevitable combination – of differences in perspectives and perceived interests, different national pressures and the influence of, and reaction to, particular political egos – that is entirely typical of European politics generally. Nonetheless, in this one part of eastern Europe, international cooperation has so far run relatively smoothly and produced real gains, from the point of view of those who dislike conflict. I would argue that this is typical of this half of the continent rather than otherwise, despite the tragedy of the Balkans in the 1990s.

Lastly, both official and unofficial challenges to the integrity and permanence of the western border are gradually producing a new situation that reduced its significance considerably even before Poland's EU entry. These cross-border activities reflect, but also contribute to, the idea of a 'Europe of regions', which is intended to prevent a return of either nationalist competition between states in Europe or authoritarianism within them. But even while the new Europe is an expanded one, it is also incomplete. On its now more heavily controlled eastern border, Poland is also contributing to an alternative idea, that of Fortress Europe, while ensuring that it will itself be within the laager. In the Europe of the future, regional, national and international identities will be worked out through the tensions between these two ideas.

Notes

1. The first period of fieldwork on which this chapter is based was carried out between February and September 2002 and funded by the Max Planck Society, through the Max Planck Institute for Social Anthropology, Halle, Germany. I am most grateful to Prof. Chris Hann, co-director of this institute, for arranging the funding during this period and supporting my research generally, as well as to his staff for their unfailing aid. Further fieldwork was carried out the following summer with funding from my then employer, the University of Oxford. I also acknowledge the invaluable aid of Maciej Irek, who acted as my field assistant during both periods. As this essay was first composed in 2005 and the situation has since changed radically, especially after Poland's EU entry, much of the present account must be considered historical.
2. The historical description in this section is based largely on Millard (1999: 53–55) and Bingen (1999: 95–98).
3. See Irek (2001). Viadrina is the Latin word for the Oder/Odra, and therefore neutral as opposed to German or Polish, as well as suggestive of the universal values associated with medieval Latin. The Polish partner is actually part of the Adam Mickiewicz University in Poznań.
4. Other people of mixed descent who have opted to become German citizens are equally feted on the other side of the border. 'Pure' descent does not seem to be a requirement for either German or Polish identity to be recognized.
5. For example, the requirement to provide the application on disc, and with an English translation, was seen as a significant impediment for an application that might only produce €1000.
6. Such losses of population on the German side of the border represent a loss of human capital and of knowledge, something that needs addressing through the education of those remaining (Jahnke 2001: 42). An earlier conference had also emphasized not economic integration but other aspects of cooperation, since mutual understanding had to be created first (ibid.: 66–67). My sense is that most Poles would regard this essentially German attitude as pie in the sky.
7. The first root in each name probably means 'brook, stream' in Old Polish and/or Slavonic. The suggestion of one official in Bobrowice, that Germans had gone from the Polish to the German village in 1945, was not substantiated in either village.
8. Wełmice won all the early matches. A local paper celebrated one such win with the headline 'Zwycięstwo integracja' (integration victory).
9. E.g., with respect to Guben/Gubin. Also, a semi-public photographic exhibition of Lubsko, today and yesterday, was housed in a cellar under the town hall.

References

Bingen, D. 1999. *Die Republik Polen: eine kleine politische Landeskunde*. Munich: Aktuell.
Donnan, H. and T.M. Wilson. 1999. *Borders: Frontiers of Identity, Nation and State*. Oxford and New York: Berg.
———— (eds). 1994. *Border Approaches: Anthropological Perspectives on Frontiers*. Lanham, MD: University Press of America.
Harvie, C. 1994. *The Rise of Regional Europe*. London and New York: Routledge.
Irek, M. 2001. 'Made-to-measure Strategy: Self-governance Initiatives in the Dreilaendereck', in D.G. Papademetriou and D.W. Meyers (eds), *Caught in the Middle: Border Communities in an Era of Globalization*. Washington, D.C.: Carnegie Endowment of International Peace and Migration Policy Institute.

Jahnke, K. (ed.). 2001. *Dokumentation zur Konferenz, 'Deutsch-Polnische und andere Grenz-städte: die Grenze als Chance', Guben–Gubin und Frankfurt/Oder–Słubice 19-21.10.2000.* Großräschen: Internationale Bauaustellung.

Millard, F. 1999. *Polish Politics and Society.* London and New York: Routledge.

O'Dowd, L. 2001. 'State Borders, Border Regions and the Construction of European Identity', in M. Kohli and M. Novak (eds), *Will Europe Work? Integration, Employment and the Social Order.* London and New York: Routledge.

Parkin, R. 1999. *Regional Identities and Alliances in an Integrating Europe: A Challenge to the Nation State?* Oxford: ESRC (Transnational Communities Research Programme Working Papers, WPTC-99-07).

Shore, C. 1993. 'Inventing the "People's Europe": Critical Approaches to European Community "Cultural Policy"', *Man* 28: 779–800.

Wilson, T.M. and H. Donnan (eds). 1998. *Border Identities: Nation and State at International Frontiers.* Cambridge: Cambridge University Press.

Chapter 3

The Skeleton versus the Little Grey Men
Conflicting Cultures of Anti-nuclear Protest
at the Czech-Austrian Border

Birgit Müller

After the radioactive cloud from the Chernobyl nuclear accident in 1986 had travelled over the whole of Europe, it was clear that the perception of danger and political treatment of risk were by no means the same from one European state to the next. The radioactive cloud seemed to have passed the states of 'real existing socialism' unnoticed to descend in force in Austria, where it provoked strong reactions among a population that had renounced the use of nuclear energy eight years before in a referendum against activating the reactors of Zwentendorf, the only nuclear power station ever built in Austria.

The construction and, in 2000, the start-up of the Temelin nuclear power station fifty kilometres from the Czech–Austrian border, brought Austrian NGOs, citizens and regional politicians to blockade the border in protest for two weeks in September. The border blockades of 2000 marked the culmination of a decade of tensions and conflicts between Czech and Austrian anti-nuclear activists about the right way to make the Czech public and politicians aware of the risks and long-term consequences of nuclear power. Although Austrian activists took pains to explain that the action was not directed against the Czech people as such but at the Czech and Austrian governments' unresponsiveness to their worries, the blockades led to Czechs' increasing identification with Temelin as a solely national

---

Notes for this chapter begin on page 88.

issue and to their rejection of Austrian interference. The issue raised questions relevant to recent scholarship on transnational advocacy networks where borders between states become permeable to international political activism (Arsel 2003: 7). What is the interrelation between proximity and asymmetry of activist groups from different countries who focus on the same campaign issues but come from different political cultures with different histories of dealing with conflict and experiencing the dangers of nuclear radiation?

For Keck and Sikkink, 'a transnational advocacy network includes those actors working internationally on an issue, who are bound together by shared values, and a common discourse, and dense exchanges of information and services' (Keck and Sikkink 1998: 2). The difficulties that Austrian and Czech cross-border anti-nuclear activists encountered in finding a common discourse and symbolism of action throw light on the difficulties of these networks in action. The social geographer Henk van Houtum usefully distinguishes three dimensions of space as the context in which people act: action space, affection space and cognition space (van Houtum 1999: 331). These spaces determine how mental borders are perceived and evolve.

Action space is constructed through the actual actions and deeds of actors. In the era of communism, the action space of Czech and Austrian citizens was limited to their respective national territories, where they developed different forms of addressing state authorities. It was possible to appeal to communist state authorities in a petition, but demonstrations, blockades or even media work were repressed as modes of action. Contrariwise, in Austria resistance to atomic energy production had become official state policy after the Zwentendorf referendum, and spectacular actions against atomic energy were officially tolerated and even supported. After the socialist system ended and the borders were opened between Austria and the Czech Republic, preferences for certain forms of action and relationships to state authorities subsisted. A further dissimilarity was that Czech anti-nuclear activists were acting against the official nuclear politics, whereas Austrians were acting in conformity with the position of their government.

Cognition space is the awareness, subjective knowledge and recognition of the characteristics and conditions in one's own or another territorial unit. The Austrian perception of nuclear danger had been shaped by the successful mobilization against the first Austrian atomic power station in Zwentendorf and the strong western media coverage of the Chernobyl accident, which contributed to the perception that the political system in eastern Europe was unaccountable for dealing with nuclear danger. Meanwhile, the worldviews of Czech citizens under communism were shaped by the imagined 'Other'. Depending on their ideological outlook, Czechs regarded Austrians as either the Western imperialist enemy or the lucky Western citizen who lived in abundance and could indulge in the luxury of criticizing the state. In Czechoslovakia, the imposition of nuclear power without public debate and the silence about the Chernobyl accident influenced how Czechs regarded the construction of Temelin. Access to information about Chernobyl, which Czechs obtained after 1989, did not affect the popular perception of nuclear danger in the same way that living through the counting of becquerels in food, avoiding rain showers and decontaminating sand pits on children's playgrounds had affected the Austrians.

Affection space is determined by feelings towards and connectedness with space, and also by the feelings citizens develop in a certain political space. For the Austrians in 1986, fear of radiation was a physical experience. For Czechs today, however, thinking about nuclear danger and calculating its probability is more of an intellectual exercise. Their strong emotional attachment lies in settling accounts with the communist system on one hand and defending national sovereignty on the other.

This chapter will examine how local activists living close to the Temelin power station and members of Czech environmental associations perceive anti-nuclear campaigns by Czech and Austrian activists. Based on interviews with villagers and local, regional and national-level Czech activists, and using materials from village chronicles compiled by local historians, I will retrace their experience with nuclear and state power before and after the Velvet Revolution[1] and their assessment of the foreign element of protesting Austrians. I will then analyse the Czech and Austrian movements' perceptions of the nuclear problem by examining visual materials used in their campaigns and the reception of certain foreign symbols, colours and slogans in the Czech Republic. In the third section, I will look at interactions and interdependencies between Czech and Austrian anti-nuclear activists and analyse their different forms of political action, focusing on the transmission and reinterpretation of forms of political action across the borders, the perception of risk and political responsibility, and the expectancies linked to the idea and practice of a (European) democracy. What impact do mental borders have on cooperation between European citizens, once political borders are softened in a unified Europe?

Nuclear Power and Civic Action
before and after the Velvet Revolution

As one drives north on the highway from České Budějovice towards Týn nad Vltavou, the four cooling towers of the Temelin power station suddenly rear up to dominate the rolling landscape of South Bohemia. Březi, the name of the hamlet that was torn down when the station was built, is readable on a rusty sign in front of the towers. The old manor house of Temelinec, now transformed into a visitors' centre for the power station, stands in front of the reactor blocks. The church was reopened for public access only after the Velvet Revolution. A photograph of its graveyard's cast-iron crosses with the cooling towers in the background figured prominently in the first Greenpeace campaign materials against Temelin.

The decision to build a nuclear power station and destroy the hamlets on the site, announced in 1980, came as a total surprise and shock to residents of the area. The totalitarian state imposed the decision without discussion or consultation. A petition against the project, signed by almost all the inhabitants, was not supported by the local village council and never received a reply from the central government. The chronicler of Litoradlice,[2] a hamlet five kilometres from the power station, likened the decision to the sudden, unexpected outbreak of war:

> Some years ago I saw a film about the invasion of the Soviet Union by Hitler's army. I was particularly shaken by the beginning of the film. In the picture were two young people, a boy and a girl, holding each other by the hand. In their faces I could see light-heartedness, joy in a life full of ideals for the future. Suddenly bombs fall, lives are destroyed, and so is everything that people have built up. This is how I would like to characterize our village until the 23rd of October 1980, except that on that date no bombs fell. Instead we realized that on the territory of our village a huge nuclear power station was going to be built.... On the 23rd of October the head of the party organisation Koubouška informed us that in the first step the hamlets Březi, Temelínec and at a later date the hamlets Podhaji and Kmín were to be liquidated. (Vrzak, 1980)

Local inhabitants experienced what was supposed to be a symbol of socialist power and progress as the end of all they had worked for and believed in. When no answer came to their petition, a delegation was sent to Prague; it returned with the message that the power station was a strong planning priority of the socialist government and indispensable to economic progress. In 1983 the inhabitants of the hamlets closest to the power station were obliged to move and accept a low price for their houses and land. Construction started in 1986, the year of the Chernobyl accident. Workers and engineers from all over the Czech Republic were brought to Temelin, changing the composition of the population and swinging the mood slightly towards favouring the power station.

In 1990, the population still living around the construction site started to petition the government again. Members of the new environmental association South Bohemian Mothers collected two thousand signatures. Politicians visited the area, promising to halt the construction, and President Vaclav Havel officially spoke out against nuclear energy. Construction nevertheless continued, slowly but steadily. The project was now limited to two reactor blocks instead of the four that were initially planned. More hamlets were destroyed, and petitions were lost or never answered – 'in spite of the fact that we were already free, that we were already a democracy', as one inhabitant phrased it. Czech television journalists came to interview the inhabitants about their opinions on nuclear energy and the resettlement. In late April 1990, the first demonstrators from Greenpeace Austria arrived bearing white banners referring to the Chernobyl catastrophe, which they hung on the outside of the cooling towers. Austrian television crews interviewed the inhabitants.

The first big joint demonstration, organized by Czech and Austrian environmental organizations Hnutí Duha, Děti Země, South Bohemian Mothers, Greenpeace and others, took place on 27 April 1991. Demonstrators met in Týn nad Vltavou to unroll a banner ten thousand metres long that symbolized the quarantine zone after a nuclear accident. The Austrian protesters brandished colourful posters painted with aggressive slogans and death skulls. The noisy, aggressive, dramatic protest they staged met with consternation among the villagers. Villagers also remembered that the protesting Austrians had nice clothing, good cars and modern camera equipment, and that they behaved as if they were at home. One of the villagers[3] recalled that German-speaking protestors had asked her why the locals did not join in the protests. She told me: 'What can we do? We don't mean anything to them.... We common people we can't change anything' (interview 14 September 2004). The spokesperson for the anti-nuclear NGO South Bohemian Mothers, characterized this reply as 'anti-activism' typical of the region. She explained that not only the communist past but also the Roman Catholic tradition of South Bohemia had traditionally kept the inhabitants out of the riots and revolts that affected regions under stronger Hussite influence. Activists in Upper Austria interpreted the local Czech population's lack of involvement in the protests as a consequence of biased reporting in the media and of fear of political repression:

> The population over there generally doesn't dare to speak up. Those who do, they then go with us, Austrians. If there is an action at the cooling towers, then Austrians are present and a few Czech People. Czechs don't come most of the time, they are afraid.... They still get locked up immediately if they do anything against the will of the government. This is not like in our country, that they would have the freedom to say what they think. They have not got that far yet. (Interview[4] with the mayor of an Austrian village 15 April 2004)

In the following years, the construction slowly progressed. The U.S. firm Westinghouse was commissioned to develop a modern Western controlling system for the Soviet reactor technology used in the power station. In the mid 1990s, the Czech Electricity Company (ČEZ) sponsored investments in village infrastructure, streetlights, a kindergarten and a home for the elderly. This flurry of construction meant odd jobs for the villagers and provided an inflow of orders for local artisans and service providers. Czech environmental groups like Greenpeace and Hnutí Duha attempted to pinpoint shortcomings in the station's security system and technical mistakes in the reactor. Greenpeace activists staged a sit-in accompanied by a howling siren at the office of reactor security in Prague to claim access to technical documents and draw media attention. They managed to attract media but got no access to documentation. In the meanwhile, local residents attempted to get the government and the company to agree not to destroy the hamlets in the vicinity of the power station, as the American security system was supposed to provide sufficient safety. Uninhabited safety zones were uncommon around nuclear power stations in western countries, they argued. They wrote letters to Prime Minister Vaclav Klaus, to the ČEZ general director, to the Department of Health and Hygiene in České Budějovice and to the regional office for construction. The answers were contradictory and inconclusive. Vaclav Klaus answered that some had the bad luck to live inside the security zone while others lived outside it, implying that nothing could be done about it. The general director of ČEZ responded that a beautiful leisure park would be constructed later in the security zone. As for the regional authorities,

> The officer of health and hygiene says that after evaluation the security area may be reduced or maybe even cancelled. And the employee of the ministry of regional development noted that we are on the side where the winds blow. Only the bureau for nuclear security answered that he will inform me after evaluating the parameters that have to be provided by the power plant. This is the current situation. (*Vrzak 1996*).

The demolitions and resettlements continued, and the chronicle enumerates the names of people resettled and the houses destroyed.

As of the mid 1990s, regular camps of protestors set up around the power station, especially towards the end of April on the anniversary of Chernobyl. Police blocked the road between Temelin and Březi, obliging locals to make a huge detour to take their children to school. Very few inhabitants sympathized with the occupants or went to see the camps. One who did told me, almost in surprise, that cultural actions, theatre and music performances were staged there, things seemed in good order and the protesters made sure to stop the cultural events at 10:00 P.M., so as not to disturb the locals. In 1997 an international blockade of the power station took a more chaotic turn. Young activists from Holland, Germany,

Bulgaria, Russia, Belgium, France and New Zealand had come together to set up camp for four weeks and block access to the construction site. However, after only four days the camp was broken up because of conflicts between Czech environmental NGOs and international participants. The Czechs claimed strategic leadership of the protests and called off the action. Moravia was menaced by floods, so they decided the protestors should go there to help. After that year's camp, the international element of the protests lost momentum and the Austrians from the Upper Austrian border zone gained more influence.

In 1997 the Upper Austrian government created its own department for anti-atomic coordination appointing a Czech émigré, as the coordinator. The task was to coordinate all activities opposing atomic energy, keep in contact with NGOs, inform them about activities by other NGOs and control the funding they received for different projects from the Upper Austrian government. The anti-atomic coordinator had to maintain contact with other regional governments, the national government and offices in Brussels. The main task was to find weak points and security problems in the nuclear projects, pinpoint economic inefficiencies and alert official bodies about these problems. The Upper Austrian Platform of NGOs against Atomic Energy set up its own office in České Budějovice to inform the Austrian public and NGOs, and coordinate campaigns in the Czech Republic.

Simultaneously and independently, the Czech environmental organization Hnutí Duha put all its energy into the anti-Temelin campaign to influence the vote of the Czech parliament in 1999. Its lobbying failed, so in early 2000 the group launched a petition campaign for a referendum against Temelin that collected 120,000 signatures from Czech citizens. The Czech government chose to ignore the petition and activated Temelin's first reactor block in the summer of 2000.

That September, anti-atomic activists in Upper Austria responded by blockading the Austro-Czech border for two weeks. The action had the active support of the regional government of Upper Austria and was passively tolerated by the federal government and the Austrian border police. Even though Austrian activists tried to organize private transport facilities for workers from the Czech Republic who had to cross the border every day to go to work in Austria, most Czechs condemned the action as an attack on their sovereignty, destroying support for the Czech NGOs' anti-nuclear campaign. When Jörg Haider, the extreme right-wing head of the Austrian Freedom Party, showed up at the border to support the protestors, the protests degenerated into a nationalist stand-off, linking the nuclear question to the Czech Republic's accession to the European community. To limit the tension, the Austrian and Czech heads of state engaged in official bilateral negotiations under the auspices of the European commissioner Verheugen – the so-called Melk process – which ended in December 2000 with an agreement promising transparency in the safety measures and early warning about technical incidents at the power station. Temelin became, according to one of the engineers at Temelin, one of the most monitored nuclear power stations in Europe. In January 2002, Haider exploited the tensions related to the safety of the nuclear reactor, which were broadly discussed in the Austrian media, by launching a petition drive for a national referendum to keep the Czech Republic out of the European Community as long as the Temelin power station was in operation. Haider's drive fell short of the one million signatures needed for a referendum and pushed support for the Temelin power station to an all-time high among the Czech population.

In 2002 the second reactor block was activated and began feeding electricity into the European grid, making the Czech Republic the second biggest electricity exporter in Europe, after France. Even Austria bought cheap Czech off–peak time electricity to pump up water levels in its artificial lakes and produce hydroelectric power that it sold at peak times. ČEZ sold the South Moravian grid to the German electricity company E.on and electricity prices in the area around Temelin rose to become the highest in the Czech Republic. ČEZ remained the owner of the nuclear power station but declined to honour its promise of low energy prices in the area. Feeling cheated, the locals petitioned the Czech Senate and Parliament in 2003, claiming the office for energy regulation should guarantee what they thought was their right to cheap electricity.

At the same time, in April 2003, four Austrian anti-nuclear activists went on a hunger strike in front of the chancellor's office in Vienna, hoping to pressure the Austrian chancellor to refuse to sign the European enlargement treaty in Athens on 16 April 2003 if the Czechs refused to abandon nuclear energy. However, the Austrian chancellor signed the treaty, which had been under negotiation for years, without posing any further conditions. Acts of protest continued nonetheless. On 9 May members of the Stop Temelin action committee offered an urn holding slightly radioactive material to EU Commissioner Verheugen, who was visiting Vienna to celebrate the European enlargement. And on 30 July 2003, the Czech outpost of the Upper Austrian Platform against Atomic Energy and the South Bohemian Mothers arranged fifty rolls of toilet paper in the shape of the number fifty in front of the gates of the Temelin power station to symbolize its fiftieth officially reported technical malfunction.

As the construction and testing phase ended in 2004, the power station started to lay off workers, especially unskilled labourers from the area around Temelin, and personnel responded by going on strike. There was no final depot for spent atomic fuel in the Czech Republic, so the site of the nuclear power station was designated as a potential intermediary storage space. Again inhabitants of the municipality of Temelin circulated a petition requesting the municipal council to arrange a local referendum on the matter. Forty per cent of the inhabitants of voting age signed, but the municipal council refused to call a local referendum in 2005.

The story of protests against the Temelin nuclear power station reveals a whole arsenal of means by which Czech and Austrian citizens tried to curb the Czech government's decision to build and run a nuclear power station at Temelin. Their petitions, demonstrations, blockades, lobbying and media work seem like a long succession of basically fruitless attempts to make their opinions heard. However, a closer look at the protests makes clear that the protestors' motives were by no means the same. Analysis of the mechanisms of power and protest from socialist times to the present shows both continuities and changes in engaged citizens' relationships to the state. It also forcefully demonstrates the impact of the opening of the Czech-Austrian borders and the difficulties citizens from different political traditions face in finding common ground for action on shared issues. In the case of Temelin, the local population, the Czech activists and the Austrian protestors framed the problems with the nuclear power station differently. According to Goffman, frames are schemata of interpretation that allow groups and individuals 'to locate, perceive, identify and label occurrences in their life space and in the world at large', allowing them to make sense of reality and project themselves into the future (Goffmann quoted in Della Porta and Diani 2006: 74).

The residents of the Temelin area initially attempted chiefly to stop the demolition of their villages and prevent resettlements. To them, the nuclear power station was a ruinous Moloch because its construction led to the physical disappearance of their villages and destroyed the harmony of the landscape. The way it was imposed reflected the structural violence of central planning and the indifference of real existing socialism for individual destinies. The locals bolstered their appeal to the government by pointing to their individual achievements and contribution to building up socialism, but the government's unequivocal reply ruled out appeal: the power station had to be built because it represented progress. Individual interests had to stand aside to further the priorities of the state.

After 1989, the general attitude in the Temelin area was that once again, 'they' – those in power in administrations, government and industry – did not listen, and even if 'they' did listen, they nevertheless did what they wanted. The local people thus experienced and framed their struggle within a continuum of powerlessness in the face of injustice. Unlike the environmentalists, they opposed not nuclear energy as such but the power station that invaded their lives, first by destroying the neighbour-hood physically and then by imposing security regulations, warning sys-tems and emergency training that contradicted the proclamations of the safety of nuclear energy.

The Czech environmental organizations founded shortly before or after the Velvet Revolution – Hnutí Duha, Déti Zemé, South Bohemian Moth-ers – initiated spectacular actions that attracted media attention but had little relation to the locals' concerns to keep their villages intact. The Czech environmental organizations wanted to raise the larger Czech public's awareness that nuclear energy created long-term problems, that other en-ergy sources could be used instead and that saving energy and using it efficiently was the order of the day. Their main addressee was in fact the government, whose information, energy and environmental policies they aimed to influence. Their actions had to be sufficiently spectacular to attract media attention without alienating the locals they wanted to convince.

For the Austrian organizations, the situation was very different. All par-ties officially supported an anti-nuclear policy. Having renounced the use of nuclear energy following the Zwentendorf referendum in 1978, Austria now felt menaced by neighbours who had not. Especially since the Cher-nobyl accident, the Austrian public was highly sensitive to the dangers of nuclear radiation. Austrian anti-nuclear NGOs could thus count on a large popular base and financial and logistic support from the government. In trying to influence decisions in the Czech Republic, however, they found themselves outside their habitual realm, needing not only to prove the le-gitimacy of their protests but also to express them in a way that resonated positively with both the Austrian and Czech publics.

Austrian and Czech Activists' Perceptions of the Nuclear Problem

> In the beginning of the 1990s Greenpeace Austria came here and they did a lot of sticking of cards and posters with very bright colors saying: 'Stop Temelin', 'Temelin is Death', 'Stop Czechnobyl' etc. It had an incredibly negative impact on the Czech population. It was not accepted at all. There were mistakes in the Czech spelling and it was considered to be something coming from outside. Not sensitive to the way in which Czech people are used to communicate, espe-cially due to mistakes in the language. (Interview Hnutí Duha, 11 March 2004)

Collective action becomes possible at the point where mobilizing mes-sages are integrated with the perceptions and interpretations of reality produced by sectors of public opinion that would otherwise remain sepa-rate from each other (Della Porta and Diani 2006: 83) Czech anti-nuclear activists pointed out that two of the most serious problems of anti-nuclear campaigning with Austrian activists were their perception of nuclear danger and lack of sensitivity to what Czechs saw as reasons for national pride. They faced the combined problem of bridging the frames of public opinion among the Czechs they were appealing to while coming to terms with the memories, prejudices and mindsets of their Austrian counterparts. Both activist networks understood that nuclear energy was too dangerous to be tolerated and that precaution was necessary, but they did not evaluate the imminence of this danger or the opportunities and constraints of the political situation – or, thus, the chances that their actions would succeed in the same way. In other words, their values coincided, but their interpretative tools did not (Della Porta and Diani 2006: 67). Austrians perceived nuclear radiation as imminently and mortally dangerous and were convinced that Czechs had the wrong appreciation of this danger and needed to be informed and educated to rightly perceive it. Czech activists criticized the campaign materials that Austrians used in the Czech Republic to educate the Czech public as highly detrimental to their own campaign, as it overemphasized mortal danger and used aggressive colours and symbols.

This observation spurred me to systematically collect Czech and Austrian campaign materials and interview Czech activists about how they perceived it. As I looked through the wonderful collection of political cartoons, posters and leaflets on nuclear energy at the Centrum Energie in České Budějovice, the campaigners pointed out to me what they thought were typically foreign materials translated into Czech and materials Czechs would use in their campaigns. They told me that when the first Austrian protestors demonstrated against the construction of the Temelin nuclear power station brandishing dramatically coloured posters comparing Temelin to Chernobyl, the Czech public was deeply shocked and angered. As the official anti-nuclear campaigner of the Upper Austrian government, a Czech émigré, explained,[5] Czechs are very proud of their technical skills, which they are convinced are far superior to the Russians'.

> I think in the Czech Republic the debate, the points of connection have to be found in the economic domain rather than in the debate about safety, because in the Czech Republic the attitude to technology is completely different than in Austria. An attack questioning the safety is unfortunately often seen as an attack on competence and skills in the technical domain and this leads to rebuttal … the Czech industrial tradition still stems from the time of the monarchy and then from the first Czech Republic where industry had an important role. Technology simply belongs to the national identity of the Czechs. (Anti-nuclear coordinator, Upper Austria interview 16 April 2004)

This pride in technical achievement did not, however, mean that the use made of the technology, or the organization of production that went with it, was uncritically accepted. Czech anti-nuclear activists may not have questioned the technical skills of Czech engineers, but they did criticize the impact of an industrial complex that concentrated economic and political power to the detriment of Czech consumers and citizens. A Vladimir Jiránek cartoon that Czech anti-nuclear campaigners used in the 1990s illustrates the line of Czech criticism (Figure 3.1).

The caption reads: 'We could make a moonscape out of the whole country, if we only had a better work organisation.'

To analyse this political cartoon I made use of the four methodical steps that Morris proposed, asking: (1) how the cartoon establishes its source as an authority labelling certain other elements as troublesome; (2) what specific frame it constructs that will create or excite interest, and what agenda it sets; (3) what normative agenda it establishes; and (4) how it stimulates a desire for action by ensuring that the preferred message resonates with the lived experiences of the audience (Morris 1993: 199–202). The 'other element' in this cartoon are three little grey men – technocrats with a narrow, instrumental world view, neither obviously capitalist nor socialist, bald and middle-aged in glasses and coats. Watching the fuming cooling towers of a nuclear power station in the background, they formulate the perfectly absurd objective of using better work organization to make a moonscape out of the whole country.

This statement frames the cartoon, setting it in the post-socialist context. Improvement of work organization had been one of the central problems of real existing socialism, but the objectives that this improvement was

MOHLi BYCHOM Z CELÉHO NAŠEHO KRAJE UDĚLAT MĚSÍČNÍ KRAJiNU.
KDYBYCHOM MĚLi LEPŠÍ ORGANiZACi PRÁCE.

Figure 3.1. 'We could make a moonscape out of the whole country, if we only had a better work organisation.' Cartoon by Vladimír Jiránek, used with permission.

to achieve did not necessarily correspond to consumers' wishes and priorities, nor were they environmentally sound. The socialist government's economic policies led to environmental catastrophes such as the lignite district in North Bohemia, which was effectively turned into a moonscape. The cartoon implies that such policies continued unabated in post-socialism. An environmentally conscious public socialized in real existing socialism – that is, the implied readership of such a cartoon – recognizes these implications and has the 'cultural familiarity' (Greenberg 2002) to relish the cartoon's absurdity. The dissident community had used the Absurd and other forms of socialist surrealism as a vehicle for struggle and a mechanism for expressing smouldering discontent (Romanienko 2007: 142). The cartoon establishes a normative agenda of creating and maintaining a viable environment by questioning the objectives promoted by industry and state bureaucracies and by contesting the priority attached to increasing productivity in post-socialism. And it stimulates a desire for action directed against the 'crazy little grey men' and their vision of, and impact on, the world. In the 1980s Czech environmental movements had fought for the environment as a way to protest against the socialist system and agitate for democracy. In the 1990s they were reluctant to attack large corporations for contributing to the destruction of the environment (Jehlicka, Sarre and Podoba 2002: 17); however, the nuclear power station Temelin, built by the state-owned electricity company ČEZ, seemed like a remnant of the old political structures and their abusive concentration of economic and bureaucratic power.

An Austrian public might not find this cartoon telling or funny at all. As Bergson pointed out: 'To understand laughter, we must put it back into its natural environment, which is society, and above all must we determine the utility of its function, which is a social one.' (Bergson quoted in Romanienko 2007 136) By comparison, the imagery used by Austrian activists was much more dramatic, almost always including symbols of death, such as skulls, skeletons, graveyards and crosses (Dejanovic and Liebhart 1999).

One cartoon (Figure 3.2), captioned 'Thank God!!!! I already thought we might loose power!!!' depicts as the Other a crazy skeleton that, although already dead from an atomic explosion, still cares about electricity. Although the caption is an absurd statement similar to the one in the Czech cartoon, the skeleton, in contrast to the little grey men, has no social specificity. It may represent the citizen or consumer who believed in or internalized the story advanced by government and industry that more energy is needed and that this energy has to be secured by building atomic power stations, or it may represent one of these decision-makers. The cartoon establishes a frame of an out-of-control consumer society that prioritizes

Figure 3.2. 'Thank God!!!! I already thought we might lose power!!!'
Illustration presented in a public exhibition at the centre against nuclear
energy in České Budějovice. (Photo: Birgit Müller)

the growth of energy consumption without regard for the lethal consequences. It is the reader's task to identify the skeleton in the cartoon as
completely mad and to associate its utterance with those of the atomic industry, which asserts the need of energy at all costs. The normative agenda
this cartoon establishes is rather vague and unsubtle: basically, it says that
life should have priority over energy consumption. It is difficult to make
out a concrete proposal for action from this cartoon, which instead has the
effect of an emotional outcry – 'Stop the insanity before it's too late!' – implying that the imminence of extreme danger requires extreme action.

It is precisely the perception of extreme danger and the need for extreme action that Austrian and Czech activists do not seem to share. Czech
activists and citizens were taken aback by the Austrians' use of death symbols. Not even the most engaged Czech activists shared the feeling of imminent danger from nuclear energy that drove the Austrians. As Ulrich
Beck (1986: 40) pointed out, the scope, urgency and even the existence
of risk depend on a multitude of values and interests. 'In contrast to the
touchable evidence of wealth, risks have something unreal. They are in a
central sense at the same time real and unreal. On the one hand many dangers and destructions are already real. ... On the other hand the actual so-

cial impact of the risk argument lies on dangers projected into the future' (Beck 1986: 44). Beck claims that in the risk-oriented society, the past loses its power of determination for the present, and the future takes its place. Thus can something non-existing, constructed and fictitious become the 'cause' of present experiences and actions (Beck 1986: 44).

However, projections into the future are but one of the causes of present experiences and actions, as is evident from the comparison between Czech and Austrian perceptions of nuclear risk and danger. The past retained all its power to determine how Czechs and Austrians felt about nuclear power in the present and what they were ready to do about it. The different political spaces created by the almost impermeable border between the socialist and capitalist blocks made for different physical and emotional experiences of the same radioactive cloud passing over both countries. These different political spaces allowed and encouraged certain modes of action but forbade and repressed others, creating repertoires of action that concerned citizens fell back on and considered the only correct way of behaving towards the state. In this case, the humour in the cartoons did not help to condense meaning or make framing and communication between Austrian and Czech activists and publics more efficient because it did not build on meanings that were already part of people's cultural and historical repertoire (Olesen 2007: 25). Concomitantly, the particular 'border landscapes' (van Houtum 1999: 329) between Austria and the Czech Republic are the product of a set of cultural, economic and political interactions and processes in space, and also of the absence of such interactions in the past. The 'mental borders' that Austrian and Czech activists experience today are the consequence of the political borders of the past.

Different Forms of Activism

Loud, violent and highly emotionally loaded actions were not well received by the Czech public. An example that was always cited as a negative one was the chaining of foreign activists to the gates of the Temelin construction site. The Czech language makes a semantic distinction between feelings (*city*) and emotions (*emoce*). In ordinary speech 'feeling' (*city*) is value-free whereas 'emotion' (*emoce*) has negative connotations (Holy 1996: 181). 'It connotes an unsuitable or inappropriate expression of feelings, unsuitable in the sense of their expression through inappropriate means. ... Particularly in political rhetoric, politicians, political commentators, and ordinary people ... condemn as irresponsible the appeal to emotions by extremists ... and they negatively evaluate "emotional solutions to problems" and emotional answers to complex questions.' (Holy 1996: 182)

After the Velvet Revolution, Austrian activists felt free to intervene in a neighbouring country that in their eyes had been passive towards nuclear danger. They did so with an urge to prevent immediate danger and also with a missionary zeal to show the Czechs how to organize civic action. Most of the Czech NGOs involved in anti-nuclear activities – Hnutí Duha, Calla, South Bohemian Mothers, Centrum Energie – received subsidies and project money from the Austrian government, and the South Bohemian NGOs in particular cooperated closely with sister organizations in Austria. The South Bohemian Mothers cooperated with the Mothers of Freistadt in Upper Austria; Centrum Energie, with the Upper Austrian anti-atomic platform. The spokesperson of the South Bohemian Mothers explained what she saw as the positive and negative aspects of this cooperation. On the positive side, her group learned from the Austrian NGOs how to influence politicians through citizens' initiatives, and that political action was possible without party politics. They also learned how to apply for project money and carry out projects. On the negative side, being financed by Austrian sources made them untrustworthy in the eyes of the Czech public and gave their position a certain ambiguity, even in anti-nuclear activism circles. They had to fight the appearance of being paid for anti-nuclear activism in the interests of Austrian industry.

In fact, the two aspects were linked. As the campaigners of the South Bohemian Mothers learned how to apply for funding, they became independent of the membership that had begun the initiative. They turned from a citizens' initiative into a NGO considered relatively wealthy by the Czech public. Thinking it unnecessary to establish a formal membership structure, they did not require the women whom they regarded as their supporters to contribute financially. Some of the latter resented that the organization did not care to accept the small financial contributions they were able to make. At the same time, the campaigners stressed the effort required to convince the media that they had their own standing and objectives, independent of Austrian influences. The controversial image they evoked of the long arm of Austrian interests came to the fore at moments of tension like the border blockades or the referendum to veto the Czech accession to the European Union, when they received vulgar or rude anonymous letters and phone calls. Meanwhile, cooperating with the Austrian groups on an equal basis was also difficult because 'the Austrians had the money and we had much less and we had to try to be equal partners nevertheless. It is not always easy to impose this, although they are intelligent people. Some time or other this feeling of power comes up' (Spokesperson, South Bohemian Mothers, 9 March 2004).

Adam Fagin (2001: 5), analysing the links between Czech environmental movements and large, internationally organized environmental movements, points to the paradox in which dependence on foreign donors made Czech environmental organizations more inward-looking rather than globally oriented in their mobilizations. Western funding and influence led to 'increased professionalism, better trained staff, offices equipped with information technology and improved information dissemination, fund-raising strategies and conflict resolution', but it did not lead to development of a more global focus for their actions. To win the support of foreign funding agencies and the public, Fagin maintains, radical strategies and ideologies had to be tempered by the need to appear as professional and conventional as possible (Fagin 2001: 5). In the cooperation between Austrian and Czech anti-nuclear groups, however, this relationship was reversed: Czech environmental groups struggled to resist pressure from their Austrian counterparts to take a more radical stand and engage in more militant forms of action. The main obstacle to the independence of Czech environmental groups was that access to foreign funding led them to neglect building a strong mass-membership base, both active and passive, that could have developed forms of action that would appeal to the Czech public. Hence, 'The result of the decade of Western nurturing of civil society is a small group of professionals with a tiny support base' (Jehlicka, Sarre and Podoba 2002: 19).

Nevertheless, the small group of Czech anti-nuclear campaigners resented it when Austrians organized actions in the Czech republic without consulting them. As the former spokesperson for Hnutí Duha, put it:

> From my point of view the cooperation does not go very well.... The problem is that the approach of the Austrian NGOs was from the beginning culturally arrogant. They were convinced that their experience and their methods are the best. They thought that Czech NGOs were stupid and cannot deal with anything.... They wanted to organize actions in the Czech Republic on their own to a large extent, blockades, direct actions, protests. They wanted to do it on their own and we thought that the right analysis was that Czech NGOs organized the Czech protests and the Austrian NGOs tried to influence the Austrian political decision-making. It was an absurd situation that the Austrian NGOs were trying to do something here, which had zero or even negative impact. (Interview Hnutí Duha, 11 March 2004)

Although he recognized that nuclear energy was a European problem because of its scale, cost, risks and social impacts, he reckoned that anti-nuclear activism in the Czech Republic should be planned and controlled by Czechs. The tensions between Czech and foreign environmental activists came out very clearly during the international blockades of the Temelin construction site in 1997. A Dutch member of the Czech Greenpeace team commented:

The structure we had agreed upon was that the 600 or 800 people would organise in affinity groups of fifteen people and that each group would elect a representative who would meet every day to make the strategic decisions, while the coordinating committee would deal with the details. Patočka from Hnutí Duha saw it the other way round. He wanted the coordinating committee to take the strategic decisions that the other groups would then carry out. This led to quite a lot of tension at the beginning of the blockades.... Patočka finally imposed himself. (Greenpeace, interview 2 November 2003)

While some of the international activists criticized Patočka's behaviour as authoritarian, Hnutí Duha's members justified it by underlining that only Czechs could understand the mentalities in the Czech lands and that foreigners would necessarily take the wrong decisions. It was thus natural that Czechs would lead the protests and give them form and content that Czech people could understand. The blockades nevertheless met with little sympathy in the Czech media. Photographs of black-clothed anarchists dominated the reports, and demonstrators were pictured as crazy extremists chaining themselves to the gates of the construction site to prevent access. This came at a time when four environmental groups had been placed alongside skinheads and anarchists on an Intelligence Service list of subversive elements as Czech environmental groups struggled to rid themselves of the stigma of extremist radicalism.

Other details also caused unease among the Czech public. Several Czech activists told me that Czechs disapproved of bringing children to demonstrations because children did not yet understand what they were protesting against; moreover, this practice reminded them of the big obligatory demonstrations in socialist times, when the presence of children was used for propaganda purposes. In Austria and Germany, however, children were commonly brought to non-violent anti-nuclear demonstrations as they symbolized the future and the altruistic concern to leave a safe environment for them. At any rate, the petition was the preferred form of political action among Czechs opposed to nuclear energy. Demonstrations against nuclear energy were generally not well attended by Czechs. The spokesperson of the South Bohemian Mothers explained the difficulty of getting her compatriots to participate:

For example big demonstrations: the Austrians always imagined that we would bring thousands of people to the street, because it had been possible in Austria in the protests against Zwentendorf. We tried to explain to them that we are not a civil society, that people don't know here that their voice is important. They have heard for forty years that they are nothing. 'Your voice does not count.' People won't take to the street. They still have to learn that. At the biggest demonstration we had a maximum of 500 Czechs. That was a big success.

To show yourself openly in the street means to sacrifice something. In a petition I only put my signature under so many other signatures and nobody wants something from me. I don't have to drive anywhere or to sacrifice even half an hour. This is different in a demonstration and it also happens that demonstrators are asked by journalists to give their opinion. That people do something themselves and stand there in public is quite rare. (Spokesperson, South Bohemian Mothers, 9 March 2004)

The spokesperson considered signing a petition, a passive form of resistance that did not oblige people to show their faces or say in front of a television camera 'I am here and I am against it.' She thus took up the Austrian critique of her compatriots for not wanting to stand up and defend their individual opinions. This critique was rather harsh as the 120,000 signatories opposing the construction of Temelin had made themselves identifiable and personally responsible by giving their names and addresses. Because 'Czech people don't participate in demonstrations', the South Bohemian Mothers turned to organizing small happenings that attract media attention and amuse the public.

The border blockades by inhabitants of the Upper Austrian border zone, supported by Austrian environmental associations and politicians of all stripes had a more differentiated reception among Czech anti-nuclear activists and Temelin locals than most Czech media reports indicated. Whereas the South Bohemian Mothers held back criticism of the blockades and received extremely negative press in the Czech Republic in the process, Hnutí Duha and Greenpeace faulted them for only amplifying animosities between the two countries and doing little to clarify the situation. The former spokesperson of Hnutí Duha admitted that the spontaneous reaction of the people living in the Czech Austrian border-zone was understandable to some extent, but had been rapidly instrumentalized by politicians.

One can understand that the NGOs and the concerned citizens really want to express the disappointment from the side of Austria that the Czech Republic is building Temelin and does not ask Austrian people at all, does not take their opinion into consideration. This makes people frustrated and upset and in Austria it has inspired a sort of direct action at the border with the blockades. At the beginning it was just a reaction of local people that were full of frustration and that wanted to do something and what they invented was the blockade of the border. But it was only a question of a few days before it was taken over by the politicians. You might have seen Jörg Haider supporting the campaign. That was rough for the Czech side. The reaction was, 'all the Austrians are stupid and we don't want to listen to them because Temelin is ours. We will not discuss this with anybody else. We can't let Austrians interfere, they are hysteric and can't understand anything.' It was like a circle that is spinning more and more. (Interview Hnutí Duha, 11 March 2004)

Inhabitants of the area around the Temelin power station, however, saw the blockade as the expression of a feeling they could share: desperation born of nobody paying attention to their concerns. The only objection one of the inhabitants had was that the Austrians would have acted more efficiently by blocking access to the canteen of the Czech parliament, as it was promise-breaking politicians who had opportunistically agreed to the construction of the power station. Prior to 1989, adoption of liberal democracy had been seen as a panacea for the environment, but the inhabitants of Temelin quickly discovered that neither liberal democracy nor European enlargement had yet been able to provide for democratic structures that gave weight to apprehensions voiced by citizens when strong economic interests went against environmental concerns.

Conclusion

Austrians have justified their anti-nuclear protests in the Czech Republic as an assertion of their universal human right to physical integrity. Living next to the border, they felt menaced by the construction of a power station just across the border, sufficiently near to threaten their lives in case of a nuclear accident. Yet they only began trying to make their voices heard after the borders of the socialist bloc opened up and the Czech Republic became a democracy. Meanwhile, most Czech activists and citizens saw the presence of Austrian activists on Czech soil as an infringement of their national sovereignty. Austrians were supposed to protest in Austria and Czechs in the Czech Republic, each using their own preferred means of protest.

But despite the national specificities in the perceptions of risk and forms of protest analysed in this chapter, international forms of anti-nuclear protest have emerged in the Czech Republic, along with international symbols (red smiling sun, the radiation symbol, etc.) and Czech specific forms of action (petitions and small, often humorous direct actions). The conflicts that Czech and Austrian protestors had to solve also contributed to their deeper understanding of one another and to a more realistic appreciation of each other's political system and culture. That is, mental borders were actually softened by direct contact and the overcoming of tensions arising from conflict. Mental borders are not fixed forever but shaped by ongoing cross-border interaction.

Since the high-flown emotions of the border blockades and the Czech Republic's accession to full membership of the European Union despite Austrian veto attempts, Austrian and Czech activists have become more careful and respectful in dealing with one another. Austrian anti-nuclear campaigners seldom come to the Czech Republic any more, although one of them decided to move to the Czech Republic altogether to promote alternative sources of energy there. Czech campaigners are aware that it no longer makes sense to do anti-nuclear campaigning in just one country. With international banks financing Temelin, foreign companies owning part of the Czech grid and European institutions discussing European guidelines for safety of nuclear energy, disposal of waste and responsibility for accidents (De Esteban 2002: 5), it is obvious that anti-nuclear campaigns need to be coordinated at the European level.

Nearly all the activists discussed what is democratic and how democracy has evolved since accession to the European Union. Their statements about democracy ranged from concerns about the politics of nuclear safety information to citizens' opportunities to have a say on mega-projects in their neighbourhoods. They also addressed the opacity of decision-making at the state level in the Czech Republic and Austria. The accession of the Czech Republic to the European Union adds a new dimension to this debate. Europeans enjoy the social and economic rights associated with European Union citizenship, but they remain excluded from political citizenship in other member countries (Aziz 2002: 1). Will a political European citizenship emerge to find formal recognition as concerned citizens confront ever denser ties at the economic and regulatory levels? Will the active protest of a Czech in Austria or of an Austrian in the Czech Republic ultimately be recognized as legitimate, even if the cultural registers they use are out of step with the national tradition?

Notes

1. The six-week period between 17 November and 29 December 1989, known as the Velvet Revolution, brought about the bloodless overthrow of the Czechoslovak communist regime.
2. Jiři Vrzak preserved the village chronicles of Litoradlice that his father wrote and gave me access to all the volumes concerning the nuclear power station from 1980 to 1996.
3. Villagers' names are anonymized; the names of elected representatives and NGO spokepersons are not.
4. The interview was conducted by Karin Liebhart and Leila Hadj-Abdou on 15 April 2004.
5. The interview was conducted by Karin Liebhart and Leila Hadj-Abdou on 16 April 2004.

References

Arsel, M. 2003. *Transnational Advocay Networks in the Mediterranean: The Case of Nuclear Energy in Turkey*. Environmental Studies Program, University of Chicago.

Aziz, M. 2002. *EU Citizenship: Spheres of Belonging and the Politics of Dispossession*. EUI Working Papers. San Domenico: European University Institute.

Beck, U. 1986. *Risikogesellschaft. Auf dem Weg in eine andere Moderne*. Frankfurt: Suhrkamp.

De Esteban, F. 2002. *The Future of Nuclear Energy in the European Union*. Background paper for a speech made to senior representatives of nuclear utilities in a European Strategic Exchange, Brussels, 23 May.

Dejanovic, S. and K. Liebhart. 1999. '"Der Osten als Bedrohung". Zur medialen Berichterstattung über grenznahe Atomkraftwerke am Beispiel der Slowakei', *SWS-Rundschau* 3: 221–37. Retrieved from http://www.demokratiezentrum.org/media/pdf/dejanovic.pdf

Della Porta, D. and M. Diani. 2006. *Social Movements: An Introduction*. Oxford: John Wiley and Sons.

Fagin, A. 2001. 'Globalisation and the Building of Civil Society in Central and Eastern Europe: Environmental Mobilisations as a Case Study', ECPR Conference, University of Kent, Canterbury, 6–8 September.

Greenberg, J. 2002. 'Framing and Temporality in Political Cartoons: A Critical Analysis of Visual News Discourse', *Canadian Review of Sociology and Anthropology* 39(2): 181–98.

Holy, L. 1996. *The Little Czech and the Great Czech Nation: National Identity and the Postcommunist Social Transformation*. Cambridge: Cambridge University Press.

Jehlicka, P., P. Sarre and J. Podoba. 2002. *Czech Environmental Discourse after a Decade of Western Influence: Transformation beyond Recognition or Continuity of Pre-1989 Perspectives?* EUI Working Papers. San Domenico: European University Institute.

Keck, M. E. and K. Sikkink. 1998. *Activists Beyond Borders: Advocacy Networks in International Politics*. Ithaka: Cornell University Press.

Morris, R. 1993 'Visual Rhetoric in Political cartoons: A structuralist approach.' *Metaphor and Symbolic Activity* 8,3: 195–210.

Olesen, T. 2007. 'The Funny Side of Globalization: Humour and Humanity in Zapatista Framing', *International Review of Social History* 52 (special issue): 21–34.

Romanienko, L.A. 2007. 'Antagonism, Absurdity, and the Avant-Garde: Dismantling Soviet Oppression through the Use of Theatrical Devices by Poland's "Orange" Solidarity Movement, *International Review of Social History* 52 (special issue): 133–51.

Van Houtum, H. 1999. 'Internationalisation and Mental Borders', *Tijdschrift for Economische en Sociale Geographie* 90(3): 329–35.

Vrzak, J. 1980–96. *Kronika Litoradlice*. Handwritten manuscript.

Chapter 4

Powerful Documents
Passports, Passages and Dilemmas of Identification
on the Georgian-Turkish Border

Mathijs Pelkmans .

Torn Passports and Dangerous Names, Part One

The collapse of the Soviet Union and the opening of the Iron Curtain
between Georgia and Turkey produced a massive flow of cross-border
movement. This movement, motivated in part by the dearth of consumer
goods in Georgia, was further stimulated by the power vacuum that
emerged upon the collapse of state structures. As with all vacuums, however, the void was quickly filled. The chaos of the early 1990s gave way
to a more ordered configuration within a still largely toothless national
legal and political framework. The central role of identity documents
in transnational movement makes them a useful focal point for exploring these changes: their official status provides insight into the political
transformations, while their individualized nature illuminates the ways
in which border dwellers and travellers engage with 'the state'. By way of
introduction, I will start with an ethnographic snapshot of a scene that occurred around 5 A.M. on 17 April 1997 in a hangar that housed the Georgian customs.

> We, thirty-some people travelling from Turkey to Georgia, were waiting along-
> side the old Mercedes bus until it was our turn to be summoned to a brightly
> lit room for interrogation. It was the last obstacle during an eight-hour border
> crossing experience. Ten people had already returned from the room, each with
> a different story of how much they'd had to pay. Apart from brief exchanges of

---

Notes for this chapter begin on page 106.

information the mood was timid and acquiescent. Suddenly an agonized shout disrupted the silence. Loud noises escaped the interrogation room – stumbling, cursing, more shouting. A few men tried to peek through the window, but it was too high to see much. Finally the door opened. A woman emerged, showing us the two parts of her torn passport. She explained that she had resisted the customs officers' sexual demands. As a result, she ended up with a passport that could no longer be used.

Although the tearing of a passport was hardly the worst that happened at the Georgian customs, it was the image that stayed with me after I had arrived safely on Georgian territory and jotted down my observations. This may have been due to my having become used to other maltreatments, or to the seeming irrationality of *Georgian* customs officers destroying a valid *Georgian* passport, or to the central symbolic and practical value of passports in cross-border passages. The event prompted many questions: *Why* had a passport been torn? Why had *this* passport been torn? And what *is* a passport? The first two questions refer to the specificities of the Georgian border regime and the position of the woman vis-à-vis the customs officers. Although none of us had managed to pass the border free of charge, there were significant differences and gradations in what was charged. As a Georgian citizen but not an 'ethnic' Georgian, and as a female, this woman had to pay a higher price than most other travellers because as a Georgian citizen arriving in Georgia, she could not threaten to report the officers' actions to the authorities of a foreign country, while her status as an ethnic Russian prevented her from playing the Georgian brotherhood card. And as a woman, she possessed something that could not be had by emptying her pockets or by searching her luggage – the officers wanted sex, and her passport, held as hostage, offered direct access to it. I never discovered why the threat to destroy her passport did not remain a threat, but the eventual deed freed this woman from further harassment by the customs officers.

The torn document challenges standard notions of passports and of bureaucratic routine. Here, passports were not simply travel documents to be inspected by scrupulous but indifferent officers who follow official guidelines. Instead, the passports and passport data were tools that were used to establish the worth of each individual and to gain access to personal belongings. The situation at the Georgian customs appears extreme in that bureaucratic routine had been transformed into a structured machine of extortion, which meant the main relevance of passports was not their official status, but instead their capacity to reveal particularities about individuals. The torn passport thus symbolizes what may happen when bureaucratic institutions transform into hierarchically organized systems of predation.

This extraordinary event raises issues with a wider significance. What this essay aims to show is that in (post-)Soviet Georgia, passports were not only tools by which the state disciplined its subjects but also documents that inculcated specific identities. As such they formed the axis around which dynamics of inclusion and exclusion unfolded, as well as the basis for asymmetric negotiations between citizens and state representatives. I argue that the situation at the Georgian customs was rooted in both the history of passports during Soviet times and the reconfigurations of power that unfolded in Georgian politics in the 1990s. To substantiate these claims, I will analyse the changing role of passports in the Georgian borderlands, both in actual border crossings and in the lives of people living along the border. First, however, I will address a basic question: What is a passport?

Passport Regimes and the Anthropology of Borders

Passports play central roles in categorization, mobility control and identification. Of crucial importance to the functioning of modern states, these issues have gained even more significance in the current age of transnational movement. Issues of categorization (e.g., Scott 1998) and identification (e.g., Bauman 2001) have, of course, been at the top of the anthropological agenda for quite some time. But whereas censuses, maps and museums have sparked interest among anthropologists at least since Benedict Anderson's *Imagined Communities* (1983), travel and other identification documents have only recently started to attract attention (see especially Navaro-Yashin 2007 and Kelly 2006). This suggests that anthropology has been slow in overcoming its sedentary perspective, which is unfortunate because, in contrast to the abstract qualities of maps, censuses and exhibitions, the personal and portable nature of identification documents directly links abstract categories to individuals, impacting their daily life.

As Torpey has documented in his important study *The Invention of the Passport* (2000), the passport in its standardized, multilaterally accepted form is a relatively modern phenomenon whose rudimentary origins are to be found in the French Revolution. Like several other inventions that are traceable to the late eighteenth century, its development can be seen as part of the 'gradual process of inclusion of broad social strata in the political order' (Torpey 2000: 2). Its history thus parallels the creation of modern bureaucratic structures and states' increasing hold over their citizens. Torpey denotes this process the state's 'embrace', which he juxtaposes to the more usual phrase of state 'penetration', arguing that the notion 'embrace' more effectively connects certain features of modern technologies of rule: categorization, identification and surveillance (Torpey 2000: 4–20). In this regard the functions of the passport run parallel to those of censuses, birth registration and cadastral mapping, all of which have been central elements in the 'state's attempt to make a society legible' (Scott 1998: 2). As modern forms of disciplinary power, these instruments link individuals to categories and thereby simplify the execution of state policies. Passports are similarly linked to bureaucratic institutions but differ from these other instruments in that passports are kept by individuals. As such they allow us to scrutinize the dilemmas of categorization as well as the ways official categories have relevance in interactions between citizens and state representatives.

Whereas passports initially resulted from the effort to produce legible populations and thus are closely linked to the idea of citizenship, the same documents have also become tools in the construction of 'ethnically pure' populations. The history of passportization in the former Soviet Union stands out in this regard. Large-scale distribution of Soviet passports, which were meant for internal travel only, started in 1932.[1] Beyond the usual personal information, these passports differed from most other passports in that they labelled the bearer according to two features: social class and ethnic status (Matthews 1993: 27). Although the label 'social class' continued to feature in Soviet passports until 1974 (Hoskings 2001: 431), its relevance soon declined in comparison to 'entry no. 5', which inscribed and indeed fixed 'ethnic nationality' by descent (only children from mixed marriages were allowed to choose upon receiving their first passport at the age of sixteen). This ethnic categorization became an important element in the creation of new hierarchies among citizens. The fixed passport ethnicities alternately helped or hindered people's access to jobs, higher education and even their possibilities for travel within the Soviet Union. Moreover, even though the categories were often contested when they were introduced, they played a significant role in the formation of collective identities. A focus on passports in the Soviet Union therefore reveals how notions of citizenship and nationality are constructed (and contested) from above and below, and offers insight into the processes of state formation, territorial delimitation and efforts to control cross-border movement.

Notions of citizenship and nationality are particularly salient in a borderland, because this is often where the ideal of the nation-state shows its most flagrant inconsistencies and collides with the loyalties and identities of local residents. Further, because these residents may easily cross the border or shift their loyalties, their actions are potentially subversive and dangerous. Since one aim of modern states is to control or channel cross-border movement and to establish people's identities to enforce this authority, the pacification of border regions is an essential precondition for the functioning of such states. The following section outlines the particularities of the passport regime in the Georgian borderlands and discusses Soviet efforts to discipline its citizens and instil specific ethno-territorial identities.

Passports along the (Former) Iron Curtain

The power and dangers inherent in passports and passport data were particularly noticeable in the border village Sarpi, located on the Black Sea shore. Nowadays the village consists of a Georgian and a (smaller) Turkish part, and has a total of approximately 1,500 inhabitants. The region on its Georgian side, the Autonomous Republic of Adjara, had considerable autonomy within the economically and politically struggling Republic of Georgia in the 1990s and up to the Rose Revolution of 2005. Since the early 1990s, most overland traffic between Turkey and Georgia has passed through the customs offices located on the sea side of the village. In 1999 and 2000 I conducted six months of ethnographic fieldwork in Sarpi, aiming to understand how relations between both sides of the village had evolved. I have traced and described the multifaceted social life of the Georgian Iron Curtain in my book *Defending the Border* (2006) and will not attempt to summarize the complete history in this chapter. Instead, I will focus on the centrality of passports in 'domesticating' the local population and in instilling new ideas of collective belonging.[2] This historical discussion also helps to show how the Soviet passport regime and its recent transformation have direct relevance for understanding the roles passports played in the border-crossing procedures that prevailed during the first decade after the collapse of the Soviet state.

Although the border in Sarpi is now an important node in transnational movement between Turkey and the Caucasus, this was not the case for most of the twentieth century. In fact, the establishment of the international border right through the middle of the village in 1921 was an 'accident' that disrupted families and socio-economic ties and placed Sarpi in the border zone (*pogranichnaia zona*) – an area closely watched by government forces. Over the next decades, the border was made virtually impermeable by a series of measures prompted as much by the ideological nature of the Soviet border as by the increasingly tense relations between the Soviet Union and Turkey during the Second World War and subsequent Cold War. Partly because of this, passports played a central role in village life. Whenever residents entered the part of the village closest to the border or left the village (e.g., to go to the nearby city of Batumi), they needed to show their passports. Also pertinent, beyond these practical concerns, was that Sarpi was the easternmost community of an area inhabited by the

Laz, who used to speak their own language (alongside Turkish) and were Sunni Muslims. Their religious, ethnic and familial ties with the population across the border made them suspect in the eyes of Soviet authorities, whose suspicions were only reinforced by the personal names that identified Laz in their passports.

By the late 1940s, all Sarpi residents were aware of the dangers of passport data. Throughout the period from 1920 to 1940, Soviet authorities had withheld or confiscated passports of individuals they deemed unreliable, making it impossible for these people to leave the village. In 1944 the Soviet government cleansed the border region of unreliable elements, exiling everyone categorized Hemshin or Kurd to Central Asia.[3] Five years later all Laz women who had been born on the Turkish side of the border and still held Turkish passports were deported to Siberia. Even though the installation of fences and surveillance mechanisms after 1937 had made the border virtually impermeable, state representatives continued to be suspicious of the villagers' possible loyalties to Turkey, their kinship relations with relatives across the border and their potential to subvert the border regime.

In this atmosphere of distrust and fear, villagers were highly sensitive to the way they were presented in their passports. Their passport ethnicities, surnames and many first names were changed in the 1940s. These changes

Figure 4.1. A view from the hills overlooking the graveyard in Georgian Sarpi and houses located on the Turkish side. (Photo: Mathijs Pelkmans)

did not simply follow a grand design for ethnic classification outlined in Moscow. For instance, although all villagers eventually had 'Georgian' imprinted in their passports, official censuses continued to classify them as 'Laz'. Another indication of the lack of coordination in ethnic categorization was that in contrast to passports held by the Laz of Sarpi, the passports of the Laz living in Mingrelia (another province of Georgia) mentioned 'Laz' throughout the Soviet period. Ethnicity, however, was only one of the categories in passports that mattered. Villagers' passports may have noted 'Georgian' ethnicity/nationality, but their personal names continued to sound Turkish and Islamic, which by definition drew negative attention in Soviet Georgia.

Inhabitants of Sarpi held differing opinions about the extent to which name changes had been externally imposed. One elderly man said: 'Nothing was forced upon us. Some people changed their name in the 1920s, some later. [The authorities] simply explained that since we were not living in Turkey and because we were not Turks, we could change our names'. Another villager, however, insisted that Lavrenty Beria had personally raised the issue of changing Turkish names in 1947. In any case, the deportations and arrests of preceding years had made it painfully clear to inhabitants that a change of personal names was desirable.

The Beria explanation (in the sense of the changes having been imposed from above) seemed largely true for the changes of first names. Zurabi, or Jemali, gave a graphic description of his own name change in 1948, when he was nine years old:

> The schoolmaster stood in front of the class and said: 'Zurabi! Open your book'. I looked around, wondering who this Zurabi might be. '*You* are Zurabi', he told me. And he explained: 'Jemali is a Turkish name and Zurabi is a Georgian name and you are not a Turk'. When I came home I told my father: 'From now on my name is Zurabi'. 'What?!' my father asked [in astonishment]. So I told him that the teacher had given me a new name because Jemali is a Turkish name. My father said that the teacher did not know anything and that Jemali was perhaps a Persian but certainly not a Turkish name. But then he said, 'It is alright, the truly important thing is that you are human'.

Similar situations occurred when people registered their newborn children. Ferine explained: 'Our son is called Suliko, after his grandfather Suleiman. But at the office they did not allow this, so officially it is Ilia. We quickly had to think of a Georgian name and we thought of the poet Ilia Chavchavadze.'

Whereas Georgian first names were first introduced by schoolteachers, the initiative to change surnames rested with the families. Most tried to stay close to the root of their old name when choosing a common Georgian name. As one person explained, 'Our old name was Kabamemetoghli and we chose Kakabadze. It doesn't mean the same thing, but it sounded somewhat alike'. In a similar vein, Bekiroghli became Bakradze, while Jevasoghli became Javakhishvili. Interestingly though, of the ten family names that were in circulation in Sarpi in the early twentieth century, only four continued to exist as single new names. The other family names split into two or even three new variants. Thus, the Memishoghlis split up into Memishishis, Dolidzes, and Lazishvilis, while Abduloghli became Abuladze and Abdulishi. The choice of different names and of either a Laz ending '-shi' or a Georgian ending '-dze' or '-shvili' followed a distinctive pattern.[4] Villagers who chose names similar to the old ones were either relatively secure in their positions or had no ambition to work anywhere besides the collective farm. By contrast, those adopting a Georgian name either were angling for a bureaucratic career or had reason to fear they would fall victim to future purges. The latter factor affected decisions in the Abduloghli family, who all were employed at the collective farm. One of the family members had been active as a mullah until the 1930s, and to make things worse, his wife had been born in Turkey. To keep a low profile, he and his wife changed their surname into Abuladze instead of Abdulishi, the name his relatives chose. Meanwhile, Memishoghli family members who worked in the village and district administrations adopted the surname Dolidze; those choosing Memishishi worked on the collective farm.

The introduction of Georgian first names caused commotion at first, but in later years villagers simply gave their children two names at birth: one Georgian and one Laz or Muslim name, each of which had their uses. Turkish-sounding names like Jemali, Hasan, Osman, Phadime and Emine continued to be used in the village, while the new 'parallel' names – like Irakli, Giorgi, Teona, Nugzar and Nino – were printed in internal passports and other official documents used in encounters with bureaucracy and in the city. The old family names similarly retained their value. As late as 1999, elderly people were still using the old names ending in '-oghli' to refer to different families. However, quite a few among the youngest generation did not know that, for example, the Kakabadzes and the Kabarias were one family group. This unawareness sometimes led to comical situations, as when children of these related family groups flirted with each other, not knowing they were related.

Obviously the new names influenced how villagers could present themselves and how others saw them. More interestingly, the adoption of new names was also seen locally as having induced changes in behaviour, thus raising questions concerning the complicated relation between naming and self-perception. Consider the following statement of an elderly woman who disliked the current practice of giving children only Georgian names: 'I am Muslim. But my grandchildren all have Georgian names. You see, everyone [is categorized] Georgian in their passports, they eat pork, drink wine and smoke cigarettes.' Of course, a Georgian name or ethnic label alone does not turn people into pork eaters, but the centrality of passports and names in presentations of self unavoidably had palpable consequences. When I discussed these issues in Sarpi, some people characterized the name changes as a learning process. Nodari, for example, described the practice of giving children Georgian names as follows: 'We did not know Georgian names. That is why the teachers decided. They had a wider knowledge and they knew Georgian names. After that we became Georgians. That is, we then became Georgians in appearance, because we had been Georgians in our hearts all along of course.' The official names and categories were integrated into ideas of selfhood among new generations, setting the stage for reinterpretations of tradition. Most significant for the purpose of this essay is that the Laz saw themselves increasingly as a subgroup of the Georgian nation, in contrast to the pre- and early Soviet period, when religious difference between Muslim Laz and Georgian Orthodox Christians precluded such identification (see Pelkmans 2006: 44–70).

In the 1990s it once again became possible to alter family names, which generated quite a bit of discussion. However, no one I spoke to mentioned having considered reinstating the old names (ending in -oghli). A small minority of elderly people had considered changing the Georgian ending of their family names (-dze) into a Laz ending (-shi). But the opposite was more common: especially young and middle-aged villagers who held Laz names told me they would like to adopt the Georgian variant of their name. Such discussions often turned to a desire to retrace pre-Ottoman Georgian origins. For example, a popular theory within the Memishoghli family held that their original family name was not Memishoghli but Diberoghli. Diberoghli was interpreted as being rooted in the Georgian name Dolidze, which is fairly common in Guria province.[5] But because no one was able to prove the genealogical links, the popularity of the name Dolidze among the Memishishoghli descendants seemed equally likely to have stemmed from the wish to have an unambiguously Georgian name, and from the better financial positions of the Dolidzes in comparison to the Memishishis.

Categorization of populations along the Soviet border and introduction of passports were some of the technologies the Soviet state used to map its borderlands and identify unreliable groups, which subsequently were removed. This pertained in particular to the Kurds, Hemshins and Greeks. The Laz, by contrast, never fell victim to wholesale deportation. Instead, they were renamed and reclassified, a process that was aimed (at least in part) at their pacification. The policies involved and their outcomes highlight the need for anthropologists to attend to how state policies and legislation anchor and mould 'identities', rather than just repeating the mantra about the contingency of identity. The categories on which states base their policies may fail to reflect how people perceive themselves, but this does not mean they are without effect. The values attached to personal names as well as to regional and ethnic affiliation were not newly invented by Soviet rule, but the associated categories, once they were actively incorporated into its policies, became reified and spilled over into everyday politics after the demise of the Soviet Union.

From Iron Curtain to International Border

From the mid 1950s to the late 1980s, the border regime in Sarpi did not change significantly. The international border was virtually impermeable, and attempts to illegally cross it were rare. Moreover, it was not Sarpi residents but Russians and Georgians living elsewhere who made such attempts. Having lived along a border of 'control and fear' for decades, most villagers accepted its impermeability and permanence. They avoided pointing to the other side, never spoke publicly of their cross-border relatives and cooperated in the maintenance and defence of the Iron Curtain. The border community had become reliable; only on rare occasions did authorities express concern about villagers' relation to the border. On the whole, the Iron Curtain mattered less in everyday life than the internal borders and checkpoints that regulated movement between Sarpi and the Georgian hinterland.

Villagers vividly remembered the constraints associated with living in the *pogranichnaia zona*. Two checkpoints and fences controlled movement from and to the village. Local residents' passports were specially stamped with the word 'Sarpi'. Still, students from Sarpi studying in Tbilisi and men and women who married outside the village needed a *propusk* (permit) to go to Sarpi, for which they often had to wait months. Arranging for such permissions – for wedding guests, for example – required extensive procedures. Villagers had to prepare all the documents in triplicate at least a month in advance. The KGB carefully checked the background of the invited guests, and invitees deemed untrustworthy were often denied access to Sarpi.

Although a nuisance, the border regime had also become predictable and stable over the decades. Several of my informants talked with amazement about the sincerity, straightforwardness and the efficiency of the soldiers and civil servants responsible for maintaining order along the

border: 'When you travelled by bus, two soldiers would enter and immediately pick out those who were not from the village. They *never* made a
mistake.' Another man recounted the time his daughter had eloped with
a man from a neighbouring village. When she did not return at night, he
went to the checkpoint to find out if she had left the village.

> The soldier who had been on duty remembered exactly which cars had passed
> during his shift, what the license plates were, and who had been in the cars.
> Then he told me that there had been a girl with a man from the [nearby vil-
> lage] Tqirnali and he even remembered his name. [The soldier] said that he
> had recognized my daughter … but that he couldn't do anything because the
> documents were in order … Such were the soldiers. Maybe they were small but
> they had a golden head.

This example reveals the nostalgia for the relative isolation and sense of
community that were a by-product of a severe border regime. This, and
the dutiful actions of soldiers, compared positively to the 'chaos' that followed, even though many villagers benefited financially from this chaos.

When the border was reopened in 1988, little happened at first. Many
Sarpi residents managed to obtain the international passports needed to
visit their cross-border relatives. Six villagers found work at the newly
established customs office. These activities prepared them well for the
massive change that occurred when the border was opened to all traffic
in 1991 and Sarpi became a gateway for international trade. Because Sarpi
residents were among the first to have international passports, because
several villagers were employed at the customs and because they lived
right on the border, they found themselves ideally positioned to profit
from the new trading opportunities. The tiny village of only a thousand
inhabitants soon got the nickname 'Little Kuwait' because its residents
were seen as sitting on an oil well – that is, becoming millionaires without
having to do much. They were among the first to set up money exchange
offices, sell refreshments to travellers and engage in various sorts of cross-
border trade. Young men did particularly lucrative business using the
'Sarpi' stamp in their passports to drive cars up to the border gate. They
could ask good money for this service because by 1992, so many people
were travelling to Turkey that the waiting time at customs had increased
to several days. My host sister in Sarpi summarized the extent to which
people profited from the border situation: 'Almost everyone made lots of
money in the beginning. That is how they furnished their houses. All the
furniture, the cars, and the televisions, those are all from that period.'

The chaos accompanying the new trading possibilities also attracted
numerous outsiders who jumped at the opportunity to make money. According to my acquaintances from Sarpi, young men from neighbouring

villages posed as Sarpi residents to demand money from travellers for a variety of made-up reasons. Others flocked to the village to sell whatever they could lay their hands on. It is worth recounting the experiences of Otari, who had been chairman of the Sarpi village council for just a few months when he found himself dealing with the chaotic situation that emerged when the border was opened to everyone in 1991:

> I wanted to bring a bit of order to the chaos down there. At the time about one hundred policemen were working here, the majority of whom had come on their own initiative to earn money. They fined people or simply demanded bribes.… I went to the commander and proposed that policemen would first register with me, so that I would know who was serving at what time. He first agreed, but later on – of course he depended on bribes as well – he dismissed the idea and told me to mind my own business.

When Otari raised the issue at a higher level, he was warned that if he did not keep quiet, he would be prosecuted for arms smuggling. Finally, during a meeting at the customs office, the commander told him: 'Whatever happens down here, that is none of your business, you stay out of it. We can give you something to shut up, but anyway you are out of it.' Not long thereafter, Otari resigned from his position as chairman.

These were basically early indications that the chaos was less chaotic than it seemed, and that people at higher levels were working hard to regulate some of the practices. But instead of aiming to curb extortion and

Figure 4.2. A Georgian *supra* with plenty of wine in the house of a former customs officer living in Sarpi. (Photo: Mathijs Pelkmans)

bribery, these efforts at regulation were intended to channel the informal money flow along patron-client lines. When I asked a well-informed Batumi official about the involvement of the political elite of the Autonomous Republic of Adjara – especially Aslan Abashidze[6] – in these practices, he told me: 'All his acquaintances approached him to get a job at the customs. The official wage was perhaps twenty dollars and what kind of a job is it anyway? This was simply part of a [money-making] structure with Aslan at the top.'

In 1995 the leadership of Adjara carried out a reorganization of the customs that made all inhabitants of Sarpi, except one particularly well-connected inhabitant, redundant. According to local sources, thereafter the (informal) fee for getting a job at the customs was around $15,000, and the bulk of trade was monopolized by a small group of people related to the political elite. Along with the changes in personnel and informal regulations, new offices and hangars were opened in 1995. The new border gate was presented as conforming to the highest international standards. Its new buildings were proudly displayed on postcards and websites and indeed looked impressively efficient. However, what had become efficient was not so much the processing of travel documents or the detection of contraband, but the streamlining of informal payments in ways that ensured the consolidation of a tightly controlled system of patronage.

Torn Passports and Dangerous Names: Part Two

Passports gained new meanings in relation to the patronage networks that pervaded the customs. As discussed above, passport names had been potentially dangerous throughout the Soviet period and had formed an intricate part of the technologies by which the state apparatus extended its control over the population. Then the ritualized power of official documents and the obscurity of Soviet-era bureaucratic procedures changed in the 1990s, and bureaucracy lost part of its symbolic and ritual abundance. In a way the involved procedures became more predictable, though in ways very dissimilar from a Weberian notion of bureaucracy. The passage across the Turkish-Georgian border exemplifies the connections between passports, citizenship and identity and their relevance in encounters with bureaucrats. The tearing of a passport was only one of the 'highlights'. A narrative of events during this night explicates the various positions and actions taken by travellers and customs officers, as well as the central role of passports in these encounters.

The bus departed at 8:00 P.M. from the Ruspazari (Russian bazaar) in Trabzon after two hours of loading and reloading merchandise and luggage. The passengers were mainly Georgian citizens with Georgian, Greek, Russian or Azerbaijani names; the few others included a Turkish couple. Most had been working at the markets or hotels of Trabzon and were travelling home. The mood was good: passengers told stories about home, ridiculed Turkish employers and passed bottles of beer down the aisle. But once we passed Hopa – the last town before the border – the atmosphere grew tense. Worries about the situation at the border started to dominate conversation. Experienced border crossers informed the rest about the latest news and the officers, speculating about who would be on duty that night.

In 1997 the border consisted of three parts: the Turkish and Georgian customs, and the Russian military post between them. The first two stages posed few difficulties. The officers at the Turkish customs routinely checked the documents and fined those who had violated visa rules. The fines were paid promptly, though occasionally they triggered a vocal protest. The next stage was an office right on the borderline, where soldiers of the Russian army checked passports, verified identities, asked a few questions and demanded a two-dollar computer fee. On the face of it, the Turkish and Russian border checks reflected disinterested efficiency, though some experienced travellers insisted this was partly a cover, and that the right approach and money would get you anywhere with the Turkish officers. Whether or not this was true, the difference from the Georgian side was clear. There, informal payments were not a possibility but something unavoidable. It should be mentioned that the bus passengers were all relatively poor and lacked personal connections that could facilitate their passage, in contrast to those who arrived at the border in expensive cars and left within thirty minutes. We had to wait another half an hour before being allowed to enter the passport control rooms one by one. I was requested to pay $10 for some kind of environmental tax I had never heard of, and I received no receipt upon doing so. Because I was smoking, an officer asked if I had an extra pack of cigarettes. I willingly handed over my pack of Camels, but when he saw they were produced in Turkey he returned them disapprovingly, saying: '*ahh, turetskie*' (yuck, Turkish ones). When I got back to the bus, which was waiting on the other side, I learned that the person behind me, a Georgian citizen and ethnic Azerbaijani, had paid $40, while the Turkish couple in front of me had been able to pass without paying anything.

I expected this to be the end of the border-crossing experience. But as soon as all the passengers arrived, a police car escorted the bus to a hangar just outside of Sarpi that had been built the previous year to expedite the checking of luggage. All the suitcases, bazaar bags and merchandise were unloaded and placed on the floor, and we passengers were summoned to stand in line and wait our turn to be interrogated in the small room described in the introduction. It was here that we had to pay the large amounts of money. My Greek neighbour from the bus (travelling without merchandise) had to pay $100. Two women (I did not find out their nationality) were accompanied by an officer to a place outside the hangar and returned half an hour later. At 8:00 A.M. we were finally allowed to enter Georgia.

My observations and the stories my fellow travellers told reveal the basic logic by which customs officers – on the basis of passports and passport data – defined the worth of each individual passenger.[7] European Union and Turkish passports were the strongest, but even Armenian and Azerbaijani passports provided more leverage than Georgian passports, precisely because we were dealing with Georgian customs officers. This differentiation calls to mind Wang's observation that passports constitute regimes of mobility: they link individuals to international rankings of governments on the basis of which access to specific territories may be granted or denied (2004: 352). The main difference at this border gate was that the regime did not concern the traveller's access to territory but the customs officers' access to money. Because the officers had to consider that foreigners might file complaints with their representatives, travellers who did not have this option – Georgian citizens – were at the bottom of the taxonomy.

A second layer of differentiation ranked Georgian passport holders according to their passport ethnicity. Ethnic Georgians seemed to be in the best position, perhaps because of a sense of collective belonging or because ethnic Georgians were more likely to have contacts that could visit reprisals on the customs officers. By contrast, my ethnic Greek neighbour had to pay excessive amounts, likely because a large part of the Greek community in Georgia had left the country and those remaining were assumed to have access to the riches of relatives in Greece. More systematic data gathering could have revealed further distinctions in the taxonomy – gender and place of residence were certainly among the factors that influenced what and how much the customs officers could demand. Despite a lack of systematic data, it is safe to suggest that passports provided customs officers with the information to judge each traveller's strength or weakness, on the basis of which they were able to claim informal payments. Since these patterns did obviously not reflect official guidelines there was room for negotiation. My fellow travellers employed tactics such as hiding the bulk of their money very carefully while keeping a limited amount (say, $30) readily available, hoping the officers would not find it worth the trouble to gain access to the rest. Just before I entered the interrogation room, I was advised to place the business card of an acquaintance, a professor in Batumi, in my passport to show that I had influential contacts in the capital of Adjara. It worked.

Corrupt practices, some contend, may stabilize bureaucratic institutions. For example, Benedict Anderson argued that in Indonesia, systems of parallel financing along the formal salary structure increased the stability of bureaucratic organizations (1990: 60). Likewise, Ledeneva argued that in Soviet Russia, informal practices turned out to be more stable than any formal system (1998: 85). Concerning post-Soviet Georgia, Christophe noted the stabilizing features of corruption in the taxation system (2003). The same might be said for the Georgian customs. The embedding of money-flows in a tight patronage network cemented relations and created an organization that was very loyal to the Abashidze regime. But such a characterization runs the risk of missing an important point: The corrupt practices at the customs did not stabilize a *bureaucratic* organization. Instead, bureaucratic *appearance* was used to strengthen and veil structured sets of relations that preyed on ordinary citizens.

Conclusion

Passports, as official documents of identification, are useful tools for studying the linkages between border drawing, categorization and the formation of collective identities. Because a Soviet passport labelled a person's ethnicity and revealed regional and religious affiliations, its power went far beyond the rights of citizenship – it literally defined the worth of its owner. In Soviet times passports were tools in the creation of a hierarchical system based on scarcity. Initially, at least, these hierarchies were unstable. The ethnographic material presented here showed that although the Laz of Sarpi did not initially identify with the way Soviet authorities categorized them, these categories became central to their ideas of collective belonging. Moreover, because they were labelled Georgians, Sarpi's inhabitants were in a position to benefit from discriminatory policies after the Soviet Union collapsed.[8]

The ultimate value of this micro-approach to passports, customs and borders is that it shows how bureaucratic mechanisms can transform into a personalized theatre of power. Bureaucratic procedures were obscure throughout the Soviet period. Their unpredictability during the Stalin era evolved in later decades into a cult of documentation and a ritualized exercise of bureaucratic power. The 1990s gave a new twist to bureaucratic efficiency: the passport – the ultimate symbol of citizenship and of state's embrace of society – became a crucial item by which officials uncovered personal details to optimize monetary or sexual gain.

The specific transformations at the Georgian customs may be unique, but there is little reason to assume that Western bureaucracies always stick to their presumed functions. As Heyman contends, 'Concrete organizations employ techniques of power for specific ends in contexts wider than the bureaucracy itself' (1995: 261). We may well ask how the current trend to incorporate biometric data in passports increases possibilities for pushing hidden agendas we will remain unaware of until they affect us.[9] Perhaps the positive thing to mention about the extortion practices at the Georgian border, then, is that they were *transparent:* their logic could be discerned by everyone and was actively discussed. Moreover, these practices did not appear to be informed by a larger agenda such as the ideological exclusion of certain groups. What we witnessed is what happens when a state system based on the categorization of its population into ethnically defined constituencies disintegrates and is replaced by patronage networks that depend on, and perpetuate, those same categories.

Notes

1. See Kotkin (1995: 100–105) for an interesting discussion of the administrative problems related to passportization in central Russia and the related emergence of a black market in official documents.
2. I am grateful to Paul Manning for drawing my attention to the ethnographic importance of passports in my book *Defending the Border* (2006), and for encouraging me to pay more analytic attention to identification documents.
3. Several Hemshin and Kurdish families used to live in the hills behind the village of Sarpi. Other groups living in the region, such as the Greeks, were also deported at this time.
4. Interestingly, the Laz in Mingrelia took the Mingrelian ending -ia, while the Ingilot in Azerbaijan changed their name depending on religious affiliation, Muslim Ingilot choosing -ev/-ov and Christians, -dze.
5. Guria province is located north of Adjara and has a Christian-Georgian population.
6. Aslan Abashidze was the leader of the Autonomous Republic of Adjara between 1991 and 2004, when he was ousted from office and fled to Moscow.
7. This rudimentary analysis is based on the described border crossing and informed by subsequent trips. For obvious reasons I could not ask all the passengers what amounts they had paid.
8. Mühlfried (2010) documents the relevance of passports in the 2008 Russian-Georgian conflict, showing how 'family names' and their specific ethnic connotations influenced people's ability to claim citizenship, despite the fact that ethnicity or nationality was no longer indicated in Georgian passports.
9. The question is particularly relevant, given that in August 2011 the Georgian government introduced a new electronic identity card that supposedly was "safe from falsification" and would contribute to the "consumer satisfaction" of citizens while also

making it possible to identify "people from a distance"! The introduction of this form of surveillance did not encounter any noteworthy resistance, despite it being much more intrusive than previous identity documents. See the following governmental website http://www.cra.gov.ge/index.php?lang_id=ENG&sec_id=49&info_id=1794, accessed 10 January 2012.

References

Anderson, B. 1990 [1972]. *Language and Power: Exploring Political Cultures in Indonesia*. Ithaca, NY: Cornell University Press.

———. 1991 [1983]. *Imagined Communities: Reflections on the Origin and Spread of Nationalism*. London and New York: Verso.

Bauman, Z. 2001. 'Identity in the Globalising World', *Social Anthropology* 9(2): 121–29.

Christophe, B. 2003. *Zwischen Fassaden der Anarchie und regulativer Allmacht - Metamorphosen des Leviathan in der georgischen Provinz*. Habilitation thesis, Frankfurt (Oder): European University Viadrina.

Heyman, J.M. 1995. 'Putting Power in the Anthropology of Bureaucracy: The Immigration and Naturalization Service at the Mexico-United States Border', *Current Anthropology* 36(2): 261–87.

Hoskings, G. 2001. *Russia and the Russians: A History*. Cambridge, MA: The Belknap Press of Harvard University Press.

Kelly, T. 2006. 'Documented Lives: Fear and the Uncertainties of Law during the Second Palestinian Intifada', *Journal of the Royal Anthropological Institute* 12: 89–107.

Kotkin, S. 1995. *Magnetic Mountain: Stalinism as a Civilization*. Berkeley: University of California Press.

Ledeneva, A. 1998. *Russia's Economy of Favours: Blat, Networking and Informal Exchange*. Cambridge: Cambridge University Press.

Matthews, M. 1993. *The Passport Society: Controlling Movement in Russia and the USSR*. Boulder, CO: Westview Press.

Mühlfried, F. 2010. 'Citizenship at War: Passports and Nationality in the 2008 Russian-Georgian Conflict', *Anthropology Today* 26(2): 8–13.

Navaro-Yashin, Yael. 2007. 'Make-believe Papers, Legal Forms and the Counterfeit: Affective Interactions between Documents and People in Britain and Cyprus', *Anthropological Theory* 7(1): 79–98.

Pelkmans, M. 2006. *Defending the Border: Identity, Religion, and Modernity in the Republic of Georgia*. Ithaca, NY: Cornell University Press.

Scott, J. 1998. *Seeing Like a State: How Certain Schemes to Improve the Human Condition Failed*. New Haven, CT: Yale University Press.

Torpey, J. 2000. *The Invention of the Passport: Surveillance, Citizenship and the State*. Cambridge: Cambridge University Press.

Wang, H. 2004. 'Regulating Transnational Flows of People: An Institutional Analysis of Passports and Visas as a Regime of Mobility', *Identities: Global Studies in Culture and Power* 11: 351–56.

Chapter 5

Proximity and Asymmetry on the Portuguese-Spanish Border

William Kavanagh

The social sciences, or at least those that, like anthropology, are less concerned with always being 'scientific', will at times accept that certain things that may seem at first sight to be purely anecdotal and unimportant may yet be capable of revealing crucial aspects of social reality. I suggest that the following is such an example.

The story has it that in preparation for a visit by the Spanish prime minister to a Lisbon school, the headmaster briefed the pupils to answer, when asked what Spain meant for the Portuguese, that 'Spaniards are our friends'. 'No, headmaster', piped up one of the younger boys, 'Spaniards are our brothers.' 'That is a very good reply', said the headmaster, 'but why "brothers" and not "friends"?' 'Because', replied the boy, 'we can choose our friends!'

Of course the story is a joke – but is it more than a joke? Another anecdote, this one apparently true, recounts that on the occasion of King Alfonso XIII of Spain's visit to the northern Portuguese city of Braga in December 1903, a canon of the cathedral, discussing with the visiting monarch why the two Iberian countries should always remain separate, commented: 'Spain and Portugal are like brother and sister … and the Roman Catholic Church does not approve of incestuous marriages.'

Like many if not most of the more interesting notions in the social sciences, 'identity' is a highly contested concept. Nationalist politicians and others may frequently believe otherwise, but the majority of social scientists do not see 'identities' as natural phenomena but rather as social

Notes for this chapter begin on page 134.

constructions that are culturally and historically specific (i.e., they change depending on context and over time), and relational (i.e., we tend to think of distinctions and differences in relation to an 'Other'). If we agree with Anthony Cohen (1985: 13) that 'consciousness of community is encapsulated in perception of its boundaries', then both 'community' and 'border' imply the idea of a relation with an Other. All identity, then, is constructed in the double sense of similarity and difference with respect to Others. And whereas Anthony Smith (1986) suggests that ethnic communities share a collective name, a myth of common descent, a shared history, a distinctive shared culture, association with a specific territory and a sense of solidarity, Hobsbawm and Ranger (1983) have shown that much of this seemingly ancient 'shared history' and 'shared culture' may have been invented comparatively recently. Benedict Anderson's (1983: 15) claim that all nations are 'imagined communities' – in the sense that they are created and invented in that their members, despite never seeing or knowing each other, believe they are somehow all related – reveals very clearly the symbolic construction of identities. Fredrik Barth (1969), meanwhile, taught that ethnic groups are categories of ascription and identification defined by the actors themselves, arguing, in his well-known phrase, that 'the critical focus of investigation from this point of view becomes the ethnic *boundary* that defines the group, not the cultural stuff that it encloses' (Barth 1969: 15).

Portugal and Spain: Historical Identities

While Spain shares land borders with four countries (five, if the 1 km border with Gibraltar is included) – 19 km with Morocco in North Africa, 63 km with Andorra, 656 km with France and 1,292 km with Portugal – Portugal has only one neighbour: Spain. And it shows. As one British historian has put it: 'Centuries of war with Castile had created deep antagonism between the Portuguese and their only land neighbours. Proverbs warned the people about the dangers of trusting Castilians and ballads emphasised the differences between the two popular cultures' (Birmingham 1993: 35). 'De Espanha nem bons ventos nem bons casamentos' (From Spain, neither good winds nor good marriages), say the Portuguese.

Compared to Spain, Portugal has only one-fifth the territory and but a quarter of the population. Unsurprisingly, the smaller country has viewed the larger with a certain apprehension ever since Portugal's origins as an independent kingdom in the twelfth century. Over the following centuries, the Portuguese often had to protect their independence from their neighbour to the east, signing treaties with England (and later, Britain) from the fourteenth century on to help ensure it. Even today, history textbooks in

Portuguese schools still refer in very negative terms to that period of some sixty years (from 1580 to 1640) when Portugal and its dominions were incorporated in the Spanish crown. The Portuguese call the time when their country was ruled by Philip II, Philip III and Philip IV of Spain (Philip I, Philip II and Philip III of Portugal, respectively) under the dual monarchy as 'the Spanish Domination' or 'the Spanish Captivity' (Saraiva 1997: 64). The Portuguese historian Saraiva (1997: 68) claims that 'a growing feeling of revulsion towards the domination of Spain had entered the Portuguese psyche, which was to remain a permanent feature'. In fact, the epithets by which these monarchs are known give us some idea as to the feelings their subjects held towards them. While Philip III of Spain is known in that country as *el Pío* (the Pius), the same man is known in Portugal as *o Cruel* (the Cruel). His son, Philip IV, known in Spain as *el Grande* (the Great), is called *o Opressor* (the Oppressor) in Portugal. And significantly, both the medieval battle of Aljubarrota (14 August 1385), in which the Portuguese defeated the Castilian invaders, and the regaining of independence in 1640 – when, in the words of Saraiva (1997: 68), 'the Portuguese had shaken off the Spanish yoke' – are still seen today 'as fundamental moments in the affirmation of national identify against the eternal Spanish enemy' (Monteiro and Costa Pinto 2003: 49).

In May 1801, during the brief conflict that came to be known as the War of the Oranges, a Spanish army crossed the border just south of the Spanish city of Badajoz and occupied the Portuguese town of Olivença, which has been Spanish ever since. Spaniards are not generally aware of the Portuguese claim to the town in the province of Badajoz that they call Olivenza, yet its loss is still a sore point for many Portuguese. And although today no one in Portugal protests when a Portuguese firm is taken over by, say, a German or French company, the popular press in Portugal will speak of 'invasion' if the takeover is carried out by a Spanish firm. *Antiespanholismo* (being anti-Spanish) is a constant in the Portuguese sense of identity. Kaplan (1991: 69) cites a Portuguese politician as stating that 'a Portuguese who dares to show open cooperation with Spain can be accused of being a bad Portuguese, even a traitor'. In a debate I watched on Portuguese television before the Portuguese legislative elections in 2009, the opposition candidate accused the Portuguese prime minister of overly favouring Spain and therefore, by implication, of being a bad Portuguese. In similar style, a Portuguese military officer cited by Kaplan (1991: 65) asserted, 'We were taught to hate Spain.' In many ways, Portugal can be said to have defined itself historically (and to do so still in many ways) precisely as being 'not Spain'.

Of course, it is only fair to mention here that at least since the eighteenth century there has also existed something known as *Iberismo*, best translated as 'Iberian federalism', which argues for the political unification of both countries of the Iberian Peninsula. The idea has found a certain amount of favour among a sector of the intellectual elite in both nations – the Portuguese writer and Nobel laureate José Saramago was a particularly vocal supporter, predicting that one day Portugal and Spain would end up forming a single country called 'Iberia' – but majorities of both countries' populations have shown little interest in the proposed union.

Moreover, though the Portuguese have historically been well aware of Spain, the Spaniards have generally ignored the Portuguese for most of the past eight hundred years. One will hear anti-Spanish jokes in Portugal (e.g., the two stories above) but not anti-Portuguese jokes in Spain, which is certainly revealing of the asymmetric relationship between these two peoples. An opinion poll taken in 2009 by the University of Salamanca's Centre for Social Analysis (Centro de Análisis Sociales [CASUS]) found that whereas 54 per cent of the Portuguese interviewed could name the head of the Spanish government, less than 2 per cent of the Spaniards asked were able to name the Portuguese prime minister. Mutual ignorance may be high and stereotypes of the other country extremely long-lived, yet the Spaniards quite clearly are far less informed about or interested in their Portuguese neighbours than the other way round.

It is also significant that some thirty years ago there were only thirteen official border crossings between Portugal and Spain. At the time there were eighteen on the border between France and Spain, which is only half the length of the Portuguese-Spanish border. Furthermore, most of the customs posts on the Portuguese-Spanish border were generally closed at 9:00 P.M., even in summer (Pintado and Barrenechea 1972: 109). It is also telling that nearly all large-scale maps of the border area produced more than just a few years ago in either country leave the territory of the other nation blank. With justification, then, one might say that until very recently, the two countries lived with their backs turned to one another. One might add, however, that the Portuguese (though not the Spaniards) also spent a good bit of their time 'looking over their shoulders'. Yet, as we shall see, much has changed since 1 January 1986, when both countries became members of the European Community (the present European Union [EU]).

Ethnography on the Portuguese-Spanish Frontier

My anthropological research[1] at three border villages – one Spanish, two Portuguese – on the part of the frontier where the northern Portuguese region of Trás-os-Montes meets the Spanish region of Galicia, is both long-term and ongoing. The original intention was to observe at close hand,

and from one specific location on a border between two EU members, the expected transformation of Europe's 'internal' international boundaries from 'barriers' to 'bridges'.[2]

The territory of the Galician village juts like a spur or wedge into Portugal, and the two Portuguese villages lie on either side of it. One of the Portuguese villages is only a few kilometres to the south of the Spanish village; the other is somewhat further to the west. All three villages are at approximately the same altitude, their soils are similar and their climates are identical. Here the border does not coincide with any sort of 'natural boundary'. Nor does the landscape appear to change in any significant way at the border, which is known as 'the dry borderline': *raia seca* in Portuguese and Galician and *raya seca* in Spanish. As for the languages spoken on either side of the border, the *Galego* (Galician) of the Spanish village does not much differ from the Portuguese spoken in the Portuguese villages. The older houses appear to be the same on both sides of the boundary, and most still have hollowed-out spaces in their walls (known as *secretas*) where smuggled contraband could be hidden when the border guards came to inspect. Yet despite their similar physical appearance, these villages have had very different national histories, different political systems and different state administrations for hundreds of years.

Many things change at the frontier. For example, the music played on either side of the boundary differs considerably: the Galicians play the bagpipes, while the Portuguese do not; the Portuguese play the accordion and the Galicians do not. The look of religious processions is also distinctive on each side of the border: in the Galician religious processions the decorations of the images of Christ, the Virgin and the saints are very simple, while those in Portugal are extremely ornate. Even time changes at the borderline, with the clocks in Portugal set an hour behind those in Spain. And the simple fact that Portuguese emigrants have preferred France or the United States as destinations, while Galicians have tended to go to Germany or to Switzerland, means that unlike the old village houses, which are pretty much identical in both countries, the new houses they build on their return home impart a very different look today to the villages on one or the other side of the border.

Meanwhile, some of the most important differences are invisible at first glance: health, welfare, education, justice, taxes, and so on differ across borders because these aspects of citizens' lives are controlled by the modern nation state. Precisely for this reason, in most countries people living on a borderline will nearly always prefer (if they have a choice, which often is not the case) to send their children to a school a good distance away in their own country, rather than a nearby school just over the border in the other country. Likewise, they will almost certainly favour the free national health doctors and hospitals on their own side of the border (which people living in a country will have paid for with their taxes) before visiting doctors across the frontier, who may very well charge fees. And – unsurprisingly, after centuries of going their separate ways – the two states have very different politico-administrative organizations. This frequently poses problems for cross-border cooperation when one state deals with a matter at a certain level and the neighbouring state at a different level. The Spanish municipality (*municipio*) in Galicia is generally both smaller and much less important politically and administratively than the Portuguese municipality (*concelho*). Similarly, the Galician parish (*parroquia*) is generally smaller than the Portuguese parish (*freguesía*). But most importantly, the Spanish autonomous region of Galicia has its own regional parliament and regional government with ample powers. There is no equivalent to this in mainland Portugal.

Virtually unchanged for eight hundred years and thus one of the oldest borders in Europe, the border between Portugal and Spain – a historically 'consecrated' yet 'artificial' barrier, as all borders are – is a peripheral area of the Iberian Peninsula, itself regarded as a peripheral part of Europe. For many years, dictatorial regimes in both Portugal (from 1926 to 1974) and Spain (from 1939 to 1975) made them politically peripheral to the rest of democratic Europe. Both nations also, until recently, brought up the rear of Europe economically. And because of the neglect the governments at Lisbon and Madrid have traditionally shown their border regions, along with the practice, already pointed out, of mutually ignoring the existence of the neighbouring state, the areas at the border were characteristically the most marginal parts of already peripheral regions. The very name Trás-os-Montes, which means 'beyond the mountains', reveals the isolation and marginality of the area, while Galicia, in the extreme northwest of the Iberian peninsula, has been characterized as 'poor, damp and difficult to reach' (Hooper 1995: 419). Both are sparsely populated agricultural regions (Figures 5.1 and 5.2) with little industry, few cities of any significant size and poor communications with their national capitals.

It has been said that 'borders are time written in space' (Rupnik 1994: 103). The Portuguese-Spanish border has not always been peaceful, as the many fortifications on both sides – their cannons aimed at the other country – show only too well. Yet it has historically been one of the most stable borders in Europe. On the particular section where the villages under study are located, the only alteration since the twelfth century was made in 1864, when Portugal and Spain signed a boundary demarcation treaty under which a Portuguese village (the one closest to the Galician village), which had previously been divided by the borderline passing through its centre (Figure 5.3), was ceded in its entirety to Portugal. The

Figure 5.1. Agricultural work at the Galician border village. The hills on the horizon are in Portugal. (Photo: William Kavanagh)

Figure 5.2. Cultivating flowers at the Portuguese village nearest the border. (Photo: William Kavanagh)

treaty stipulated that the boundary would skirt the Portuguese village at a distance of a hundred metres from the last house facing Spain. This was expressly done to control the inevitable smuggling that – with many houses directly on the borderline having one door giving onto Spain and another onto Portugal – was the order of the day. As García Mañá (1988: 12) puts it: 'This circumstance created situations of mockery of the customs authorities and conflicts gravely prejudicial to the good harmony of the villagers and the customs authorities.' The village, along with two nearby villages also divided by the border between the two countries, was known as a *povo/pueblo promíscuo* and is recorded as having been so since at least the beginning of the sixteenth century. The village had enjoyed no special privileges and was not exempt from taxes: the part of the village that had belonged to Spain had paid taxes to Spain, and the part belonging to Portugal had paid taxes to Portugal. Nor was there any doubt as to the nationality of the inhabitants. For the villagers, the only advantage of living where they did was the ease with which they could carry on their smuggling activities. The 1864 treaty, by which all three divided villages passed in their entirety to Portugal, made that slightly more difficult.

Figure 5.3. The stone cross marks where the borderline went prior to the 1864 demarcation treaty. The frontier passed through the line of houses on the right. (Photo: William Kavanagh)

From the point of view of Lisbon and Madrid, the Treaty of 1864 was also important for doing away with another 'anomaly' known in Spanish as the Coto Mixto and in Portuguese as the Couto Misto. This was the territory of another three small villages (Santiago, Rubiás and Meaus) not far from the three I have been studying. Since the origin of Portugal in the twelfth century, it had been neither part of Portugal nor part of Spain. Inhabitants of the Coto Mixto / Couto Misto enjoyed a number of privileges: they had a right to choose whether they wished to be Spaniards or Portuguese; they did not have to pay taxes to either country, nor could they be called to serve in the armed forces of either state; they needed no licence to bear arms; they could grow what they liked, including tobacco, whose cultivation was strictly controlled in both Spain and Portugal; they did not have to use the official stamped paper that at that time was obligatory in both countries for every sort of agreement and contract; they could bring whatever they liked, without danger of being stopped by the customs guards of either nation, along the six-kilometre neutral road that went from the Coto through territory of Spain and Portugal to the Portuguese village of Tourem. In essence, the Coto Mixto was a self-governing independent territory whose maximum authority was a judge or mayor elected annually by the inhabitants of the Coto, who upon election would then appoint six subordinates, two men from each of the three villages, who were known as *homes de acordos*, which may be translated as 'men of agreement or harmony'. All the important documents of the Coto were kept in a large wooden chest that was, and still is, kept in the sacristy of the parish church of Santiago. The document chest has three locks and three keys. Each of the villages kept one of the keys, so opening the chest required the presence of representatives of all three villages and all three keys. The Treaty of 1864 gave the Coto Mixto, in its entirety, to Spain in compensation for its ceding the other three villages that had been divided by the borderline (the *povos/pueblos promíscuos*) in their entirety to Portugal.

Nation states usually dislike anomalies at their borders, since a common characteristic of borders is that they are liminal areas where control by the authorities is more easily eluded. García Mañá (1988: 39) says that in the twelfth century during what is known as the Reconquista, when the Christians in the north of the Iberian Peninsula moved south, recapturing territory lost to the Muslims at the beginning of the eighth century, the monarchs of the Christian kingdoms repopulated the border area by creating what were known as *coutos de homiciados*, enclaves within which certain criminals (and not just murderers, as one might conclude from the name) could obtain a conditional freedom, expiate their crimes and eventually be pardoned by settling there with their families. García Mañá

(1988: 90) believes that the Coto Mixto may originally have been one of those *coutos de homiciados.*

Local Actions and the State

What is special about living on an international frontier? Firstly, nearby cross-border villages may form an unusual sort of unrecognized 'community' in the sense that although its residents are subject to very different jurisdictions (a reality known to those living across the border), one personally knows the people on the other side (they may be the Other, but they are not strangers), with whom one has frequent relations at many different levels. Secondly, even though living near an international border may pose a set of difficulties not experienced by those living far from such a border, at the same time it offers a set of opportunities (principally associated with the practice of contraband trade) that people elsewhere in the nation state do not normally have access to. Thirdly, awareness that things are very different just across the border may lead to a feeling that the laws of one's own country are arbitrary and that flouting those laws is therefore a perfectly normal thing to do. But since people generally do not like to feel that what they do is relative or arbitrary, they may very well also resort to stereotypes to overstate the differences between themselves and the Other across the border to reinforce their own sense of identity.

Smuggling, more than any other activity, exhibits border dwellers' tendency to live 'outside the law'. Referred to by border villagers as 'night work', smuggling is culturally acceptable behaviour on the border. And it was certainly not an exclusively male occupation. 'It was lovely', one Portuguese woman told me of her years as a smuggler from age fourteen to eighteen, when she went to Paris to work. She had made various journeys each night with rucksacks of whiskey and tobacco weighing some twenty-five to thirty kilos, and had also (the part she says she never told her mother about) been shot at by the border guards. Such 'night work' entailed other risks as well. A local doctor confided to me that he had detected a higher incidence of cirrhosis among people, especially women, who worked as smugglers for long periods. He put this down to the quantity of brandy they needed to drink to ward off the night chill during their smuggling operations. The priest of the two Portuguese villages, writing in the December 1992 issue of the monthly newspaper that he edited at the time, complained – without the slightest hint of the possible illegality or immorality of such activity – that the imminent disappearance of the border would mean that his villages 'would lose their most important business and source of employment and wealth, which was smuggling'.

Border people structure much of their lives around their relations with 'foreigners'. In this sense, the border is a bridge and not a barrier. The border dwellers always felt the laws against contraband, passed by distant politicians insensitive to the local realities of the border, to be unjust and unreasonable. The borderland villagers are a 'we' group to whom the authorities are 'they' – especially given knowledge that state officials themselves have cashed in on the illegal border trade. Many villagers on both sides of the frontier tell stories of knowing full well that the pair of shoes for their child or the few kilos of rice or the dozen eggs the border police had confiscated from them were almost always kept by those very same policemen.

Many stories tell of how border guards on both sides frequently abused their position of power and not infrequently acted with brutality towards villagers, who for their part regarded their own smuggling activities as totally normal, not reprehensible. While villagers on both sides of the frontier say that the Spanish and Portuguese border guards were both bad and would confiscate whatever was carried into their respective countries by those crossing the border (whether foreigners or their own co-nationals), they admit that there was a certain asymmetry in the treatment meted out by the guards. People on both sides of the border told me that the Portuguese Guarda Fiscal (popularly known as the *guardinhas*) were more likely than the Spanish Guardia Civil to beat smugglers up after seizing what they were bringing from the other side. When asked why this was so, a Portuguese villager – in a clear comment on a perceived asymmetry – replied: 'Because they were poorer, more backward.'

Another Portuguese man told me that when he was fifteen, the Guarda Fiscal had stopped him on the borderline and accused him of smuggling. Although he was carrying nothing, he said, one of the *guardinhas* hit his head hard enough to knock him unconscious. When the teen's family went to complain, the head of the border post asked the guard involved why he had hit the boy so savagely. 'Because I thought he was a Spaniard', the guard is said to have replied. He was expelled from the corps. This story might lead to a conclusion that border guards sometimes gave harsher treatment to smugglers from the other country than to their own countrymen. Yet most people I asked about this point denied that the guards were any more lenient with one side or the other. Portuguese villagers tell stories of having had to sell their fields on the Spanish side of the border because of difficulties imposed by the Portuguese border police. Not only were farmers required to obtain a special permit to work their land and allowed to cross the border only during daylight hours, they stated, but the guards would often, on the slightest pretext, confiscate recently harvested crops the farmers were bringing home from their fields just over the border.

A Galician woman married to a Portuguese man told me that on the day after her wedding in the Galician village some forty years earlier, she had accompanied her new husband to visit his relatives in the nearby Portuguese village only to be stopped at the border by a Portuguese border guard, who sent her back to her village but let her husband cross into Portugal. She explained that it was only upon mentioning the incident to her village priest that she learnt she had a right to enter Portugal as the wife of a Portuguese man.

Other stories tell of smugglers shot dead on the borderline by the border guards. One Galician man was a bit luckier: he told me how his contraband group had been challenged near the border by a patrol of *guardinhas*. His companions had bolted off in different directions and escaped arrest, but he had tried to push his way past the guards and one of them had shot him in the testicles, though luckily he suffered no permanent injury. What angered him most, he told me, was that he was 'already some two hundred metres into Spain, where the *guardinhas* have no jurisdiction whatsoever'.

One of the elements repeated among the villagers' stories is the ambivalent position of the border police. They had power over aspects of villagers' lives, but they were never really part of the village, since they were nearly always, in the case of the Portuguese *guardinhas*, and always, in the case of the Spanish *guardias*, from some other part of the country. The authorities are always to be distrusted – many people told me the border police 'were hated by everyone' – except when they can be shown to be human, that is, when they are prepared to accept bribes to look the other way. And sometimes even that is not sufficient. One Galician man told me angrily that, despite having taken the precaution of bribing the corporal at the Portuguese border post, he had had a large load ('five thousand kilos', he said) of bananas confiscated by the Portuguese *guardinhas*. He did admit, however, that it was probably thanks to the bribe that in the end he was allowed to keep half the load of smuggled bananas. Some villagers claim that smugglers were the only people who would ever risk going past the border post – they had to, to pay bribes to the border guards. However, villagers do speak of one newly arrived border guard who – incredibly – had refused to accept any bribes and had even tried to arrest some smugglers who had previously paid off his companion guards to look the other way as the contraband went through. Apparently his fellow guards quickly taught him the rules of the game and thereafter he took his cut like the rest of them. Villagers tell the story with the clear implication that non-corrupt police were considered arbitrary and cruel to attempt to stop what was, from the point of view of the villagers on both sides of the line, considered to be 'clean trade', whereas the guards who accepted bribes were thought to be more 'human' because they were acting more reasonably. Here we see the 'unreasonable' laws and rules of both national states forced to come to terms with the 'reasonable' practices of the local border community.

And while on the one hand people at times give excellent 'reasons' for despising people of the other country, on the other hand both sides had, until very recently, the same interests in outwitting the authorities. Villagers are fond of telling stories of tricks they used to fool the ever-vigilant guards. The Galicians tell of the time a man of their village was caught on the borderline by the *guardinhas*. On the pretext of showing them where he had hidden the contraband, he led them across the border and straight into the arms of a patrol of the Spanish Guardia Civil, who sent the *guardinhas* packing, saying the Portuguese had no right to be arresting anyone on Spanish soil. In this case, one authority was played off against the rival authority. In another story that made the border guards look ridiculous, a Portuguese woman told me about her great-aunt, who was caught by the Guarda Fiscal while bringing in two dozen eggs from Spain. As they escorted her to the customs post to pay a large fine – apparently a fine was levied for each egg confiscated – the woman desperately wondered how to rid herself of the eggs. It was impossible to simply throw them away, with one guard in front of her and another walking her. In the end she took the eggs one by one, sucked them, crushed the shells and dropped the bits of eggshell in the tall grass along the path without letting the guards notice what she was up to. When the guards got her to the post, she was found to be carrying nothing and the *guardinhas* had to let her go without a fine. Finally, if all else failed, one could resort to reliance on divine intervention to save oneself from the border police. A splendid mural painted on an inside wall of the church of the Portuguese village closest to the borderline depicts three *guardinhas* on horseback in full gallop. The object of their chase is not shown, but the mural speaks of the *milagre* (miracle) of a smuggler's escape from the guards thanks to the intervention of Santo António (St Anthony). The mural, which probably came at considerable cost to the man who commissioned it, openly depicts the expectation of divine protection of smuggling activities (clearly not regarded as immoral) as perfectly normal.

Since smuggling was so very profitable, a common distrust of authority brought together people living on the border. People say that when there was *confiança/confianza* (trust), they were all good partners. They state categorically that 'money would never change hands at the borderline'. The goods would be delivered and payment would be made later. A good example of this 'cooperation' and 'trust' was the smuggling of wolfram (tungsten ore) during the Second World War. The Germans used a mine near the Galician village as a front for smuggling the mineral, used in the making of bombs and aircraft, from Portugal to Spain. As Britain's oldest ally, Portugal was unable to export the wolfram directly to Germany, so the mineral was smuggled into Spain and then legally exported from Spain to Germany. At night, groups of sixty to a hundred men would move sacks of wolfram loaded on donkeys and horses. The Portuguese brought the wolfram to the border and handed it over to the Galicians, who would then take it to the mine. The border police of both sides were bribed to look the other way, though only in a figurative sense, as we have seen: since the bribe was usually a percentage of the contraband, the guards always counted the number of loads. The following day the sacks of mineral were openly loaded onto lorries and shipped out. Villagers who worked in the mine at the time say the amount of wolfram actually produced by the Galician mine was tiny in comparison to the amount of mineral shipped out as if coming from the mine.

In troubled times the border provides the perfect escape for those in difficulties. Timely border crossings saved quite a few lives during the Spanish Civil War (1936–39). Even after the war, a number of Spaniards were living in Portuguese villages along the border. Those who had been identified as politically suspect by the regime of General Franco were there merely for their safety, but others were operating as anti-Franco Maquis, crossing the border to murder members of the Spanish Civil Guard and local heads of the Franco regime's single party, the Falange, and then returning to their bases in Portugal. Later, during the 1960s, Portuguese men who wished to avoid military service in the colonial wars in the former 'African provinces' of Angola, Mozambique and Guinea-Bissau would necessarily first make their way to Spain on the overland route to safety in France.

Even today, the border retains, at least in part, some aspect of an 'escape valve'. A few years ago, a man from the Galician village, well known as a smuggler, popped over the border into Portugal when the Spanish police came to arrest him. The somewhat hastily 'retired' ex-smuggler later made his way to Brazil, where he lives as a free man. Villagers talk of the impunity of those who, having committed a crime in one country, escape punishment by fleeing to the other. Nowadays, though, this historically important role of the border as a provider of instant sanctuary is limited by Article 41 of the Schengen Agreement, which authorizes the police of one Schengen state to penetrate into the territory of another Schengen country while engaged in 'hot pursuit' of suspected criminals. Here the once-rigid frontier has become elastic, thus losing one of its main roles, that is, provider of instant safety for those seeking to escape the rules or the justice of one of the two countries.

Further demonstrative of the liminality of a border is another form of 'escape' taken by the last two members of the Galician village to commit suicide. They did so by drowning themselves in a pool of the river that, for a short distance, marks the border between the two countries. In this case it would appear that the location of the 'escape' was clearly chosen for its symbolic value. This could be just coincidence, but the villagers who told me about the suicides did not appear to think so. I had the clear impression that they regarded the border as a bit of a no man's land, though no one actually used those words. And is it just coincidence that the Portuguese villagers who live on the borderline dispose of their rubbish by throwing it onto the Spanish side of the border?

In some circumstances, border dwellers make use of the fact that the Church is the same on both sides of the border. A woman of the Galician village whose husband was killed in the Spanish Civil War has been receiving a war widow's pension ever since, despite her living with another villager for many years. She did not lose the pension through remarriage, because their marriage took place in the Portuguese village. Thus, as far as the Spanish State is concerned, the woman remains an unmarried widow, while in the eyes of the Roman Catholic Church and of their neighbours, the couple are not 'living in sin'. Another example is that of a young Portuguese couple who got married in the Galician village and immediately left for the United States – separately. The woman had no trouble getting an entry visa, as her parents were already working there and she applied as a single woman. Her husband likewise applied as a single man. Apparently a visa for a married couple would have been much more difficult to obtain. Their Spanish marriage meant that neither the Portuguese state nor the U.S. immigration authorities knew the couple's real situation. These cases demonstrate some ways people manipulate the border to their advantage, a privilege enjoyed by those living at an international frontier.

Border Encounters Before and After 1992

The undeniable need to cooperate and trust those on the other side of the border still does not mean that people always speak well of those in the other country. Villagers' attitudes towards their 'foreign' neighbours are often ambiguous. Very close friendships sometimes form between men[3] from different villages – I once witnessed a Galician break down in tears upon hearing that one of his Portuguese friends had been attacked and killed by his own bull – and people will speak admiringly of individuals from the other country. However, when people are asked how they feel about those of the other country generally, rather than about inhabitants of a specific village, mutual dislike is often the first thing to surface, and stereotypes come thick and fast: 'Galicians are loud, stuck up and live off the dole instead of working' (the last part a reference to a perceived economic asymmetry between the two countries); 'Portuguese are backward, appear to be *muy formales* [very serious, responsible], but are really *falsos* [deceitful]'. 'You can never trust a Galician', the Portuguese say. 'You can't trust the Portuguese', the Galicians say, 'they are just like the Gypsies'. 'The Galicians beat their wives', say the Portuguese. 'The Portuguese beat their wives', say the Galicians, and so on. Yet some people do observe, correctly, that 'they probably say the same thing about us'.

When speaking of their nearest Portuguese neighbours, the Galicians say, 'The best person at X is Jesus and even he is behind bars', referring to the image of Christ behind the grilles on the windows of the chapel at the entrance to the village. The Portuguese claim that a Galician would never be generous, whereas a Portuguese would. On their side, the Galicians tell the story of the Portuguese who invites some Galicians to dinner but gives his guests very little to eat. They cheer up when they hear the man tell his wife to 'Bring out the chicken' – until they realize that it is a live animal brought in to clean up the few crumbs dropped on the floor. The main character in this legendary tale, told in many places, is generally 'a poor man', but at the border he becomes the Other. Something similar happens in the story of a woman – again, a Portuguese, as it was a Galician who told the tale – talking to an image of St Anthony in church. She is annoyed with the saint because she has prayed long and hard to be sent a husband, to no avail. In anger and frustration, she throws a stone at the statue, which gives off a small cloud of dust when hit. 'There you are', says the woman, 'smoking without burning and here I am, burning without smoking'. In the Portuguese version of the same story, the protagonist is naturally a Galician woman.

When asked whether they would like to see a child of theirs marry someone from the other country, people on both sides of the border most frequently reply, 'No, they are very different from us.' Yet mixed marriages are not unknown (see Figure 5.4). When I began research in the Galician village in 1990, it was home to four couples in which the wives were all from the Spanish village while their husbands originally hailed from the nearest Portuguese village. A few people at the Galician village spoke of these marriages with disdain, saying that the men had been landless poor in Portugal and married their wives simply to gain access to a bit of property. This opinion would appear to underline the perception of asymmetry and Portugal's economic inferiority to Spain.

Figure 5.4. A woman (her back to the camera) from the Galician village on a visit to her Portuguese husband's family at their village across the border. (Photo: William Kavanagh)

Even the apparently true stories the borderlanders tell about each other frequently underline their mutual dislike of each other. Yet it is not totally clear whether such expressions of dislike are real or feigned. As noted above, people may very well use stereotypes to overstate differences with the Other and thereby reinforce their own sense of identity. And although many of the Galician villagers maintain a certain attitude of superiority to their Portuguese neighbours, some of these same Galicians have proudly boasted to me that they are sometimes mistaken for Portuguese when they are in Portugal because they speak the language so well.

In many ways the nearest neighbouring village is treated as exactly that, without taking the political boundary into account. Whereas the people of the Galician village sometimes speak badly of their Portuguese neighbours, they have worse to say about their Galician neighbours in the village just down the road. Then again, they characterize the Portuguese village just beyond the one opposite them as full of excellent people who make the best sort of friend. Since the second Portuguese village is, as one might expect, the traditional rival of the first Portuguese village, the Galicians' affinity for the Portuguese of the second village is understandable along the lines of 'the enemy of my enemy is my friend'. In this respect, the trans-frontier 'community' and communities elsewhere inside the nation state exhibit quite similar patterns of behaviour.

The following true story is an example of something that is 'normal' at a border but impossible elsewhere. As I heard it, a man from the Galician village was working in his field on the border when his Portuguese neighbour in the adjoining field began shouting insults at him. The Galician told his neighbour to watch it or he would let him have it with his shotgun, which he happened to have with him as he had been out hunting rabbits. The Portuguese jeered and bent over, turning his backside to the Galician, who snatched up his shotgun and blasted the Portuguese in the arse. The Portuguese cried out and fell. The Galician, suddenly aware of what he had done and certain he had killed the Portuguese, ran back to his village and asked the mayor what to do. The mayor wanted to know whether the villager had shot the Portuguese in Spain or in Portugal. When the Galician replied 'In Portugal', the mayor is said to have told him, 'Ah, then you needn't worry. Let the Portuguese bury him', clearly reflecting the belief that the border, as the limit of the state's jurisdiction, is a provider of immunity.

However, that was not the end of the story. Luckily, the Portuguese had not been killed but had managed to limp back to his village. He was taken to hospital and operated on, and survived. Yet he took no legal action against the Galician who had shot him. Here the explanations of the Portuguese man's behaviour vary. Some say his pride was more injured than his bum, and he feared becoming a laughing stock if he reported the incident to the police. Others, though, emphasize the feeling that legal consequences for any crime or misdemeanour committed in one country are easily avoided by simply crossing the borderline. This story presents an extreme example of a feature that distinguishes a trans-frontier 'community' from any other: a crime may be committed in one country (where the offender would normally be accountable for it, but in this case is not) while its effects are suffered in another (where the authorities have no jurisdiction to prosecute the offender, who acted across the border and thus outside their jurisdiction).

This impunity provided by the border is illustrated by another story in which the young men of the Galician village and the young men of the nearest Portuguese village got into one of the periodic stone-throwing fights that appear to have been a regular custom on fair Sunday afternoons in former times. The border guards generally ignored these fights between rival villages. One day during the usual Sunday skirmish, however, a young Galician fired a few shots from his father's pistol in the direction of Portugal. This was a bit too much for the lieutenant of the Guarda

Fiscal, who came over to the Civil Guard post that existed then to have a word with his Spanish colleague. The Spanish Guardia Civil lieutenant summoned all the rowdy young Galician men involved in the border incident to his office and gave them a stiff dressing-down in the presence of his Portuguese colleague. As soon as the Portuguese border policeman left, though, the Spanish lieutenant is reported to have told the Galician youths, 'Well done, lads, only next time hit them even harder' in another example of rampant impunity at the border.

Until just a few years ago, people on both sides of the border were telling me that they felt 'a Europe without borders' was something they would never see during their lifetime. The border was a part of their lives that they had always known as a politico-administrative reality imposed from outside. Only a few years ago, it was nearly impossible to have an hour's conversation with any villager without the subject of the border coming up. When they spoke of their past, of their present, of almost anything, the border was always there somewhere. Today, however, the local trans-frontier 'community' has lost one of its main defining features: all the border guards are gone, as are the chains across the roads, and what were once dirt tracks crossing the border are now proper roads surfaced with tarmac.

The priest of the two Portuguese villages, writing in the December 1992 issue of the monthly newspaper that he edited at the time, called on villagers on both sides of the border to meet at the border on the night of 31 December 1992 'to shoot off rockets and burn the boundary markers that separate us from Galicia'. In the paper's February 1993 issue, he reported that on the night of 31 December, Portuguese and Galician villagers had met on the border and lit a bonfire to show 'the union of peoples, protesting against the dictatorial obscurity of governments indifferent to the atrophy of the interests of distant villages of the mountain periphery'.

The disappearance of the border has brought many changes, not all of which are seen as positive from the local people's viewpoint. Most obviously, despite all the inconveniences and risks of living on an international border, the very existence of the border had provided villagers with their main source of income, smuggling. Now the trade in contraband has all but disappeared, except for the movement of drugs such as heroin and cocaine, which most people in these villages regard as quite unlike the 'clean trade' of the smuggling in the past. Shortly after border controls were removed in 1992, in the Portuguese borderline villages there circulated numerous rumours of sinister activities carried out by Spaniards (the Other), made possible by the opening of the border. One that apparently had some truth in it and points to the underlying economic asymmetry between the two sides of the frontier was that Portuguese girls from poor families in the borderland were being tricked into going to Galicia with the promise of a job and then drugged, kept prisoners at roadside brothels and forced into prostitution. The other rumour, for which no evidence was ever produced, had it that 'Spaniards in high-powered motorcars' were coming to Portugal to kidnap children 'for their organs'. At one point the level of hysteria was such that the priest of the Portuguese villages told me he had stopped his car – admittedly a Mercedes, but with Portuguese number plates – at another border village to talk with some children and found his car suddenly surrounded by angry villagers armed with sticks. Luckily, the priest was recognized in time.

What has not changed very much over the past twenty years is that the Galicians still attend the annual religious gatherings known as *romarias* at four local shrines just over the border. The Galicians at these Portuguese *romarias* are so affluent that two masses are celebrated, first one in Galician and then another in Portuguese. When Galician villagers are asked why they are so keen to go to these religious ceremonies at sanctuaries in another country, the answers they give seem to indicate that they believe these border saints to be particularly powerful, not at all 'foreign' and just as much theirs as they are of the Portuguese. This interesting religious asymmetry is somewhat balanced by the fact that quite a few Portuguese border villagers cross the frontier to consult the many *curanderos* (folk healers) in the nearby Galician villages. When asked why they visit these Galicians rather than the *curandeiros* in their own country, the answer appears to be that they consider them to be especially powerful. All this seems to imply that the border, which divides so many mundane things, does not divide when it comes to spiritual matters. This does not refer simply to the fact that both the Portuguese and the Galicians of these villages are all officially members of the Roman Catholic Church. No, what is most interesting is that when they negotiate the supernatural realm in their particularly local ways, the people of these border villages appear to do so as a spiritual community that is not separated by any borderline. The trans-frontier 'community' has this fundamental feature: it is a religious and spiritual community with a shared devotion to the same saints and shrines. The reality of this community is clear from the story the villagers tell of the time some years ago, before border controls were lifted, when a crowd of Galicians on their way to one of these shrines for the annual *romaria* was stopped at the frontier by the Portuguese border guards, who refused to let them pass. When word got to the nearby shrine that the *guardinhas* were keeping some Galicians from crossing the border to attend the religious ceremony, the Portuguese villagers took the decision to bring the image of the saint from his shrine up to the very borderline, so that the Galicians would be able to participate.

Something else that has not changed much is that people from both sides still go to the *ferias* (market fairs) held at the nearby Portuguese city of Chaves every Wednesday and at the Galician town of Verín on the third, eleventh and twenty-third of each month. On the other hand, whereas before the 'disappearance' of the border in 1992 it was common to see people from the other side at the village shops looking for the things that were cheaper there than in their own country – the Portuguese would go to the Galician village to buy rice and noodles, while the Galicians would go to the nearest Portuguese village to get sugar and insecticide – this trade, which was a reflection of an interrelated and complementary 'commercial community', stopped after the border was opened and the same products appeared, at about the same Euro prices, on both sides of the border.

Another aspect of change is that neither economy is as insulated as it was before the opening of the border. A certain asymmetry pertains here, as this particularly affects the Portuguese, who, having had far less competition when the border was closed, in some cases had permitted themselves to be less efficient than Spanish firms just over the border. For example, a Portuguese border villager who owns his own small welding firm (he was trained as a welder in Germany, where he lived for a number of years) told me he prefers to buy his material across the border in Galicia, not because the quality is any better but simply because he finds the Spaniards to be 'more responsible' than his fellow countrymen. The Spaniards deliver when they say they will, unlike the Portuguese, who don't even bother to deliver; you have to go to their shops to get what you want, he said. He also complained that when he was expanding his business and needed to take on two extra workers, he was unable to find any young men in the Portuguese villages in the area who were willing to work as apprentice welders and learn the trade. However, he had no trouble finding the two young men he needed in the Galician village just across the border. The welder's wife pointed out that now that her husband has Spanish, not Portuguese assistants, 'even his Portuguese clients take him more seriously', although she added that some people in their village are annoyed 'because having hard-working Galicians coming every day shows up the Portuguese as being lazy'. What the woman was clearly telling me was that one of the advantages of living on a border is the possibility of being able to choose workers from one side or the other.

One recent development that was unexpected, at least by the anthropologist, is that the disappearance of border controls, instead of bringing the Portuguese and the Galicians in these border villages closer together, seems in some cases to have pushed them apart, especially the younger generations. At the weekends the young people of both sides often cross the border in groups to go to bars and discos in nearby towns and cities of the other country, but they appear to stick very much with their own groups, not mix with those of the other nation. When these same young people are asked if they have friends on the other side of the border, the most frequent reply is that they do not. Yet their parents and grandparents, when asked the same question, will almost always talk about their good friends in this or that village across the border. This apparently paradoxical situation can be explained by remembering the importance of smuggling in the past. Having trustworthy partners on the other side was of crucial importance for the older generations but is now totally superfluous for the younger generations. This apparent paradox demands reflection on how the 'disappearance' of the border may have caused the weakening or even the disappearance of the previously vigorous trans-frontier 'community' that used to be knitted by the need to complement economic activities: smuggling, local markets, and so on. People who once experienced the limitations the border imposed on their 'community' as hardship now find the disappearance of such limitations almost irrelevant.

Also irrelevant and superfluous today are the former customs posts from which the Portuguese Guarda Fiscal and the Spanish Guardia Civil once controlled the border areas. After the 'opening' of the border in 1992, these buildings were all abandoned. Later, a number of them were turned to other uses. A few have become town halls, while others have become, of all things, museums dedicated to the history of smuggling. It is amusingly ironic that what for hundreds of years was the economic base of the frontier and often a matter of life and death has now become part of the tourist industry, with the old smugglers' routes made into trails for walkers and bikers. During the summer months, a number of villages on the border celebrate so-called Fiestas de Contrabando (smugglers' fairs), when the local people dress up as smugglers and border guards to re-create episodes of their not-so-distant past. It is unclear to what extent they do this for themselves, for the visiting tourists or for both.

Other interesting developments have taken place over the years. Immediately after the complete opening of the border in 1992, the previously unmarked dirt tracks formerly used only by local farmers and smugglers – who, as we have seen, were often the same people – were all paved and were posted with signs reading 'To Spain' or 'To Portugal'. Where these new, post-Schengen roads crossed the border, large blue European Union signs were put up featuring each country's name encircled by twelve gold (or yellow) stars. Significantly, however, many of these 'nation state' signs were either gone or defaced by the late 1990s. In their place today are much smaller signs indicating the border, or only road signs bearing the names of the local villages or, occasionally, a signpost showing that the traveller was entering the Spanish autonomous community of Galicia (as mentioned above, mainland Portugal has no such administrative divisions). At times, only a simple stone boundary marker, half-hidden in the grass by the roadside, shows travellers that they are going from one country to another. But even more frequently, the only hint that an international frontier is being crossed is the change in the surface of the tarmac (Figure 5.5) – and sometimes not even that. So the situation today is that outsiders often cross from one country to the other unawares, which reveals the complete artificiality of an often imperceptible border dividing fields in the middle of the countryside. The locals, of course, know very well where the border runs. But even outsiders, once they reach a village, know perfectly well which country they are in, since apart from the evident marker of the signs being in one language or another, one need only notice how the streets are paved: tarmac in Spain, cobblestones in Portugal.

The complete disappearance of border controls and a visible borderline – 'the line on the ground' – after 1992 has not, however, meant the disappearance of what we might call the 'border in the mind'. Eight centuries of history are not wiped away overnight, and the nation state is still, despite the overly optimistic predictions of some who favour the European

Figure 5.5. An abandoned border post on the Portuguese-Spanish border today. The change in road surfacing reveals the borderline. (Photo: William Kavanagh)

Union, the primary source of welfare, authority, identity and loyalty for the foreseeable future. Talking with a friend at one of the border villages a few years ago, I asked him what he thought of the changes brought about at his village by a 'Europe without frontiers'. He thought for a moment and then, carefully and repeating his words, he replied: 'You may remove the door, but the doorframe remains ... you may remove the door, but the doorframe remains.' He went on to explain that he thought it would take many years, 'perhaps a hundred or more ... or never' for differences between one side and the other to disappear. My friend's comment seems to clearly underline the persistence of perceived asymmetry between the two Iberian countries.

Though it seems a likely conclusion that the task of 'constructing Europe' on this particular section of one of Europe's internal frontiers may not be as easy or rapid as some have hoped, things may very well be changing. Many initiatives are afoot – most, if not all of them, financed by the European Union through the various INTERREG programmes of the European Regional Development Fund (ERDF) [FEDER in Spanish and Portuguese] – in the direction of eliminating the bureaucratic and administrative barriers generated by borders in favour of common policies on education, health and transport for regions on the 'internal' frontiers of the European Union. An example of this would be the so-called 'Euro-city' of Chaves (Portugal) and Verín (Galicia), where the citizens of both cities have, as 'Euro-citizens', been given a card that entitles them to use the municipal libraries, municipal swimming pools and other facilities of both their own city and the neighbouring city across the border.

The following story hints at another possibly different future for the inhabitants of this part of the Portuguese-Spanish border. A Portuguese journalist in the border town of Montalegre, reporting in the local newspaper *Noticias de Barroso* (15 July 2010: 7) on the Spanish national team's victory in the 2010 Football World Cup in South Africa under the headline *E Viva a Espanha!* (Long Live Spain!), wrote that whilst always remembering that one should expect 'neither good winds nor good marriages' from Spain, 'the truth is that the Spaniards have never been anything else but brothers to us'. Although the schoolboy in this chapter's opening story was only too aware that one cannot choose one's brothers, it is also true that one can share in the glory of their successes.

Conclusions

My principle conclusion concerns both a false assumption and an apparent paradox. The false assumption is the generalized tendency to believe that the disappearance of a frontier leads inevitably to closer relations with those on the other side. The apparent paradox is that the 'beloved friends' of yesteryear – formerly kept distant by the perceived will of both states to maintain a 'closely watched' frontier with border guards and controls – are no longer as close as they once were, even though it is precisely now that physical proximity is greatest. In other words, in the past physical proximity (through ease of communication and travel) was controlled and frequently difficult and social proximity (understood as relations of friendship and cooperation) was high, whereas today, when no barriers whatsoever impede the physical movement and proximity of those on the border, social proximity is much less intense. There lies an apparent paradox.

Considering the transformation of the material conditions of these borderlanders' lives over the past twenty years, enormous changes are obvious on both sides of the frontier. Most strikingly, however, the great asymmetry in the material conditions of previous decades has almost entirely disappeared. When I began fieldwork in the summer of 1990, I was impressed by the clearly noticeable differences between one side of the frontier and the other. At that time it was quite easy to tell a Portuguese from a Galician by their dress and general appearance: rural Galicians tended to dress and do their hair following urban patterns of fashion, while the attire of rural Portuguese tended be more 'old-fashioned' (and in the case of the women, more 'prudish'). Today both the rural Portuguese and the rural Galicians look and dress largely alike, as is the case for people everywhere else in Europe.

As discussed above, the subsidies Portugal and Spain received from Brussels after 1986 significantly reduced the economic gap between themselves and the countries of northern Europe. Both countries have also been noticeably equalizing economically; nice cars and nice clothes are seen on both sides of the frontier. But there has been an equally important tendency towards similarity in behaviour and customs in general. One might, then, imagine that these factors of convergence would lead to ever closer ties between people living so physically close to each other on the border. Yet this has not been the case. Economic and other sorts of asymmetry between the two Iberian countries may have decreased, but this has resulted in less, not more, communication with those on the other side of the border. Why is this so?

The answer lies in the traditional economic and social importance of smuggling for the people of these border communities. As we have seen, those in the contraband trade need partners on the other side who can be trusted. When men (principally, since they were the ones most involved with smuggling) formed friendships based on *confiança/confianza* (trust), they socialized a lot, visited each other and frequently ate and especially drank together. Though these relations were certainly dictated by economic necessity, it would be unfair to say that they were merely 'utilitarian' and not 'real' friendships. The fact that people needed these partners does not mean they were necessarily insincere or cynical to say and believe that the others were their friends.

Before 1992, when the border was 'really a border', villagers on both sides often complained that they were 'kept apart' from their 'beloved friends' on the other side of the frontier by the unreasonable restrictions of both states (in the shape of the local border guards and their regulations) and often declared to me that they would certainly visit the other side much more often if such limitations no longer existed. However, this discourse of 'They [the border authorities] don't let us [get any closer]' is no longer valid, and ever since this excuse has evaporated and the villagers are free to travel across the border as they please, such visits are nowhere near as frequent as they used to be. So they now have had to invent a new discourse. When asked why they no longer visit the other side, they often answer: 'Why should we? We have no reason to go.'

In sum, when the very existence of the border was crucial to these villages' economies – in that smuggling really only happens at borders – and certain goods were much cheaper on one side or the other and therefore worth the bother (and the risks) of being brought across illegally, the creation and maintenance of social relations with the Other were of paramount importance. Today, on the other hand, when the same products are sold in the same supermarket chains at the same Euro prices on both sides of the frontier, maintaining strong social relations with the Other is no longer useful. Living in 'Schengenland' has redefined the relationship to the Other. Before, the Other was different, but extremely useful. Today, the Other is much less different, but no longer very useful.

Interestingly, the only possible exceptions to having 'no reason' now to visit the other side actually reinforce my argument, though they apparently qualify the conclusion that social contacts have declined since the removal of border restrictions: The Galicians still appear to attend the Portuguese *romarias* (the gatherings at a local shrine) with very much the same devotion as in the past, and the Portuguese still visit Galician *curanderos* (folk healers) with more or less the same enthusiasm as ever. There are three possible explanations for this. The first is that those who go to the *romarias* and *curanderos* are almost exclusively older people – those for whom partners in the smuggling trade were essential – who are merely continuing customs and behaviours of many years. The second is that, as illustrated above, the people of these border villages appear to apprehend the supernatural realm in particularly local ways as a community – that is, a spiritual community that is not separated by any borderline. The third, most important explanation is that the villagers still 'need' the spiritual protection of the shrines and the services of the healers. Both saints and healers remain useful to them, with or without a 'border'. The general conclusion, therefore, is that although the 'meaning' of a border changes radically depending on whether those on the other side are needed, 'need' cannot be confined to material needs but must also include the spiritual needs of a border community that endures despite changes in the nature of the border.

Notes

1. Research at the Portuguese-Galician border began in the summer of 1990 thanks to a three-year grant from the Universidad P. Comillas, Madrid, and continued after 1992 with regular short visits to the area. From October 2007 to May 2011, the research was supported by funding from the Spanish Ministry of Science and Innovation, Award SEJ2007-66159/CPOL, Project 'El discurso geopolítico de las fronteras en la construcción socio-política de la identidades nacionales: el caso de la frontera hispano-portuguesa en los siglos XIX y XX'.
2. Part of the ethnography presented in this essay has previously appeared in Kavanagh (1994, 2000, 2009). An earlier, less developed version of this chapter appeared as Kavanagh (2011). All translations from Portuguese, Galician and Spanish are mine.
3. But, very possibly due to the gendered division of labour, not women.

References

Anderson, B. 1983. *Imagined Communities: Reflections on the Origin and Spread of Nationalism.* London: Verso.
Barth, F. (ed.). 1969. *Ethnic Groups and Boundaries: The Social Organization of Culture Difference.* London: George Allen and Unwin.
Birmingham, D. 1993. *A Concise History of Portugal.* Cambridge: Cambridge University Press.
Cohen, A.P. 1985. *The Symbolic Construction of Community.* London: Tavistock.
García Mañá, L.M. 1988. *La frontera hispano-lusa en la provincia de Ourense.* Orense: Museo Arqueolóxico Provincial.
Hobsbawm, E. and T. Ranger (eds). 1983. *The Invention of Tradition.* Cambridge: Cambridge University Press.
Hooper, J. 1995. *The New Spaniards.* London: Penguin Books.
Kaplan, M. 1991. *The Portuguese – The Land and Its People.* London: Penguin Books.
Kavanagh, W. 1994. 'Symbolic Boundaries and "Real" Borders on the Portuguese-Spanish Frontier', in H. Donnan and T.M. Wilson (eds), *Border Approaches: Anthropological Perspectives on Frontiers.* Lanham, MD: University Press of America, pp. 75–87.

————. 2000. 'The Past on the Line: The Use of Oral History in the Construction of Present-day Changing Identities on the Portuguese-Spanish Border', *Ethnologia Europaea* 30(2): 47–56.

————. 2009. '"Se puede quitar la puerta, pero se queda el marco": Identidades, Cambiantes y no Cambiantes, en las Fronteras Europeas', in H. Cairo Carou, P. Godinho and X. Pereiro (eds), *Portugal e Espanha – Entre discursos de centro e práticas de fronteira*. Lisbon: Edições Colibri, pp. 155–72.

————. 2011. 'Multiple Encounters on the Portuguese-Spanish Border', *Journal of Mediterranean Studies* 20(1): 27–52.

Monteiro, N.G. and A. Costa Pinto. 2003. 'Cultural Myths and Portuguese National Identity', in A. Costa Pinto (ed.), *Contemporary Portugal – Politics, Society and Culture*. Boulder, CO: Social Science Monographs, pp. 47–62.

Pintado, A. and E. Barrenechea. 1972. *La Raya de Portugal – la frontera del subdesarrollo*. Madrid: Cuadernos para el Dialogo.

Rupnik, J. 1994. 'Europe's new frontiers: remapping Europe', *Daedalus* 123 (3): 91–114.

Saraiva, J.H. 1997. *Portugal: A Companion History*. Manchester: Carcanet Press.

Smith, A.D. 1986. *The Ethnic Origins of Nations*. Oxford: Basil Blackwell.

Part II

Strengthening Borders

Chapter 6

Asymmetries of Gender and Generation in a Post-Soviet Borderland

Laura Assmuth

Introduction

It should be obvious that women and men experience borders differently in their daily lives. This is because women and men are differently positioned vis-à-vis the state's routine management and maintenance of power. The associations of structure and belonging between the state and its gendered subjects have been relatively little theorized. As Wilson and Donnan (1998: 20) suggest, 'the links between the border, sexuality, gender and the state are not relationships readily referred to by other scholars of the state, but are the kinds of association which anthropology's twin focus on identity and locality is especially good at revealing'. As in the case of gender, it is intuitive that belonging to a particular generation[1] should make a difference in people's experiences of and practices in borderlands. Many studies of post-socialist societies in rapid transformation have fruitfully applied a generational perspective. For example, in their fine studies of youth in Russia, Fran Markowitz (2000) and Alexei Yurchak (2006) show how fundamentally different the outcomes of the break-up of the Soviet Union have been for the young and the old. However, studies of post-socialist borders have not focused on generational differences.

This chapter aims to show how the intertwined perspectives of gender and generation can shed light empirically on the analysis of borders and life in borderlands. It does so by presenting an ethnographic case study from an eastern European area where state borders are relatively recent re-

---

Notes for this chapter begin on page 161.

sults of political, economic and social changes brought about by the end of state socialism. My studies at the post-Soviet borderlands between Russia, Estonia and Latvia focused on everyday practices and ideals connected with new state borders. I observed local men and women of different generations in their practices of border crossing, cross-border trade and shopping, and other transnational activities, and I asked all these people how the new border affects their lives and what they think of it.

In this essay I discuss new kinds of asymmetries that developed in this Baltic border area in the years following the break-up of the Soviet Union. Some asymmetries clearly traceable to the Soviet period persist, while new kinds of dividing lines have emerged between individuals and groups of people. Border-related activities are deeply gendered: women's activities are most certainly different from those of men, whether regarding employment, trade, smuggling, shopping, cross-border social networks, religious activities – indeed, almost anything people do in a border area. Borders also mean very different things to people of different age groups, as will become evident from the interview and essay materials. Gendered and generation-related changes are evident not only in the everyday practices of the borderland residents but also in the ways they understand and experience the border and the social realities on the other side of it. I argue that the nature of face-to face encounters across the border has changed fundamentally, with wide-ranging implications for both perceptions of the neighbouring peoples and relations between the neighbouring states.

An anthropological micro-perspective on borders and border crossings that investigates both the overlap and the limits of state action and authority highlights the agency of the subjects under study. In their everyday actions, borderland dwellers often defy, counteract or subvert rules and regulations defined by state actors, as in illegal crossings or informal cross-border trade. But even when they behave legally, the meanings local residents attach to the border differ significantly from those ascribed by actors at other levels. For example, local actors often see borders as more porous than state actors would usually expect. Even extremely guarded borders can be crossed in some ways, and through many different activities (Wilson and Donnan 1998; Verdery 1998; Donnan and Wilson 2003).

Our research projects[2] explored how the states' attempts at nation building with and at their borders concretely affect the everyday lives of women and men, young and old, who live in the peripheral area of the former Soviet Union where Estonia, Latvia and Russia meet. The research team examined local residents' efforts to adapt to, support or oppose the workings of the respective states and their representatives in a situation where the recently enacted state borders are an important part of everyday life. Because issues of borders, border crossings, citizenship and ethnic/national identity were vividly present in local people's acts and conversations, we used them in our analyses as clues to studying the local actors' relationship with the state. The findings are based on observation of everyday interaction, thematic interviews and conversations with local residents, and written materials collected for the purposes of this research.[3]

The Setting

The disintegration of the Soviet Union created numerous borders between states in places where there previously had been only borders between Soviet republics. The borders between the Soviet Republics were administrative; for example, instead of border controls or posts, only a road sign informed visitors that they had just entered the Socialist Republic of Estonia. One of the priorities each new state faced after the dissolution of the Soviet Union was to institute functioning border regimes with its neighbours. For Russia, the borders with its Baltic neighbours manifested and confirmed a new political reality that Russia has had some difficulty dealing with. Nevertheless, Russia's relations with its new Baltic neighbours have stabilized and improved, and the borders in question have become the least of Russia's borderland and ethnic worries (see Valuev 2003). For Estonia and Latvia, small countries that regained their independence in 1991 after having been forcefully annexed to the Soviet Union for almost fifty years, the state borders with Russia are of special political and symbolic significance. Both of these countries have also had serious disagreements with Russia about the proper location of the borderline. In both cases the border as a physical and politico-juridical reality is a factor that strongly divides the people who now happen to live on its opposite sides.

The initial porosity of the Estonian-Russian and Latvian-Russian borders in the 1990s gave way to stricter and more uniform border regimes that have been enforced since 2000. Since 2004, Estonia and Latvia have been members of both the European Union and NATO, and the borders in question have become the EU's new borders with Russia, as well as Russia's new land border facing NATO countries. Flexible borderland identities, statuses and practices are not encouraged by the respective states or powerful agents like the EU and NATO, which want their new borders facing Russia to be efficiently controlled. Today, when everyday personal contacts across these borders are much more difficult and costly than before, local residents have to make decisions and plans concerning their residence and citizenship that would have been unnecessary or irrelevant in the Soviet period or the early years of new independent statehood.

We conducted case studies[4] on borderland living in a multi-ethnic Estonian-Russian border area called Setomaa or Petserimaa in Estonian and Pechorskii raion (Pechory district) in Russian. Setomaa means 'the Setos' land', and Petserimaa / Pechorskii raion is named according to the district's main town, Petseri/Pechory, where there is a famous Russian Orthodox monastery. The Setos are a Finno-Ugric people numbering approximately 15,000. Seto culture can be said to form a link between the Estonian and Russian cultures: their vernacular language, a dialect of South Estonian, connects Setos with Estonians, and their religion, Russian Orthodoxy, with Russians. Religious practices, especially celebrations of patron saints' holidays and visits to family graves at cemeteries, also firmly connect Setos with the Russian side of the border, where many of their most important churches and graveyards are located. Lay religious activities are highly female dominated (Figures 6.1 and 6.2): women actively attend church, sing in church choirs, do voluntary work for their congregations and visit and tend the graves of family members, relatives and friends. Women have no official position in the organization and hierarchy of the Russian Orthodox Church, however.

Figure 6.1. A woman taking care of a country chapel, Pechory district, Russia, 2006. (Photo: Marina Hakkarainen)

Figure 6.2. Selling home-made articles at the gate of Pechory monastery, 2006. (Photo: Marina Hakkarainen)

Estonia's citizenship laws grant automatic citizenship to all persons who were citizens of the pre-annexation Estonian republic (1918–1940) and their descendants. Crucially for my discussion here, this includes those citizens who resided at that time in the province of Petserimaa, which during the first Estonian republic was part of the territory of Estonia. The Estonian government encouraged ethnic Estonians to move to the province, where the population was quite mixed at the time, mainly with Setos and Russians. It also set up an extensive programme for educational, cultural and economic development in hopes that development of the area would eventually 'Estonianize' and 'civilize' the 'backward' Russian Orthodox Setos (Jääts 1998). When Estonia was annexed by the Soviet Union in 1944, the province first became part of the new Socialist Republic of Estonia, but in 1945 the border between the two socialist republics was moved further west and the province of Petserimaa was joined to the Socialist Federation of Russia as the Pechory district.

Setos have traditionally lived on both sides of the present Estonian-Russian state border, so changes in borderlines and border regimes affect their everyday lives more than they do local Estonians' or Russians'

(Jääts 1998; Berg and Oras 2003). On the Russian side in the post-Soviet situation, villages in the countryside around the town of Pechory have in effect become Russian-speaking as most Estonians and Setos have moved to richer Estonia. The few Setos and Estonians who continue to live in the Russian Pechory district are typically elderly women, often widows, who refused to relocate to Estonia with their relatives because, as I have heard many of them explain, they 'want to die peacefully in the homeland'.

Trading at and across the Border, Soviet-style

Our studies of phenomena such as cross-border trade and exchange, of both goods and people, reveal that trade carried out by women differs from the trade carried out by men. Borderland markets and other forms of near-border or cross-border informal trade often seem to be dominated by women traders. And women of all ages have been very much involved in trade activities in our research areas, most often on an informal, small-scale level. This is the case in the Russian town of Pechory, two kilometres from the Estonian border, where the busy daily market appears to be very much female dominated. Especially the part of the market where all kinds of goods, from seasonal garden products to knitwear and various cheap junk, are sold in the open is the domain of elderly women (and their grandchildren).

Anthropologist Pernille Hohnen (2003), who studied a Lithuanian open market outside the capital city of Vilnius, also notes that although at first glance the market seems to be dominated by female customers and traders, it is actually the less visible men who are have control of the business, both wholesale purchasing of goods and the phenomenon of racketeering. The same hierarchy applies in the market of Pechory. Professional Russian-Estonian cross-border trade is also a male domain, in part because men have better access to cars, vans and lorries. The same assumption can be made of large-scale smuggling and other criminal activities, although of course it is difficult to gain reliable information on such phenomena. As at many other state borders,[5] the price differential between Estonia and Russia for petrol, cigarettes, alcohol and many other products makes smuggling and petty informal trade lucrative businesses here. On the other hand, women are the most frequent border crossers, and every time they cross in either direction they bring goods with them. Who would suspect an innocent-looking female pensioner crossing the border on foot of smuggling? She is much less likely to be stopped for thorough inspection than is a young man in a black leather jacket and sunglasses driving a beat-up van. However, since a pedestrian can smuggle only negligible amounts of any illegal goods across the border, it is fair to assume (as the border guards do) that the elderly of either sex do not engage in any significant criminal activity.

Frances Pine's (1996) work on the Górale, a Polish mountain people who live close to the Polish-Slovak border,[6] is also instructive in this regard. Pine shows that even during socialist times, when crossing the border legally was difficult if not impossible, Górale women were the expert cross-border traders of petty goods. Of course this trade has flourished even more since the opening of the border, changing form to become more official, with concomitant changes in the role of women. According to Pine, the despised Górale people managed to find themselves a favourable informal niche in the socialist economy by exploiting their marginality in society and their location by the border. Women, as the most marginal and unthreatening of all, could engage in informal activities with less risk (and less visibility) than men.

Whereas the Górale women had to and could adapt to a newly opened border and its opportunities, in the Baltic border areas the situation was almost the opposite. In Soviet times people could travel and move about freely inside the Soviet Union, and shopping in the neighbouring Soviet republics was an important activity, for women especially. Also, both women and men often went to the other Soviet republics to sell their garden plot goods at the few existing legal private markets. Both activities, shopping and small-scale trade, have changed fundamentally since the state borders were enacted. Women on the Estonian side have quickly entered a consumer society, albeit a limited one characterized by a very popular saying: 'Once we had a lot of money but no goods to buy; now we have all the goods you could dream of but no money to buy them.' Still, to compensate for their lost economic opportunities across the border, new kinds of opportunities are plentiful in the new EU Estonia. On the Estonian side of the border, therefore, it is rare to hear expressions of 'Soviet nostalgia', in which people compare their living conditions in the Soviet Union favourably to their present situation.[7]

On the Russian side, the new border's effects on local lives have been more clearly negative. Access to the nearby 'Soviet West' of the Estonian Socialist Republic has ended, and nothing has yet replaced it. Comparing their lives 'back then in the Soviet times' and now, middle-aged and elderly female informants on the Russian side usually found that their lives had become more local, more restricted and definitely materially poorer. It is no wonder that longing for the Soviet past abounds, when so many people see themselves as worse off than before.

One telling example is the way people on different sides of the present border portray the Russians' shopping trips to Soviet Estonia. In an economy of scarcity such as the Soviet economy, people had to be ready for a shopping spree whenever the opportunity arose. As soon as some rare consumer product (e.g., toothpaste, nylon stockings, sanitary towels, children's shoes or washing machines) became available a rumour started spreading, and within minutes a long line of people, mostly women, would gather outside the shop in question. People queued during their working hours, they waited patiently for hours or they took turns queuing through an ad hoc wait list system. Elderly women – pensioners – were the experts in this practice as they had both the time and the endless patience.

Burdened by systemic shortages, local people had a powerful incentive to exploit differences in supply and quality across the Soviet republics. This led to an important gendered phenomenon of the former Soviet Union: inter-republican shopping. Shopping stories can be read as an important key to local discourses on change: what everyday life was perceived to be like in the Soviet Union and how it is perceived now. A first noteworthy aspect is that women and men tell different stories about their Soviet-era shopping and trading experiences in the neighbouring republic: women complain much more about their decreased freedom to shop (and sell) where they choose, and where they once were used to going.

Secondly, the way shopping is talked about differs greatly between Estonia and Russia. Estonian stories relate to a more general national discourse that stresses the two countries' fundamental economic, social and cultural differences. The current gap in living standards and overall development, so much in Estonia's favour, is seen as but one proof of the success story of independent Estonia and its reunification with Europe. On the Russian side, however, the stories are told in the context of a nostalgic discourse about the Soviet Union. This explains why a single phenomenon, Russian women's shopping trips to Soviet Estonia, can be interpreted in completely opposite ways on the two sides of the border.

An Estonian woman in her forties described Russian women's shopping trips to her village grocery store in Soviet times, referring to practices in the early 1980s, when there were many dire shortages of consumer goods:

> They would come in hordes, buses full with people. They were all women, of course. They didn't come just from the villages bordering our [Soviet] Republic, that would have been more acceptable. For example, there are villages right across the lake from here that don't really have proper shops, and of course we even knew many of the people who came from those villages. They usually came by boat or over the ice in winter. But the buses would come from the towns also, to look for some product that was missing there. They had even more shortages than we did, see? Oh well, they would simply empty our village shop, buy out everything. Oh, it is no wonder that such people were re-

sented. And of course, they had to be addressed in Russian, everything always went on in the Russian language. They were completely monolingual, nobody knew any Estonian. I was of course used to that but I never liked it. After all, they had taken our country.[8]

But from the perspective of a Russian woman in her fifties, the shopping trips she and her fellow villagers made to an Estonian village across Lake Peipus, a few kilometres away, look very different:

It was so convenient at that time [in the 1970s] that we could go shopping across the lake to the Estonian side. The border was open then; we were all in the great Soviet Union back then, but the Estonian and Russian sides were still very different, in every respect. When our village shop had nothing, absolutely nothing, sometimes not even bread, the supply was much better in Estonia. And sometimes you could even find some good quality stuff there, like shoes made in Finland! We would never have such things on our side of the lake, those things were only sold in Moscow or Leningrad. Some Estonians some-times complained when a big crowd of us women went to a local shop; the Es-tonians aren't usually very friendly to Russians, you know. They grumbled that we were emptying the whole shop. And sometimes they resented us speaking Russian, you could feel that even if I couldn't understand what they were say-ing in their language amongst themselves. But for us the small village shop was like a shopping paradise! I remember once *choosing* between different kinds of children's toys, that felt incredible. But now the border is closed, I haven't been to Estonia since they broke away from us.

What is interesting in both stories is how they relate to an undefined So-viet period, 'at that time'. Decades or years were almost never mentioned directly in the interviews, and people often spoke about very different periods of Soviet rule as if 'it was all the same'. Informants were also not very forthcoming about the nature of everyday-life practices in the Soviet Union because they assumed that the interviewers had shared their expe-riences.[9] Ethnic (national) and linguistic tensions are also evident in both stories, but such feelings of dislike or distance were not allowed to come into the open in the Soviet Union, which was officially 'the happy home of a multi-ethnic Soviet people'.

After 1991, when the Baltic States proclaimed independence from the Soviet Union, the border practices at the new Estonian-Russian border did not change overnight. On the contrary, the border was not even demar-cated until 1994 when, besides withdrawing the remaining Soviet military forces from Estonia, Russia started to treat the formerly inter-republican border as its new, international border with Estonia. At this time the Es-tonian state was also willing to accept this borderline as its de facto state border, even though the demarcation line cuts right across the historical province of Petserimaa, which was part of Estonian territory from 1920 to 1940. In effect, the Estonian state was willing to concede a tenth of its former territory to Russia in order to secure its eastern border, stabilize its relations with Russia and become eligible for membership in the European Union.

The Seto people regard the whole historic province of Petserimaa as their homeland. In practice, Estonia long ago gave up its demands for the reincorporation of this area into its territory, and as of 1997 Estonia was ready to sign a border agreement with Russia in which this district would legally remain part of Russian territory. The border treaties were finally signed in May 2005 in Moscow. The Estonian parliament ratified them in June 2005, but the government of the Russian Federation (as of April 2013) has not yet presented the treaties to the Duma for final ratification.[10] Besides the vocal Seto activists, of course, quite a few residents on the Estonian side of this border area still hold out hope for the reincorporation of the Pechory district into Estonia, but by now most people have adjusted to the present situation and no longer expect it to change. The actual border is stable and demarcated, and for all practical purposes accepted and recognized by both sides (Berg and Oras 2003).

Over more than ten years of an existing, stable borderline between Russia and Estonia, Estonian citizenship or a border resident's multiple-entry visa has become a very valuable asset; without it, cross-border shopping is neither possible nor profitable. On the Russian side, those who have an Estonian passport or multiple-entry visa are often envied for their increased opportunities and freedom of movement. In the town of Pechory (two kilometres from the Estonian border), it even appears that the new dividing line between groups of people is their relationship with the border. On one hand, those lucky ones whose employment, family relations and/or citizenship allow them to maintain frequent contact 'with the other side' are able to profit from this. On the other hand, the town is populated by people, often originating from other parts of the former Soviet Union, whose lives are not touched by the closeness of the border (Hakkarainen, 2005). Needless to say, the negative stereotypes about a hostile Estonia are widespread precisely among this group of people, which has been deeply influenced by Soviet and post-Soviet anti-Western nationalistic propaganda. Attitudes remain xenophobic: the Soviet Union's fear of foreign influences and contacts very much lives on in this area, and people are still highly suspicious of or hostile to such 'Western' phenomena as trade (termed illegal and immoral speculation in the Soviet Union).

Vladimir is in his thirties and lives in Pechory. The bilingual son of a mixed Estonian-Russian family with a Seto grandfather, he is permanently employed by the town administration. However, typically for a Pechory man of his generation, he has recently accepted a lucrative second job offer from Estonia that will allow him at least to triple his present earnings. The new manual job involves frequent travel back and forth, but this is not a problem since Vladimir has both Estonian and Russian passports. We talked at length about his commuting plans and about his other cross-border trips. Vladimir has a truly transnational lifestyle.

On the Estonian side of the border there is some resentment and envy of those who travel frequently to the district of Russian Pechory. People who said they were either too busy to go or lived too far from the border-crossing points sometimes made a point of disapproving of those "who tell you that they go there because they have a grave to take care of; but all the same, they all stop at the Pechory market place for cheap cigarettes and booze!" On the other hand, few people disapprove of buying cheap petrol smuggled in from Russia, easily available to knowledgeable locals.

Border Crossings, Post-Soviet–style

While conducting fieldwork in this Baltic border area of the former Soviet Union, we heard numerous descriptions of how the new border regime concretely affects local people's lives. The right to visit monasteries, churches and graveyards is a particularly acute problem for many ethnic Setos. Until 2000, Estonian citizens living in border municipalities facing Russia had been allowed to cross the border without a visa on certain important religious holidays, like Easter or local patron saints' days, if they provided proof of close relatives in Russia, living or dead, and applied for inclusion on the official list of such visitors. This practice of simplified border crossings succeeded in easing the situation of practising Russian Orthodox Setos, most often elderly women, who have been by far the most regular visitors to the Russian side.

Since 2000, a full, mutual visa regime has been in force between the two countries, and Estonia and Russia have regularly exchanged lists of border-area residents receiving free or reduced-price entry visas for the neighbouring country. Visa exemptions for borderland residents lingered even after Estonia and Latvia joined the European Union in May 2004, but the practice ended in March 2008, in accordance with the requirements imposed on Estonia and Latvia upon joining the Schengen Agreement. The agreement stipulates, among other things, external border checks by a common standard for all the implementing countries, so Estonia's and Latvia's national visa policies and border checks of third-country nationals like Russian citizens have changed accordingly. Locally this means that

Figure 6.3. The Latvian-Russian border at Pededze, 2005. (Photo: Aija Lulle)

internal borders between EU member states are vanishing, whereas the external border towards Russia is increasingly impermeable.

Külli, a 37-year-old Seto woman who lives on the Estonian side of the border in a village just ten kilometres from the border-crossing point, is a frequent visitor to the Russian side. When I interviewed her for the first time in late August 2000, she had crossed the border fifty-seven times so far that year (she actually counted her visits). She travels to visit her sister, who is married to a Russian man, whose children speak Russian and who has decided to continue living in Russia. But it is equally important for Külli to visit and tend her father's and grandparents' graves. With tears in her eyes, she spoke of her need to visit both living and dead relatives as often as she could, despite the hardships, 'because my heart is still there, in the village where I was born; somehow I feel that I still *belong* to that side, although I've lived here [on the Estonian side of the border] for nineteen years.'

Other borderland people, regardless of their ethnicity, have also used these opportunities to cross from Estonia to Russia for practical purposes. Those who have recently moved from Pechory district to Estonia need to care for their old houses and gardens or help relatives still living in Russia; anyone living in the border area might want to take advantage of cheaper shopping in the town of Pechory while doing business on the Russian side, and so on. But many ethnic Setos simply feel that Petserimaa as a whole is their homeland, and they expect to be able to visit it freely, regardless of the new state border that cuts through the historical district. For Setos, the notion of home and homeland is very much connected with the burial place of one's family members, which explains the utmost importance of visiting, tending and praying at relatives' graves.

At the Estonian-Russian border, people are always carrying goods in both directions. Younger men carrying petrol, building materials and the like almost always cross the border in cars and vans, but elderly people go on foot or by bicycle. A typical fieldwork encounter at the border-crossing point was with an elderly Seto woman, Aino, who was crossing the border on foot with big bags. She answered my question while we were both waiting in line:

> Why do I travel? I go there [to the town of Pechory] mostly to tend the family grave. If I have time, I also try to visit the church, even on an ordinary day. And when I pass by the market square on my way to the graveyard I stop by to make some purchases. And I always take some toiletries with me when I go, because I know they are in short supply there.

Like inter-republican travel in Soviet times, any movement across the state border in this area includes at least some shopping. But Aino, and other pensioners like her who cross the border frequently, cannot really be considered 'cross-border shopping tourists' for that. Although Aino always makes short day trips only and always takes advantage of the considerable price differentials on her way, she would not go to the trouble of an arduous trip on foot, were it only for the commodities. I conclude that the incentive to travel locally across the border derives from something other than the lure of cheaper prices.

The student essays from Misso, a municipality in south-eastern Estonia that borders both Russia and Latvia, are full of personal and family stories about the everyday difficulties of visiting relatives and family graves on the Russian side. There are only slight gender differences in the style, length and content of the essays. Girls express more nostalgia for the things that have been lost, but boys' descriptions are equally touching in their realism. Interestingly, these 17- and 18-year-old students make comparisons with both the times of the non-existent border (Soviet times) and the early years of independence (1991–1994), when the border was still porous enough to be crossed freely in practice. Many of the memories the students relate are actually those of their parents and grandparents, which shows how urgent and much-discussed the theme of the border actually is, in these borderland families. An 18-year-old girl writes: 'State borders are very important in the lives of me and my family. It is because my mother was born in the area that used to belong to Estonia which is now part of Russia'. Another 18-year-old girl explained:

> When there wasn't a border regime yet my parents went very often to Latvia and Russia. A couple of times a week. Everything was much cheaper there. They bought clothes, carpets, food. It was much cheaper to go by bus to Latvia and Russia than to Võru or Tartu [towns in southern Estonia]. It was a shorter distance and much more comfortable for people who live in the borderland. They couldn't even imagine a different kind of life.

In some discussions and interviews on both sides of the border, people complained about the actual practices at frontier crossing points: long lines and waiting times, the need to present endless documents, the hassling and outright harassment by border guards and customs officials. Most people seemed to take such inconveniences for granted, however. Frequent border crossers like Külli could tell impressive 'horror stories' about bad experiences at the border and 'hero stories' about how they patiently endured the hardships, but their complaints, worries and anger were directed at a higher level, usually the neighbouring state (some blamed their own state as well). None of our informants ever castigated individual Russian or Estonian officials for ethnic or other discrimination. Only one Russian female student wrote in her essay that 'for many of my village-mates the actual crossing of the border causes pain; it is a very unpleasant experience'.

The theme of loss – of young people's escape from the country villages in Petserimaa to a better future in Estonia – is a substantial presence in our interview and essay materials. Women and girls in particular often express deep regret about how things are going. For example, a 17-year-old Seto girl who attends the Estonian-language school in Pechory, Russia, writes almost poetically about her personal feelings of loss:

> And sooner or later the grandparents have to move to where their children are. The children, of course, live in the town or somewhere far away in Estonia. And so the homes are left empty, homes which used to be so beautiful, with big gardens, apple tree orchards full of flowers in blossom. Just empty. The home gradually falls into disrepair or maybe some stranger is found who will buy it. How sad, but so it goes. And on top of all this, visiting between parents and relatives has become more difficult because of the border. You need all those documents just to cross the border, and it takes so much time, money and energy.

The acute problems of who has the right to visit the other country, who gets to have a visa and who does not feature clearly in the youngsters' descriptions. An 18-year-old boy writes:

Many people who live in Petserimaa district have close relatives who have come to live in Estonia. Now these people can't visit each other anymore. Many elderly people have their adult children in Estonia and it is very expensive now for the children to go back to see their parents. But it is even more expensive for the parents, with their poor Russian pensions!

The possibility of visiting and tending family graves is a recurrent and pressing problem also for the younger generation, as one 18-year-old girl elaborated:

All those who are not allowed to go to Pechory cemetery to their relatives' graves feel this deep pain. Graves need to be taken care of, don't they! For example my family, we have more than ten family members buried there, and now we can't even go and see the graves. We fear that some hooligans have again been vandalising the graves as they did last year – I don't think it is right that only those whose parents, children, sisters or brothers are buried there will get a visa for free. Myself, to go to my grandfather's grave I would need to buy a seventy-five dollar visa. That's much too expensive for me.

Despite these local people's deeply felt concerns, the border regime on the two Baltic borders facing Russia is unlikely to become more relaxed or better tailored to the needs of borderland residents. On the contrary, the easternmost border of the European Union is and will remain strictly controlled. Local residents' complicated visa exemptions have become a thing of the past, and visa-free travel between the EU and Russia is still a long way from becoming a reality. The present situation considerably complicates spontaneous, informal and personal interaction and trade across the Estonian-Russian border (cf. Kuldin 1999; Berg and Oras 2003), but despite the difficulties, and with various motives, borderland residents do engage in such interaction (for other Russian borders see Valuev 2003).

Ethnicity, Gender and Generation

In this section I explore the importance of ethnicity for men and women of different generations. A discourse about ethnic identities is of course present in the borderland context, but ethnicity is usually presented and understood as one significant identification among many. Borderland people may think of themselves primarily as Estonian or Russian citizens, as Estonian, Seto or Russian by ethnicity or as inhabitants of their respective regions, towns and villages. Often they make reference to several such identities, in different situations and in different contexts. Seto ethnicity certainly has become more pronounced and appreciated in the post-Soviet context, so much so that one can even speak of a Seto cultural revival. Political scientist Robert Kaiser and sociologist Elena Nikiforova have linked the flourishing of Seto ethnic identity and Seto cultural movement specifically to the establishment of the present state border (Kaiser and Nikiforova 2006). Our Estonian-speaking informants in both Estonia and the Russian Pechory district frequently said they had always felt themselves to be Estonians, even in Soviet times. Language and customs (and the obligatory designation of ethnicity/nationality on one's personal documents[11]) had clearly marked that basic distinction in a multicultural environment. Thus, ethnicity had always mattered and ethnic boundaries had always been there, but only lately had a specific Seto sub-ethnicity come to the fore. People were now making finer distinctions than before: 'gradually I began to realise that I was and I had always been Seto, not just Estonian', as one male informant put it.

Külli, the Seto woman who travels very frequently to Russia, also started to think about her ethnic identity only recently:

Interviewer: Do you consider yourself a Seto? Does Seto identity mean anything to you?

Külli: Well... When somebody asks me that you are a Seto, aren't you – well, then I realise, I guess I am. But what about it?

Interviewer: Wouldn't you call yourself Seto then?

Külli: Well, you know... we don't usually discuss such things. We just are what we are.

...

Interviewer: But earlier, in Soviet times, you didn't think in those terms, whether you are Seto or not, it didn't seem important or how?

Külli: Well you know, we used to think in terms of Estonians and Russians only, only in terms of those peoples.

Interviewer: People didn't talk about Setos in those days, then?

Külli: No, we didn't really.

Külli's hesitant words about her 'real' ethnic identity show that the Soviet practice of imposing an obligatory choice of nationality from a list of approved, officially existing nationalities had a profound effect on how people placed and understood themselves. Earlier, Külli and many others did not think of themselves in terms of a Seto nationality/ethnicity, because Seto was not an official designation but was regarded only as a subgroup of Estonians.

And how are ethnicity and gender intertwined? In the case of the Seto, women are unquestionably seen (and regard themselves) as bearers of Seto culture. They are the more active participants in all kinds of folklore presentations of Seto culture: they dress and dance in folk costumes, perform in festivals, sing in traditional Seto all-female choirs. Leini, a 42-year-old woman who works as a guide in a Seto folklore museum on the Estonian side of the border, is conscious and proud of being part of a cultural revival of her people. She talked at length about her desire and duty to carry the traditions over to her own children, especially her daughters. Many male informants also link women with ethnicity. While interviewing a male Seto activist, I commented that women always far outnumbered men among the active participants in Seto folklore performances and festivals. This university-educated man answered:

> But that is because women *are* the natural bearers of culture! If it were not for the women, women as mothers, who would keep our traditions alive? Who would teach them to our children? Who would sing our songs to them? Who would they go to church with? And most importantly, who would speak Seto language to the children if not the mothers? Why do you think each and every person's first language is called the mother tongue? Precisely, the *mother* tongue. So yes, I agree, women have an absolutely crucial role in all this. All women of course, but especially the mothers. And grandmothers. [Emphases in original.]

Women of the younger generations too see it as their task to pass on Seto culture to their children. Kaia, thirty-six years old, is a mother of four children. She is not Seto by birth but Estonian, and she comes from another region of the country. However, she is married to a Seto and the family lives in the husband's home village less than a kilometre away from the state border. Kaia told me that she sees it as her duty as a mother to make sure her children learn 'to become Seto, learn the beautiful customs of our people and be proud of our heritage and [Russian Orthodox] religion'. Kaia also described many cultural activities that involve her and her children in the practice of Seto folklore, whereas her Seto husband hardly ever participates in the numerous festivals and choral and folk dancing events. Kaia's case shows that it is possible to take on and embrace Seto identity by way of marriage. She herself stressed the importance of her conversion to the Russian Orthodox religion as an integral part of 'becoming Seto', since 'language and religion together make [form] a Seto'.

It must be emphasized again that ethnic identity is not the only kind of identity that is important to our informants in the border areas. Although ethnic identity is very significant to most Setos, they also stress the importance of the home village, home area or homeland (*koduküla, kodukant, kodumaa*) (see also Võro Instituut 1998). Many Estonians in the area take their Estonian-ness entirely for granted; for them, other distinctions, such as language (south-east Estonian dialect, *võro keel*) and locality (being *võrokene*, resident of Võrumaa) are identity markers at least as important as ethnicity (Võro Instituut 2000). The general finding – from all the interviews and discussions with Estonians, Setos and Russians alike – is that informants are keen to stress similarities and links between people of different ethnicities/nationalities and do not want to emphasize the differences and uniqueness of a particular group. A typical example of this multicultural local discourse is from Anna, born in 1950, who had this to say about ethnic differences:

> Interviewer: You are of Seto ethnicity?
>
> Anna: Yes, sure I am.
>
> Interviewer: Is being a Seto important to you?
>
> Anna: I'm not sure, I'm not so inclined to stress my ethnicity.... The thing is, I simply have nothing against anyone because of his or her ethnicity. I remember when I went to work together with the Russians, some people [Estonians] would tell me, Oh dear, how dare you go there with all those Russians around... Well, I don't have that attitude. I don't care about who is Russian and who is something else, what nationality each of us belongs to – we are all alike, we are all humans. The Russians were actually better in many respects! All the time they tell you, 'spassibo, spassibo' [thank you in Russian], they are so nice and friendly [laughs]...
>
> Interviewer: Very hospitable?
>
> Anna: Oh yes, yes, very!

Ethnic Russian informants living in the Pechory district also have a wide variety of ideas about what it means for them to be Russian. In just one village, Lavry, which is close to both the Estonian and Latvian borders, opinions and ideas range from extreme, chauvinistic Russophilia to idealization of the village's Latvian heritage and culture. In the first case, Russian-ness is constructed in opposition to other identities and peoples, and is seen as superior to either Estonian-ness or Latvian-ness. In the second case, Russian-ness is constructed on the basis of a multicultural local identity, which means it is flexible and changeable. Again, women are the active agents in ethnic groups' 'tradition work': in the families of Latvian origin, women pass on the stories, pictures and documents that relate to Latvian-ness and are the most likely speakers of Latvian. Among the Russian population it is the female librarian/local museum curator who collects and preserves the Latvian heritage of the village.

Conclusion: Asymmetric Encounters, or No Encounters at All?

Our research process convinced us of the enormous importance of the new state borders in many local people's lives. The borders and border regimes do not impact all borderland residents equally, but they definitely affect those who, for whatever reason, need and want to cross the border. In this chapter I have described who these border crossers are, how and why they go to the other side and what kinds of ties they try to maintain or develop. Some interestingly overlapping differentiation or polarization processes are discernible in our material. Gender polarization has occurred, as the new borders have functioned to make many borderland women's lives more local, insular and static. This is especially true of older generations of women living on all sides of the borders discussed here. Infrastructure is poor, social services are inadequate and pensions are small. These women have thus taken on the traditional subsistence activities of maintenance and reproduction of the private sphere. 'Someone's got to take care of the [grand]children, the kitchen garden plot and the cow', we often heard female pensioners remark (even in the town of Pechory). Younger women and educated women of all ages have left for the towns and cities in search of employment. The luckiest ones have found employment locally as border or customs officials, especially on the Russian side; indeed, these steady, ill-paid occupations attract women more than men. Men, on the other hand, have taken on the traditional role of the male breadwinner involved in various formal and informal activities or, in numerous cases, given up trying altogether and turned to an alternative pastime, drinking. Alcoholism is a very serious social problem in this area, as elsewhere in the post-Soviet peripheries.[12]

Another significant asymmetry is that young, middle-aged and elderly borderland residents live very different lives indeed, with young people on all sides increasingly turning their backs on the border and the social realities beyond and seeing their future prospects in their respective nation states or even abroad (in the West). One Estonian, middle-aged resident of a village close to both the Latvian and the Russian border expressed his concern about the effects of declining face-to-face interaction across the borders thus:

> In my generation, we were all 'children of the great Soviet Union' as we used to say. I used to have friends from all nationalities, not just Estonians. And everybody knew at least some Latvian people, if not otherwise then we met them at the markets. And of course everybody knew the Russian language, we were required to. But my children, what do they know? My daughter is twenty and she cannot speak a word of Russian – she will not speak it! She's been in Sweden now for a year. And they are not interested either! This is what really worries me, you know, that they know absolutely nothing about how it is in Russia, about the people, the culture.... It's like a different world to them, just like the West was a different world to us. But still it is not the same thing, because we were so keen to find out, but this generation of my children … they couldn't care less. They've turned their backs towards Russia. And it really worries me.

As this informant notes, changes in language use play a significant role in the widening of a 'mental gap' across the border. The Russian language has lost the status of regional lingua franca that it had in the Soviet Union, when every Soviet citizen of every nationality was supposed to be fluent in Russian. Although the obligatory study of Russian in schools was much resented, it nevertheless assured that people of the different republics, and of different ethnic and age groups, could communicate with each other. This communication was never on an equal basis, of course, because most Russian speakers were monolingual, whereas citizens with other mother tongues had to be bilingual or even trilingual. Today, when Estonian and Russian children do not learn each other's languages[13] but instead study English, German, Finnish or something else, it is easy to see that the cross-national feelings of closeness that the informant describes for his generation are dying out.

The decline of personal, face-to-face encounters has had other, generation-related effects. A generational gap in cross-border, cross-national relationships and interests also means that young people increasingly know only media representations of the neighbouring countries and peoples (cf. Manakov 1999: 131). This makes them more prone to prejudiced views and attitudes about the inhabitants of the neighbouring country. Various opinion polls and surveys conducted in the three countries show that negative stereotypes about Russia and Russians are indeed very common both among ethnic Estonian and ethnic Latvian youth. Young Russians in Russia tend to take a more positive view of Estonia and Estonians than of Latvia and Latvians, which again reflects the very negative media representations of Latvia in Russia (Kuldin 1999). Increasingly, young people's opinions about 'what the Russians/Estonians/Latvians are like' are formed in the national capitals, not through relationships of proximity among the borderlanders themselves.

When the border impedes actual physical proximity, family unity becomes even more important to people who feel the new border has severed their social networks. Paradoxically, then, in the intimate context of family and kin relations, the border unites family members of different generations and genders, at least temporarily. This comes out well in one 18-year-old Seto boy's school essay about the border's effects on his family life. His story is an apt reminder of the absurdities of borderland living from the viewpoint of local residents:

> We have lots of relatives who live in Russia. The one who lives the closest is my aunt. When we count the distance between our home and where she lives it is about seven hundred metres. You can see the border with Russia from our doorstep. If it wasn't for a small forest we could even see my aunt's house. She herself lives about fifty metres from the border. She lives on her own, all alone.

Sometimes, when the weather is good, one of us goes to the border to meet with the aunt, especially in summer when the weather is warm. Sometimes we do it altogether. What makes us sad is the fact that she can't hear so well. We have to stand at about fifty metres distance from each other. It's a terrible sight, really. But if we want to really meet her, talk to her and comfort her we have to travel thirty-five kilometres through the border crossing point. It is so sad.

From an individual and family point of view, such experiences are sad indeed. A deep melancholy is perceptible, not only in such stories, written or told, but also in casual encounters with local people at different kinds of gatherings and events in this border area. And yet, in the many hours I have been lucky enough to spend talking with wonderful elderly women and men who told me their sad life stories with tears in their eyes, I have noted that they still managed to laugh and have fun, and to be warm, affectionate and optimistic. They have undoubtedly lived hard, often tragic lives, but the prevailing mood among the borderland elderly is nevertheless not tragic. Perhaps, to people who have withstood the harsh life experiences that were the lot of many Soviet citizens, all the difficulties and problems entailed in the establishment of the border are just another inconvenience or nuisance. The experiences shared by millions of Soviet citizens of their generation form a basis of common understanding across the state border.

However, deep asymmetries divide even the older generations. This is evident with regard to not only material circumstances such as the adequacy of pensions and social services, but also attitudes towards the future. On one side, in Estonia and Latvia, the state and its residents are busy building new lives for themselves and their children, and there is a lot of optimism. For example, elderly Seto women, who have suffered the most from the new border cutting through their ancient homeland, may be sad and melancholic, but they are not bitter and nostalgic. Instead, they turn their hopes and aspirations towards the future, which they see as bright, at least for their children and grandchildren. On the other side, in Russia, the elderly see few grounds for optimism, and an ambience of decay and apathy has fallen over the slowly emptying countryside. Also, the Russian state and many of its residents seem hurt and offended by the ingratitude Estonians and Latvians showed by wanting to break free. In the Estonian and Latvian perspective, the dissolution of the Soviet Union meant freedom and independence; from the Russian side, the same historical event is seen as a break-up with the unappreciative Balts and a loss of 'western provinces'. The Balts have gained much from the break-up, whereas many Russians still tend to see it as a loss, in line with the president of the Russian Federation, Vladimir Putin, who called the break-up of the Soviet Union 'the biggest tragedy of the twentieth century'.

Here I have described various relations of increasing asymmetry and decreasing proximity in the Baltic borderlands of the former Soviet Union, pointing to a growing gap in living standards, increasing feelings of distance among the inhabitants and a declining number of personal, everyday contacts. In sum, people of the three states that share a border are growing farther apart from each other, and the distance is slowly increasing with the passing away of the older generations. However, such tendencies need not lead to animosities and actual estrangement. It should be emphasized that in a comparative perspective, these Baltic border areas have been remarkably peaceful and well-functioning; the inhabitants have neither witnessed nor been party to any kind of ethnic, religious or political aggression or violence. In fact, this area's achievement of a fully peaceful dissolution of the Soviet Union and continuously non-violent relations between post-Soviet states can be seen as a considerable achievement. Meanwhile, cross-border cooperation is finally emerging within the new frameworks of sovereign states and other equal partners collaborating with each other.

Thus, in my predictions for the future of this border area I concur with the quiet optimism of Olga, a Seto woman born in 1921 who has lived through five different political regimes[14] in her homeland on the western shore of Lake Peipus:

> As long as I can remember there have been Setos, Russians and Estonians living in this land, my homeland. Just think of these three neighbouring villages of ours: we've got a Seto village, a Russian village, another one which is for the Russian Old Believers. All these people with different languages and religions have lived here together in peace. This is how it should be, and I don't think that will ever change. It did not change in Soviet times either! Nor did it change during the war. After all, I don't think we are so very different from each other.

These 'words of wisdom' from the periphery should be a powerful reminder to those actors – often influential actors at the state level – who wish to stress and promote ethnic, religious, cultural and other differences. Unfortunately, even in the hitherto peaceful Baltic post-Soviet borderlands some have attempted to politicize 'identity issues' such as ethnicity and increase estrangement across ethnic and state barriers. I believe that politicizing ethnic and other differences and demonizing those who are conceived and represented as different become much more difficult when there are practices of, and possibilities for, everyday face-to-face encounters, communication and cooperation across ethnic lines and across the border. However, an atmosphere of trust and familiarity among neighbours cannot be created and maintained by itself, or by local actors alone. Formal and informal plans, initiatives, actions and funding, by actors and networks at different levels, are needed for this and other EU border areas to develop as borders of peace and cooperation.

Notes

1. Here I use the concept of generation in a non-genealogical sense to refer to individuals belonging to a distinguishable age group that includes several cohorts (by definition, a cohort usually includes all who are born within the arch of the same time period). On this, see Kertzer and Keith (1984); Bertaux and Thompson (1993).
2. The research projects 'Ethnic Identity and Everyday Life in the Borderlands between Estonia, Latvia and Russia' (1999–2001) and 'Russia and the New EU-neighbours on a local level: A Comparative Ethnography of the Border Area between Estonia, Latvia and Russia' (2004–2007) were funded by the Academy of Finland and University of Helsinki Network for European Studies, respectively. Besides the author, the researchers were Dr Jeanna Kormina and Dr Marina Hakkarainen from the European University at St Petersburg, Sanita Vanaga and Aija Lulle from the University of Latvia, and Dr Aili Kelam, Tallinn University.
3. The discussion is based on fieldwork on the Estonian and Russian sides of the borders in question. See Assmuth (2003, 2004, 2005) for detailed descriptions of the three research areas. The main research data are transcripts of long theme interviews conducted during 2000, 2004 and 2005 with men and women of different ages, nationalities, citizenships and social positions. Besides the transcribed interviews, the other large body of research data is essays ($N = 110$) written in 2000 by students (17- to 18-year-olds) from the study areas on the themes of ethnic and local identity and the border. These were collected by way of a writing competition organized in local schools by interested teachers. Here I use 24 essays (13 by girls, 11 by boys) written in schools in Estonia and Russia.
4. Mostly materials from the Russian/Estonian borderland were used for this essay. For the Latvian/Russian borderland see Assmuth (2005, 2012) and Lulle (2006).
5. E.g., Hann and Bellér-Hann (1998) and Pelkmans (2006) have produced fine studies of comparable cases at or near the Turkish-Georgian border.
6. Until 1993, the Polish-Czechoslovakian border.
7. 'Soviet nostalgia' refers to a tendency, especially among elderly people, to romanticize and glorify memories and practices typical of the Soviet Union. In the interviews done on the Russian side, nostalgic references to the Soviet period frequently took the form of expressions like 'in the Soviet times we were all united', 'in the old days when Estonia hadn't yet broken free from the union', or 'Why did the Estonians want to leave? What did we do to them? I don't understand. We were always so good to them'.
8. The direct quotations are from the following materials: interviews conducted in 2000 and 2004 by the author in Estonian, transcribed by Uno Saar; interviews conducted by the author and Uno Saar in Russian, transcribed and translated from Russian into Estonian by Uno Saar; interviews conducted and transcribed by Jeanne Kormina and Marina Hakkarainen in Russian; and essays written in 2000 by students of schools on the Estonian and Russian sides of the borders in question. Translations from Estonian into English are by the author; from Russian into English by Kormina, Hakkarainen and Svetlana Kirichenko.

9. Except for the author, all the team members did indeed have years of 'inside informa-
    tion' about the Soviet Union and have been Soviet citizens. The author's understanding
    is based on frequent visits, a long-term research interest in everyday life in Soviet and
    post-Soviet Estonia, and reading. However, the informants were right in assuming that
    a middle-aged Finnish woman academic would have at least some knowledge of every-
    day living conditions in the Soviet Union.
10. Russia took exception to Estonia's preamble to the law – which refers to the Estonian
    state's uninterrupted legal continuity during the Soviet period and indirectly references
    the Soviet occupation of Estonia – and announced that it is revoking its signature and
    desires to restart negotiations with Estonia. Estonia has said that there is no need to
    renegotiate the border and that it has no land claims against Russia (http://www.estemb
    .ru/est/eesti_ja_venemaa; retrieved 27 February 2012).
11. At the age of sixteen, every Soviet citizen had to choose his or her nationality
    (*natsional'nosti*). This permanent choice was inscribed in one's internal passport and other
    official documents. The list of available nationalities did not include Seto, which was
    considered a subgroup of Estonians (cf. Humphrey 1983; Anderson 1996; Jääts 1998).
12. Alcoholism and high levels of alcohol consumption were, of course, extremely wide-
    spread in the Soviet period as well. The Soviet authorities, and also the Russian Or-
    thodox Church, tolerated and even encouraged consumption of alcohol. Sanctions and
    penalties were mild. Attitudes towards heavy drinking and drunkards continue to be
    very lenient, and women's drinking is also tolerated. However, men are much more
    likely to be unable to work, become seriously ill or die due to drinking. A full discus-
    sion of this topic is beyond the scope of this chapter, but alcoholism and alcohol-related
    illnesses and deaths are definitely gendered phenomena that need to be considered in
    any account of rural areas in the post-Soviet world.
13. Until 2005 there was an Estonian-language school in Pechory where instruction in all
    school subjects was in Estonian. Nowadays the school operates as a 'foreign-language
    school specializing in an intensive study of Estonian'. See Assmuth (2007).
14. The first Estonian republic, 1918–40; annexation by the Soviet Union, 1940–41; occupa-
    tion by Nazi Germany, 1941–44; second annexation by the Soviet Union, 1944–91; the
    Republic of Estonia, 1991–present.

References

Anderson, D. 1996. 'Bringing Civil Society to an Uncivilised Place: Citizenship Regimes in
    Russia's Arctic Frontier', in C. Hann and E. Dunn (eds), *Civil Society: Challenging Western
    Models*. London and New York: Routledge, pp. 99–120.
Assmuth, L. 2003. 'Nation Building and Everyday Life in the Borderlands between Estonia,
    Latvia and Russia', *Focaal: European Journal of Anthropology* 41: 59–69.
———. 2004. 'Ethnicity and Citizenship in the Borderlands between Estonia, Latvia and Rus-
    sia', in R. Alapuro, I. Liikanen and M. Lonkila (eds), *Beyond Post-Soviet Transition: Micro
    Perspectives on Challenge and Survival in Russia and Estonia*. Helsinki: Kikimora Publica-
    tions, pp. 128–47.
———. 2005. 'To Which State to Belong? Ethnicity and Citizenship at Russia's new EU-
    borders', in T.M. Wilson and H. Donnan (eds), *Culture and Power at the Edges of the State:
    National Support and Subversion in European Border Regions*. Münster: Lit Verlag, pp.
    255–88.
———. 2007. 'Politicizing Language at a Post-Soviet Border: An Estonian School in Russia',
    Suomen Antropologi [Journal of the Finnish Anthropological Society] 32(1): 36–46.

————. 2012. 'Rural Belongings: Baltic Russian Identities in Estonian and Latvian Border-land', in A. Aarelaid-Tart and L. Bennich-Björkman (eds), *Baltic Biographies at Historical Crossroads*. London and Oxford: Berghahn Books, pp. 107–24.

Berg, E. and S. Oras. 2003. 'The Estonian-Russian Border: Ten Years of Negotiations', *Estonian Foreign Policy Yearbook*. Retrieved 27 February 2012 from http://www.evi.ee/lib/valispol2003.pdf

Bertaux, D. and P. Thompson (eds). 1993. *Between Generations: Family Models, Myths and Memories*. Vol. 2 of *International Yearbook of Oral History and Life Stories*. Oxford: Oxford University Press.

Donnan, H. and T.M. Wilson. 2003. 'Territoriality, Anthropology, and the Interstitial: Subversion and Support in European Borderlands'. *Focaal: European Journal of Anthropology* 41: 9–20.

Hakkarainen, M. 2005. 'On the Margins: Minority Groups in Pechory Borderland', presented at the conference *Defining Region: Baltic Area Studies from Sociocultural Anthropology and Interdisciplinary Perspectives*, Klaipeda University, Lithuania, May 2005.

Hann, C. and I. Bellér-Hann. 1998. 'Markets, Morality and Modernity in Northeast Turkey', in T.M. Wilson and H. Donnan (eds), *Border Identities: Nation and State at International Frontiers*. Cambridge: Cambridge University Press, pp. 237–62.

Hohnen, P. 2003. *A Market Out of Place? Remaking Economic, Social and Symbolic Boundaries in Post-communist Lithuania*. Oxford Studies in Social and Cultural Anthropology. Oxford: Oxford University Press.

Humphrey, C. 1983. *Karl Marx Collective: Economy, Society and Religion in a Siberian Collective Farm*. Cambridge: Cambridge University Press.

Jääts, I. 1998. *Setude etniline identiteet*. Tartu: Tartu Ülikooli Kirjastus.

Kaiser, R. and E. Nikiforova. 2006. 'Borderland Spaces of Identification and Dis/location: Multiscalar Narratives and Enactments of Seto Identity and Place in the Estonian-Russian Borderlands', *Ethnic and Racial Studies* 24(5): 928–58.

Kertzer, D. and J. Keith. 1984. *Age and Anthropological Theory*. Ithaca, NY: Cornell University Press.

Kuldin, S. 1999. 'The Border Influence on the Conscience and Economic Behaviour of the People along the Pskovsko-Chudskoe Lake', in O. Brednikova and V. Voronkov (eds), *Nomadic Borders*. St Petersburg: Centre for Independent Social Research, pp. 138–40.

Lulle, A. 2006. 'Social and Cultural Consequences of Newly Established Border in Latvian and Russian Border Areas', *Lineae Terrarum, International Borders Conference, State University of New Mexico, USA, April 2006*. Retrieved 27 February 2012 from http://research.utep.edu/Portals/379/lulle,%20aija.pdf

Manakov, A. 1999. 'Border factor in the life of the population of the Petchory area (Pskov region, Russia)', in O. Brednikova and V. Voronkov (eds), *Nomadic Borders*. St Petersburg: Centre for Independent Social Research, pp. 130–133.

Markowitz, F. 2000. *Coming of Age in Post-Soviet Russia*. Urbana, IL, and Chicago: University of Chicago Press.

Pelkmans, M. 2006. *Defending the Border: Identity, Religion, and Modernity in the Republic of Georgia*. Ithaca, NY: Cornell University Press.

Pine, F. 1996. 'Redefining Women's Work in Rural Poland', in Ray Abrahams (ed.), *After Socialism: Land Reform and Social Change in Eastern Europe*. Providence and Oxford: Berghahn Books, pp. 133–155.

Valuev, V.N. 2003. *Russian Border Policies and Border Regions*. Nordic Network for Security Studies. Retrieved 27 February 2012 from http://www.nnss.org/index_documents.htm

Verdery, K. 1998. 'Transnationalism, Nationalism, Citizenship, and Property: Eastern Europe since 1989'. *American Ethnologist* 25(2): 291–306.

Wilson, T.M. and H. Donnan. 1998. 'Nation, State and Identity at International Borders'. In T.M. Wilson and H. Donnan (eds), *Border Identities: Nation and State at International Frontiers*. Cambridge: Cambridge University Press, pp. 1–30.

Yurchak, A. 2006. *Everything Was Forever, Until It Was No More: The Last Soviet Generation*. Princeton, NJ: Princeton University Press.

Võro Instituut. 1998. *Ku kavvas Setomaalõ seto rahvast jakkus?* Võru: Võro Instituudi Toimõtisõq 2, 1998.

———. 2000. *A kiilt rahvas kynõlõs… Võrokeste keelest, kommetest, identiteedist*. Võru: Võro Instituudi Toimõtiseq 8, 2000.

Chapter 7

'We Are All Tourists'

Enduring Social Relations at the Romanian-Serbian
Border in Different Mobility Regimes

Cosmin Radu

This chapter explores the implications national and supranational policies have for cross-border mobility. It illustrates relations between state
central institutions and peripheral administrative units, between regional
policies and local practices. In particular, it tries to show how mobility at
the Romanian-Serbian border has been challenged by changes enacted in
the border regime in the 1960s and 1970s, 1989 and 2004. The visas introduced in 2004 have temporarily stifled the hopes of people who previously
circulated throughout the area, accustomed to a 'border economy' developed since the outset of socialism through cross-border seasonal labour
and small-scale trading, various forms of smuggling, cross-border marriages and shared industrial activity. Yet the chapter insists on the dual
nature of the restrictive border regimes. Expectations about crossing were
initially gloomy, but social relations and practices emerged in context to
both permit and restrict mobility. Taking the evidence further, the essay
articulates the interpretive limits and possibilities enabled by conceptual
elaborations of migration, transnationalism and the 'mobilities turn' in the
context of changing proximities and asymmetries at borders.

The essay begins with some theoretical considerations to clarify the
central theme and argument. Next it relates the recent history of border
crossings from Romania to Serbia, pointing out the forces that shaped
mobility in socialism and post-socialism and the border regimes that
developed in those periods. Further, it describes changes during the EU

Notes for this chapter begin on page 190.

pre-accession period and responses in terms of consequent cross-border mobility. A large part of the chapter concerns the analysis of border cross-ers' practices as sites of relation making. Here the essay aims to show re-lations between localities and persons from each side of the border, with respect to forms of labour, trading and cross-border marriages.

Ethnographic research for this essay was carried out mainly in Febru-ary 2002 and July 2004 in the Romanian border villages Balta Verde and Gogoşu, funded by a grant from the Romanian Ministry for Education and Research. Additional research with people waiting in queues to purchase visas was conducted around the premises of the Serbian consulate in Bu-charest in July–August 2004 and April–May 2005. Insights from fieldwork done in summer 2006 in Dušanovac and Negotin, Serbia, funded by the Open Society Foundation, Bucharest, have also been used here.

Introductory Argument

Theoretical framing of cross-border mobility between neighbouring Eu-ropean countries might be a difficult task, especially if the emphasis is on the movement itself. This section insists that the cross-border mobility discussed in the chapter cannot be accurately grasped and theorized in terms of migration. Also, it cannot be seen as transnationalism or mobili-ties alone. To distinguish cross-border mobility in the context of changing border regimes from other forms of corporeal and (non)bodily movement, I have elsewhere proposed the notion of 'crossing' (Radu, forthcoming), arguing that whereas crossing the border from Romania to Serbia does not make an absolute difference from living and staying in place, it works as a compensation for dwelling conditions marked by unemployment, poverty and everyday hopelessness. Although crossing confers only minor mate-rial benefits, it connects apparently different worlds, living standards and class divisions, and makes changes in the imaginations of borderlanders.

On the other hand, crossing as both individual and collective practice is linked to everyday processes of belonging and political contestations of place. From this point of view, crossing is itself an active force in making the border and its 'geography', in terms of space-time, and interacts vari-ously with both restrictive and permissive regimes of mobility. In periods of frontier-(re)making and changing asymmetries and proximities, border crossings become practical, affective domains of intense (inter)subjectivity. In the present, crossing activates domains of experience the borderlanders have had with, for example, the harsh restrictions on mobility enforced between the late 1940s and early 1970s, when illegal flight was the only way to cross the border. It also generates hope and multiplicity in the spaces of mobility.

As a general point of departure, the cross-border mobility the chapter speaks about is, unlike other analytical focuses concerning forms of movement, a process that flexibly acknowledges the political, the spatial and the temporal at various scales, while insisting on its relational and subjective aspects. Mobility, in the context of border crossing, is an expression of the agentive capacity of the border projected beyond the institutional dimension or presence of the state (Radu 2012). The border regimes designed to regulate the flows across the border are treated here as relational constructs, negotiable categories of experience that themselves are part of the processes of crossing. In this context, border regimes are both enabling and restricting. Mobility, then, challenges constructions of class at borders and produces various processes of redistribution, proximity and asymmetry that are conceived beyond notions of fixity, permanence and physical distance. An implicit argument of this chapter is that mobility, and the interplay of crossing and dwelling, should be taken as key notions in the anthropology of borders, a specialized area of studies with huge potential for conceptualizing movement beyond the scholarly 'canons' already established.

Migration, Transnationalism, Mobility?

In parallel with the debates on globalization social sciences have designed three cross-disciplinary, competing narratives on movement: international migration, transnationalism and mobilities. These narratives focus on global movement of persons and objects through different underlying, enclosing assumptions.

Accounts of migration, systematically developed after the Second World War, have privileged distance over proximity of contacts, and long over seasonal or short-term stays. Adding to these, the so-called international migration perspective (Massey et al. 1998; Massey and Taylor 2004) produces views of economic and institutional resonance, emphasizing interactions between different labour markets and between sending and receiving societies. Also, it draws attention to interplays between 'migration policies' and multiple migrating actors, causes and effects of flows, and policies aimed at regulating the flows. This perspective, heavily influenced by economics, usually addresses processes of migration from a top-down approach. In search of regularities of movement, international migration scholars have often spoken about 'push and pull' factors, 'migration systems', 'South-North' migration, networks, 'chain migration', and so on. In this perspective, adaptation and assimilation – or their failures, visible in the formation of immigrant enclaves – are key notions and points of reference.

More recent developments, as of the 1990s, have offered a less deterministic approach, the so-called transnational migration perspective (Glick Schiller 2003). This draws attention to migration spaces themselves, taking a fresh look at the ways migrants belong to these spaces (Glick Schiller and Fouron 2001). It ceases to consider 'origin' and 'destination' as fixed analytical categories and elaborates ideas about simultaneity of belonging (Levitt and Glick Schiller 2004). The transnational turn has been constructed on the grounds of post-positivist, post-structural and post-national contention with migration studies (King 2012), and anthropology has had the leading voice in this scholarly endeavour. Basch, Glick Schiller and Szanton Blanc (1994: 7) have defined transnationalism as the process by which migrants develop and sustain 'multi-stranded relationships – familial, economic, social, religious and political – that span borders and link their societies of origin and settlement'.

Whereas 'international migration' holds that movement is the product of malfunctions within sending societies and discrepancies and asymmetries between the migrants' points of travel, 'transnational migration' shows that movement in societies is rather natural, irrespective of structural differences between economies and state apparatuses. Instead of the strict division of the world prompted by the international migration perspective, transnationalism favours 'multiple connectivity' and has focused more on individuals' feelings and practices in relation to the various spaces enabling connections. But by overemphasizing connections, transnationalism has somewhat lost contact with processes of exclusion, poverty, inequality and the restricting entities within the landscape of the global movement of persons – states, borders and migration controls (King 2012). Among the scholars who have warned against the idealist position taken in the transnational migration perspective, Portes (2003) has shown that migration processes are highly selective in nature and that most of the people moving across the globe cannot be characterized as transnational, precisely because escalated restrictions and the precarious lives of the migrants disallow sophisticated attachments or detachments from transnational spaces spanning national borders. Transnationalism's different emphasis and epistemological position have thus enabled further debates on hypermobility and deterritorialization of space and place in migration.

The international migration perspective has sought to explain the structuring of the world through movement, while transnationalism has focused attention on the more inclusive middle ground of transnational spaces.

However, neither seems to consider short-distance, short-term movement. The so-called mobilities turn, developed in the 2000s by sociologists and geographers, is an approach closer to these particular forms of movement. The challenge was to conceive movement beyond the influential trope of presence and corporeality. Urry (2007) considered that whereas social science takes a metaphysics of presence as a primary assumption, the social world is in fact composed, and sometimes dominated, by absence. The mobilities turn formulated the need of a 'sociology beyond societies': 'movement, mobility, and contingent ordering' must transcend 'stasis, structure, and social order' (Urry 2000: 18). This perspective also explicitly introduced the question of varying proximity and inequality within movement. 'Mobilities themselves can generate social exclusions that reduce social proximity, social trust and social capital. The relations of co-presence always involve nearness and farness, proximity and distance, solidity and imagination" (Urry 2002: 265–66).

According to King (2012), the mobilities turn downplays corporeality and embodiment of migration, which should be still important references. Yet from another point of view, the mobilities turn favours an understanding of movement in the framework of sedentarism – formerly rejected by transnational migration scholars – which happens when migration is seen as stability-within-movement (Halfacree 2012). In the same line of thought, Urry (2000) has spoken of 'mobility landscapes'. On the other hand, though, as Halfacree (2012) points out, the mobilities turn provides a subtle understanding of mobility in its multiform nature and transcends the limiting analysis of movement as a discrete event.

Emplacement and/or Mobility: The Anthropology of Borders

Although the three narratives on movement emphasize the importance of a separate, dependent (and independent) variable of movement, and stress important aspects that can advance the ethnographic study of mobility, proximity and asymmetry, all of them seem to become anxious and lose contact with place. Halfacree (2012) argues that mobility studies, particularly in geography but also in other disciplines, need to enable accounts of place. A particularly helpful notion that can help reposition place in the landscapes of mobility is Massey's (1991, 2005) 'throwntogetherness' – the 'global sense of place', 'the event of place':

> If everything is moving, where is here? ... 'Here' is where spatial narratives meet up or form configurations, conjunctures of trajectories which have their own temporalities ... But where the successions of meetings, the accumula-

tion of weavings and encounters build up a history.... what is special about place is not some romance of a pre-given collective identity or of the eternity of the hills. Rather, what is special about place is precisely that throwntogetherness, the unavoidable challenge of negotiating a here-and-now ... the coming together of the previously unrelated, a [temporary] constellation of processes rather than a thing. (Massey 2005: 138–41, quoted in Halfacree 2012: 211)

On the other hand, both the anthropology of borders and border studies in general are in a privileged position to counterbalance mobility with place and staying in place, as they have emphasized frontiers as territorial sites of relatively fixed patterns of cultural and institutional negotiations (Radu 2012, 2010). Although borders are sites of permanent short-term, recurrent crossing that takes different forms, they have been widely depicted as sites of separateness and rigid impositions of power from above. Therefore, whereas narratives of mobility tend to lose the sense of place and proximity, border studies are rather place-bound and (physical) proximity-focused, losing sight of mobility. As argued earlier, even in the context of strict, restrictive border regimes, the examination of the interplay between 'crossing' and 'dwelling' and their everyday politics can explain borders and their transformations, including the changes in proximities and asymmetries.

From the 1970s until 1989, Romanians and Serbians circulated between each other's countries, mainly for small commerce. Since 1989, vast numbers of Romanians from the more deprived eastern regions and the borderlands have worked in Serbia. Even these days, more than six years after Romania joined the EU, producing a new geopolitical and economic asymmetry between the two countries, there are poor people from border areas who subsist on their contacts with the Serbian Vlachs. In the same period – especially in the 2000s, when the oil contraband stimulated by the international embargo upon Serbia ended – Serbians have generally shown less interest in coming to Romania for work or business.

This chapter argues that cross-border mobility in the context of this kind of combination of changing proximities and asymmetries is poorly addressed in accounts of international, transnational migrations and the mobilities turn. Paradoxically, the growing cross-disciplinary field of border studies (Wilson and Donnan 1998; Donnan and Wilson 1999) also tends to be of little help. As already emphasized, the anthropology of borders focuses less on movement itself than on borders and borderlands as geographical areas of concentrated state apparatuses (Heyman 1994, 1995; Sahlins 1998; Cole and Wolf 1974; Chalfin 2006), or as hybrid sites of contact and fluid cultural encounters (Rosaldo 1988; Anzaldua 1987; Alvarez 1995). In neither case is mobility stressed as an important analytical issue, although some outstanding studies about borders have tried to introduce mobility as a more vigorous agenda (Donnan and Wilson 2010; Green 2009, 2005; Konstantinov 1996; Williams and Baláž. 2002; Cunningham and Heyman 2004).

But what forms of mobility do border crossings constitute, or not? International migration theories have long emphasized that processes of migration can be subsumed into 'patterns', 'flows' and 'systems' spanning over long periods of time: East-West, South-North, Mexico-U.S., circulatory or 'push-pull' migrations. Wallace and Stola (2001), for example, treated post-1989 migration in east-central Europe as 'patterns', examining previously non-patterned short-distance, cross-border mobility and looking, for instance, at Ukrainians going to Poland or Romanians to Hungary. They also discussed cross-border trading in terms of patterns of migration. Yet whereas relying on the analytical terminology of 'pattern' makes it difficult to address the fluid nature of the cross-border mobilities examined, basing the focus almost exclusively on patterned practices leaves little room for understanding the subjective, variable constructions of experience with mobility, proximity and asymmetry. In addition, accounts of border regimes as alternating closings and openings of borders provide a simplistic perspective on the relational and intersubjective character, spanning institutional spaces, of the impositions of power. To sum up, the anthropology of borders has to be cautious with the treatment of crossing as patterned mobility.

In relation to this, the point of this chapter is that in the cross-border mobility between Romania and Serbia, characterized by changing border regimes in both countries, fluid border events and spaces of cross-border creativity give mobilities very particular yet changeable histories, embedded as they are in social relations and political subjectivities of various temporal references. This point is consistent with recent attempts to affirm spatio-temporal dimensions of mobility at and across borders. Donnan and Wilson (2010) have recently emphasized the prevailing aspect of mobility as a process that causes us to speak about, and sometimes become anxious about, borders. Green (2009) has proposed looking at borders through the metaphors of line, trace and tidemark. Whereas the anthropology of borders has so far favoured the representation of the border (or 'borderli-ness') as a 'line' – a barrier, a fence, an interruption of communication and movement – Green points out that borders are best described as 'tidemarks' in permanent transformation and movement, implying both divisions and connections within sites of ongoing reterritorializations. Similarly, Radu (2010) has emphasized the dimension of 'becoming' at borders, which encapsulates and produces space-time beyond the territorial trope. The events of mobility and crossing are part of these processes of becoming, as opposed to dwelling.

Anthropology of Borders: Mobility, Proximity and Asymmetry

The question of proximity and asymmetry is an assumption from which an anthropology of borders can start a systematic analytical treatment of mobility. Border crossings, especially in cases of populated borderlands, involve pre-existing physical proximity between people, localities, and so on. However, physicality is further complicated by a changing sense of presence and absence, 'sedentarism', emplacement and mobility. Simmel (1950) referred to proximity as an important aspect of social space – of closeness and distance between individuals – able to produce intimacy, purity and 'alienated objectivity'. Although there is a 'compulsion of proximity' (Boden and Molotch 1994), the mobilities turn draws attention to society as a set of occasional, imagined and virtual co-presences (Urry 2002). In terms of sociality, then, physical proximity, in various ways, can only be a fiction. Trying to bring politics back into the mobilities turn, Pellegrino (2011) initiates a relevant discussion on mobility and proximity by emphasizing the fluid, changing and relational nature of proximity as part of mobility. Proximity changes as the routes and permissions to mobility change. Proximity can thus be enforced and prohibited, fixed or negotiable. Therefore, it is clearly not the physical distance that primarily matters in giving sense to proximity, but mobility and journeys to each other, that is, the corporeality and the intermittent direct contact.

Because mobility can foster inequality and asymmetry, it is important to note that proximity in the form of co-presence already contains asymmetry. According to Levinas (1998), asymmetry is one of the most important aspects of face-to-face relationships. Levinas's asymmetry of proximity – or 'distant nearness', in Habermas's terms – is the primary sense of ethics (Erman 2006), the context in which the social actors realize that they are 'all unequal before the other' (Alford 2004). Proximity and its production of asymmetry are also the means to create intersubjectivity. This is sensed, rather than known, for proximity is not understood as a way of knowing but as a sensibility and vulnerability – and, in a way, a breakup of identity (Horowitz 2002). For Levinas, proximity does not evolve in the amalgamation of the self with the other but remains a space in-between, 'a never being close enough … outside myself, yet not within another' (Horowitz 2002: 232–33). From this point of view, proximity is an open question with no clear, fixed or permanent configurations of identities. Proximity is itself asymmetry, and the relation between them is always changing. This chapter considers border regimes and crossings as agents of transformations at borders, changing senses of inequality and class divisions as well as everyday notions of citizenship and belonging.

A whole series of theoretical assumptions, therefore, both enable and restrict anthropologists' understanding of how borders and mobility across them change significantly in relatively short periods of time and how they change, or are produced by, the border 'geographies' of social relations with their inherent proximities and asymmetries. One example of such change is the workings of a border regime initiated during the Romanian pre-accession to the EU. As a candidate country, Romania had to start implementing a series of security measures at its frontiers, including new visa regimes. This chapter looks into this and other changes occurring in recent socialist and post-socialist history. In addition, it reveals and ethnographically expands the diversity of forms of cross-border mobility in relation to changes in border regimes. Concluding that strong connections between these forms are materialized in social relations between Romanian citizens and Serbian Vlachs that span various border regimes, I emphasize that cross-border mobility is not entirely dependent on changes in border regimes. Border crossings emerged in informality and, rather than ceasing now to exist, enter a different context of informality. Wallace (2002: 621) has made a somewhat similar point: closing borders is likely to 'drive migration underground'. Another important argument that derives from this is that border 'enclosures', or the border regimes themselves, are actually combinative processes with no single assumptions.

Border Crossings before 1989: Mobility Rediscovered

A crucial event that seems to have shaped social relations across the border, and consequent senses of proximity and asymmetry, was the launch of the construction of the Iron Gates I hydropower plant. The formalities took place in 1964 at a meeting between Gheorghe Grheorghiu Dej and Jošip Broz Tito, the respective presidents of Romania and Yugoslavia, in Gura Văii, a periphery of the town Drobeta Turnu-Severin, on the Romanian side. Large crowds of Romanians and Serbian Vlachs, whose mobility across the border had been completely restricted for many years, improvised a bridge of boats on the Danube to attend the meeting. The new industrial enterprise significantly changed the landscape of the border: some islands on the Danube were flooded, the stretch of river-border from Orşova to the Southern Romania generally widened, and several villages and towns were relocated. Atop the dam that crosses the Danube approximately between Gura Văii and Novi Sip (Kladovo) on the Serbian side is a bridge for car traffic. Two border checkpoints, one Yugoslavian and the other Romanian, were opened at the ends of this bridge in the early 1970s.

Figure 7.1. The Danube at Orşova in 2010. Before the construction of the Iron Gates I hydropower plant, the river was narrower between Romania and Serbia. (Photo: Cosmin Radu)

The checkpoint at Iron Gates I is one of the most important on this border, as it is the area's only passage for car traffic over the Danube.

The construction project marked the start of a new era for organized, legal cross-border mobility, which, even though restricted, accounted for much of the (re)making of social relations and the trading ethos at this border. The two sides signed a bilateral agreement on border crossings stating that border dwellers were allowed to cross and circulate freely within a certain number of kilometres' distance from the borderline in the neighbouring country for approximately eight days per month, without visas and even without passports. The only travel document required was a special permit for border crossings, issued by local authorities.

Tourism was the official rationale for these crossings. However, apart from visiting relatives, the reason for both Romanian and Serbian citizens' crossings was to sell merchandise they carried into the other country. Large marketplaces hosting the traders soon sprang up on both sides of the border. *Piaţa Sârbilor* (the Serbians' market) in Drobeta Turnu-Severin is still known by this old name in everyday talk today. Kladovo, Negotin and other Serbian towns also had markets for the Romanian border crossers. In the 1980s, when consumer goods shortages were at their peak, trips across the border provided Romanians with foodstuffs, jeans, coffee, shoes, cigarettes and electronics. The regular success of cross-border trade and traders has always been accepted, and to some extent protected, by customs officers and border guards, who tend also to have relatives involved in this mobility.

For many villagers from Balta Verde and Gogoşu, the sites of my early fieldwork on the border, cross-border commerce was a monthly routine. Every Saturday evening, groups of people headed 65 km north to Iron Gates I, the nearest checkpoint[1], to depart for Negotin or Pančevo, the Yugoslav border towns with the largest marketplaces. At the Yugoslav marketplaces there was great demand for crocheted and other handmade fabric items, carpets, porcelain, housewares, and the like. A single home-made fabric decoration could bring a woman as much cash as a monthly worker's wage (3,000–4,000 Lei – more than an average salary in socialist Romania). Shopping and retailing at those markets were accompanied by intense socializing and relation making with Romanian-speaking Serbian Vlachs. Shopping was more than necessary, as the crossers were not allowed to pass with foreign currency at the checks in the border post. To keep an exchangeable value for their cross-border activity, some of them were purchasing gold, hiding it carefully from the border checks.

During their stays in Serbia, my informants slept in the homes of Vlach families who were also keeping safe the goods that were not sold, even for long periods of time. Some say that almost every Vlach household had a special room to hold the merchandise of its Romanian friends. Keeping merchandise in this way presupposed regular visits and contacts with hosts and unprecedentedly strong ties between Romanian and Yugoslav citizens. Some things purchased from the Yugoslav markets and shops were for personal use; others were traded informally at the markets at home or through personal contacts, while still others were offered as gifts and small 'attentions' to customs officers, doctors, border guards, socialist managers, workplace colleagues or siblings.

To sum up, cross-border mobility and relations were reactivated for approximately twenty years before 1989. Despite the Romanian socialist regime's anxious reluctance to tolerate private entrepreneurial activity, mobilities thus enabled a certain widespread sense of consumerism and petty capitalism in the area. Economic and exchange relations stimulated the maintenance and development of long-term social relations and certain degrees of trust. Naturally, these counted for a lot in the liberalized context that came up later. It was not only access to common resources and a sort of equality that developed in the border regime of the 1970s and 1980s. To reiterate Simmel's terms, horizontal trust and equality were rather instantiations of an 'alienation of objectivity'. Cross-border mobility in those times fostered an anxious sense of proximity and asymmetry. The differences between the relatively open Yugoslav economy and the 'closed' Romanian one, coupled with the freedom of movement to Western Europe that Yugoslav citizens were enjoying then, infused the experience of the Romanian border crossers. Before the early 1970s, proximity between Romanians and Serbians was produced in absence and imagination. But once mobility across the border was permitted, proximity and asymmetry accentuated and changed ways of contesting a disappointing dwelling, place and belonging at home. Thus mobility into Serbia until 1989 became a medium for everyday politics and a subject-making process that was well reflected in the border class 'system' so obvious after 1989.

Border Crossings after 1989: Diversification and Informalization of Mobility

After 1989, the unrestricted opening of the Romanian border provided my informants with opportunity to further develop their contacts with the Vlachs. Long stays in Serbia were no longer restricted, so they managed to spend much more time there, trading and working in construction, agriculture, housekeeping and forestry. This was probably the first time they were able to derive advantage from the affluence of the Serbian Vlachs. Inlanders, especially those from the more deprived eastern parts of the country, also came to cross the border to Serbia. The border Vlach localities were attractive because of their wealth, produced over years of migration, remittances and capital accumulation by Vlachs in Austria, France, Sweden, Germany, Denmark and other prosperous destinations since the 1960s (Schierup 1990; Kohlbacher and Reeger 1999). Because many Vlach households' younger members were working abroad in the 1990s, those remaining behind faced severe labour shortages. Hiring Romanians became a generalized, inexpensive solution to the problem. In 2001, a day's labour for Romanians working in Serbia paid between 15 and 30 German marks — three times what Romanian citizens could earn at home doing the same job.

Until 2004, ever increasing numbers of Romanian citizens worked seasonally in Serbia. The combination of stringent requirements for Western European visas and a much more permissive border regime with Serbia, alongside good 'salaries' and growing opportunities at the border – such as when the Yugoslav wars turned oil embargoes into thriving contraband – plus gradual lay-offs at the border's major industries all made cross-border mobility a real everyday enjoyment and fantasy for many.

As an enduring practice, mobility created premises for different processes concerning social relations. Numerous seasonal workers in Serbia went further – into Austria or Germany – out of loyalty to their Vlach friends. Other Romanian border dwellers, together with Serbian Vlach partners, started larger businesses, such as arranging massive transports of Moldavian labourers into Serbia. Still others intermediated workforces for large construction sites in Serbia. Many housekeepers married their Vlach employers, thus creating families with mixed citizenship. Meanwhile, huge illicit gas transports crossed the Danube or the 'green frontier', largely 'authorized' by the state.

Border regimes on the Romanian side facilitated mobility in different ways. Until 2002, border crossings were not restricted in any way. Contraband itself was subject to 'appropriate' control by border guards or local police only in cases of quarrels between smugglers or on occasions of institutional supercontrols from the centre. By the end of that period, however, the newly acquired status of EU candidate meant important changes to Romanian institutions of border control. Border guards, as a special branch within the army, had to transform into 'border police'. This change in the ways the border was controlled minimized the presence of the border patrols but made it more difficult for borderlanders to carry their petty smuggling across the border as new forms of surveillance were intensified. In 2002, upon enforcement of the Schengen Agreement at the external borders of the member or associated states, cross-border mobility became a subject of increased legal ambiguity. Deposits and cash guarantees were required to cross into Serbia. And now that visa renewals were necessary, workers in Serbia had to take monthly trips back to the checkpoint to get new stamps in their passports.

In February 2002, when I conducted my first fieldwork in the region, the villagers of Balta Verde and Gogoşu were rather hopeless about future prospects for journeys to Serbia, although the cash proofs legally required in the border post amounted to only about €250. Many informants said they would have to find another livelihood. On my second trip to the field in 2004, people were still going to Serbia with the help of bus and taxi drivers from Drobeta-Turnu Severin or Serbia, who lent them money for the border crossing. Bus drivers would distribute cash to passengers and then retrieve it after the checks. The central role that working or trading in Serbia still played for many of my informants in 2004 is evident in their ability to pay the drivers well for this service – up to €50 for lending just €250. In 2006, during my fieldwork in the small village of Dušanovac, Serbia, I met some thirty Romanian day labourers and numerous housekeepers, some of whom were from Gogoşu and Balta Verde. In 2009–10, even though many were changing their mobility routes into Western Europe, some were still going or considering going to Serbia, attracted by the €20 daily pay (less than in Italy or Spain, but still better than in impoverished Romanian areas of the border, especially in agriculture).

The concluding point of this section is that mobility became a massive movement after 1989. Numerous villages on both sides of the border have depended on the 'supply' and 'demand' of labour and services for many years. Also, many businesses in major towns along the entire border - Drobeta Turnu-Severin, Timişoara - often relate directly to crossing the border to Serbia. Mobility has further accentuated both proximity and asymmetry between the Vlachs and their hired workers. Importantly, the years since 1989 have also been a time of mobility and crossing going underground. Whereas before 1989, these were mainly connected to addressing shortcomings of the socialist system of goods provision, since 1989 mobility has been guided by the desire for accumulation, or poverty and lack of sources of income at home. Under socialism, cross-border travel of people and goods was a legal facility under the careful inspection of the state, but after 1989 it was subject to increased 'illegality' governed by both everyday social relations and the state (Radu 2009). Official and unofficial rule at the border, dictated by poverty, deindustrialization, embargoes and pre-EU accession requirements, were followed by new forms of social relatedness that drove mobility into informality.

To understand better how mobility has been consolidated over the years, the following sections elaborate ethnographically on social relations and their emergence and growth in border situations of work.

Relations and Mobilities at the Border

In what follows I deal with the expansion of work in Serbia in the 1990s and most of the 2000s. Particular emphasis lies with housekeepers – women permanently hired by Vlach households – and male day labourers who commuted seasonally, especially in spring and summer, to work in different households and villages. This approach allows me to single out the different potentialities for social relations in each occupation.

First, the pay was different for each occupation. A housekeeper had the security of a fixed monthly income, while the day labourer's earnings were uncertain. Day labourers exercised their 'freedom' to move from landlord to another, and from village to village; housekeepers were bound to a single household in which, if they showed loyalty, they might in some respects become equal to family members.

Second, workers at Vlach homes on the border came from different Romanian regions and were ranked accordingly in the eyes of their employers. Being a border native seemed more advantageous than coming from Moldavia. Border dwellers were usually offered good pay and working conditions on the basis of 'privileges' that derived from proximity and previous relations with Vlachs. Interestingly, the asymmetry between Serbian Vlachs and Romanian borderlanders, which developed over decades of socialism through the Vlachs' guest work and labour migration into Western Europe, was somewhat minimized by the shared experience of border crossings and mobility of both Vlachs into Romania and Romanians into Serbia. Reciprocal visits, mixed marriages and other opportunities for intersubjectivity between border dwellers on each side have always been present to some extent. Also, shared experiences of shortages and of material and symbolic consumption under socialism certainly accounted for actual close relationships between Romanian borderlanders and Vlachs. Even the Romanian Rudars (Roma), who otherwise would have been clearly differentiated from Romanians on the basis of popular prejudice, were well inserted in the Vlach 'border economy' and appreciated for their skills more than were workers from Moldavia, Dobrogea and Eastern Oltenia. Therefore, a certain 'border identity' apparently helped consolidate monopolist positions and relations with the affluent Vlachs. Among workers, Moldavians were viewed as a distinct group with different work ethic and collective solidarities. In contrast, border natives' 'ethnic' or 'cultural' distinctiveness was often ignored. In this respect, the Romanian-Serbian border appeared to have a 'classifying mission' (Kearney 2004). The interplay of proximity and asymmetry at the border, paralleled by heightened mobility, created classificatory practices well suited to class relations encompassed in work situations.

Similarities between Vlachs and their labourers, as the latter perceived them, went so far as to blur the boundaries between informal and formal, worker and employer, with labour arrangements generally produced by reciprocal dependence. Especially where there was a long-lasting relation, for example when a woman worked in a Vlach household for many years, the roles lost many of their different meanings. A woman from Gogoşu explained that besides her regular work, she was permitted to do everything she wanted in the household, such as hiring day labourers on the land of her 'host' and often taking over the tasks of arranging things with village neighbours and more distant kin. In relation to this, housekeepers tended to refer their Vlach employers as *gazde* (hosts), whereas day labourers usually called Vlachs *patroni* (employers). The two forms of relation (employer and day labourer, host and housekeeper) produced contrasting forms of embeddedness in the local border economy, with relevant consequences for continuing mobility. Securing a more or less permanent host or employer in Serbia assured not only a stable living, but also recurrent

Figure 7.2. Romanian traders from Timişoara carrying bags of merchandise at Pančevo railway station, Serbia (2005). (Photo: Cosmin Radu)

mobilities animating the border. In a different register, especially between Romanian border dwellers and Vlachs, people seemed eager to develop long-term, stable relations imbued with intimate feelings, often unspoken, of asymmetry and inequality. For instance, I was quite surprised to hear a woman from Balta Verde who was repeatedly mistreated by her Vlach host say she would return to him as soon as possible.

Housekeepers, Cross-border Marriages and Mobility

Rodica is a 56-year-old woman from a Romanian-Serbian border village. She has worked for Serbian Vlachs since the late 1990s. She made her first trip – to a village near Pančevo, where she found her first host – without a passport, getting over the Danube to Serbia in a car transporting workers from Iron Gates II (a hydropower plant on the Danube south of Drobeta Turnu-Severin, built in the 1980s): 'I looked for work for three months, I got the cash and then I got back to my village.' Compared to the present, it was easier then to find a host, and mobility was facilitated by diffuse regulations. 'Registering with the police in Serbia was not required and warranties by the host were sometimes not honoured.' 'I was able to make money every year because I had a good relationship with my host.' Why did she leave her home to work in Serbia? 'I was a single mother with four schoolchildren; I was fired from my job, so I was forced into this. Immediately after December 1989, everybody wanted to make their way to Serbia'.

In 2006, when I saw her in Dušanovac, Serbia, her host was paying her €200 a month. 'It is much better than in Romania. In my village, there are no rich families at all. Therefore, everybody works for himself. And, when available, the day-labour pays three times less than in Serbia', she told me then. Other hosts paid their housekeepers less – €100 per month – which in turn gave them opportunities to supplement their income with day labour for other households in the village: 'They [the hosts] sometimes say that it is good for us to get additional "black" jobs.' Nevertheless, most of the workers permanently hired by Vlachs were strictly prohibited from working with other households, as their willingness to stay on was seen as a question of allegiance. What were the regular costs of her stay in Serbia? None. Her host provided her return ticket, meals as long as she stayed, and monthly pay. Since July 2004, when expensive visas were introduced, the host has supplied her with cash for the visa as well (€27 for a one-month visa).

Even though permanent housekeepers, as compared to other labourers, certainly enjoy privileged positions in the border economy, housekeeping is a challenging job for many women because they have to do everything to keep the house and garden in order as well as assume additional tasks involving intensive participation in their hosts' families. Cooking, washing, shopping, organizing other practical activities: these were the daily activities of a woman like Rodica. Many women, after staying with their host families for a time and getting to know the families' relatives abroad, followed younger Vlachs to Austria. At first they were happy about this, as they expected to earn more for easier work. But upon getting there, they usually discovered that they were paid the same for more work for a larger and much more pretentious family. 'There were cases when such hard-worked women have not received any money for their efforts. You cannot do anything in such cases because you only have a tourist visa for three months', Rodica told me. Many young women chose this path thinking of a possible marriage to a rich Vlach and a permanent relocation to Vienna or elsewhere. Although there were successful arrangements of that kind, many other women got cheated – even upon marrying a Vlach, the situation did not really change. It is noteworthy that the experience of the Vlach women trying to get ahead in Austria was an object lesson for Romanian women too. While single Vlach women strove to marry older Austrians, attracted by their pensions, Romanians were trying the same with elders in border villages. Some pensioners retreated to their houses on the border to benefit from the Austrian or German social insurance systems, having been guest workers and labour migrants in those countries since the 1960s. Sometimes such arrangements failed, as women were not eligible to receive the pensions of husbands who died within the first five years of marriage. Listening to such cynical calculations made by housekeeping women struggling for a better living has been a mainstay of my fieldwork. At least in Balta Verde, almost every new border crossing by women was based on this calculus.

Going to Serbia was very much valued among the Rudars from Balta Verde too. When Roma cross-border mobility involved marriage arrangements, the strategy differed from Romanian women's. An important rationale for the mobility of Roma women from Balta Verde to Vlach villages concerned local evaluations of bride price, as cross-border marriages between Roma were primarily based on the lower price of Roma girls from the Romanian side of the border. Serbian Roma families periodically came to Romanian border villages to look for suitable wives for their sons. According to my 2004 fieldwork, bride prices among the rich Roma in Serbia ranged from €50,000 to €100,000, while the poorer Romanian Roma parents were happy to marry their girls for about €1,000. However, it was not only the bride price that led them to marry their daughters off to Serbia. Again, mobility was at stake. Through marriages with Serbian Roma, girls became part of the mobility arrangements of their husbands and friends, accompanying their new families to Austria or Germany. To get to more Western destinations, girls without arranged marriages to Serbian Roma would rely on already-married women, appealing to these intermediaries to find them cleaning jobs or cheap housing.

In general, relations between housekeepers and their hosts make for an interesting case of proximity and asymmetry. While these women were certainly exploiting a gendered segment of an informal labour market,

thus supporting their families and communities back home and contributing to a counter-geography of globalization (Sassen 2000), they were
also highly personally exploited and subject to the cross-border economy,
deepening its inequalities. Mobility and border crossings, coupled with
changing border regimes, not only produce imaginings and senses of
proximity and asymmetry, but reproduce them on various 'geographical'
scales, from the regional to the local to the workers' and women's bodies. Consistent with this is the 'gendered geographies of power' model
proposed by Mahler and Pessar (2001). First, it says that gender works at
multiple and different spatial levels. Second, migration or mobility can
change the fixed socio-economic statuses held by men and women at their
initial locations. Third, a mutually constitutive process joins these micro-
and meso-level operations of gender to the so-called power geometries
(Massey 1993) that signal the activity and influence of macro-processes
that produce, for example, deindustrialization, unemployment and the re-
treat to agriculture in the border area. Economic informality and precari-
ousness (and the wide availability of hard, low-paid labour) (Anderson
2000), sustained by the state and markets, is a key mechanism through
which the gendered geography of power and consequent particular experiences of proximity and asymmetry are enforced.

Cross-border Day Labour and Mobility

Whereas women tended to be hired for housekeeping, day labour was
more common to men. In recent years, though, so many of the rich Vlach
families already had Romanian housekeepers that newcomers could
hardly find available hosts. Thus women also became active in agriculture
as day labourers or seasonal workers. Borderland and inland Romanians
alike were taken on in agriculture, construction and other unskilled or
semi-skilled activity. Coming mostly from rural areas, they were usually
hired for no more than a couple of days. Compared with other temporary
labourers in Serbia, the day labourer was much more exposed to regular
police harassment and bad treatment by employers. Their work was based
on easily violated verbal agreements. Vlach employers had various ways
of keeping their workers in a subordinate position without control over
payment, work conditions and so on. Meanwhile, the random character of
this occupation meant that earnings were lower than those of housekeepers. As of 2004, a housekeeper might save up to €200 monthly, whereas a
day labourer usually brought home around €100 and counted it a lucky
break to garner €200 or more. The differences between savings were due
to living costs, which the latter covered themselves. For example, Vasile,
a 36-year-old Rudar from Balta Verde, stayed in Serbia working as day la-

bourer for a year around 2003, netting between €100 and €200 monthly. He considers himself very lucky to have retained this much, given that four to seven days per month were workless and accommodation cost around €1 a night.

Immediately after visas were introduced for border crossings in July 2004, the pay for a day's labour in agriculture or construction rose from €10 to €15 or even €20 due to the labour shortage that suddenly struck Vlach border villages. These unskilled workers had to pay certain local insurance taxes of approximately €15 per person, but for Romanian border dwellers, employers usually covered this cost plus accommodation expenses. This was not the only site of differentiation between workers. Vlachs referred to day labourers from the border as friends and neighbours, and accorded them priority when looking for a hire. Moldavians, on the other hand, were negatively privileged as day labourers. As compared with housekeepers and border dwellers, Moldavians were usually unskilled summertime day labourers who could not enter into close relationships with Vlachs. According to my informants, the *patroni* in search of labourers carefully examined not only 'candidates'' bodily appearance but also their origins and relations, asking questions about place of origin, or how many people did they know in Serbia.

Many Vlachs and Serbians at the border who had no labour migration experience and thus did not share in their neighbours' affluence undertook to provide housing for Romanian labourers. 'You might even find five Romanians living at once in one (or two) rooms', an interlocutor told me. Romanian cross-border labourers therefore constituted not only cheap labour but also a fairly stable source of income for impoverished Vlach and Serbian families.

When it came to working conditions, day labour in Serbia was no easy task. 'For example, when someone hoes, the Serbian [Vlach] sits right behind him and eventually tells him how to work better. It's really stressful', a man from Balta Verde told me. Furthermore, harsh treatment by employers was often encouraged by the frequent disputes between different groups of labourers. Conflicts often erupted between workers from the border and Moldavians, as the latter 'are so desperate that they sometimes agree to work for food only', someone stated. Their Vlach bosses were then happy to lower day-labour payments to the more experienced workers, who consequently became very angry at the underbidders who had stymied their income potential.

The typical Vlach employer in a Serbian border village was from a family that owned 30–40 ha of land and a big house. Local labour shortages continuously forced Vlachs to hire Romanian workers, the most available labour force, to run their extended agricultural lands. The ongoing need to maintain or refurbish their villas – which serve and materialize symbolic struggles between neighbours – also created demand for Romanian construction workers.

For most of the labourers, the 'profession' was taught in Serbia, and everyone was available to make some cash doing any kind of work, be it agricultural or construction. The lack of practical skills contributed significantly to day labourers' vulnerability. It is often said that journeywork in construction was very risky, and not only because the workers did not receive the insurance payout in the event of accident. They might receive no money at all for working ten or twelve hours a day, as was sometimes the case when the labourers were supervised by skilled workers at the building site, who usually were acting as intermediaries between landlords and day labourers. When the houses were finished, landlords paid these *majstors*, who were supposed to remunerate the day labourers in turn. Establishing work agreements with these intermediaries was always relative. Unskilled workers like the Moldavians and Eastern Oltenians were usually less experienced in bargaining. Day labour has often been seen as a kind of slavery, as the many stories circulating in the Romanian border villages well document.

Yet day labour was not without certain advantages. Especially face-to-face relations between *patroni* and labourers, where they existed, could develop to the advantage of both. Many Vlachs owned town flats in Negotin or even Belgrade, and even someone without such an urban residence could still have friends or relatives living there. For Romanians, this was an opportunity to make bigger money in the city and to extend their social networks. When these connections developed, they were attractive to many of the lucky ones' workmates and friends. The importance of these relations was most apparent when they facilitated further cross-border mobility. At best, day labourers in Serbia could become day labourers in Austria or Germany through their connections to Vlachs.

To conclude, it was not only cross-border marriages that could lead Romanians to a Western destination. Although labour relations between employers and workers in Serbia often generated stressful proximities and asymmetries, they were another effective source of short- and long-distance cross-border mobility.

Border Regimes and Mobility

In an attempt to harmonize the border with EU mobility regulations, in July 2004 the Romanian government made visas compulsory for citizens of Serbia and Montenegro travelling to Romania. Serbia imposed the same conditions on Romanians travelling to Serbia. In the same period, similar agreements were concluded between Romania on the one hand, and Turkey and Ukraine on the other. Visas for Serbia were expensive, between €27 and €60. Commentators suggested that these costly visas would entirely terminate good relations between border localities and lead to deterioration of political, social and economic contacts. Here is a clearer image of the language of the limited public debate that arose over the issue:

> From Tito up to the present, the Western frontier of Romania has lain outside bureaucratic control, a weird combination of regionalisation and commerce, a large family within which both Serbians and Romanians on each side of the border related to each other through kinship ties. Actually, Romania-Serbia relations form the background of a real Euro-region with no official status, projects or political will. Transforming improvised economic relations into economic and commercial effectiveness would only be a question of political initiative. Nevertheless, in an unaccountable manner, Romania and Serbia build up artificial barriers against regionalisation in this part of Europe. At first sight, the introduction of visas is a blow to small border crossers – thousands of people getting their living from the border. The effect of introducing visas is actually more global: it re-establishes bureaucracy by removing the freedom of movement. At national and regional level, visas induce suspicion. While the international context seems to be auspicious for the abolishment of frontiers, Romania builds a barrier right on our most friendly borderland. (*Evenimentul Zilei*, 29 June 2004)

According to the media, negative economic consequences were apparent within the first two weeks. In mid July, Romanian tourism and transport companies downsized their activities dramatically. Tourism decreased by around 90 per cent compared to the previous period (*Evenimentul Zilei*, 13 July 2004), former tourists to Serbia having been mostly day labourers, seasonal workers and traders. One day after the implementation of the visa regime, a border policeman at the Moraviţa checkpoint stated, 'If the number of travellers exceeded 57,000 in May 2004, the current situation is that nobody has crossed the border to Serbia in the last ten hours' (*Evenimentul Zilei*, 2 July 2004). The same mood should have prevailed at Iron Gates I. When I was back in Gogoşu and Balta Verde in July 2004, many people were at work in Serbia, waiting to come back to purchase new visas from consulates in Timişoara or Bucharest. Those remaining at home had very dim expectations about future work or trading in Serbia.

Before the introduction of visas, the average daily number of people crossing the border to Serbia through Moraviţa was around 1,400. The opposite flow from Serbia to Romania had not exceeded 400 people a day (*Evenimentul Zilei*, 29 June 2004). Most of the Serbians still travelling to

Romania were kiosk owners or shopkeepers who replenished their stocks from the wholesale markets in Bucharest and other Romanian cities.

Long queues of hundreds of people appeared at the Serbian consulate in Bucharest and Timişoara shortly thereafter. Prior to visas, people who worked regularly in Serbia had been used to travelling without making bureaucratic arrangements apart from bribes paid to drivers and at checkpoints. But from 2004 to 2007, they paid cash at consulates to get visas on their passports – and this took time. The consulates' processing of visa applications usually lasted between fifteen and thirty days. Another serious obstacle posed by the visa regime was that not everyone received the letter of invitation from a Vlach employer that was required for the visa. Again, the workers most likely to receive the document were the border dwellers.

Still, massive numbers of visas were issued. For example, the Timişoara consulate issued around 8,500 visas during the four weeks of July 2004 (*România Liberă*, 31 July 2004). This quantity indicates the importance of Vlach localities in the lives of Romanian border dwellers. Favourable social relations between workers and employers, as well as labour supply and demand, sped up the circulation of invitations.

When I met Rodica in July 2004, she was waiting to receive an invitation letter from her host. Some cross-border workers regarded the invitations that employers had to send to workers after July 2004 as a boon, as they relieved workers of the need to go to the checkpoint to renew their one-month visas. Some expected the new regulations to lead to more secure work arrangements. They could stay in Serbia until their consulate-issued visas expired. The invitations were to be delivered by licensed drivers who regularly crossed the border to supply their shops. Otherwise, the host came to Romania in person to hand the letter of invitation to the worker. A few days after the visa regime was introduced, the returning workers themselves were carrying out this mailing service, getting three or four invitation letters from various employers to distribute to neighbours in their village. For example, a woman I talked to in the field in 2004 had, upon her last return from Serbia, brought three letters of invitation from a single Vlach host addressed to some of her neighbours.

The first thing Rodica had to do when she got back to Serbia was to prove she was a documented 'tourist', that is, a person paying a visit to Serbian Vlach acquaintances for one month or so. This meant she had to show her papers, especially the visa, to the local police. From the police she got a kind of Serbian identity card bearing her name and the hosts' identity. With money enough to prove ability to sustain the living of several people, a 'host' could send invitations to several Romanian workers.

Upon arriving in Serbia, workers usually spread all over the village looking for real 'hosts' to stay with or work for. The Vlachs who were eligible
to invite more people than they needed for themselves were usually former guest workers benefiting from Austrian or German pensions.

The available means of transport have undergone important changes
and adaptations too. July 2004 marked a sudden decline in the business
of tour operators. As most of them had no transport licenses, they were
replaced by private drivers engaged in transporting small groups of up
to four persons through the checkpoints. Workers, even those from Eastern Oltenia or Moldavia, knew all the details about this new opportunity.
Drivers' names and phone numbers circulated widely around consulates and in small villages and border towns. In May 2005, while hanging
around with a group of Moldavians waiting for their visa appointments
in Bucharest, I witnessed the spontaneous formation of a small group of
'tourists' looking for such cross-border transport facilities. A man from
Bacău came around and asked who was interested in crossing the border at Iron Gates I. After several people showed interest, he said he was
in close contact with a driver who could arrange a safe trip through the
border checkpoint. Several people in the queue said they knew that driver
very well and confirmed that he was trustworthy. Although they had been
total strangers until this moment, the men left the queue to arrange the details of the trip. It took them five minutes to decide which bus to take from
Bucharest to Drobeta-Turnu Severin, where to stay overnight, and so on.

Conclusion

By pointing out several border events and responses to them, this chapter
described the state and the EU's recent attempt to change the Romanian-
Serbian border and its subjective, practical and relational implications
for cross-border mobility. In the first weeks and months after July 2004,
changes in the visa regime created discontent in border villages and towns,
changed life projects and mobility routes and, most important for the argument here, reactivated creative social relations between Vlach *patroni*
and Romanian workers so they could both surmount the obstacles posed
by the new regulations. Flows of persons and goods were thus restored,
demonstrating that in the decades after socialism, border crossers subjec-
tively appropriated the changing border regimes and transformed them
into highly adaptive, informal codes of knowledge.

The Romanian-Serbian border should, I suggest, be seen as a particular place characterized by local socio-economic asymmetries that do not
necessarily reflect interstate comparisons based on national indicators,

international rankings or media constructions. What I have covered here is a particular instance of organizing production, distribution and consumption as conducive for social relations, proximities and asymmetries that in turn maintained and adapted cross-border mobility in the context of changes in the border regimes. I tried to show how socialism initiated a process of forging social relations across the border, and how the border regimes, as highly negotiable and relational constructs, allowed traders disguised as tourists to enter into regular mobility. The chapter also pointed to how social relations went further underground and expanded after 1989, consolidating an interconnected world of cross-border mobility based on trade, contraband, work and marriages at the 'margins' of the EU. Post-2004 adaptations in social relations, such as circulating invitations and recently devised approaches to cross-border transport as well as the continuity of cross-border trading and work long after the Romanian EU accession in 2007, are illustrative. In addition, the border's ability to resist the European and global geographical and political rescaling desired for EU accession in this region of Europe (through a multitude of processes known collectively as cross-border securitization and external EU border making) is a nice metaphor of the state's and Schengen's limits.

The transnationalism, migration and mobility theories discussed earlier in the chapter show limits but also provide interesting conceptual categories for studying border crossings and border regimes, and their transformations and rerouting. The chapter has argued that the anthropology of borders is a privileged body of knowledge that can expand and develop understanding of cross-border mobility and its relations to border regimes. Proximity and asymmetry, both imagined and present in everyday practice within class and gender divisions and the border's working situations, appear as key notions facilitating this understanding. In different border regimes, proximity indicates different processes of subject making and different social relations. It is consequently conducive to different senses of asymmetry, which are already at the root of any face-to-face relationship. The border regime and the form of mobility undertaken by the border crossers, as both possibility and action, are interpersonal, intersubjective processes based on historical developments of proximity and asymmetry on different scales, from the national and regional to the body, senses and ideas about the other. Proximity is thus definable as much more than physical distance or closeness. It is a domain of experience intricately linked to ongoing permissions and restrictions to mobility (and immobility). Sometimes it is realized in physical absence, as virtual co-presence; other times it is based on real co-presence. Border-crossing, mobility and the border regimes are ways to help organize proximity, but they are also constituted by the senses of proximity and asymmetry, and by relations at the border - all developed and experienced in different periods of time.

Meanwhile, the question whether mobility and border regimes were resources or boundaries at the Romanian-Serbian border is still open. Interestingly, cross-border mobility appears to have mired some crossers in exploitative, reproductive, precarious labour for a long time, preventing their making better decisions for further movement associated with better pay and working conditions. In a different register, this chapter invites anthropologists of frontiers to consider processes of mobility and their relations to the dwelling in place. This involves consideration of various scales of practice and action that could open borders more to subjectivity, practical experience and alternative spatio-temporalizations.

Acknowledgements

The author thanks Jutta Lauth Bacas, William Kavanagh, Gideon Kressel, Dumitru Sandu and the Berghahn anonymous reviewers for their critical comments on different versions of this chapter.

Notes

1. The Iron Gates II checkpoint, which is situated just nearby the two villages, opened in December 2011.

References

Alford, C.F. 2004. 'Levinas and Political Theory', *Political Theory* 32(2): 146–71.
Alvarez, R.R. 1995. 'The Mexican-US Border: The Making of an Anthropology of Borderlands', *Annual Review of Anthropology* 24: 447–70.
Anderson, B. 2000. *Doing the Dirty Work: The Global Politics of Domestic Labour.* London: Zed.
Anzaldua, G. 1987. *Borderlands/La Frontera: The New Mestiza.* San Francisco: Aunt Lute Books.
Basch, L., N. Glick Schiller and C. Szanton Blanc. 1994. *Nations Unbound: Transnational Projects, Postcolonial Predicaments and Deterritorialized Nation-States.* New York: Gordon and Breach.
Boden, D. and H. Molotch. 1994. 'The Compulsion of Proximity', in R. Friedland and D. Boden (eds), *Nowhere: Space, Time and Modernity.* Berkeley: University of California Press, pp. 257–86.
Chalfin, B. 2006. 'Global Customs Regimes and the Traffic in Sovereignty: Enlarging the Anthropology of the State', *Current Anthropology* 47(2): 243–76.

Cole, J.W., and E.R. Wolf. 1974. *The Hidden Frontier: Ecology and Ethnicity in an Alpine Valley*. New York and London: Academic Press.

Cunningham, H. and J. Heyman. 2004. 'Introduction: Mobilities and Enclosures at Borders', *Identities: Global Studies in Culture and Power* 11: 289–302.

Donnan, H., and T.M. Wilson. 1999. *Borders: Frontiers of Identity, Nation and State*. Oxford: Berg.

Donnan, H., and T.M. Wilson. 2010. 'Ethnography, Security and the "Frontier Effect" in Borderlands', in H. Donnan and T.M. Wilson (eds), *Borderlands: Ethnographic Approaches to Security, Power, and Identity*. Lanham, MD, Boulder, CO, New York, Toronto, Plymouth, UK: University Press of America, pp. 1–20.

Erman, E. 2006. 'Reconciling Communicative Action with Recognition : Thickening the "Inter" of Intersubjectivity', *Philosophy & Social Criticism* 32(3): 377–400.

Glick Schiller, N. 2003. 'The Centrality of Ethnography in the Study of Transnational Migration', in N. Foner (ed.), *American Arrivals: Anthropology Engages the New Immigration*. Sante Fe, NM: School of American Research Press, pp. 99–128.

Glick Schiller, N., and G. Fouron. 2001. *Georges Woke Up Laughing: Long Distance Nationalism and the Search for Home*. Durham, NC: Duke University Press.

Green, S. 2005. *Notes from the Balkans: Locating Marginality and Ambiguity on the Greek-Albanian Border*. Princeton, NJ, and Oxford: Princeton University Press.

———. 2009. 'Lines, Traces and Tidemarks: Reflections on Forms of Borderli-ness'. East-BordNet, COST Action IS0803 Working Paper.

Halfacree, K. 2012. 'Heterolocal Identities? Counter-Urbanisation, Second Homes, and Rural Consumption in the Era of Mobilities', *Population, Space and Place* 18(2): 209–24.

Heyman, J. 1994. 'The Mexico-United States Border in Anthropology: A Critique and Reformulation', *Journal of Political Ecology* 1: 43–66.

———. 1995. 'Putting Power in the Anthropology of Bureaucracy: The Immigration and Naturalization Service at the Mexico-United States Border', *Current Anthropology* 36(2): 261–87.

Horowitz, A. 2002. '"By a Hair's Breadth": Critique, Transcendence and the Ethical in Adorno and Levinas', *Philosophy & Social Criticism* 28(2): 213–48.

Kearney, M. 2004. 'The Classifying and Value-filtering Missions of Borders', *Anthropological Theory* 4(2): 131–56.

King, R. 2012. 'Geography and Migration Studies: Retrospect and Prospect'. *Population, Space and Place* 18: 134–53.

Kohlbacher, J. and U. Reeger. 1999. 'Polonia in Vienna: Polish Labour Migration during the 1990s', in G. Crampton (ed.), *Regional Unemployment, Job Matching and Migration. European Research in Regional Science* 9. London: Pion, pp. 111–42.

Konstantinov, Y. 1996. 'Patterns of Reinterpretation: Trader-Tourism in the Balkans (Bulgaria) as a Picaresque Metaphorical Enactment of Post-totalitarianism', *American Ethnologist* 23(4): 762–82.

Levinas, E. 1998. *Otherwise than Being or Beyond Essence*. Pittsburgh, PA: Duquesne University Press.

Levitt, P. and N. Glick Schiller. 2004. 'Conceptualizing Simultaneity: A Transnational Social Field Perspective on Society', *The International Migration Review* 38(3): 1002–40.

Mahler, S. and P. Pessar. 2001. 'Gendered Geographies of Power: Analyzing Gender across Transnational Spaces', *Identities* 7: 441–59.

Massey, D. 1991. 'A Global Sense of Place'. *Marxism Today* (June): 24–29.

———. 1993. 'Power Geometry and Progressive Sense of Place', in J. Bird, B. Curtis, T. Putnam, G. Robertson and L. Tickner (eds), *Mapping the Future: Local Cultures, Global Change*. London: Routledge, pp. 59–69.

———. 2005. *For Space*. London: Routledge.

Massey, D.S., et al. 1998. 'New Migrations, New Theories', in D.S. Massey et al. (eds), *Worlds in Motion: Understanding International Migration at the End of the Millenium*. Oxford: Oxford University Press, pp. 1–16.

Massey, D.S. and E.J. Taylor. 2004. 'Introduction', in D.S. Massey and E.J. Taylor (eds), *International Migration: Prospects and Policies*. Oxford: Oxford University Press, pp. 1–14.

Pellegrino, G. 2011. 'Introduction: Studying (Im)mobility through a Politics of Proximity', in G. Pellegrino (ed.), *The Politics of Proximity: Mobility and Immobility in Practice*. Surrey: Ashgate.

Portes, A. 2003. 'Theoretical Convergencies and Empirical Evidence in the Study of Immigrant Transnationalism', *International Migration Review* 37: 814–92.

Radu, C. 2009. 'Border Tricksters and the Predatory State: Contraband at the Romania-Serbia Border during the Yugoslavian Embargoes', *Focaal: Journal of Global and Historical Anthropology* 54: 49–63.

———. 2010. 'Beyond Border-'dwelling': Temporalising the Border-space through Events', *Anthropological Theory* 10(4): 409–33.

———. 2012. 'Frontier Effects and Tidemarks: A Commentary in the Anthropology of Borders', in M. Canevacci (ed), *Polyphonic Anthropology – Theoretical and Empirical Cross-cultural Fieldwork*. InTech, pp. 19–32. Available from: http://www.intechopen.com/books/polyphonic-anthropology-theoretical-and-empirical-cross-cultural-fieldwork/frontier-effects-and-tidemarks-a-commentary-in-the-anthropology-of-borders

———. Forthcoming. 'Dwelling and Crossing the Frontier: Political Subjectivities and Moving Landscapes at the Romania-Serbia Border', *New Europe College Yearbook*.

Rosaldo, R. 1988. 'Ideology, Place and People without Culture', *Cultural Anthropology* 3(1): 77–87.

Sahlins, P. 1998. 'State Formation and National Identity in the Catalan Borderlands during the Eighteenth and Nineteenth Centuries', in T.M. Wilson and H. Donnan (eds), *Border Identities: Nation and State at International Frontiers*. Cambridge: Cambridge University Press, pp. 31–61.

Sassen, S. 2000. 'Women's Burden: Counter-geographies of Globalization and the Feminization of Survival', *Journal of International Affairs* 53: 503–24.

Schierup, C.-U. 1990. *Migration, Socialism and the International Division of Labour: The Yugoslav Experience*. Avebury: Aldershot.

Simmel, G. 1950. *The Sociology of Georg Simmel*. New York: Free Press.

Urry, J. 2000. *Sociology beyond Societies*. London: Routledge.

———. 2002. 'Mobility and Proximity', *Sociology* 36(2): 255–74.

———. 2007. *Mobilities*. Cambridge: Polity.

Wallace, C. 2002. 'Opening and Closing Borders: Migration and Mobility in East-Central Europe', *Journal of Ethnic and Migration Studies* 28(4): 603–25.

Wallace, C. and D. Stola. 2001. 'Conceptual Challenges from the New Migration Space', in C. Wallace and D. Stola (eds), *Patterns of Migration in Central Europe*. Basingstoke and New York: Palgrave Macmillian, pp. 45–71.

Williams, A.M. and V. Baláž. 2002. 'Trans-border Population Mobility at a European Crossroads: Slovakia in the Shadow of EU Accession', *Journal of Ethnic and Migration Studies* 28(4): 647–64.

Wilson, T.M. and H. Donnan. 1998. 'Nation, State and Identity at International Borders', in T.M. Wilson and H. Donnan (eds), *Border Identities: National and State at International Frontiers*. Cambridge: Cambridge University Press, pp. 1–30.

Chapter 8

'We Used to Be One Country'
Rural Transformations, Economic Asymmetries and
National Identities in the Ukrainian-Russian Borderlands

Tatiana Zhurzhenko

In 1991, the administrative boundary between the two Soviet republics Ukraine and Russia became an international border.[1] The process of border making (introduction of passport and customs controls, reorganization of transport routes, restructuring of labour markets) made the territory of the neighbouring state less accessible and more 'distant' for the population of the Ukrainian-Russian borderlands. As a consequence, people have learned to adjust their social networks, mobility routes and shopping and leisure habits to the new situation and take the fact of the border into account in their labour market and education strategies. At the same time, the new situation of being a periphery, a borderland territory, is perceived differently on the different sides of the Ukrainian-Russian border. Not only do schoolbooks and national media give different interpretations of the same historical facts and quite recent events (such as the Orange Revolution), but the new border and related economic asymmetry also create additional opportunities and/or disadvantages for local inhabitants, thereby contributing to the shaping of new national identities – Ukrainian and Russian. Bordering and reordering of habitual spaces, combined with nation-building policies on both sides of the border, challenge the traditional cultural proximity inherited from the Soviet era. These changes in the individual and collective mental maps are reinforced by radical social and economic transformations – land reform, dismantling of the *kolkhoz*es (collective farms) and emergence of private

Notes for this chapter begin on page 211.

agricultural companies, rising unemployment and social insecurity. Now, in the eyes of the local population, market transformations and their negative effects are inseparable from the fact of the new border. Spatial and temporal boundaries are closely related: the new border manifests the irreversibility of the post-1991 political and social changes, thus separating not only Ukraine from Russia, but also the new Ukrainian state from an imagined Soviet Union.

This chapter analyses narratives of border crossing and border encounters, as well as perceptions and images of the new border, among Ukrainians and Russians living in its close vicinity. It focuses on the particular experience of people who became 'borderlanders despite themselves' due to the collapse of Soviet Union while also being confronted with the market transformations and nation building policies of the new post-Soviet states. The concepts of 'asymmetry' and 'proximity', which are key to my interpretation of the ethnographic material, are not entirely new in border studies. For example, in his study of the U.S.-Mexico border cultures, Josiah M. Heyman (2010: 22) poses the question 'how the asymmetries in power and prosperity affect the formation of culturally distinctive groups and the relations between such groups'. The new economic and power asymmetries in Ukrainian-Russian relations and the asymmetry caused by the de facto dominant role of the Russian language, culture and media in Ukraine have a direct impact on the everyday life of the borderlanders, their pragmatic choices and national loyalties. Proximity in border interactions manifests itself through routine encounters with the neighbours across the border, representatives of state power (border guards, custom officers, police) and smugglers. But in this chapter I also refer to the concept of 'cultural proximity' to characterize the culturally homogeneous, still non-differentiated post-Soviet space of the Ukrainian-Russian borderlands.

Therefore, the key question I try to answer in this chapter is how the new asymmetries resulting from the fact of the border and from the different economic and social dynamics in both countries challenge cultural proximity between Ukrainians and Russians living in the borderlands and contribute to the formation of new national identities. The chapter is based on focus groups and individual interviews conducted in the summers of 2003 and 2004 in three villages of the Kharkiv oblast in Ukraine and in two villages of the Belgorod oblast in the Russian Federation (RF). The focus groups consisted of people from various occupations: teachers, village administrators, medical personal, bookkeepers, lorry drivers, workers in agricultural enterprises and small farmers as well as pensioners, students and the unemployed. The focus group interviews involved three groups of questions. The first concerned local history and the Soviet past, particularly issues of language, ethnic and national identities. The second dealt with the economic and social aspects of near-border life: job and business opportunities, social infrastructure, pensions and salaries, small cross-border trade and contraband. The final, third set of questions was about feelings and emotions related to the border and border crossing.

The first section of the chapter introduces the reader to the political, economic and cultural context of the Ukrainian-Russian borderlands, focusing on new and old asymmetries created or reinforced by the new international border. The second section addresses the local population's regular encounters with state actors such as border guards, customs officers and police, and analyses the new relations of proximity emerging from these interactions. The third section focuses on local narratives of social change and continuity with the Soviet past. It argues that economic asymmetries resulting from the different dynamics of rural transformations in the Kharkiv and Belgorod oblasts are reflected in local discourses about 'Russians' and 'Ukrainians' as new national collectives. The final section shows how new national identities have emerged despite the inherited cultural proximity in the Ukrainian-Russian borderlands and points to the role of the cultural and sociolinguistic asymmetry resulting from the still-dominant status of the Russian language in this process.

Asymmetry and Proximity in
the Ukrainiàn-Russian Borderlands

Before 1991, the border between Ukraine and Russia existed on maps, but not for those who crossed it. Russians and Ukrainians carried the same Soviet passports, and personal information contained in them (place of birth and current place of registration, as well as 'nationality') did not have symbolic links to the territory. There were, of course, limitations on freedom of movement caused by the system of forced registration (*propiska*) and other significant barriers that structured the social spaces and life worlds of the Soviet people: military zones, so-called closed cities and highly protected near-border areas were not easy to enter (Brednikova and Voronkov 1999: 20). But in practice the administrative boundaries between the Soviet republics did not matter in everyday life – people worked, studied, shopped and visited friends across the 'virtual' border.

In Eastern Ukrainian oblasts bordering Russia, many people saw the collapse of the Soviet Union and the materialization of the new border as a dramatic change that threatened their mobility and social networks. Of course the border did not emerge overnight, and hopes of some kind of reunification or substitute for the USSR remained in the early 1990s. Russia's position that the borders inside the Commonwealth of Independent States should stay 'transparent' certainly corresponded to the mood of the local population. But Ukraine saw national borders and the ability to control them as an important attribute of state independence. In 2003, the Agreement on the State Border between Ukraine and Russia was signed, finalizing four years of negotiations on the delimitation of the Ukrainian-Russian border (the land part). The official demarcation of the border on the ground started only in 2012. Border and customs controls were established at the Ukrainian-Russian border in 1992, above all on the main highways and railways with the urgent purpose of preventing massive smuggling caused by the uneven effects of price liberalization and the sudden disruption of economic ties between Ukrainian and Russian enterprises. But it took a long time to tighten border control enough that people accepted the new border as 'serious and for a while'.[2]

The border significantly changed the economic and social situation in the near-border villages, creating new hierarchies and inequalities. For example, for Udy and Zemlianky (both in Ukraine) the new border, combined with the long distance to Kharkiv and worsened transport connections, means further marginalization and economic stagnation. At the same time, the inhabitants of Hlyboke (Ukraine) and Zhuravlevka (RF) instead profit from the new border. The village of Hlyboke, located only 35 km from Kharkiv, is in a particularly advantageous position: its residents can use a regular bus route connection to work and study in the city. Neighbours in Zhuravlevka on the Russian side once worked in Kharkiv too, but now the border makes this impossible. Fortunately for them, the new crossing point and the big Nekhoteevka transport terminal on the Moscow-Crimea highway were built just 5 km away. The terminal provides Zhuravlevka's inhabitants with various jobs, from customs and border controls to technical services, shops and petrol stations.

These new local hierarchies and inequalities overlap with economic and power asymmetry in Ukrainian-Russian relations, which is also reflected in different economic and social dynamics in the Kharkiv and Belgorod oblasts. At the time of this field research, the Belgorod oblast was definitely more prosperous than the Kharkiv one. Belgorod's economic revival had started earlier and moved faster due to a more balanced economic structure and the advantage of a relatively late modernization (Kolossov and Vendina 2002: 24–26). The average salary in the Kharkiv oblast in the early 2000s was only 80 per cent of that in Belgorod. Correspondingly, on the Russian side pensions and other social benefits were higher, and many social indicators, such as housing provision, medical services and crime rates, were better. A survey conducted in June 2001 among residents of both oblasts who were interviewed when crossing the border showed that the level of social optimism and satisfaction with the social and economic situation in their country was higher among Russian citizens (Kolossov and Vendina 2002: 39).

These differences concern populations both urban and rural. In the 1990s, the agricultural sectors in both Ukraine and Russia suffered from economic recession. Peasants got shares of land after the kolkhozes were dismantled, but only a small percentage of families managed to launch private farms before big agricultural firms swallowed up the remnants of the kolkhozes. Now most agricultural workers lease their shares of land to these new monopolists in the village, which also provide them with seasonal work. People earn a living from their household plots, which cost little to farm and are intended to provide food just for the family. In many cases, however, part of the produce goes to the market: primarily milk and milk products, but also vegetables and meat. Rural transformation in Russia's Black Earth region has followed a similar path (Allina-Pisano 2008), but in the Belgorod oblast the agricultural decline of the 1990s was less dramatic than in Kharkiv. Moreover, private investments and local policies led by the agricultural lobby made Belgorod one of the most economically successful Russian provinces. At the time of my research, this Belgorod agricultural 'miracle' was especially visible in Shchetinovka (RF), a village just 5 km from the border with Ukraine. Part of the Frunze kolkhoz, which prospered in the 1970s and 1980s, it was not dismantled after 1991 but adapted successfully to the new market conditions. To the envy of its Ukrainian (and Russian) neighbours, the Frunze kolkhoz invested in the social infrastructure of the village, provided jobs, helped pensioners and offered higher salaries to teachers.

The border has also created new cultural and sociolinguistic asymmetries, challenging the cultural proximity inherited from the Soviet era but rooted deeper in history. In the seventeenth century this territory was a vast, thinly populated frontier zone between the Muscovy state, the Tatar Khanate and the Polish-Lithuanian Commonwealth. Russian and Ukrainian ethnic settlements historically coexisted in this area (Chizhikova, 1988). Cultural boundaries between the two ethnic groups (clothing, elements of house design and decoration, religious holidays) almost disappeared in the twentieth century, especially under the pressure of Soviet rural modernization. In the 1920s, the administrative border between Soviet Ukraine and the Russian Federation was drawn generally according to ethnic and linguistic criteria, but each republic had some ethnic enclaves left on the other side of the border. The Soviet nationalities policy encouraged ethnic differentiation at that time, so the administrative division of territory down to the village councils and kolkhoz level was based on ethnic criteria in both Ukraine and Russia (Martin 2001). But from the end of the 1920s on, ethnic Ukrainians in Russia were subjected to intensive Russification. They did not have access to Ukrainian-language education or press, unlike ethnic Russians in Ukraine, who could usually attend Russian or bilingual schools. As a result, most people on the Ukrainian side of the border now have some competence in both Ukrainian and Russian and understand both languages without difficulty. Surzhyk, a mixture of Ukrainian and Russian, is widespread there (Bilaniuk 2005) and is also spoken in many border villages on the Russian side, where assimilated ethnic Ukrainians form a significant part of the population. Mixed marriages between ethnic Ukrainians and Russians are common, and most people have relatives in both countries. Finally, most residents of Ukrainian and Russian villages alike consider themselves Orthodox and belong to the Orthodox Church of Moscow Patriarchy.

The arrival of state independence raised the status of the Ukrainian language, but Russian still dominates in Eastern Ukraine – a top problem on the agenda of many Ukrainian politicians. However, politicization of the language issue is confined to the big cities; the rural population usually stays indifferent to the cultural wars of the urban elites. Since 1991, the Kharkiv oblast has experienced a half-hearted Ukrainization of education and the administrative system, which has left room for compromise and flexibility for local actors. In Udy, formerly an ethnic Russian village, the Russian language still dominates today (some old people still speak the local Kursk dialect of Russian). Moreover, the language of instruction in the local school is still officially Russian, making it the only Russian-language school in the district. In Zemlianky the local school has always been Ukrainian, and the Hlyboke school switched from Russian to Ukrainian in 2000. Compared to this complexity, the linguistic policy on the Russian side is less ambivalent: Ukrainian language is not in the curriculum, even as an option, though Ukrainian folklore is usually welcomed. The persisting asymmetry of the Russian and Ukrainian languages remains a problem in relations between the two countries. On the local level, it overlaps with other asymmetries and hierarchies emerging from the growing relevance of the cultural and language issues. The best example is Udy, which, having gained special exceptional status as an 'ethnic Russian village' under Ukrainian law, is allowed to keep Russian in the local school and administration. Many village inhabitants regard this exceptional status with ambivalence and would prefer assimilation to Ukrainian as a better option for their children (Zhurzhenko 2010: 309–14).

Encountering State Power in the Borderlands

In social anthropology, a border is seen not as a line but as a special zone with its own rules, an area where the power of the state is particularly concentrated, visible and felt by people in their everyday lives. 'To the inhabitants of an area adjacent to a state boundary, the degree of compulsion is partially higher than that of residents of the interior of the country' (Lunden and Zalamans 2000: 2). In her study of the Russian-Estonian border, Olga Brednikova highlights 'the effects of a border as a political tool of state building on restructuring of the habitual social space, destroying old ties and developing new social networks' (Brednikova 1999: 19). In this section I trace similar processes at the Ukrainian-Russian border by showing how state power manifests itself in the borderlands and how people respond to it.

Geographic proximity to the border (all five villages – Udy, Zemlianky and Hlyboke in Ukraine and Zhuravlevka and Shchetinovka in Russia – are situated in the special near-border zone) makes encounters with border guards, custom officers and police a matter of routine. For local residents, the main impact of the new border is that they need to be always ready to show identification. In other words, the new border means carrying a passport, even if one does not intend to cross the border but only to go, for example, to one's own vegetable garden. The constant presence of

Figure 8.1. Kozacha Lopan, a railway station halfway between Kharkiv and Belgorod on the Ukrainian-Russian border. The border guard patrol is on its way to check the local train. (Photo: Tatiana Zhurzhenko)

this institution of state power – border guards who define the new rules of behaviour – has changed the habitual space of everyday life. Mobile patrols can stop anybody on the way to the border and search a private car; they can temporarily block the road or enforce a detour. Regulations in the near-border controlled zone oblige agricultural workers to submit information about their fields and cultivated crops to local border control offices. Some crops, such as maize and sunflower, are not allowed at the border because smugglers can hide among the plants. The official announcements displayed at villages' administrative offices – warnings about the danger of illegal migration, possible crimes and serious diseases linked to illegal migrants; calls for local inhabitants to report strange or unknown people seen in the village or its surroundings; requests for voluntary fingerprinting – reminds people that their village now belongs to a special zone with extraordinary rules.

Crossing the border by private car is no trivial matter because any car, even with an empty trunk, has to pass customs control. Customs control points are installed only on main roads, which means a significant loss of time and petrol for the local population. The unpredictable wait time at the border and the sometimes humiliating routine of border checks make people feel the disadvantage of their new situation. From the perspective of border guards, however, construction of a new border requires special efforts to discipline and educate the local population so as to bring order to the 'chaos' of free movement (in the official rhetoric these unpopular practices are justified as building a 'civilized border'):

> Once my husband and I, we went by car to visit our friends. They stopped us ... and I had only a student ID, I had left my passport for registration in the administration. So, they forced me to get out of the car ... and said: go back and bring your passport. We'll keep your husband with the car ... so I turned and walked back through the fields ... then, some minutes later, they reconsidered and said [to the husband], 'OK, go drive her home and then come back'. Imagine the situation, what they were saying was: 'We will seize your car and you go by foot and bring your passport.' (f., 26 years, Hlyboke).

Local administrations usually support the border guards' attempts to 'educate' and discipline the local population. Not surprisingly, an affirmative discourse on the new border is common among local administration workers in both Ukraine and Russia. For them, 'state interests' and economic benefits justify the border. Deliberately or not, Soviet connotations are often evoked when the authorities call for the 'responsibility' and 'vigilance' of ordinary citizens:

> Border guards ... they make announcements. For example: please tell people who are registered here that they should always carry their passports with them.

> We understand, this is a border zone [*pogranzona*] ... in a way, we are proud ...
> we feel responsible, we are a border zone ... so we got used to it. If we go some-
> where we should have our passports on us. (f., administrator, 54, Hlyboke)

> It is a status or something ... pride or some kind of responsibility ... you know,
> now the village symbol ... it turns out to be a border post ... others have, for
> example, a chicken – they have a chicken farm ... and we have a border post!
> (f., 40, Zhuravlevka).

To mobilize support from within the local population, the border guards
willingly cooperate not only with village administrations but also with the
schools. Special lectures are given to make children aware of possible near-
border threats (illegal migration and contraband) and encourage them to
cooperate with the border guards. This is maybe the most effective way
to anchor the border in the human heads and make its presence natural
for the next generation, since for older people it will always remain rather
artificial. School administrations usually find such cooperation with the
border guards useful and adapt it to its own needs.

How do people react to this interference by state power in their lives?
Usually, it seems, they just try to ignore it as irrelevant. In their narratives,
local inhabitants tried to 'normalize' the new situation using phrases such
as 'we are an ordinary village'; 'they [the border guards] have their business, and we do not know much about it'; 'we got used to them'; 'nothing
has changed'. Attempts to cope with the new proximity of the state power
are reflected in the use of the pejorative term *pograntsy* (deriving from the
Russian *pogranichniki*) for border guards, and in the numerous jokes about
them. At the same time, local inhabitants, especially schoolteachers and
public servants, often internalize the arguments of the state. In the next
extract, the head of the village administration in Zhuravlevka (RF) tries to
challenge what she thinks is our assumption that the border plays a negative role in village life. Her narrative avoids the contradiction between
'state interests' and the interests of the village inhabitants:

> All this talk about open borders ... you know ... in the end ... we do not really
> care. I feel nothing special ... in fact this border ... it does not limit me ... it does
> not press ... it was a moment ... psychological ... we overcame it. The thing is
> ... why can't the Russian state give up the borders? It is not a secret ... I think
> you know ... the customs provides the state budget with money ... and this
> is teachers' and doctors' salaries ... who would give this up? Now it is rather
> comfortable to cross.... With the border our people, population, found jobs. (f.,
> 53, Zhuravlevka)

In no way are local residents merely passive objects of border construction policies. One anthropological study on state power at the border has
argued that 'the powerless, among others, have a variety of behavioural

options at their disposal, including violence, avoidance, resistance, inclusion and exclusion, many forms of which have been called by James Scott (1985) the "weapons of the weak"' (Donnan and Wilson 1999: 63). For many reasons, people do not always obey the formal rules for crossing the border. Often they are just following routine and do not see illegal crossing as a crime. They do it to save time or to avoid contact with the border officials, especially when they are engaged in petty contraband or do not have the required documents on them. One can better understand such an attitude by recalling how important informal practices were in the Soviet economy: for example, petty theft of kolkhoz property (a packet of seeds or food for animals) legally qualified as a crime but was widely tolerated by the authorities as a kind of informal economic stimulus. In his research on the Belize-Mexico border, Bruce Wiegand has shown how perceived notions of social justice rooted in the social class system determined the popular opinion of the legitimacy of smuggling as well as political willingness to enforce laws against such criminal behaviour (Wiegand 1993). The local population at the Ukrainian-Russian border sees the existence of large-scale organized contraband and corruption as justifying their right to adapt the border regime to their own needs. In their narratives people use various euphemisms for illegal crossing: to go 'through the fields' (*poliami* or *ogorodami*), by 'goats' paths' (*koz'imi tropami*), by 'partisans' paths' (*partizanskimi tropami*).

People are convinced, probably not without reason, that the informal (or even illegal) way is simpler and cheaper. It is easier to make a deal with a personal representative of the state authorities than to follow the formal rules. This makes sense, for these rules are often changing and unclear, and therefore leave space for various interpretations, which in turn invites harassment and bribery. The interviews indicate that people often perceive crossing the border as a matter of luck (indeed, one of the local newspapers used to publish a weekly horoscope for those who were going to cross the border). But at the same time, everyday informal practices of dealing with the border are grounded in rational knowledge of a particular kind: for example, which border police unit is on duty today, when they take their lunch break, and so on.

This local situational knowledge is also a valuable resource that can be offered to smugglers in exchange for a material benefit. Some interviewees tried to convince us that the organized smugglers now have perfect maps, 'made from space' (i.e., based on satellite photographs), and are equipped with advanced military devices to orient themselves in the territory, so that they no longer need the help of the locals. But accidental encounters with professional smugglers are another aspect of border life in any case. Facing a choice of whose side to take – the state represented by the border guards, or a stranger – local inhabitants often help the latter, in hope of material benefit or just motivated by solidarity:

> The people's mood ... the population is inclined to help the smugglers rather than the border guards. People do not trust the police ... and this is projected onto the border guards. If they see a guy around the corner with huge bags, full of stuff ... everybody will come and tell him: there are *pograntsy* [pejorative nickname for border guards] over there [people laugh]. So with us it's the opposite attitude ... we have pity for these people: 'poor people ... they have to earn money'. Nobody will go to the border guards and tell them: look, now my neighbour will go ... no, this will never happen ... despite all these assistance groups. Nobody will inform about the neighbours... Or even about strangers (f., housewife, 26, Hlyboke)

Illegal crossing, petty contraband and sometimes collaboration with professional smugglers are typical forms of opportunistic behaviour among the near-border population. As some people admitted, these activities are rooted in a deep distrust in state institutions, an attitude inherited from Soviet times.

Narratives of Continuity and Change:
The Border as a Temporal Boundary

As mentioned above, the construction of the new border after 1991 coincided with a decade of radical economic transformation and land reform in both Ukraine and Russia. These rural transformations are hardly irrelevant to the local residents' perception of the new border, their loyalty to the state and their new national identities. In this section I compare the local narratives of social change in Shchetinovka (RF) and Udy (Ukraine). These neighbouring villages, only 5 km apart, are now separated by the border, but people maintain regular personal contacts with relatives and friends on the other side. As already noted, the economic and social dynamics since 1991 have differed between the two sides of the border. The prosperous kolkhoz in Shchetinovka, managed by an experienced and influential director, has successfully adapted to the new market conditions and is able to preserve a relatively high level of social security, including guaranteed employment and regular payment, and to maintain and even develop the social infrastructure. But in neighbouring Udy the kolkhoz was dissolved, and the new, private agricultural companies offer only seasonal jobs to agricultural workers and do not take on any social obligations. Unemployment is high, and the infrastructure of the village is in decay. By answering our question 'What has changed in the village since 1991?' people connected the emergence of the new border with the new social and economic asymmetry and in this way related their collective identities to new national communities of 'Russians' and 'Ukrainians'.

In Shchetinovka, a narrative of stability and continuity dominated the discussion. From a certain point of view, time stopped in this village somewhere in the early 1980s, during the 'golden age' of the kolkhoz system. In comparing their situation with their neighbours', people stressed the advantages of the kolkhoz, mainly as a provider of social security:

> Our kolkhoz – it is still the same as it was in Soviet times. Our director is a twice 'Hero of Socialist Labour' ... here people really get paid. ... I have worked for twenty years here ... it has never happened that people were not paid in time ... they get wages, additional payments, rewards [*premia*] – everything as it should be. Farmer is farmer, kolkhoz is kolkhoz ... in kolkhoz you are paid if you are sick ... farmers do not have this ... in kolkhoz you have holidays... a farmer has to work with his family from the morning to the evening. (m., foreman, 48, Shchetinovka)

Of course, this 'socialism in one village' is rather limited. People are aware that their situation is exceptional, and that things might change when the kolkhoz's eighty-year-old director dies. Besides, the modern-day economic oasis of the Frunze kolkhoz exists in a completely different political and economic environment with new opportunities and challenges: one can buy a car without the requisite years-long wait of Soviet times, but children's education has become expensive, even unaffordable, for many families. Shchetinovka residents seem well adapted to this new economic situation; they are not at all passive recipients of kolkhoz welfare relying on Soviet-like paternalism. Burawoy and Verdery (1999) remind us that 'what may appear as "restorations" of patterns familiar from socialism are sometimes quite different: direct *responses* to the new market initiatives, produced *by* them, rather than remnants of an older mentality'. As in neighbouring Udy, agricultural workers' households in Shchetinovka are also partly market-oriented, and many combine kolkhoz jobs with some kind of private farming or other small business. At the same time, people in Shchetinovka are not really protected from the new economic and social risks. What they seem to appreciate is not so much the level of income, but the fact that the norms of social life were not totally devaluated in the transition, and that some kind of coherence and 'order' was preserved. This was possible thanks to a policy 'from above', not because of people's own initiative, and this fact is reflected in the interviews ('We were lucky' was a common descriptor of the exceptional situation in Shchetinovka).

The narrative of stability and continuity in Shchetinovka is crucial for defining 'us' and 'them' (the neighbours across the border), the Russians and the Ukrainians, in terms of economic success or failure.

> With Ukraine ... with Udy and others ... until Zolochiv [small town in Kharkiv oblast] ... we always had friendly relations. We visited each other, exchanged spare parts, especially during harvesting.... Now this all has stopped because ... this is ours, this is yours.... I tell you ... we do not suffer much ... at least we have a successful kolkhoz and live better, it is not a secret.... But the Ukrainians suffer ... they cannot come anymore ... although we cannot give much ... but some used spare parts. (m., agronomist, 47, Shchetinovka)

What was earlier a friendly mutual exchange of help between two collective farms is now an act of charity, the paternalism of the rich to the poor neighbour. This attitude was made clear to us as guests from Ukraine: 'The border did not affect our well-being, but yours!' In Shchetinovka, the new border therefore is embedded in this collective narrative of economic stability and continuity with Soviet times, as opposed to the (negative) changes across the border. The border as a symbol of the new times corresponds to a view of the collapse of the Soviet Union as being induced by non-Russian republics: it is Ukraine that has 'separated' (moved away) from Russia (which stayed where and as it was). A kind of justice is seen in the fact that now the Ukrainians have to deal with the consequences of their recklessness and egoism. That the border 'does not matter' in Shchetinovka (as was claimed in the interviews above) only underlines the village's relative prosperity. The 'poor Ukrainians' on the other side of the border who would be happy to get help are not cultural 'others' yet; they are rather perceived as economic losers. People in Shchetinovka apply this new asymmetry not only to Shchetinovka and Udy, but also to Belgorod/Kharkiv and sometimes to Russia/Ukraine in general. Ukrainians in the Belgorod oblasts are perceived either as seasonal workers or small traders, forced to cross the border out of economic necessity:

> 'Kharkiv residents come every day to our markets to sell. In Belgorod ... if you go from the stadium to the central market ... it is only Kharkiv there ... they stand in a row...' (m., agronomist, 47, Shchetinovka).

During the interviews in Udy, on the Ukrainian side of the border, the theme of decay and crisis dominated the collective narrative of village life, and unlike in Shchetinovka, past and present were radically opposed. As in Shchetinovka, in the 1970s and early 1980s people in Udy enjoyed the advantage of working in a rather successful kolkhoz. People in the focus group interview enthusiastically indulged in memories about that time. The kolkhoz could afford to build a two-storey trade centre, a 'palace of culture' with a 200-seat hall and a public library, a hospital and a kindergarten with a swimming pool. Apart from the kolkhoz, employment opportunities included the so-called ATS (auto transport station), a small clothing industry and six state-run shops. As one woman illustrated, in

1985 the Udy telephone book had listed over a hundred phone numbers of firms and organizations; at the time of fieldwork there were only twelve.

In Udy, the discussion of the present situation was structured around comparison with the neighbouring Russian village of Shchetinovka on the one hand, and with the Soviet past on the other, as is evident in the following extracts from the focus group discussion:

> In terms of economy, of course ... all of Ukraine, not only our village ... I go to Russia regularly, and literally after 10 km you can see ... their fields ... those reforms that are implemented on the Russian territory ... and our fields, you cannot even compare. The roads are good, and even if it comes to clothes ... if I have to go there for a wedding, it is always a problem – what to wear? Because I have fifty-six adult relatives there, and every year somebody gets married. (f., medical assistant, 44)

> I have relatives in Russia ... we visited them. They live much better than us, better 'obespecheni' [provided for]... They consider us ... just as poor. An ordinary worker there earns more than I do.... And I am a kind of boss in the village council! What then do our peasants earn? They [the Russians] are just surprised how we can live with our money. (f., administrator, 46)

The Udy residents seem to reproduce the same opposition heard in Shchetinovka, but the other way round ('the neighbours' are prosperous, and 'we' are poor). But in Udy, 'border matters' and the neighbouring Russian village is an important point of reference. The situation in Udy, as residents described it in the interview, is partly seen through the neighbours' eyes: 'What do they think of us', 'we are ashamed'. Interestingly, some interviewees said that 'reforms are going faster in Russia', while others were convinced that 'everything is still working orderly there as it was under Soviet rule'. For middle-aged people, the Belgorod oblast (and Russia in general) represents a more dynamic development, more successful in terms of both economic growth and social security. For the elder generation, however, Russia still represents the Soviet Union, and the border with Russia is also a symbolic boundary separating the idealized past (guaranteed employment, social infrastructure, salaries paid on time) from the problematic present. The border separates Udy inhabitants from their past Soviet life, as well as from the better life in Russia they also would be sharing in, had the Soviet Union not collapsed. The border therefore turns out to be temporal as well as spatial.

Cultural Proximity and National Identities in the Making

In the Soviet era, cultural proximity in the Ukrainian-Russian borderlands was reinforced by rural modernization, voluntary assimilation into the

Figure 8.2. A monument commemorating the liberation from German fascist occupation dominates the central square of Udy. Five hundred six inhabitants of the village died in the Second World War. (Photo: Tatiana Zhurzhenko)

Russian language, a high level of mixed marriages and a significant population of migrants from other oblasts of Ukraine and Russia. In our fieldwork, however, this proximity found quite different expression on the two sides of the border. In Ukrainian villages, when asked about ethnic identities, people often made use of the old Soviet discourse of 'internationalism' and 'people's friendship'. Young people used the same language, though in some cases such references were ironic and rather sceptical. In Udy (an ethnic Russian village) and Hlyboke (a rather new settlement founded after the Second World War), people often described their native village as 'multinational', or as a 'small Soviet Union'. In fact, here 'Soviet' did not refer to a particular political system, ideology, or way of life; rather, it signified the absence of other terms for a disappearing common political and cultural space.

> This border … we did not feel it at all … we felt ourselves as one people … maybe we did not feel we were separate republic … later of course, when the border was built … it has changed … the border mood: there is Russia and we

are Ukraine … it was a bit painful that we do not belong to Russia … we would like to … we would so like to stay together [*ostat'sia obshchimi* – to belong to both Ukraine and Russia at the same time]. (f., teacher, 40, Udy)

In some sense this common Soviet space was preserved by the dominance of Russian media, particularly Russian television. People at the border with Russia do not need expensive satellite antennas to watch Russian TV; they have access to more or less the same channels as the residents of the Belgorod oblast. Given this opportunity, many people indeed prefer to watch Russian TV. Thus, some people virtually live in Russia, rather than in Ukraine. The role of Russian media is also observable in big cities such as Kyiv, but it was still more visible in small near-border villages. Some interviewees exaggerated this situation, telling us local anecdotes:

Children come to school and tell me: 'Valentina Ivanovna, do you know that today is Putin's birthday? The ORT channel showed it' … Larissa Viktorovna [a colleague] asks: 'Children, do you know who is our president?' 'Yes! Putin!' 'And what is our flag?' 'Red!' [people laugh]. And the day before I had just told them: blue and yellow! (f., teacher, 34, Udy).

When asked about their affiliation to the new Ukrainian state, local inhabitants often gave rather uncertain answers: 'We live here … and the passports are Ukrainian … so we are Ukrainians' (f., pensioner, 60, Hlyboke). It sounded as if the new national identity still needed time (and positive social change associated with the new state) to be internalized by the population – in other words, 'Ukrainians' still had to be made out of the post-Soviet population.

People also referred to their mother tongue and place of origin in the discussions about national identity. Those with Ukrainian roots pointed to the voluntary assimilation to Russian, due to its higher status as an 'urban' language and the better prospects proficiency offered for education and professional careers. Many interviewees would call themselves 'Russian-speaking Ukrainians', a highly disputable (and politically charged) ethnic category in Ukraine (see Wilson 1998). Some have discovered their Ukrainian identity retroactively, as the following example shows:

I am also from Russia… We were neighbours of Savchenko, who is today a governor of the Belgorod oblast. Then we moved here with my parents [to Udy, Ukraine], I was in fifth grade in school. The interesting thing is that in Russia … our village, they were Ukrainians there, a Ukrainian-speaking population … a kind of Zolochiv dialect. But school was in Russian. … So many years have passed, almost thirty-five, and now I realize, there was discrimination by the teachers, they always accused us of speaking Ukrainian outside the school. (m., administrator, 49, Udy)

Various options are still open to the 'Ukrainians in the making' living at the border: to be assimilated into Ukrainian, to try to keep their ethnic Russian identity using the new status of national minority or to opt for a range of interim solutions by switching between situational identities. Ethnic Russians and Russian speakers in Ukraine still profit from the former superior status of the Russian language in the Soviet Union and its still-important role in post-Soviet Ukraine. This factor (and the proximity of Russia) means that the option of combining Ukrainian citizenship with a 'private' Russian or Russian-speaking identity might stay attractive for a long time. The example of Udy shows that the language of schooling (Russian, in this case) can play an important role in preserving or transforming ethnic identity. Not only are children educated in Russian, but the local school also attracts newcomers who have reason to look for a Russian-speaking village or a school with Russian as a language of instruction:

> I came to this village in 1995, after attending the Kharkiv pedagogical college. The first thing I was interested in when I came to this Ukrainian oblast was if there was a Russian village here with a Russian school. Because I am Russian, I almost did not know Ukrainian. I just had no chance to learn it in school. ... Two years in college, but I knew very little. ... And thank God I was sent to this Russian village. (f., primary school teacher, Udy, 40)

In Hlyboke Russian dominates everyday communication, but the language of schooling is Ukrainian, and the administration of the village has switched to Ukrainian as well. Local inhabitants combine their new political loyalty and the official use of Ukrainian with their private use of Russian. In the interviews, they stressed the virtues of adaptability and flexibility:

> I worked in a crèche as a nursery teacher ... and sometimes brought children to school. So we go and speak Russian. ... As soon as we reach the school, they see the fence and immediately switch to Ukrainian: 'when do we have a break' and so on. They adapt so quickly ... good children! (f., 60, Hlyboke)

However, there are also some proponents of assimilation to Ukrainian in Udy, as many Russians are concerned with their children's educational and career opportunities in Ukraine, especially given the government's insistence on Ukrainian as the only language allowed in school-leaving examinations.

The discourse of Soviet 'multinationalism' is present on the Russian side of the border too: in Zhuravlevka and Shchetinovka, many villagers have ethnic Ukrainian roots, as local residents noted. But at the same time, ethnic background seems rather irrelevant to the feeling of belonging and loyalty to the post-Soviet Russian state, whereas the new Russian

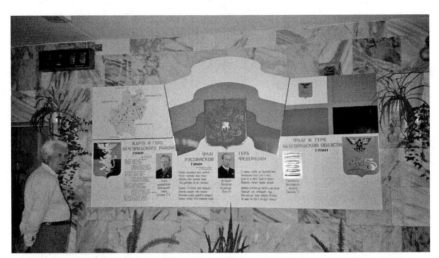

Figure 8.3. National and oblast symbols in Shchetinovka's school. (Photo: Tatiana Zhurzhenko)

national identity is less ambivalent than the Ukrainian one. Here, Russian as an official state language does not have to compete with Ukrainian, which has the status of a local dialect. For example, the Zhuravlevka school has a Ukrainian-Russian Friendship Club but offers no Ukrainian language courses, even though around 30 per cent of its inhabitants came from Ukraine and the school's director is an ethnic Ukrainian. Residents attributed the absence of such an opportunity to the passivity of the local Ukrainians:

> 'Our Ukrainians … they do not want Ukrainian to be taught … if they wanted it… something could be done … but they don't make such demands…. Why? They forgot their language. They came here as seventeen-year-olds …' (Zhuravlevka, group discussion).

In Soviet times, young people from Belgorod oblast often pursued higher education in Kharkiv, where the range of opportunities was wider than in small, rather provincial Belgorod. Now this is rather an exception. A Kharkiv University diploma or academic degree, which is still prestigious in Ukraine requires additional formalities for recognition in Russia (the same is true for Russian academic qualifications in Ukraine). Therefore young people from Belgorod oblast usually prefer to study in their home town (where a new ambitious university has recently opened) or other Russian cities. Considering also the lower salaries in Ukraine, young Russian citizens (even of Ukrainian origin) have no incentive to learn Ukrainian and to go to Ukraine for studying.

Conclusion

The border between Ukraine and the Russian Federation can serve as a laboratory for studying the complex processes of market reforms, rural transformations and nation building at the margins of the post-Soviet state. The new 'borderlanders despite themselves' – Ukrainians and Russians living in the immediate vicinity of the new border – try to adapt to the limitations it has imposed while also making use of the new opportunities it has created. Spatial and cultural proximity to cross-border neighbours and routine interactions across the border provide them with enough information for comparison and discussion. New economic and social asymmetries resulting from the different dynamics of rural transformation in the Kharkiv and Belgorod oblasts are thus reflected in local discourses about 'Russians' and 'Ukrainians' as new national collectives. The new social hierarchies in the borderlands add to the asymmetry between the Russian and Ukrainian languages and cultures, with its long history going back to Soviet and Russian imperial times. But neither Russian nor Ukrainian citizens perceive the new border as a cultural boundary. Rather, it is different social provisions related to citizenship and the labour market situation that make the border 'real' in their eyes.

This research is by no means representative of the whole Ukrainian-Russian border, but it shows that residents of the Ukrainian villages, especially the Russian speakers, often find it difficult to affiliate to the new nation. For them, the new border represents the irreversibility of the post-1991 political and social changes, separating not only Ukraine from Russia but also the present Ukraine from the imagined Soviet Union. Meanwhile, although the new border seems artificial to the residents of the Russian villages (many of whom are of Ukrainian origin), the better economic situation makes it easier for them to accept the new reality.

Notes

1. This chapter is based on research conducted from 2002 to 2004 under the auspices of the Lise Meitner Fellowship Program of the Austrian Science Fund (FWF).
2. The rules for crossing the border have been tightened since the end of the 1990s. In addition to passport and customs controls, migration cards were introduced in both Ukraine and Russia in 2003, and in 2004 car insurance for the neighbouring country became obligatory on both sides. The summer of 2003 saw the launch of a widely advertised experiment in simplified border crossing (the 'green corridor') on the Kharkiv-Belgorod part of the border, but it turned out to be a rather short-lived political campaign.

References

Allina-Pisano, J. 2008. *The Post-Soviet Potemkin Village: Politics and Property Rights in the Black Earth.* Cambridge: Cambridge University Press.

Bilaniuk, L. 2005. *Contested Tongues: Language Politics and Cultural Correction in Ukraine.* Ithaca, NY, and London: Cornell University Press.

Brednikova, O. and V. Voronkov. 1999. 'Border and Social Space Restructuring (the Case of Narva/Ivangorod)', in O. Brednikova and V. Voronkov (eds), *Nomadic Borders.* St. Petersburg: CISR Works (7), pp. 19–25 (in Russian).

Burawoy, M. and K. Verdery. 1999. 'Introduction', in M. Burawoy and K. Verdery (eds), *Uncertain Transition: Ethnographies of Change in the Postsocialist World.* Lanham, MD: Rowman & Littlefield, pp. 1–17.

Chizhikova, L. 1988. *Russian-Ukrainian Borderlands: History and Traditional Everyday Culture (XIX–XX Centuries).* Moscow: Nauka (in Russian).

Donnan, H. and T.M. Wilson. 1999. *Borders: Frontiers of Identity, Nation and State.* Oxford and New York: Berg.

Heyman, J.M. 2010. 'US-Mexico Border Cultures and the Challenge of Asymmetrical Interpenetration', in H. Donnan and T.M. Wilson (eds), *Borderlands: Ethnographic Approaches to Security, Power, and Identity.* Lanham, MD: University Press of America, pp. 21–34.

Kolossov, V. and O. Vendina. 2002. 'Social Gradients, Identity and Migration Flows (by the Example of Belgorod and Kharkiv Oblasts)', in S. Pirozhkov (ed), *Migration and Border Regime: Belarus, Moldova, Russia and Ukraine.* Kiev, pp. 21–46 (in Russian).

Lunden, T. and D. Zalamans. 2000. *Boundary Towns: Studies of Communication and Boundaries in Estonia and Its Neighbours.* Stockholm: Stockholm University.

Martin, T. 2001. *The Affirmative Action Empire: Nations and Nationalism in the Soviet Union, 1923–1939.* Ithaca, NY: Cornell University Press.

Scott, J.C. 1985. *Weapons of the Weak: Everyday Forms of Peasant Resistance.* New Haven, CT: Yale University Press.

Wiegand, B. 1993. 'Petty Smuggling as "Social Justice": Research Findings from the Belize-Mexico Border', *Social and Economic Studies* 42(1): 171–93.

Wilson, A. 1998. 'Redefining Ethnic and Linguistic Boundaries in Ukraine: Indigenes, Settlers and Russophone Ukrainians', in G. Smith et al. (eds), *Nation-building in the Post-Soviet Borderlands: The Politics of National Identities.* Cambridge: Cambridge University Press, pp. 119–38.

Zhurzhenko, T. 2010. *Borderlands into Bordered Lands: Geopolitics of Identity in Post-Soviet Ukraine.* Stuttgart: Ibidem.

Part III

Crossing Forbidden Borders

Chapter 9

Under One Roof

The Changing Social Geography of the Border in Cyprus

Lisa Dikomitis

The Green Line

The Green Line, as the partition line on Cyprus is called, is a de facto 'border' – a controversial term in the Cypriot context. It is a militarized border that runs 180 km across the island, cutting right through the heart of the capital, Nicosia. It consists of a variety of formal and informal barricades, manned by United Nations peacekeepers and always bearing the omnipresent 'forbidden zone' sign. Cyprus has been divided since the Turkish invasion of 1974, which followed a brief Greek Cypriot coup orchestrated by the then military Greek regime. Greek Cypriots living in the north had to flee southward, and Turkish Cypriots living in the south had to move to the north. Consequently both displaced groups became refugees in their own country (Dikomitis 2012; Loizos 1981, 2008). Since 1975 there have been several diplomatic attempts to resolve the conflict, but for various complex reasons no solution was found and the island remains divided.

Once Cyprus obtained its entry ticket to the European Union in December 2002, more peace talks were held and the pressure was on to resolve the long-standing partition of the island. This climate triggered the unexpected opening of some checkpoints at the partition line. On 23 April 2003 the border was opened for a limited amount of movement in a surprise gesture by Rauf Denktaş, the then Turkish Cypriot leader.[1] For the first time in almost three decades, Cypriots could cross from one side of their

Notes for this chapter begin on page 230.

divided island to the other. Since the easing of the border crossing restrictions in the spring of 2003, Cyprus has undergone more dramatic changes. On 24 April 2004 a referendum was held on the Annan Plan, a reunification model drafted by the United Nations. Turkish and Greek Cypriots voted in opposite directions, with 76 per cent of Greek Cypriots voting against the plan and 65 per cent of Turkish Cypriots voting in favour of it. The final outcome was that the 'Cyprus Problem' remained, and only the Greek Cypriots entered the European Union.

In this chapter I explore how Greek and Turkish Cypriots dealt with the possibility of crossing the Green Line and draw some tentative conclusions about six years of border crossings (2003–2009). To do this, I will analyze several fieldwork vignettes to show how perceptions of the border and possible visits to 'the other side' have shifted over the course of recent years.[2] My aim is to show how the border crossings became part of the Cypriot experience and shifted from an excited, emotional event into a routine.[3]

The Dilemma of Crossing

One of the reasons fewer Greek Cypriots than Turkish Cypriots cross is that the former are more ambivalent about the border. Greek Cypriot policy itself maintains a contradictory attitude towards crossing the Green Line: on the one hand, Greek Cypriots are discouraged from crossing because it implies political recognition of the regime in the north; on the other hand, meetings between Greek and Turkish Cypriots are encouraged as a way of preparing the ground for future unification. Non-crossers validate their decision by reciting the many impediments at the checkpoint: they have to show their identity card, complete a one-day visa form stamped by border officials and buy special car insurance from one of the Turkish Cypriot companies there. Their refusal to spend money in the north or show identification in their own country reflects a common way of thinking among Greek Cypriots. The argument is that by doing so, one supports the Turkish Cypriot regime. Crossing as 'a tourist in their own country' – an often-heard phrase in the official rhetoric of Greek Cypriot refugeehood – would imply recognizing the illegal Turkish Republic of Northern Cyprus. According to Webster and Dallen (2006), 57 per cent of Greek Cypriots do not cross because they do not wish to show identification at the checkpoints. A survey in 2008 (Jacobson et al. 2009: 9) confirmed this statistic.

Some individuals cross often and curse every time they near the checkpoint. They comment on the Turkish flags and feel annoyed by the many uniformed Turkish Cypriot representatives at the checkpoint, but these do not stop them from crossing. Others experience equal annoyance at all the hurdles but put it aside because 'their need (*anangi*) to go is too strong'. Manolis, a Greek Cypriot refugee in his early fifties, explained this to me using the metaphor of theatre for the checkpoints: 'I don't feel anything, because it is a piece of theatre they are playing, without an audience. Nobody says "well done" (*pezoun theatro choris na exoun theates, kanenas enlalei 'mbravo'*). If I had to pass in front of a machine, it would be the same (*an itan ena aftomato, to idio mou ekane*).'

I encountered many Greek Cypriots who were still debating with themselves whether to cross. Maria, a sixty-year-old refugee from Famagusta and a psychiatrist, told me in May 2007: 'I did not go to my village … yet [*sighs*]. I think I will be very disturbed by it. I am sure I would feel down for months. I will be the one they will have to treat for depression!' Others hesitated for months, even years, but then decided to cross. Theodoros, a Greek Cypriot in his late twenties, did not want to go to the north because of all the bureaucratic impediments. He explained to me many times that he *wanted* to go but *could not* because he felt it was not right to 'ask permission from the Turks' to visit his mother's village. But one summer day in 2005, news spread of a miracle (*thavma*) in one of the monasteries in the north – a paralysed Greek Cypriot could walk again after visiting the monastery – and Theodoros decided to cross:

> I took my passport and I drove to Ledra Palace. Nobody knew I was going to cross. I needed to do this by myself. I walked in the old town of Nicosia. It was a good experience. I will go and visit my mother's village soon and I will take up my uncle's invitation to go for a day-trip in the north with his Turkish Cypriot friend.

Theodoros continued to go on day trips to the north, crossing the checkpoints early in the morning. He came to know the town of north Nicosia inside out and even bought an old bicycle from a Turkish Cypriot trader he befriended. To date, however, Theodoros's older brother persistently refuses to cross the border, for the same reasons his brother recited for two years.

Beyond the hurdle of bureaucratic formalities lies another reason that crossing is especially difficult for refugees: practically all refugees' houses in the north are now occupied by Turkish Cypriot refugees, mainland Turks and, in some cases, foreigners who bought the houses from Turkish Cypriots. Visiting their house is often the cause of anguish for refugees, who have to knock on their own front door and ask permission to enter. In other words, they can only *visit* their house. Meanwhile, some Greek Cypriots do not understand why their fellow villagers are unwilling to take the opportunity to see their houses and visit, at least once, the place they were forced to leave.

Greek Cypriot crossers and non-crossers do share one conviction, though: they do not recognize the border as a legal boundary. Paradoxes and dilemmas are involved in both cases: by not crossing, people acknowledge the existence of the border; indeed, refugee crossers *need* the border to make sense of their status as refugees.

Turkish Cypriots, on the other hand, *seem* to have fewer problems with crossing the border, but as I will show, they too express ambivalence. Ahmet, a 29-year-old Turkish Cypriot engineering student who closely followed news about the crossings, claimed in February 2005 that

> there is no Turkish Cypriot on this island who has not crossed yet. Turkish Cypriots do not hesitate to cross, no matter what political orientation they have. We all crossed, without faltering. Everybody crossed at least once, in order to get an identity card [from the Republic of Cyprus]. Moreover, Turkish Cypriots cross very regularly for all sorts of reasons.

All the local Turkish Cypriots I met after 2003, urbanites and villagers alike, had crossed at least once. Turkish Cypriots named work, shopping, study, medical care and leisure activities as reasons for crossing to the south.

In the first three years after border restrictions were loosened, Turkish Cypriot crossings increased in number every year (from 1,371,099 in 2003 to 2,222,199 in 2005), but then they decreased rapidly (1,638,734 in 2006 and 1,116,990 in 2007).[4] This change was reflected in the interviews I conducted with Turkish Cypriots. Kasim, who used to cross very often, expressed his view on the border as follows:

> I lost my motivation to cross. I do not want to cross to the south anymore. It annoys me that some of my Greek Cypriot 'friends' [*gestures to indicate quotation marks*] did not even cross once. I crossed to get an identity card, to see friends, to travel from Larnaca airport and to buy things. I have to say that the Greek Cypriot yoghurt is more tasteful than ours [laughs]. We do not want more checkpoints to open. We see the border as a security. (February 2006)

I heard similar comments from the Kozanlılar when I lived among them. Although many of the village's households depended on a man's income from manual work in the south (as builder, painter, carpenter, etc.), I heard a lot of sceptical remarks. One sunny morning in July 2006, I was chatting with the men sipping coffee in front of Kozan's *bakkal* (grocery). Mete (48), who used to live abroad, spoke confidently in English and paused often so I could take careful notes: 'It is not nice that you feel the borders. In a European country you should not feel the borders. I am a Cypriot. I hate borders.' About half an hour later he said something else that caught my attention: 'Of course we feel safer on this side of the border, given everything that happened.'

This was not the first time I heard Turkish Cypriots saying something along that line. Murat (54) told me several times that 'although things are better now because we are free to go anywhere we want, it is good the Turkish army is still present. In the same vein we see the border as a form of security.' When there was talk of opening more checkpoints, such as the Ledra Street checkpoint (opened on 3 April 2008), I heard many Turkish Cypriots remark that there was no need to open up more 'gates' (*kapılar*). At the same time I frequently heard complaints about the practicalities of crossing at the checkpoints: the long wait, preparation of insurance documents, showing identification and car searches by customs or the police.

Like the Greek Cypriots, many of my Turkish Cypriot informants wanted to cross without impediment. The main difference between the two standpoints was that Greek Cypriots demanded permanent elimination of the border and absolute certainty that no kind of boundary would divide the island. Illustrative of this is a frequently seen graffiti slogan painted outside army posts: 'Our borders are in Kyrenia [a coastal town in the north].' My Turkish Cypriot informants, by contrast, always emphasized the need for a form of tangible, visible security. This tied in with their communal past of fear and insecurity. 'Greek Cypriots do not understand why we feel safer with the presence of the Turkish army', Fahri (62) explained on one occasion:

> Greek Cypriots have not been through the same long-term suffering as we have. I was displaced several times, I lived in enclaves, tent camps and in an army base. I want to feel safe on our side (*bizim taraf*). It is very good that we can cross now but we need the Greek Cypriots to understand why we want to stay here [in his village in the north] and cannot move back to Paphos.

It was perhaps my informant Salih (67) who most poignantly phrased his view of the situation on Cyprus and its future:

> Cyprus is a house with two rooms (*iki odalı bir ev*) where Turkish Cypriots live in one room and Greek Cypriots in the other. As a result of our past experiences, I believe that it will be better for both parties to stay like that.

It was no coincidence that Salih used the metaphor of a house to describe the division of Cyprus. Houses are an important symbolic asset in the small-scale Cypriot society, because a successful person is somebody who owns his own house. Turkish Cypriots wanted to live under one roof with Greek Cypriots, but in separate rooms. As is clear above, Turkish Cypriots would like to retain at least a notional border marking off an area in which they run their affairs, like the wall between the two rooms in Salih's metaphor.

A first conclusion of this section is that for Turkish Cypriots, crossing does not pose the same sort of ethical dilemma it poses for Greek Cypriots, although some Turkish Cypriots might have crossed infrequently or stopped doing so as time passed. Graffiti slogans such as 'Tourists or refugees?', used in the south to reproach Greek Cypriots who cross, are not found in the north of Cyprus. A second conclusion is that Greek Cypriots perceive the border as illegitimate and its complete removal as the only just course of action. Turkish Cypriots would prefer to retain a notional border symbolizing a form of security.

Of Pilgrims and Tourists

Just as Greek Cypriots undertook 'pilgrimages' to their lost villages, so too did Turkish Cypriots visit the villages they had left behind (see Dikomitis 2009 for a detailed analysis of Greek Cypriot 'pilgrimages'). I accompanied both Greek and Turkish Cypriots on these journeys and found that many aspects of their experiences were similar. For example, both groups of refugees often took things back with them – tangible reminders such as soil, plants, fruits, a stone from their house and so on. Ayhan (70) took a branch from a tree in his former field and planted it in his garden in north Nicosia. He told me that fellow villagers had found some of their old household things in the village and brought them over, as Greek Cypriot refugees had done.

I joined a few Turkish Cypriot refugees on their first return visit, and they were as emotional as Greek Cypriot refugees. I remember a visit by a Turkish Cypriot couple who lived in Yukarı Bostancı (Zodia) paid to a Limassol village. Mustafa (64) and Neşe (60) shed copious tears while visiting their former house, and Neşe stayed a long time in her former fields and picked a large bunch of wildflowers. In the first months of my stay in Kozan, the villagers asked me where I was from and where my house was, and told me in turn where they came from and what their first visit to their village was like. Thus I came to understand that Greek Cypriots who thought Turkish Cypriots did not care about their former houses and villages were wrong. Mehmet (56), for instance, loved to talk about the village he had left behind, praising the water, the trees and the landscape of his home village just as Greek Cypriots would do. He reinforced his stories by reciting songs and poems, in both Greek and Turkish Cypriot dialects, about the place he came from. Salih (67), a refugee from Polis tis Chrisochou, narrated his first return visit in April 2003:

I found my old neighbours and my friends. They were very happy to see me after thirty years. Also people whom I did not know gave me a warm welcome. It saddened me to see that they built a car park where my house used to stand. I was angry with the Greek Cypriot government. Why was my property turned into a car park? Why Turkish Cypriot property? Then I looked for the field I used to guard for hours in order to shoo away the birds that ate the watermelon seeds. I found the trees under which I used to sleep and I sat there for a while.

However, there were also differences between Greek and Turkish Cypriots' 'pilgrimages'. First, Greek Cypriots were very reluctant to spend money in the north. Even six years after the borders opened I witnessed Greek Cypriot refugees carrying everything they needed to make their own coffee (a thermos, Nescafe, sugar, cups and spoons, biscuits and a tea towel). Numerous Greek Cypriots, refugees and non-refugees alike, also opposed participation in any form of leisure activity in the north. As Webster and Dallen (2006: 175) have pointed out, 'The majority [of Greek Cypriots] is also against fee-based sightseeing, eating in restaurants and going to the beach. Interestingly, about one third of respondents are even against sightseeing without a fee and visiting places of origin.... It appears that most of the [Greek Cypriot] tourists did not really act like tourists, spending money to enjoy themselves.'

Turkish Cypriots, by contrast, would always visit new places and certainly have a drink or a meal in a local restaurant. On the occasions when I joined Turkish Cypriots, I did not hear any political talk about 'spending money in the south'. On the contrary, many of my Turkish Cypriot informants spent money readily. Three years after our conversation about his first visit, Salih told me about it again, now emphasizing other aspects. He wanted to illustrate that Turkish Cypriots were not 'poor', as Greek Cypriots often portrayed them, and that they could afford to do what Greek Cypriots did:

> We left with a full bus and drove to our villages in the Paphos district. After I had seen my house, I wanted to go to the cafés in the touristy harbour of Paphos. I sat there and I ordered an expensive drink. There was a television crew present and I made sure they got a good shot of me. (February 2006)

A second difference was that, unlike Greek Cypriot refugees, Turkish Cypriots did not seem to visit their villages, fields and houses every time they crossed. They were definitely eager to explore other places in the south and always took the opportunity to stop in other villages and touristic hotspots. In this respect, Turkish Cypriots were more 'tourists' than 'pilgrims', a conclusion confirmed by a Turkish Cypriot tourist guide who had befriended a Greek Cypriot who owned a bus company and organized regular one-day trips to the Baths of Aphrodite and other sightseeing venues in the Polis area for Turkish Cypriots. By 2007 most of my Turkish Cypriot informants, both urbanites and villagers, were crossing to visit places in the south unrelated to their villages (such as the Troodos Mountains). As one informant put it in the summer of 2007: 'When you have been a couple of times back to your village the moment comes that you decide not to go anymore. Two to three per cent of the Kozanlılar did not even go once back to their villages. They do not see the point.' This statement tied in with the Turkish Cypriot refugees' view that their village in the north was now their home, a perception on which I will elaborate at length below.

A final difference between Greek and Turkish Cypriot refugees concerned their children. The original Turkish Cypriot refugees had transmitted to their children a sense of freedom and permanence of their new home in the north, as reflected in, among other things, the fact that they knew little about their parents' lives in their villages in the south. For example, during my fieldwork I asked Sema (23), who had recently moved to Kozan after marrying a Kozanlı, whether her parents were refugees. She told me her father was from Limassol. I asked whether he was from the city or from a village, and she answered that he was from a village near the city of Limassol but she did not remember the name (in either Turkish or Greek). Sema added that I should ask older people if I wanted to know details, implying that younger people were little concerned with the past. This was also the case with the four children of the family I lived with in Kozan. Unlike Greek Cypriot youngsters, they could not tell me much about their parents' lives before they became refugees. This indifference was certainly reflected during return visits, when some young Turkish Cypriots declined to join their parents to visit their former villages or found it a rather boring experience when they did. They certainly did not express the strong emotions their Greek Cypriot peers did.

To conclude this section, Greek Cypriot crossings were clearly more the 'pilgrimage' type of visit to what had been lost, whereas Turkish Cypriot crossings, if they were unrelated to work, medical emergencies or obtaining government documents, were more of the 'tourism' type, as if they were visiting another country. Turkish Cypriot border crossers seemed to be more interested in meeting people – old and new friends, for instance – but Greek Cypriots more often crossed with the purpose of visiting specific places, such as their former villages or specific religious sites.

Shopping the Border

It was mainly Turkish Cypriots who crossed the border to engage in everyday activities: working, shopping, doctor's visits and all kind of other services. 'Borders are economic resources, to be consumed like other resources in a variety of ways. This is especially apparent to those who use the border as one way to add value to their own products, or who market themselves as masters of the border in order to entice people to use their services' (Donnan and Wilson 1999: 122).[5]

A small number of Greek Cypriots, however – primarily working-class women who lived close to one of the checkpoints – engaged in weekly shopping across the border. One of their favourite places to buy groceries was the Tuesday market in Gönyeli and the nearby supermarkets, where they would chat with Turkish Cypriot traders about their goods and about daily things. For instance, Eleni, Agathi and Petros, Greek Cypriot refugees in their early sixties, crossed the border every week in the summer of 2004. Petros would have his morning coffee at the local coffee shop while the women compared the prices of goods with those in the markets in south Nicosia in colourful detail, chattering loudly as they checked out a watermelon or a bunch of grapes. When I asked them why they went to the trouble of crossing in order to shop, Agathi replied that if she went there, the Turkish Cypriots would see things in a better way (*to vlepoun me pio kalo mati*). She described establishing relationships between Greek and Turkish Cypriots as the right thing do to, using the word 'friendship' (*filia*) a lot. And Agathi had indeed befriended some of the female sellers. On a later occasion she told me she would buy goods there – cigarettes, petrol, fruits – when they were cheaper (*tha agoraso an einai pio ftina*). (As discussed above, many Greek Cypriots opposed the practice of spending money in the north.)

Besides grocery shopping, these cross-border shoppers also went to Turkish Cypriot hairdressers, beauticians and dentists. They would praise the service – Turkish Cypriots allegedly invested more time in each client – and the cheaper rates. From the winter of 2005 onwards, two years after the border opened, I observed a steep decline in the number of Cypriot cross-border shoppers. Women complained that prices had risen and it was not worth crossing anymore. But long after the weekly border shopping stopped, my Greek Cypriot informants were still going to the north to buy cigarettes and petrol.

A small number of Greek Cypriot men would cross the border to frequent casinos and private nightclubs. This practice generated many negative comments among Greek Cypriots. One woman told me, regarding gambling or visiting brothels, '*Arostia einai*' (it is a disease). Gambling establishments are forbidden in the south of the island. Driving at night along the coastal road near Kyrenia, I saw many Greek Cypriot cars in the huge casino parking lots.

In contrast to Greek Cypriots, many Turkish Cypriots cross the border for economic reasons, for instance, to shop at the big supermarkets in the south of Cyprus. This is not because the goods are cheap – on the contrary

– but because many of the goods there, mostly European brands, cannot be found in their local shops. One of my Turkish Cypriot language teachers, a 25-year-old upper-class girl, told me: 'I want to buy clothes from Zara and Mango! My mother buys perfumes and nappies from the brand Pampers. All these things we cannot find here. Although we support the Denktaş regime, we cross in order to buy those goods' (July 2004).

In June 2007, Greek Cypriot supermarkets were still full of Turkish Cypriot shoppers, but their numbers decreased thereafter, although one still saw Turkish Cypriots in the big supermarkets in south Nicosia. In the spring of 2009, Mustafa (66) told me that more international chains had opened in north Nicosia and Kyrenia in recent years, and more products from international brands had become available. Turkish businesses had obtained licenses and opened branches, or exported the products to north Cyprus. Mustafa emphasized during our conversation that some Turkish Cypriots still crossed to the south to shop as a form of protest against the political and economic situation in the north: 'They want to show their disappointment and dissatisfaction because things have not changed drastically enough.' During my fieldwork in Kozan I was often asked to bring goods from the south. The women I had my daily coffee with marvelled at, for instance, the deodorant I used, and asked me to bring them such deodorant, as well as tampons and many other toiletries. Aware that my host liked Greek Cypriot brandy and other alcoholic beverages, I would take them with me to the village. Also, many diabetes patients in the village asked me to bring medicines and needles for equipment they had purchased in the south. For instance, Ceylan (80) suffered from diabetes and needed to check her blood sugar on a daily basis. She used a glucose meter that somebody had brought her from the south, and her alcohol pads, sterile finger lancets and test strips were also purchased in the south.

Another reason why Turkish Cypriots crossed was to be treated at private clinics, specialized medical centres and especially the general hospital, where, unlike many Greek Cypriots, they are entitled to free medical care. Before the border opened, Turkish Cypriots would go to Turkey or the United Kingdom for specific operations or treatments, or they were treated in the south in certain urgent cases. Many of my Turkish Cypriot informants explained that access to a variety of doctors and clinics was one of the most significant benefits of the border openings. Another group of Turkish Cypriots crossing the border daily consisted of those attending a private, English secondary school or one of the private English-taught universities, often on scholarship.

However, the main reason for Turkish Cypriots' frequent crossings, and for the significantly higher number of crossings from the north was that many of them were employed in the south of Cyprus. Women worked as hairdressers and cleaners. Turkish Cypriot men worked mainly at construction sites and petrol stations. Every day around four in the afternoon, the queue at the Ledra Palace checkpoint was jam-packed with Turkish Cypriot workers going home. All the sons and sons-in-law of my field family in the village worked in the south, waking before dawn to drive to the checkpoint and from there all over the island to work as painters, builders and carpenters.

In the first years I heard only positive comments about their work: they were pleased to have found work – complaining there were no jobs for them in the north – and were on very good terms with their Greek Cypriot employers. The latter would visit their house in the north on Sundays and attend their engagement and wedding parties. In an interview, Ali (33) explained that they were paid different wages according to seniority and position:

> We work more or less eight hours per day. We leave Kozan at six in the morning. Sometimes we have to leave earlier, depending on where we work [they used to work in many places in the south]. We start working at about 7h30 and finish around 15h. My brother Orhan (26) earns thirty-five Cypriot pounds per day, because he works already two years in the south. The fiancée of my sister, Zafer (20), just finished his army service last month and joined us recently [working in the south]. He earns twenty-eight Cypriot pounds per day. I earn forty Cypriot pounds per day because I am a skilled workman (*usta*). (July 2006)

A year later (in autumn 2007), however, I increasingly heard criticism in the Turkish Cypriot community. Fatma (50), mother of three sons working in the south, grumbled about the working conditions in the south. I paraphrase what she told me:

> Two of my sons found work now in our areas [north Cyprus]. You know, the work was dangerous and they were not well insured. People were dying: some Turkish Cypriot fell off the scaffolds while working. There were too many accidents. I think it is better they work on our side. Only my youngest son still works over there, he did not find a job here yet.

In winding up this discussion of cross-border economic activities, I want to stress the main difference between Greek and Turkish Cypriots' behaviour. The overwhelming majority of Greek Cypriots saw crossing north for economic reasons as a political act that legitimized an illegal regime (Webster and Dallen 2006). There remained but a few Greek Cypriot border shoppers, and I knew of no Greek Cypriots who sought employment across the border. Many of my Turkish Cypriot informants spoke

very positively about the benefits conferred by the opening of the borders,
such as (free) medical care, access to specific consumer goods, employment and schooling. Not all Turkish Cypriots took up all these opportunities, but on several occasions people expressed a strong feeling that
the suffering of their isolated community was now somewhat eased. The
behaviour of Turkish Cypriot border crossers might at first seem uncom-
plicated and innocent, but their activity certainly had political significance
as well. For many Turkish Cypriots, it indicated the beginning of the end
of their economic isolation.

Stereotypes across the Border

Ceylan (80) was a small, wrinkled woman with bright blue eyes and skin
tanned from a life of hard work in the fields. She was born a deaf-mute. The
first time she came over to the house where I was staying, my field mother
explained that I was a Greek Cypriot by tapping her index finger on her
nose and making a wave gesture. When Ceylan repeated the gesture after
pointing towards me, my hostess explained that it meant 'Greek Cypriots'
because 'Greek Cypriots have a big idea about themselves'. One morning
over coffee, Ceylan and her husband Beyit explained some of their other
makeshift gestures – always brief, fleeting hand movements. One sign,
pinching her nose as if responding to a stench in the air, also meant 'Greek
Cypriots'. Her husband explained that Ceylan's former neighbours in her
Paphos village had been Greek Cypriots with a pig farm. Making a cross
with two fingers was another way to indicate Greek Cypriots, whereas
making a crescent shape with her fingers meant she was talking about
Turks or Turkish Cypriots. Some signs were private between her and her
relatives, but the sign of 'those with their nose in the air' was known by
many Kozanlılar, and indeed, I often heard that 'Greek Cypriots are pretentious, they think they are everything'.

Both Turkish and Greek Cypriots hold entrenched stereotypes about
each other that became apparent in everyday language and in cartoons.
What struck me, now that Cypriots could cross the border and actually
meet the Other, was that the stereotypes I had heard over the past decades
were now supported with fresh observations. Meetings with the Other
were often occasion to maintain and reinforce popular stereotypes. Negative comments about Turkish Cypriots were rife. It was most common to
typecast Turkish Cypriots by saying 'they are behind' (*poli mbiso*) compared to Greek Cypriots. Yiannis, a Greek Cypriot refugee living in Germany, told me what he had thought upon visiting his former house in the

area of Varosha (Maraş) for the first time: 'Where is the hate? Where is this thing we are afraid of? The killers?' During our conversation he repeated the phrases 'Nothing had changed' and 'It was as if I were waiting for my friends to come out of their houses to play football' up to seven times.

But when I asked him about his contact with the local Turkish Cypriots and Turks, he said they had annoyed him: 'They do not keep their houses clean. They are behind. It was like I travelled with a time machine and went thirty years back in time. The inhabitant of my house was so proud to show me his fridge and the new flush toilet (*niagara*). Can you imagine?' Greek Cypriot refugees firmly believed, and continuously reproduced, the cliché that Turkish Cypriots neglect fields, trees, houses and whole properties and do not care where they live – 'they just live'. Younger Greek Cypriots too reiterate this stereotype. A twenty-year-old Greek Cypriot told me in an interview about her grandmother's visit to her former village:

> She was very sad because when she was living there the fields were evergreen (*ta chorafia itan kataprasina*). Now none of the inhabitants cares about the environment (*kanenas apo tous katoikous den asxolitai me tin fisi*). They do nothing. They just live there (*apla katoikoun*). My grandmother was happy and emotional. She cried at times from joy and other times from sadness (*eklege pote apo chara pote apo lipi*).

Yet there had been, and still were, amicable meetings as well between Greek and Turkish Cypriots. Panikos (59), a non-refugee, often donated blood and was called one day for a direct transfer of blood during an operation on a Turkish Cypriot boy. I paraphrase what Panikos told me:

> I went to the general hospital at 7 in the morning. I was brought into the operation theatre where there were two beds. The boy was already on one of the beds and I had to lie down on the other one. It felt good to be able to do this. You see, my blood has very good qualities. After the operation the boy's parents came up to me. They did not stop thanking me. The mother wanted to kiss my hands but I refused. I did what I had to do. They invited me several times to go to their house in the north.

On a later occasion I asked Panikos whether he had taken them up on their invitation. He had not. He said he had been a couple of times to the north but disliked having to show identification at the checkpoints. I asked him whether he had any Turkish Cypriot friends, and he mentioned having some acquaintances he had met through his work. Panikos explained that a Greek Cypriot and a Turkish Cypriot could never be as close (*demeni*) as two Greek Cypriots or two Turkish Cypriots could because 'it is too much trouble to cross at a checkpoint in order to have a coffee together', as Panikos phrased it. I too got the impression that although there were many contacts between Greek and Turkish Cypriots, solid friendships between them were rather exceptional.

In addition to the revival of old stereotypes, I found that on both sides of the border, new clichés were developing in relation to how the Other dealt with the opening of the border. Greek Cypriots would say that most Turkish Cypriots were only interested in the benefits of the Republic of Cyprus. A common stereotype was that Turkish Cypriots were not only able to use Greek Cypriot properties but now were asking for more on top. I rarely heard Petros speak negatively about Turkish Cypriots, but when it came to money and economy he was very bitter and repeated what I had often heard before. What bothered him most (*afto pou me pirakse perisotero*), he said, was that his best field, which once gave him good produce, was now left uncultivated. Instead of making a livelihood out of the field, as he used to do, they left it bare and 'then they complain they do not have any money'. Turkish Cypriots, on the other hand, would generally comment on the Greek Cypriot refugees who wanted their houses and properties back, typecasting them as greedy and selfish. Greek Cypriots were also pretentious, according to many Kozanlılar, who indicated this with the same gesture I saw Ceylan use. Here is how Ahmet (29) pictured Greek Cypriots in an interview in 2008:

> My father always warned me that I am too much of an idealist. He tells me that I am thinking in a very rosy way and that I will lose my passion soon. He was right after all. At first, I enjoyed crossing the border to meet my new Greek Cypriot friends, but now I am annoyed with them. It is always me who had to cross. Some of my 'friends' did not even cross once! It gets on my nerves that Greek Cypriots assume that Turkish Cypriots do not care about their lost properties and they believe we will not claim our houses. Greek Cypriots are always whining: 'My home, my home, my fields! What will happen?' They are so selfish. We also care for our lost houses and show interest in them. But the thing that upset me the most is that a lot of Greek Cypriots, even my friends, they call me Ahmet*is*. My name is Ahmet! There is no need to 'Greekify' my name. I am not Christak*is*, Vassil*is* or whatever. ... They want me to become like them, they do not accept me as I am.

In conclusion, the ethnic stereotypes that Greek and Turkish Cypriots had held about each other prior to the border openings were still very much alive and had, if anything, been strengthened by contact between members of the two communities. Despite the many examples of positive contacts across the border, Greek Cypriots and Turkish Cypriots each felt the other lacked understanding of their position.

Conclusion

At one time, the traffic at the checkpoints was so dense that there was no space between cars and the people waiting to get a visa had to fight their way through passport control. By the time of my later fieldwork, the rush and excitement of the first crossings were long past. Over the past six years the number of Greek Cypriots crossing the Green Line had decreased by almost 50 per cent (from 1,123,720 in 2003 to 708,656 in 2008). The number of Turkish Cypriot border crossers had more or less remained the same (1,371,099 in 2003 and 1,298,325 in 2008), having peaked in 2005 at 2,222,199 Turkish Cypriots crossing to the south.[6] The crossings had become a normalized, routine event on the island, and in the year 2009 a general disappointment lingered over both communities.

Greek Cypriot attitudes towards the border were unified by a common theme. Whether they had seized or resisted the opportunity to cross the border, none of my informants *accepted* the legality of the border. Greek Cypriots refused to recognize the division of the island as legitimate. However, and significantly, this refusal was expressed in different ways. Even as those Greek Cypriots who refused to cross denied the existence of the border, in a certain paradoxical sense they also reproduced it: the border was illegitimate, but they refused to cross it. This refusal to cross the border was also paradoxically an acknowledgement of its existence. Meanwhile, the few Greek Cypriot border shoppers who 'recognized'[7] the border did so in a way that denied it: there was a border, but they ignored it by crossing to do everyday things that did not normally require crossing a border. The Greek Cypriot refugee-pilgrims 'recognized' the border because through it they recognized themselves as refugees. Crossing the border allowed them to emphasize this identity and re-create the community they had lost. Yet at the same time, the emphasis on their refugee status and lost community pointed to the illegitimacy of the border.

The Turkish Cypriot community did not have ethical objections to crossing the border. However, this did not mean they accepted the legitimacy of the border as it is now. For Turkish Cypriots, the opening of the border signified that their long-term isolation was starting to break down. It offered them many opportunities: employment, education, access to certain consumer goods and most importantly official membership of the Republic of Cyprus and the European Union in the form of documents such as ID cards, passports and driving licenses. Turkish Cypriots also perceived the border as it is now as problematic and illegitimate because they had to go through the process of showing identification at the checkpoints, but unlike Greek Cypriots, most of my Turkish Cypriot informants argued in favour of a notional border remaining on the island. They wanted to live under one roof with the Greek Cypriots, but in two separate rooms of the same house.

Acknowledgements

I would like to thank Xenios Anastassiades for his constant support during my several fieldwork rounds.

Notes

1. The Turkish Republic of Northern Cyprus, declared unilaterally in 1983, is not recognized by any state other than Turkey, whereas the Republic of Cyprus is legally recognized by the international community.
2. The northern part of the island is variously coined by Greek Cypriots as *sta katexomena* (the occupied areas), *potji* (over there), *sta Tourtzika* (in the Turkish [areas]), *stin alli plevra* (the other side) or to a lesser extent *sta voria* (the north) and *sto psevdokratos* (the pseudo-state). My Turkish Cypriot informants referred to the south of Cyprus variously as *güney Kıbrıs'da* (south Cyprus), *güney'de* (in the south), *öbür tarafta* (on the other side). The word *Urum* is used mostly by the elderly: *(U)Rum tarafında* (the Greek Cypriot side) or *(U)Rum'da* (to the Greek Cypriots).
3. Data are based on several rounds of ethnographic fieldwork conducted between 2002 and 2009 on both sides of the island (Dikomitis 2005, 2009, 2012). I primarily worked with two groups of refugees linked by their histories of displacement to a single place. The Larnatsjiotes, the original Greek Cypriot inhabitants of the village Larnakas tis Lapithou, have been scattered all over the south of Cyprus since their displacement during or just after the war of 1974. The present inhabitants of the village (now called Kozan), the Kozanlılar, are Turkish Cypriot refugees originally from a handful of villages in the Paphos district in the south of Cyprus who moved to Kozan in 1974 and 1975.
4. Numbers provided by the Republic of Cyprus police. The number of Turkish Cypriots crossing to the south increased again in 2008 (1,298,325). For a detailed table see Jacobson et al. (2009: 10).
5. The heading of this section is borrowed from Donnan and Wilson (1999).
6. Numbers provided by the Republic of Cyprus police.
7. When I use the term 'recognize', I mean it in an individual, subjective sense, since under international law only a state can recognize another state.

References

Dikomitis, L. 2005. 'Three Readings of a Border: Greek Cypriots Crossing the Green Line in Cyprus', *Anthropology Today* 21(5): 7–12.

———. 2009. 'From the City to the Village and Back: Greek Cypriot Refugees Engaging in "Pilgrimages" across the Border', in R. Pinxten and L. Dikomitis (eds), *When God Comes to Town: Religious Traditions in Urban Contexts*. Oxford: Berghahn Books.

———. 2012. *Cyprus and Its Places of Desire: Cultures of Displacement Among Greek and Turkish Cypriot Refugees*. London: I.B. Tauris.

Donnan, H. and T.M. Wilson. 1999. *Borders: Frontiers of Identity, Nation and State*. Oxford: Berg.

Jacobson, D., et al. 2009. *The Opening of Ledra Street/Lokmacı Crossing in April 2008: Reactions from Citizens and Shopkeepers*. PRIO Report 2/2009.

Loizos, P. 1981. *The Heart Grown Bitter: A Chronicle of Cypriot War Refugees*. Cambridge: Cambridge University Press.

———. 2008. *Iron in the Soul: Displacement, Livelihood and Health in Cyprus*. Oxford: Berghahn Books.

Webster, C. and T. Dallen. 2006. 'Travelling to the "Other Side": The Occupied Zone and Greek Cypriot Views of Crossing the Green Line', *Tourism Geographies* 8(2): 162–81.

Chapter 10

The Birth of a Border
Policing by Charity on the Italian Maritime Edge

Maurizio Albahari

Nota di geografia
Le coste del Mediterraneo si dividono in due,
di partenza e di arrivo, però senza pareggio:
più spiagge e più notti di imbarco, di quelle di sbarco,
toccano Italia meno vite, di quante salirono a bordo.
A sparigliare il conto la sventura, e noi, parte di essa.
Eppure Italia è una parola aperta, piena d'aria.[1]
—Erri De Luca, *Solo andata*

'Our hope is that our land of Apulia,[2] the *gate of the Orient*, and for centuries a *gate of civilization and culture*, becomes a *gate of legality*, but most importantly, a *gate of charity*' (Ruppi 2002: 14; original emphasis). This statement by an influential Catholic[3] archbishop synthetically indexes the intersection of moral geographies, religious charity and sovereignty distinctively emerging in the Italian governance of borders and migration.[4] The pages below trace the foundational phases of Italy's border enforcement vis-à-vis the earliest instances of mass maritime migration in contemporary Europe.[5] To do this, they sketch the discordant activities of two key public figures, Don Giuseppe and Don Cesare. For more than a decade at the turn of the century, these Catholic clergymen were primary actors in Apulian, national and transnational state and charitable endeavours relating to migration. By focusing on intersections of state policing, humanitarian assistance and Catholic charitable activities in south-eastern Italy, I am able to account for the first instances and institutionalization

---

Notes for this chapter begin on page 249.

of Italian migrant confinement – which proved indispensable to the symbolic legitimacy and logistical sustainability of maritime patrolling and migrant processing.

Afghans, Kurds, Pakistanis, Egyptians, Palestinians and others, having transited Greece, Turkey or Egypt, are occasionally able to survive their smugglers and the maritime journey, slip away from FRONTEX[6] and Italian maritime patrolling, and disembark in Apulia. Small groups of migrants might be noticed walking from the coast towards larger cities, hoping to catch a train to northern Italy or northern Europe. Local residents might offer them food, drinks and even shelter. More and more often, though, residents' first impulse is to just report the presence of newly arrived migrants to police authorities. The approach presented in this chapter helps account for these novel reactions, and for the broader European reconfigurations of solidarity, hospitality and social proximity they reflect. By mapping a newly dominant aesthetics of migration that deals with spatial, moral and social ideas of proximity and distance, as well as military patrolling, administrative detention and charitable assistance, these pages help discern and analyse novel forms of humanitarian and emergency-based governance.[7]

Early Encounters on Italy's Shores

La Gazzetta del Mezzogiorno, one of the most respected regional newspapers in southern Italy, in 1999 proposed 'la gente del Salento' (the people of Salento, the southern part of Apulia) as possible candidates for the Nobel Peace Prize (Quarta 2006). The idea was discussed in the official venues of the European Parliament and the Italian Senate, as the arrival of migrants to Italy and the EU through this coastal back door was increasingly under the spotlight. Although ultimately unsuccessful, the proposition stands as the self-celebratory crowning achievement of a decade of humanitarian work by residents and church institutions vis-à-vis daily maritime migration. Thus, at the regional level, the former Governor of Apulia Raffaele Fitto celebrated Apulia's 'effectiveness as regards solidarity; [and] efficiency in the cooperation with Albania' (*Gazzetta del Mezzogiorno*, 26 June 2004). At the national level, sociologist Vittorio Cotesta critically rendered one of the contemporary refrains of national identitarian construction, writing 'it is true that Italians cannot make war; but they can give solidarity as efficiently as others make war' (Cotesta 1999: 393; see also Favell 2002). And finally, then Prime Minister Silvio Berlusconi, addressing the European Parliament, noted that 'our European Christian tradition brings us to look to these immigrants with a spirit of reception worthy of

Figure 10.1. Port of Gallipoli: sailboat used by Kurdish migrants, confiscated by the coastguard. (Photo: courtesy of Guardia Costiera, Gallipoli)

our level of civilization' (*Gazzetta del Mezzogiorno,* 23 October 2003). These paradigmatic statements index a lived narration of popular charity, religious compassion and institutional solidarity. A benevolent trademark of overarching *accoglienza* (reception) essentializes what is in fact a complex architecture of contingent and often controversial practices. In the remainder of this section, I highlight the early foundations of this architecture. They bear on the formation, implementation and legitimation of the Italian south-eastern maritime border and more generally of Italian migration governance.

In 1990, eight hundred political dissidents sought refuge in the Italian and several other Western embassies in communist Albania. The Italian government organized the passage of many of these people into Italy (Dal Lago 2004: 182). In neighbouring Apulia, as in the rest of Italy, local institutions such as municipalities offered hospitality. Mass media waxed enthusiastic for these Albanian *profughi* (refugees), portrayed as heroes of anti-communism (Perrone 1996: 33) fleeing a dictatorial regime, though in its final days. This event inaugurated a conspicuous flow of migrants originating in Albania and transiting that country to cross the Strait of

Otranto. The Schengen Agreement's implementation in Italy (1997) would make this strait, traversed especially by Albanians, Kurds, Afghans and people from the countries succeeding Yugoslavia, a de facto border region of the EU.

'I could often see the mountains of Albania across the strait when I was a young student in Otranto. I don't see the strait as a border, but as a door or a window', said Don Giuseppe (personal interview, 11 August 2004), a Catholic priest in his mid fifties. Those mountains are certainly visible, on a clear day. To coastal residents they serve as an occasional reminder of the spatial proximity of the other side of the Strait of Otranto, and of what they refer to as the East, the Orient, Albania, the Balkans and so forth. Yet interviews in Apulia delineate a certain disinterest towards nearby Albania and neighbouring countries. Historically, complex factors have discouraged Italian popular and institutional understanding of the Strait of Otranto as a consequential international border, and of Albania as a notable neighbour. Among such factors are the geopolitical, economic and infrastructural choices and internal imbalances of Italy and Western Europe due to the 'cold war,' which certainly orient southern Italians' gaze and aspirations northward, rather than eastward. Also to be taken into account is the fact that until 1990, emigration from Albania was legally prevented by that country's isolationist authorities. Today, as in this recent past, spatial proximity is shadowed and overpowered by political, social, economic and geopolitical asymmetries perpetuated by the Italian and EU regime of border enforcement, visa policies and migration management.

The Strait of Otranto, in the accounts of several Italian informants, represents a liminal temporal gate as well, a virtual time machine. In the words of a high-ranking police officer, 'an imaginary door separates and divides, just as a temporal gate, our civilization and our culture from those of our closest neighbour, Albania' (D'Alessandro 2002: 24). Similarly, Luca,[8] a lawyer and a volunteer, said that a visit to Albania in the early 1990s gave him the impression of experiencing the miserable conditions of late eighteenth-century post-revolutionary France (personal interview, 14 January 2005). What lies on the other side of the Strait of Otranto – Albania, and more generally what a pervasive Orientalism[9] still lumps together as 'the Balkans'[10] – is relegated to a condition of backwardness and archetypical violence. In Luca's morally charged account, migrants from Albania sheltered in a public gym in Otranto 'ate even the soap bars' (ibid.). And a tailor, in commenting on a picturesque postcard from Tirana, regretted that 'it is useless that they build these new and nice architectures: sooner or later they are going to destroy everything anyway' (personal interview, 14 August 2004).

The Albanians' gaze, on the other hand, has been more conspicuously (although not exclusively) directed towards their neighbours across the strait. Italy and the Italian language have often entered Albanian homes on a daily basis through radio and television channels.[11] Providing Albania (and Italy) with a glossy, celebratory, simplified version of 'Italy', Italian mass media contributed to the creation of Italy as the closest 'America' for Albanians.[12] More generally, economic, legal and geopolitical inequalities have long made distance/proximity a function of direction: seen from Italy, Albania seems quite far and foreign. Seen from Albania, Italy seems close and familiar. Ironically, these asymmetries have granted indifferent Italians and western Europeans discretionary access to Albania and other Balkan countries, conversely making Italy and the EU accessible to deeply motivated people only at great cost and peril.[13]

Early in March 1991, about 25,000 Albanians arrived at the Apulian ports of Bari, Brindisi and Otranto (Perrone 1996: 33). This time, however, only a few days after the official end of the 1990–91 Gulf War, opinion makers in Italy were starting to articulate concerns about the alleged 'Islamic danger' inherent in such migration. Others were making similarly arbitrary connections between the Ottomans' brief and brutal conquest of Otranto (1480–81) and contemporary migration, rhetorically asking, 'Wasn't Vlorë [in Albania] the port from which in 1480 Mehmed II moved to conquer Otranto, the same city to which Albanians are pouring today?' (in Dal Lago 2004: 182). Still others worried about the threat to the body of the nation after a few cases of scabies were reported.

The Don Giuseppe mentioned above is the former director of Otranto's diocesan branch of Caritas, a large international relief, development and social services organization inspired by Catholic social teachings. Recalling the first instances of his personal and institutional involvement with migration, he stated that for three months starting in March 1991, 1,200 newly arrived migrants from Albania were kept in the tourist camping ground of Frassanito near Otranto, under the authority of the police prefect (*prefetto*).[14] During this time, Don Giuseppe and Caritas provided humanitarian assistance but refused to directly administer the camp on behalf of the state. Especially concerned about the 200 children who were in the camp, Caritas arranged for the local juvenile court to temporarily entrust them to Caritas's care. Discussing this point in an interview, Don Giuseppe, red in the face, remarked: 'ma la Caritas non si fece venire in mente di aprire un campo!' (but Caritas did not come up with the idea of opening a camp for them!) (personal interview, 11 August 2004). Here, Don Giuseppe's use of the conjunction *ma*, his tone and the context of the interview suggest a critical stance towards the choices of other Catholic actors who, as explained below, later privileged the encampment solution.

These children, Don Giuseppe continued, were brought into the province's villages, close to parishes and Caritas branches, and on weekends local families got involved by welcoming them into their homes.

Don Giuseppe's recollections certainly raise several questions concerning the potentially arbitrary and authoritarian nature of humanitarian decision-making. Were these children orphans? Had they lost contact with their relatives during disembarkation, or had the police randomly and forcibly separated them from their families? Rather than merely celebrating diffused popular solidarity or problematizing Caritas's concern and care for the children, these questions interrogate the state's inexperienced, improvisational management of these arrivals during what were routinely defined as 'emergencies', and its response to the need to humanely cope with the considerable impact of an influx of numerous new non-citizen subjects.

In August 1991, as many as 10,000 Albanians, many of whom arrived on the dangerously overcrowded commercial ship *Vlora*, were interned in the old soccer stadium of Bari, Apulia's capital. Surrounded by armed police forces, the stadium held the migrants under the scorching sun for a week. The police refreshed the detainees by spraying water on them, helicopters dropped food rations and bottled water was thrown to them from outside the soccer field's fence. Several hundred detainees who had been promised residence permits were instead deported to Albania. Albania was no longer communist, and its immigrants were no longer represented as heroes. At the national level, the image of these Albanians was now that of violent, ragged beggars whom one at best needed to rescue, nourish and clean (Dal Lago 2004: 183.)

Quite significantly, detention in the stadium arguably constituted an important early step in Italians' acquisition of cultural knowledge and moral evaluation of migrant 'difference' (and of 'self'). Symbolically, but also materially in terms of logistics, this early instance of 'emergency' internment anticipated successive permanent forms and structures of internment in Italy and the EU, and the enforceability of the border as instrumental to national security.

With the benefit of hindsight, Don Giuseppe stated that Otranto's Caritas had realized as early as the early 1990s that large migrant camps were not 'humane' and were organized only to facilitate police control, which was something that 'it is not my duty [as a priest] to contribute to' (personal interview, 11 August 2004). On the other hand, religious and lay residents of Apulia participated wholeheartedly and sincerely in providing necessary assistance. Very rarely were the main actors of this solidarity the elite, notable or wealthy members of the local community. As several interviewees emphasized, 'it is the poor who care for and give to other persons in need', if only by offering 'a box of cookies, a quart of milk, a jar of jam'. On chilly nights coastal residents brought blankets, clean clothes and homemade meals to migrants on the shores. Hundreds of persons, both children and adults, were privately sheltered by families and priests. Medical, police and other personnel worked after hours or volunteered their time and expertise. According to the Minister of the Interior (2002), between 1990 and 1999 '209,500 foreigners have been assisted' in Apulia, including 67,000 Albanians, 3,000 Croats, 14,000 Somalis, 80,000 Yugoslavs and Bosnians, 15,000 Kurds and 30,000 Kosovars.

As further explained below, the state solicited the involvement of local volunteer and Catholic services, and for more than a decade they proved indispensable to the management of such migration. But with very few exceptions, these volunteer forces were unable to take full advantage of the political leverage ensured by the state's dependency on their services. In short, they were unable, or unwilling, to try to foster a legislative shift in the state's 'public order' approach to migration. Like Fassin (2005: 375), I can say that episodes of compassion towards migrants 'appear as privileged moments of collective redemption eluding the common law of their repression'. Still, for many Catholic and lay individuals, migrant disembarkations (*sbarchi*) of the 1990s were the beginning of an involvement that was cultivated and extended into other arenas of volunteer work with migrants. Several volunteers who began working within parish activities or other religious frameworks later used that expertise working for state or local institutions of migration management. Thus it was unexceptional for priests to be involved in migration issues and the resulting mass media coverage. The social and charismatic role of Catholic priests and bishops in the local communities, their moral and intellectual authority and prestige, and their charitable mobilization first for Italian emigrants and then for immigrants contributed to their becoming public 'experts' on migration.[15] In addition, parishes have often worked as shelters for migrants and as meeting venues for associations trying to elaborate forms of migrant assistance or even resistance to policies seen as exclusionary and unjust. Indeed, there is little doubt that state immigration policies and practices have often contributed to a culture of emergency towards '*stranieri*' (foreigners). Intentionally or not, they have fostered an exclusionary 'knowledge' of migration as a 'threat' to security and public order,[16] as the following examples demonstrate.

Decree No. 152 of 2 May 1995 established the Salento army mission. Between May and November 1995, about five hundred patrols were conspicuously dispatched to the Salento coastline with the purported objective to 'obtain a more pervasive control of public order and guarantee citizens' security' (Esercito Italiano n.d.). According to the Italian Army, the mission, featuring the following specifications, was considered an 'important' operation:

- 1,650 places of observation
- 767 vehicle controls
- 2,604 procedures of identification
- 3,029 arrests of clandestini (clandestine migrants)
- 10 arrests of suspicious persons
- Total deployment of 1,713 soldiers.
  (Esercito Italiano n.d.)

The army had previously been deployed to southern Italy on missions targeting Mafia and other organized crime. However, this time 'the threat to be faced is different: not strictly internal anymore, but rather coming from abroad' (ibid.).[17] In line with this stance, fishermen rescuing migrants at the mercy of the sea have been prosecuted for complicity in illegal immigration. This is an institutional way to de facto discourage the solidarity that every sailor is ready to extend to *any* fellow seafarer (Delle Donne 2004; Albahari 2006).

March 1997[18] was a major turning point in the institutional reception of migrants and in migration policies. After the arrival in Apulia of 15,000 Albanians, in a situation again defined as an emergency, Decree No. 60 of 20 March 1997 authorized police prefects to expel any foreigner deemed 'undesirable' (Dal Lago 2004: 203, n. 33). Don Giuseppe, who at the time was involved in providing assistance to some of these migrants, recalled that the police prefect of Lecce, on behalf of 'the state,' asked local volunteer forces and the Catholic dioceses of Otranto and Lecce to help find sleeping quarters for at least 600 migrants. Otranto's diocese and Caritas managed to find the 600 places, but in twelve different locations. The prefect rejected that offer because, as Don Giuseppe explained, 'immigration was considered more as a problem of public order than as a social-political issue' (Don Giuseppe, personal interview, 11 August 2004). In other words, migrants could not be dispersed because that would not ensure their manageability by the state. Opposing this idea of migrants' concentration and control, in several conversations with me Don Giuseppe emphasized how he and his Caritas branch repeatedly proposed to state authorities that individual migrants be hosted in the homes of local families, and migrant family groups housed in small autonomous apartments. This, he was convinced, would help them access the social, administrative, legal and economic networks and resources necessary for everyday life.

Meanwhile, the diocese of Lecce, guided by Archbishop Ruppi, offered a *single* site with up to 500 potential places (Don Giuseppe, personal interview, 11 August 2004) – the Regina Pacis, a former seaside resort for children on the Adriatic coast near Lecce, donated to the diocese by a private citizen. The state accepted this diocese's offer of help, and 500 migrants were sent to the centre, marking the institutionalization of the cooperation of church and state in managing migration. Don Cesare, a dynamic young priest, became the director of the Regina Pacis centre on behalf of the diocese of Lecce. As an 'expert' on immigration management and human trafficking, Don Cesare has given hundreds of interviews to Italian and European mass media. Various institutions, some at the EU level, have invited him as a consultant, and he has been a panellist at conferences and meetings all over Europe. What follows is his account of the early phases of the centre at the Regina Pacis and of state-church cooperation, which deserves to be quoted at some length:

> My service to migrants began with migrants, in the sense that it is they who came to our house. Especially in 1997, it was a reality that deeply affected our Salento region: many people arriving, no organised welcome and reception, no presence of the state. Even voluntary forces were scared by a phenomenon that featured extremely high numbers. Christian humanism doesn't fear numbers, because it makes available what it's got, and tries to turn a difficult moment into an opportunity for doing good to others. In 1997 we had a migratory phenomenon welcomed in ways rich in charity. Maybe there was little organisation, but certainly there was a shelter and a meal, and assistance and guarantees not offered by others, and certainly not by the state. It is evident that the transition from emergency to a situation of ordinary migration influx has brought migration facilities to grow as well. At the beginning we were an improvised camp of migrants, with time we have become a facility of welcome and reception with rules and several methodologies of specialized intervention.... Moreover, the Regina Pacis has carried the moral weight of being the first facility of reception in Italy, [and] therefore of having the duty to dictate the rule to other facilities, through forms of dedication to the human being made up of small things, but anyway of value. It is obvious that the interpretation of reception that the [immigration] legislation has provided is completely different. The understanding of migration is completely different. Because following that kindness of reception we witnessed, since 1998, a legislation that has used a completely different interpretive key. This key is related to preoccupations about social order and security, invasion, Islamisation and to many readings that have changed the politics vis-à-vis migration.

(Personal interview, 22 September 2004)

Here Don Cesare was expressing the consensus that emerges from additional interviews, archival research and participant observation I did in conference settings and in migrants' assistance venues: prior to the 1998 establishment of institutionalized and publicly financed migration centres, charity and solidarity were represented as disorganized, isolated efforts to compensate for the state's inactivity. The 'Turco-Napolitano' immigration law (40/1998) institutionalized previously informal shelters and charitable activities, structuring and financing the allegedly disorganized and isolated charitable grassroots efforts. Thus it was generally well received by Catholic and other voluntary organizations, even though it focused on policing and regulation rather than on proposing organic policies of integration. The law legally defined the Regina Pacis and similar centres oxymoronically as '*centri di permanenza temporanea e assistenza*' (centres for the temporary permanence and assistance of migrants), giving shape to a national and EU network of migrant-processing facilities. The 'Bossi-Fini' immigration law of 2002 (189/2002) further restricted the channels of legal migration, including asylum and work residence, and reinforced the policing function of centres, sanctioning them as the only legitimate and functional shelters for most types of migrants. Most recently, legal dispositions on security (Law No. 125/2008) formally changed the name of the old '*centri di permanenza temporanea e assistenza*' to '*centri di identificazione ed espulsione*' (CIE, centres for the identification and expulsion of migrants).

At present, the Italian state network comprises thirteen such identification and expulsion centres and additionally twelve centres of *accoglienza* (reception) formally intended for immediate assistance (CDA, *centri di accoglienza*) and for the reception of asylum seekers (CARA, *centri di accoglienza per richiedenti asilo*).[19] The identification and expulsion centres, which independent cooperatives and NGOs run and manage on the state's behalf, are essentially administrative detention facilities. They hold several 'categories' of people for periods of up to eighteen months before deportation or before a migrant is notified of an expulsion decree. Detainees may include migrants who, for example, were discovered on the Apulian coastline or rescued off the coast of Sicily and might or might not be able to submit an asylum application, have been caught with expired residence permits or forged documents, or have just been released from prison (after serving time for common crimes) and transferred to migration centres to await deportation or the expulsion decree. About 60,000 individuals stayed at the Regina Pacis centre between 1997 and the end of 2004, when its convention with the Italian state was terminated.

Charity behind Bars

From 1997 to 2000, the Regina Pacis centre was managed by the diocesan Caritas of Lecce. In 2000, the newly established Regina Pacis Foundation, headed by Don Cesare and the archbishop, assumed control of the centre, replacing the diocese. In several interviews and in other venues, Don Cesare underlined the charitable nature of the diocese's and the foundation's efforts at the Regina Pacis, emphasizing that 'migrants' reception entails openness, charity and sacrifice.' He often insisted on explaining that 'it is not us who wanted gates and bars outside the centre, but the Law' (*Gazzetta del Mezzogiorno*, 19 August 2004). Indeed, interviews with migrants and extensive participant observation suggest that everyday life behind bars in immigration facilities is inherently frustrating and entails an experience of time as cyclical and uneventful. Oleg, for example,[20] a 35-year-old Ukrainian man formerly detained at the Regina Pacis, lamented the emptiness of daily routine: 'All you do is eat and sleep, and you cannot but ruminate all the time.' Ahmad, a Tunisian fisherman and long-time resident of Italy with his family, also spent some time in the Regina Pacis wearily waiting for a police interview. He said that though he did not have any interaction with the management, he knew the centre's director to be a Catholic priest and was certainly not bothered by that. Ahmad stressed his opinion that the material conditions at the centre were adequate. By contrast, the Regina Pacis was a 'terrible experience' for Olga, a Moldovan woman in her late twenties who speaks Italian, Romanian, Russian and Ukrainian. She told me she had come to Italy on a tourist visa (for which she paid €3,000) and worked near Naples as a maid paid by the hour for nearly two years. She complained that the separate quarters for men and women at the centre did not stop men from harassing women. Some of the female inmates, allegedly former prostitutes, were continuously baited by army guards (*Carabinieri*). And at any rate, all the *Carabinieri* in the facility were men.

Clearly, both running these immigration centres and being detained in them necessarily entail coping with the institutional and discretionary demands of law enforcement. Migrant detention and identification facilities cannot but harbour a structural situation of psychological, verbal, legal and potentially physical abuse,[21] regardless of the possibly good intentions of the management. In one example I observed a small group of young Kurdish Iraqi men who, having arrived at the Apulian port of Brindisi hidden in a truck, were taken to one of the region's migrant identification facilities. There, when they declined to have their fingerprints taken, a high-ranking police officer threatened them, saying their continued refusal would result in their being charged and jailed as Islamic terrorists. During long waits for deportation, police interviews or the outcome of legal appeals, detainees experience resignation, frustration, vandalism and self-destruction, including political gestures of protest such as sewing lips together or scarring oneself on the arms and chest with razors or glass. Moreover, the guards are often inexperienced – and unmotivated, as they go about their duties dealing with unarmed civilians with whom they are often unable to speak.

The Church as the State's Nurse: Politics of Charity

The Catholic Church, according to Don Cesare, has built a net of solidarity and reception working as *'l'infermiera dello Stato'* [the state's nurse] (Don Cesare, *Movimento Cristiano Lavoratori* Conference, Lecce, 21 January 2005). He deplored the absence of any serious state policy of migrants' inclusion and criticized the institution of migration facilities – such as the Regina Pacis itself – as responding only to a logic of control and public order. In this framework, he said, charity is exploited and its operators, himself included, become bureaucrats of exclusion. The church as 'the state's nurse' is a phrase that can help us articulate a wider discussion on the relationship between church, state and charity work as regards such bureaucracy of exclusion and border management.

Charitable institutions, often under church control, have historically been called on to govern the 'accidents, infirmities, and various anomalies'[22] (Foucault 2003: 244) the modern state encounters in its continuous labour of self-formation and sustenance. In this case, the church, together with all other Catholic and lay organizations involved, has in effect been working *for* and *as* the state by assisting, processing, managing and detaining subjects on the state's behalf. In doing so, it has been working to cure, support and nourish the state itself.[23] As I stated above, without the practical and moral contribution of non-governmental actors including dioceses, the Misericordia confraternity, parishes, the Red Cross and myriad other organizations, the state would have been unable to manage its south-eastern border region and more broadly migration on its territory.

In summary, the prolongation of migrants' lives through food and shelter – in Apulia, in Lampedusa and throughout the Italian and EU network of migrant detention facilities – might very well be due 'to charity and not to right', to use Arendt's insightful words (1958: 296), and to the implementation of 'humanitarian' tenets. But this also serves political and police ends, as I turn now to discuss.

Because all centres are rigorously closed to the public and to journalists, the network of centres is often accused of 'hiding' migrants and information about their condition from public engagement. I am politically sympathetic towards this stance, yet I contend that these centres do not merely 'hide' ready-made information or knowledge but rather also *produce* knowledge and information essential to state mechanisms of governance and self-sustenance. Migrants are privileged objects of knowledge and management (Ngai 2004; Inda 2005), and the camp and centre structure enables such knowledge production. Documentary accumulation, medicine, psychiatry, anthropology, photography and bureaucracy have traditionally gained access to migrants, including refugees, because they

Figure 10.2. The entrance of the centre for the identification of asylum seekers in Otranto. It is currently functioning as a centre of immediate assistance (CDA). (Photo: Maurizio Albahari)

are placed in camps (Malkki 1992). To this series of gazing practices, we can add charity. The Regina Pacis and similar centres, while materially enabling the immediate bureaucratic and physical control of migrants, also work symbolically by mass-producing frames of reference, and in this sense they are doing cultural work. They help produce an *aesthetics of migration* that is political and conveys a clear political message.

To explain: the centres, anticipated and epitomized by the Regina Pacis and the Bari soccer stadium in 1991, mentioned above, ensure the categorization and recognizability of the 'masses' they create. Thus migrants' proper place – their almost natural environment, once they have trespassed national borders – becomes the gated, fenced centre.[24] Migrants' internment is constructed as beneficial to both the larger society, which allegedly confines social instability and illegality, and the migrants, who find a place in a 'humanitarian' environment where their physical needs are met. In the process, the inmates' condition of administrative (and occasionally extrajudicial) detention, suffering and isolation is disembodied from 'the totality of human miseries and burdens' (Illich 1987: 16). It becomes insignificant to the larger society, whose fragmentation and inequalities wither vis-à-vis national-identitarian and security concerns about 'immigration'.

Conversely, the humanitarian legitimacy of confinement is also reinforced, for example by regional and national newsmakers.[25] Both in print and on television, journalists rarely refer to immigration centres by their proper (admittedly changing and oxymoronic) bureaucratic definition. Rather, for years they have inadvertently used the implicitly celebratory *centri di accoglienza* (reception centres), defining inmates as *ospiti* (guests) instead of *trattenuti* (arrestees). Even the police, in official documents I have seen, routinely call these centres *centri di accoglienza*. Meanwhile, many local residents understand these simply as centres *for* 'immigrants'. There is little effort to use more precise legal terminology. In fact, that usage is understandable less as a sign of popular ignorance than as an outcome of an essentializing governmental and mass media aesthetics of migration. The implications of using such euphemisms to describe migrants' detention are evident. If these centres provide *accoglienza* in the eyes of Italians, then they must be run with a humanitarian spirit and purpose, and have been established for the migrants' own good. And if 'guests' rebel against their benefactors, they are just ungrateful. Vibrant critical voices are often expelled from mainstream public discourse and are usually attributed to

Figure 10.3. Political graffiti in Lecce. 'Everybody free! Migrants out of concentration camps!' Note the anarchist symbol. (Photo: Maurizio Albahari)

the alleged radicalism and utopianism of leftist, anarchist and even Catholic groups.

Meanwhile, several members of the Italian parliament, ministers and prime ministers, and even then President of the Republic Carlo Azeglio Ciampi have approvingly visited the Regina Pacis. Such high-profile visits, well publicized by local and national media and by the Regina Pacis Foundation itself, have helped celebrate the centre, the church of Lecce, and the people of Salento's worthiness of Nobel candidacy. Perhaps more importantly, media representations of the visits have circulated as icons showcasing the state's institutionalization of 'charity' and 'solidarity' to manage its borders and migration at the fringes of the EU. That is, they have celebrated the state itself.

In reality, as detailed above, long before 11 September 2001, 'exceptional' dispositions and policies, such as the creation of camps and the deployment of the army, had been established as governmental tools to handle the alleged humanitarian and public order 'emergencies' of 1990, 1991 and 1997. Rather than rolling back the state in the neoliberal predicament, or the state ceding some of its power to non-governmental actors, the case under investigation shows the state sustaining itself through a strategic use of religious and lay organizations. This is most evident in the state's contracting with NGOs, cooperatives and foundations – whose work is often explicitly guided by principles of human rights, charity and nongovernmental independence – to perform the labour of assisting, detaining and sheltering migrants. Nevertheless, this contracting of public functions differs from the old concordat tradition that aimed at sharing well-bounded spheres of influence between church and state (Ferrari 2005). Instead, it requires continuous negotiation between public institutions and religious groups that then 'share the regulation and management of the multiple areas of social life at all administrative levels' (Ferrari 2005: 7). Indeed, the dynamics at play here are strategic to larger neoliberal governance, and are locatable within the ongoing global commodification of salvation.[26]

No reasons were officially and publicly offered to explain the Regina Pacis Foundation's unwillingness to renew the centre's convention with the state in December 2004. In his latest public statements Don Cesare has again argued, as he did privately with me, for the need to cooperate with legislators, thus anticipating Benedict XVI's call for apolitical 'practical commitment here and now' in relation to the 'neighbour', who is 'anyone who needs me, and whom I can help' (Benedict XVI 2006: par. 15):

> It's evident that when you find yourself operating within a [immigration] law that puts many limits to your activity, that tells you 'if you want to work in

the reception of migrants, then you must respect certain rules', then you must choose: either you act as a revolutionary kicking the law, or you act as a revolutionary remaining close to the [migrant] human being, even accepting the pressure of the law. (Don Cesare, personal interview, 22 September 2004)

But Don Cesare has also expressed exhaustion – at working as a bureaucrat of exclusion, at the church becoming a servant of the state and at 'charity' being increasingly exploited by 'politics'. Along the same lines, at a national conference on migration organized in Lecce by the Italian Christian Worker Movement, Archbishop Ruppi ultimately conveyed the incompatibility of migrants' reception, detention and growing political pressures: 'Reception (*accoglienza*) and legality are two sides of the same problem, and are both necessary. Reception is a human, civic and Christian duty. Reception is such when it is free of physical and political bars. Christians are such when they welcome the other, when they remember that the first immigrant is Christ' (Ruppi, *Movimento Cristiano Lavoratori* Conference, Lecce, 21 January 2005).

Indeed, several bishops, missionary orders such as the Comboniani; national Caritas, other Catholic and lay NGOs; and even state prosecutors have long expressed serious concerns over the church's involvement in the management of migration for the state. It should also be noted, though, that along with the structural violence of the centres noted above, processes of migrant assistance, processing and even detention, such as those enacted at the Regina Pacis, engender legal identities and power relations that are sometimes difficult to predict.[27] Thus, Don Cesare and the lawyer for the Regina Pacis proudly emphasized that through their intervention,[28] in 2003 around 37 per cent of the centre's inmates who had received an expulsion decree were able to successfully appeal it or to have the expulsion suspended or revoked for health or other reasons[29] (personal interview with the lawyer, 24 September 2004). Also, the Regina Pacis is open as a shelter to homeless or destitute asylum seekers and migrants (regardless of their often 'illegal' status), for which it is not reimbursed by the state (ibid.).

Conclusion: Edges and Centre Stages

Based on the ethnographic case of south-eastern Italy, this chapter argues that contemporary borders are a modality of power working not merely through classical sovereign surveillance, but also through knowledge production and moral precepts[30] that include spatial and aesthetic imageries, forms of charity and humanitarian assistance. The biopolitical governmental concern with migrants' survival nourishes and effects the material, territorialized and militarized nature of enforced geopolitical borders, detention and deportation. In other words, migrants surviving border militarization and unauthorized transport are certainly rescued, fed and sheltered in border locales. But through these very processes they are also fingerprinted, identified, interned and deported. It is in fact these material, moral and legal mechanisms of administration of territory and bodies across it that constitute the fulcrum of Italian and EU power to 'allocate, classify, categorize, and formalize categories of the human' (Ong 2003: 17).

What is usually categorized under the shorthand of 'the border' is therefore a broad assemblage of meanings, practices and engagements. Becoming highly significant in the spectacle of enforcement that renders law and migrant 'illegality' visible and natural (De Genova 2002: 436; see also Pottage 2004), the border as the solidified, legitimate and iconic[31] container of national and EU citizenry is institutionally constructed, maintained and related to certain popular perceptions and experiences of proximity, distance and inequality.[32] My ethnographic focus on such institutional mechanisms also helps to reveal the identitarian, administrative and political labour through which hegemonies of nationhood and supranational community are *being* produced.[33] In Apulia, for example, soldiers and immigration centres' staff – as southerners subjected to the disparaging moral geography that normatively describes southern Italy as culturally, socially and economically inferior to northern Italy[34] – now tend to position themselves both as rigorous and compassionate gatekeepers, and as full-fledged members of Italy, the EU and 'the West.'[35]

Police forces at the border have pointed out to me that it is clearly impossible to 'control' the maritime border in its entirety. Indeed, I would argue that the rhetoric of 'fortress Europe'[36] is less an insightful descriptive and analytical device than it is a normative trademark of sovereignty, one that is arguably losing some of its credibility and legitimacy. This is partly due to the evidence of continuous landings, and to the relative disquiet with which Italian citizens and EU institutional actors take in the daily chronicle of migrant death in the Mediterranean. The case study I have presented, then, suggests that charity and humanitarianism might symbolically provide a novel moral-aesthetic institutional trademark that ostensibly legitimizes the Italian state's large-scale, unrewarding, often lethal project of human mobility regulation. Logistically, charity and humanitarianism have also allowed for the implementation of exclusionary national and EU practices of patrol, surveillance and administrative detention.

Ethnographic and historical analysis of the south-eastern Italian case suggests that the (Italian) state and the EU, rather than being merely 'challenged' by migration, function as partly overlapping, complementary networks that form and maintain themselves in part through border discourses and activities vis-à-vis migration. In this sense, the edges of the Italian state and the EU are not merely marginal spaces but rather centre stages[37] of liberal-democratic myths of self-legitimation effected through sovereignty and humanitarianism.

Acknowledgements

This work draws on my larger doctoral research, completed at the University of California at Irvine, Department of Anthropology (2006). Writing was made possible by a 2006–07 Carey Postdoctoral Fellowship at the Erasmus Institute, University of Notre Dame; a 2005–06 Visiting Research Fellowship at the Center for Comparative Immigration Studies, University of California at San Diego; and a 2006 University of California Regents' Dissertation Fellowship. Fieldwork was made possible by a fellowship grant of the Institute of European Studies at the University of California at Berkeley (2002), and by numerous fellowship grants generously awarded by the Department of Anthropology and the School of Social Sciences at the University of California at Irvine (2001–05). I am also indebted to everyone in Italy who shared their time, expertise, frustrations, opinions, everyday lives and a glimpse of their worldviews with me, and to the helpful and insightful readers of this chapter's drafts: Jutta Lauth Bacas and William Kavanagh, Bill Maurer, Victoria Bernal, Leo Chavez, Tamara Stojanović Albahari, Allison Fish, my anonymous reviewers and copyeditor. I alone am responsible for any errors in fact or judgement associated with this work.

Notes

1. *'Note on Geography.* Mediterranean coasts are divided into two / of departure and arrival, but with no balance: / more beaches and more nights of embarkment, than of disembarkment; / fewer lives touch Italy than the many that embarked. / Misfortune parts the bill and us, who are part of it. / And yet Italy is an open word, full of air.'
   All translations from Italian poetry, newspapers, scholarly literature, personal interviews and conferences are mine.
2. The administrative Region of Apulia comprises the south-eastern peninsular part (the so-called 'heel') of Italy, stretching into the Ionian and Adriatic Seas and facing the Balkan Peninsula. Together with Sicily and Calabria, it has been at the forefront of the

reception of maritime migration since 1990, largely because of its accessibility from Albanian, Montenegrin, Greek, Egyptian and Turkish ports.

3. Throughout the chapter, 'Catholic' stands for 'Roman Catholic'.

4. 'Migration' and 'migrants' are hereafter used to include those persons who, arriving in 'mixed flows' to the southern Italian territory on vessels or as stowaways, are categorized as asylum seekers, economic immigrants or even 'clandestine' immigrants in contingent and state-centred taxonomies. Areas of origin include Northern and sub-Saharan Africa (especially Somalia and Eritrea), the Middle East (especially Palestine, Syria, Iraq, Iran, Turkey and Afghanistan), southern Asia and, prior to recent concessions in visa regimes, the Balkan Peninsula (including Albania, Kosovo/Serbia and Bosnia-Herzegovina).

5. This chapter is supported by extensive and transnational ethnographic field research (2001–2006). In Italy, I focused on partly overlapping Catholic-migrant and state-migrant interfaces, and on how knowledge about migration, Islam and Catholicism is produced (e.g., in conferences, roundtables, demonstrations). I used methods such as participant observation and in-depth interviews in the local community in Apulia, in conference settings, and in the border apparatus of police control and migrants' assistance, processing and detention; systematic monitoring of national and European media; archival research and textual and visual analysis. The chapter alone cannot account for the full complexity of citizens' and migrants' predicament in southern Italy – the bibliographic section is intended to complement the chapter. For example, space limitations do not allow me to include a discussion of important cosmopolitan practices resisting the border under scrutiny.

6. The European Agency for the Management of Operational Cooperation at the External Borders of the Member States of the European Union, or FRONTEX, is the EU agency for external border security.

7. Scrutinized by a burgeoning anthropological scholarship, exemplified by Fassin and Pandolfi (2010), Fassin (2011), Dumbour and Kelly (2011) and Bornstein and Redfield (2011).

8. A pseudonym.

9. In Edward Said's (1979) understanding of the term.

10. As detailed by Todorova (1997).

11. It is also worth noting that fascist Italy invaded Albania (1939–1943), that Italian tobacco smugglers collaborated with Albanian communist authorities from the 1970s to 1990, that republican Italy sent its army to Albania on several missions during the 1990s and that Italian entrepreneurs look to Albania for cheap labour and outsourcing opportunities.

12. See Pajo (2001) for an introduction to Albanian articulations of belonging and longing to travel 'West;' see also Kosic and Triandafyllidou (2003). For a fictional account, see the movie *Lamerica* by Gianni Amelio (1994).

13. As I detail in Albahari (2006, where I provide data and references on smuggling routes, military patrolling and casualties), the recent history of the Strait of Otranto is a history of death at sea. See also Leogrande (2011).

14. The police prefect operated on behalf of and under the Ministry of the Interior.

15. And although pseudo-Christian arguments, in Italy and elsewhere, are increasingly used by non-religious pundits in nativist, anti-Muslim and xenophobic 'crusades', 76 per cent of migrant respondents declared that 'the Italian Church supports immigrants' (Cotesta 2002: 106).

16. See Foucault (2003) for a discussion on public order, social security and governance.

17. During 1997, the Italian Army was also deployed in Albania itself. Moreover, the Italian Military Navy enacted a naval blockade in the Strait of Otranto. See Albahari (2006).

18. The social, political and military upheaval that characterized Albania in early spring 1997 was largely due to the collapse of pyramid financial schemes, the consequent

widespread loss of savings and the popular suspicion of government corruption and involvement in the schemes.

19. On these centres, see Sossi (2002); Amnesty International (2005); Rovelli (2006); Sciurba (2009); Medici Senza Frontiere (2010). On immigration laws in Italy see Calavita (2005); Zincone (2006).

20. Oleg, Ahmad and Olga are pseudonyms.

21. Given this structural situation, it is relatively unsurprising that starting in 2001, Don Cesare faced judicial prosecution for several abuses. In 2005 he was convicted, along with two doctors, five staff members and eleven army officers, of physical violence perpetrated on inmates who had tried to escape. Testimonies of physical violence throughout CIE facilities abound.

22. In a world of nation-states, migration interrogates the naturalized overlap of 'the nation' and 'the state,' and is therefore represented as the anomaly *par excellence.* The pervasive discourse of humanitarian and security 'emergency' on the Apulian coast is evidently mutually constituted with this representation of migration as a disrupting and challenging anomaly.

23. For a comparative understanding of the intersection of state, faith-based services and politics, see Wuthnow (2004). Holmes (2000: 47) explores the historical roots of the EU as deeply related to Catholic ideas of subsidiarity and of the common good.

24. In this respect, the centres resonate with the neoliberal penal system recently analysed by Wacquant (2009).

25. On the ideological impact of news making see Chavez (2008); Cook (2005).

26. A theme pioneered by Comaroff and Comaroff (2000). For comparative purposes, and for an excellent historical survey of the relationships between salvation, charity and morality in North America, see Loseke (1997).

27. Coutin (1994) points out some of the ambiguous effects of migrant 'assistance' in the U.S. context, focusing on the Californian Sanctuary movement, a grassroots religion-based network that formed in the early 1980s to aid and support undocumented Central American refugees (see also Cunningham 1995). The differences from the Italian case are obvious, as Italian centres work for the state whereas these sanctuaries worked in direct defiance of it. Practices of sanctuary thus resisted the exclusionary and restrictionist policies of U.S. asylum. Yet they also reinforced the distinction between legal and illegal immigration, objectified Central Americans, subjected them to screening and created a hierarchy between people who were defined as refugees or otherwise and the defining workers (ibid.: 300). In so doing, Coutin proposes, these practices also reinforced the official U.S. policy that sought to constitute these immigrants as 'illegal aliens'. This is to argue, in Coutin's case as well as in mine, that the practical and political implications of charitable practices in border settings 'derive not only from their ultimate goals, but also from the practices themselves' (ibid.; see Fisher 1997). Ethnography is therefore methodologically indispensable.

28. Indeed, a discretionary one.

29. The high rate of successful appeals shows the weak basis of expulsion decrees in the first place. The lawyer in the appeal procedure is paid by individual inmates, or by the state if the latter loses the case.

30. A growing body of literature (e.g., Heyman 1998; Carens 2003; Seglow 2005) is addressing the ethics of immigration.

31. My use of 'iconic' follows Herzfeld (1992: 107ff.).

32. To gain a comparative perspective on these perceptions, see Darian-Smith (1999); Suarez-Navaz (2004).

33. And contested: see Albahari (2008a, 2008b).

34. See, for example, Gramsci 1971 (especially pp. 55ff.); Teti 1993; Cole 1997; Schneider 1998; Albahari 2008b.

35. For accounts of identitarian and political interplays in Italy, see Carter 1997; Agnew 2002; Sniderman et al. 2000; Albahari 2007, 2008a, 2008b; Lucht 2011.
36. Used pervasively, for example by Geddes (2000).
37. A similar argument has been articulated by Talal Asad (2004).

References

Agnew, J.A. 2002. *Place and Politics in Modern Italy.* Chicago: The University of Chicago Press.

Albahari, M. 2006. 'Silent Death and the Moral State: Making Borders and Sovereignty at Europe's Southern Maritime Edges', Working Paper 136, University of California at San Diego: Center for Comparative Immigration Studies. Retrieved 25 April 2013 from http://ccis.ucsd.edu/wp-content/uploads/2012/07/CCIS-Albahari-death-and-the-moral-state-june-15-2006.pdf

——. 2007. 'Religious Symbols: Made in Italy', *ISIM Review* 19: 30–31. Retrieved 25 April 2013 from https://openaccess.leidenuniv.nl/handle/1887/17124

——. 2008a. 'Staging Cosmopolitanism', *ISIM Review* 22: 12–13. Retrieved 25 April 2013 from https://openaccess.leidenuniv.nl/handle/1887/17261

——. 2008b. 'Between Mediterranean Centrality and European Periphery: Migration and Heritage in Southern Italy', *International Journal of Euro-Mediterranean Studies* 1(2): 141–62. Retrieved 20 July 2010 from http://www.emuni.si/press/ISSN/1855-3362/1_141-162.pdf

Amnesty International. 2005. 'Italy: Temporary Stay - Permanent Rights'. Retrieved 20 July 2010 from http://www.amnesty.org/en/library/info/EUR30/004/2005

Arendt, H. 1958 [1951]. *The Origins of Totalitarianism.* Cleveland and New York: Meridian Books.

Asad, T. 2004. 'Where Are the Margins of the State?' in V. Das and D. Poole (eds), *Anthropology in the Margins of the State.* Santa Fe: School of American Research Press, pp. 79–88.

Benedict XVI. 2006. Encyclical Letter *Deus Caritas Est.* Vatican City: Libreria Editrice Vaticana.

Bornstein, E. and P. Redfield, eds. 2011. *Forces of Compassion: Humanitarianism Between Ethics and Politics.* Santa Fe, NM: SAR Press.

Calavita, K. 2005. *Immigrants at the Margins: Law, Race, and Exclusion in Southern Europe.* Cambridge: Cambridge University Press.

Carens, J.H. 2003. 'Who Should Get In? The Ethics of Immigration Admissions', *Ethics & International Affairs* 17(1): 95-110.

Carter, D.M. 1997. *States of Grace: Senegalese in Italy and the New European Immigration.* Minneapolis: University of Minnesota Press.

Chavez, L.R. 2008. *The Latino Threat: Constructing Immigrants, Citizens, and the Nation.* Stanford, CA: Stanford University Press.

Cole, J. 1997. *The New Racism in Europe: A Sicilian Ethnography.* Cambridge: Cambridge University Press.

Comaroff, J. and J.L Comaroff. 2000. 'Millennial Capitalism: First Thoughts on a Second Coming', *Public Culture* 12(2): 291–343.

Cook, T.E. 2005. *Governing With the News: The News Media as a Political Institution,* 2nd ed. Chicago: University of Chicago Press.

Cotesta, V. 1999. 'Mass Media, Ethnic Conflict and Migration. A Research on the Italian Newspapers in the Nineties', *Studi Emigrazione* XXXVI(135): 387–499.

——. 2002. *Lo Straniero: Pluralismo Culturale e Immagini dell'Altro nella Società Globale.* Rome and Bari, Italy: Laterza.

Coutin, S. 1994. 'Enacting Law through Social Practice: Sanctuary as a Form of Resistance', in M. Lazarus-Black and S.F. Hirsch (eds), *Contested States: Law, Hegemony, and Resistance.* New York and London: Routledge, pp. 282–303.

Cunningham, H. 1995. *God and Caesar at the Rio Grande: Sanctuary and the Politics of Religion.* Minneapolis: University of Minnesota Press.

D'Alessandro, A. 2002. *La Porta d'Oriente.* Bari, Italy: Uniongrafica Corcelli.

Dal Lago, A. 2004. *Non-Persone: L'Esclusione dei Migranti in una Società Globale.* Milan: Feltrinelli.

Darian-Smith, E. 1999. *Bridging Divides: The Channel Tunnel and English Legal Identity in the New Europe.* Berkeley: University of California Press.

De Genova, N.P. 2002. 'Migrant "Illegality" and Deportability in Everyday Life', *Annual Review of Anthropology* 31: 419–47.

Delle Donne, M. 2004. *Un Cimitero Chiamato Mediterraneo: Per una Storia del Diritto d'Asilo nell'Unione Europea.* Rome: DeriveApprodi.

De Luca, Erri. 2005. *Solo andata: righe che vanno troppo spesso a capo.* Milan: Feltrinelli.

Dembour, M. and T. Kelly (eds.). 2011. *Are Human Rights for Migrants? Critical Reflections on the Status of Irregular Migrants in Europe and the United States.* New York: Routledge.

Esercito Italiano. n.d. 'Operazione Salento'. Retrieved 20 July 2010 from http://www.esercito .difesa.it/Attivita/OperazioniinTerritorioNazionale/Pagine/Salento.aspx

Fassin, D. 2005. 'Compassion and Repression: The Moral Economy of Immigration Policies in France', *Cultural Anthropology* 20(3): 362–87.

———. 2011. *Humanitarian Reason: A Moral History of the Present.* Berkeley, CA: University of California Press.

Fassin, D. and M. Pandolfi (eds.). 2010. *Contemporary States of Emergency: The Politics of Military and Humanitarian Interventions.* New York: Zone Books.

Favell, A. 2002. 'Italy as a Comparative Case', in R. Grillo and J. Pratt (eds), *The Politics of Recognizing Difference: Multiculturalism Italian-style.* Aldershot: Ashgate, pp. 237–48.

Ferrari, S. 2005. 'Religions, Secularity and Democracy in Europe: For a New Kelsenian Pact', Jean Monnet Working Paper 03/05. New York: New York University School of Law. Retrieved 20 July 2010 from http://centers.law.nyu.edu/jeanmonnet/archive/ papers/05/050301.rtf

Fisher, W. 1997. 'Doing Good? The Politics and Antipolitics of NGO Practices', *Annual Review of Anthropology* 26: 439–64.

Foucault, M. 2003 [1997]. *'Society Must Be Defended'. Lectures at the College de France, 1975–76,* trans. D. Macey. New York: Picador.

Geddes, A. 2000. *Immigration and European Integration: Towards Fortress Europe?* New York: Manchester University Press.

Gramsci, A. 1971. *Selection from the Prison Notebooks,* ed. and trans. Q. Hoare and G.N. Smith. New York: International Publishers.

Herzfeld, M. 1992. *The Social Production of Indifference: Exploring the Symbolic Roots of Western Bureaucracy.* New York: Berg.

Heyman, J.M. 1998. *Finding a Moral Heart for U.S. Immigration Policy: An Anthropological Perspective* (American Ethnological Society Monograph Series). Arlington, VA: American Anthropological Association.

Holmes, D.R. 2000. *Integral Europe: Fast-Capitalism, Multiculturalism, Neofascism.* Princeton, NJ: Princeton University Press.

Illich, I. 1987. 'Hospitality and Pain', paper presented in Chicago at the invitation of David Ramage of McCormick Theological Seminary. Retrieved 20 July 2010 from http://www .davidtinapple.com/illich/

Inda, J.X. 2005. *Targeting Immigrants: Government, Technology, and Ethics.* Oxford: Blackwell.

Kosic, A. and A. Triandafyllidou. 2003. 'Albanian Immigrants in Italy: Migration Plans, Coping Strategies and Identity Issues', *Journal of Ethnic and Migration Studies* 29(6): 997–1014.

Leogrande, A. 2011. *Il Naufragio: Morte nel Mediterraneo*. Milan: Feltrinelli.

Loseke, D.R. 1997. '"The Whole Spirit of Modern Philanthropy": The Construction of the Idea of Charity, 1912–1992', *Social Problems* 44(4): 425–44.

Lucht, H. 2011. *Darkness before Daybreak: African Migrants Living on the Margins in Southern Italy Today*. Berkeley: University of California Press.

Malkki, L. 1992. 'National Geographic: The Rooting of Peoples and the Territorialization of National Identity Among Scholars and Refugees', *Cultural Anthropology* 7(1): 24–44.

Medici Senza Frontiere. 2010. 'Al di là del muro. Viaggio nei centri per migranti in Italia'. Retrieved 20 July 2010 from http://www.medicisenzafrontiere.it/Immagini/file/pubbli cazioni/ITA_sommario_aldila_muro.pdf

Minister of the Interior of Italy. 2002. 'L'Emergenza Immigrazione: L'Intervento del Prefetto Michele Lepri Gallerano'. Retrieved 20 July 2010 from http://www.interno.it/minin terno/export/sites/default/it/sezioni/sala_stampa/interview/Interventi/altre/notizia_ 17865.html_8783103.html

Ngai, M.N. 2004. *Impossible Subjects: Illegal Aliens and the Making of Modern America, 1924–1965*. Princeton, NJ: Princeton University Press.

Ong, A. 2003. *Buddha Is Hiding: Refugees, Citizenship, the New America*. Berkeley: University of California Press.

Pajo, E. 2001. 'Longing and Belonging: The West as Territory of Nationness in Albanian Cosmologies', *Anthropology of East Europe Review* 19(1): 98–107.

Perrone, L. (ed.). 1996. *Naufragi Albanesi: Studi, ricerche e riflessioni sull'Albania*. Rome: Sensibili alle Foglie.

Pottage, A. 2004. 'Introduction: The Fabrication of Persons and Things', in A. Pottage and M. Mundy (eds), *Law, Anthropology, and the Constitution of the Social*. Cambridge: Cambridge University Press, pp. 1–39.

Quarta, S. 2006. 'Images of the Kosovo War: The Dichotomous Vision of Children', *The International Communication Gazette* 68(1): 93–103.

Rovelli, M. 2006. *Lager Italiani*. Milan: BUR Rizzoli.

Ruppi, C.F. 2002. 'Prefazione', in A. D'Alessandro, *La Porta d'Oriente*. Bari, Italy: Uniongrafica Corcelli, pp. 7–15.

Said, E.W. 1979. *Orientalism*. New York: Vintage Books.

Schneider, J. (ed.). 1998. *Italy's 'Southern Question': Orientalism in One Country*. Oxford: Berg.

Sciurba, A. 2009. *Campi di forza. Percorsi confinati di migranti in Europa*. Verona, Italy: ombre corte.

Seglow, J. 2005. 'The Ethics of Immigration', *Political Studies Review* 3(3): 317–34.

Sniderman, P.M., et al. 2000. *The Outsider: Prejudice and Politics in Italy*. Princeton, NJ: Princeton University Press.

Sossi, F. 2002. *Autobiografie Negate. Immigrati nei Lager del Presente*. Rome: Manifestolibri.

Suarez-Navaz, L. 2004. *Rebordering the Mediterranean: Boundaries and Citizenship in Southern Europe*. New York and Oxford: Berghahn Books.

Teti, V. 1993. *La Razza Maledetta: Origini del Pregiudizio Antimeridionale*. Rome: Manifestolibri.

Todorova, M. 1997. *Imagining the Balkans*. Oxford: Oxford University Press.

Wacquant, L. 2009. *Punishing the Poor: The Neoliberal Government of Social Insecurity*. Durham, NC, and London: Duke University Press.

Wuthnow, R. 2004. *Saving America? Faith-Based Services and the Future of Civil Society*. Princeton, NJ: Princeton University Press.

Zincone, G. 2006. 'The Making of Policies: Immigration and Immigrants in Italy', *Journal of Ethnic and Migration Studies* 32(3): 347–75.

Chapter 11

Managing Proximity and Asymmetry in Border Encounters
The Reception of Undocumented Migrants on a Greek Border Island

Jutta Lauth Bacas

Introduction

On a beautiful summer day in 2007, a local newspaper on the Greek border island of Lesbos published the following item: 'Ten foreigners (three men, three women and four children) were detected on Petalidi beach on Lesbos by coastguard officers at 5:45 A.M.'[1] Those foreigners were boat migrants whose inflatable dinghy washed up on the remote Greek beach from the opposite Turkish shores. The arrival of undocumented migrants on Lesbos was not only daily news in the local newspaper; it was also, in a nutshell, a border encounter entailing all the topics tackled in the present essay: migration movements, cross-border contacts, the intimacy of the face-to-face encounter and the hierarchical standing of the actors involved. Undocumented migrants in trainers and jeans, strangers who have left home and country to flee war and social injustice and the Greek coastguard officers in their blue uniforms: these are the actors in the social scene this chapter will investigate.

The following case study on proximity and asymmetry in border encounters focuses on the Greek island of Lesbos, which is situated on the border between Greece and Turkey in the eastern Mediterranean Sea. The essay aims to analyse irregular border crossing and its consequences at

one of Europe's easternmost borders, where the blue waters of the Mediterranean Sea divide not only two countries, but also the Schengen and
non-Schengen worlds.[2] Since 2000, when Greece first implemented the
Schengen Agreement, its land and sea borders with Turkey have also
become external borders of the Schengen zone at which strict checks on
people exiting or entering the area are obligatory.

The following analysis gives special emphasis to the interaction between foreigners and Greek nationals in the framework of the reception
structure that has been established for so-called boat people: men, women
and children who manage to cross the maritime border and enter Greece
clandestinely. The argument presented here is based on an anthropological research project on the arrival of undocumented migrants on a Greek-
Turkish border island that collected quantitative and qualitative data concerning the means and forms of irregular border crossing and the local
reception structure for handling irregular boat migrants.[3]

The presentation below follows the pattern of this clandestine border
crossing and its consequences. First, border regulations and the binational
framework for legal border crossing between Greece and Turkey are analysed to enhance understanding of the patterns of irregular border crossing in the North Aegean Sea that this chapter investigates and describes.
The second part of the essay analyses the social framework and practical consequences of receiving undocumented migrants on the island of
Lesbos. It describes the procedure of arrest and detention in a detention
centre at Mytilene, the island's capital, with special emphasis on the types
of interaction occurring between locals and foreigners. Then it presents
recent data on the composition of the group of undocumented migrants,
moving into a more detailed analysis of their social profile. The last section of the chapter discusses the question of proximity and asymmetry
in border encounters with regard to the case presented here. The Greek-
Turkish border can be understood as a social scene – a meeting point for
actors from completely different worlds and cultures: undocumented boat
migrants on the one hand and Greek civil servants on the other. The closing remarks address some consequences of the actors' hierarchical standing, particularly the systematic misunderstanding of the needs and best
interests of the boat people who arrive on the island.

Patterns of Border Crossing between Greece and Turkey

The particular border situation of Lesbos has to be understood in relation to its geographical position. A narrow strait five to ten nautical miles
(6.5–12 km) wide separates the island from the mainland opposite, and

the borderline between Greece and Turkey lies exactly in the middle of the strait. Distances are short: the coast of Asia Minor is so close that the lights of Turkish villages are easily seen from many parts of the island. Mytilene, the island's capital and commercial heart, is on the eastern side of the island facing Asia Minor and two provincial Turkish towns. A tradition of small-scale cross-border contacts has existed since the foundation of the modern Greek and Turkish states, when Mytilene was established as a port of exit with police and custom posts, permitting residents and foreigners to leave the country and travel to Turkey on a regular basis.

A discussion of the Aegean Islands should note that until 1912, the Greek islands lying off the coast of Asia Minor were not part of Greece but were still included in the Ottoman Empire (Tzimis et al. 1996: 196f.). The maritime border between Greece and Turkey in its present form was defined and agreed upon by both countries only in 1923, through the Treaty of Lausanne (Clogg 1992: 101). Having been completely closed during World War II, the border crossings and ports of entry reopened in 1946, but strained interstate relations between Greece and Turkey kept cross-border contacts and trade on a small scale for decades. Since the beginning of the new millenium, bilateral political relations have improved, especially now that Greece strongly supports Turkey's application for EU membership. The Greek-Turkish rapprochement led to an increase in cross-border contact at diplomatic and private levels, and to increased volumes of tourism and trade (Lauth Bacas 2003: 249).

Today, traffic of persons and goods between the two countries is governed by both binational legislation and EU regulations on the Greek side. The result is that visa requirements for EU nationals entering Turkey differ from those applying to Turkish nationals entering Greece (and the Schengen area of the European Union). Today, Greeks and other European tourists can legally enter Turkey with ease by presenting valid identity cards, which are the sole visa requirement. Mytilene is a port of exit providing customs services that allow people to leave Greece and enter Turkey as tourists without further complications.[4]

Traffic and legal border crossing from Turkey to Greece is more regulated under the Schengen Agreement signed by EU member states in 1985 (Baldwin-Edwards 2006: 117), which Greece implemented in the year 2000. Since then, to legally enter Greece, Turkish nationals need a visa, which is obtainable only at the Greek embassy in Ankara and the Greek consulates in Istanbul and Izmir. Consequently, Turkish residents of Ayvalik or Dikkili (the provincial towns opposite Lesbos) wishing to travel ten kilometres to Mytilene for a temporary visit must first travel a hundred kilometres to Izmir to queue for a Schengen visa at the Greek consulate. This procedure is costly and time-consuming, so only a very few inhabitants of Turkish coastal towns and villages acquire the needed visa, sometimes after receiving invitations from the Greek side.

Unauthorized entry from Turkey to the Greek islands occurs alongside the authorized way of entering the national territory. In the case of Lesbos, literally unauthorized border crossing is easy by boat because the common frontier is most difficult to guard, especially at night. In those cases, the water channel of five to ten nautical miles serves as a bridge for undocumented migrants hoping to begin a new life in Europe. The departure points for illegal exit from Turkey are usually tiny fishing harbours (where the Turkish coastguard are not present) or remote beaches on the mainland of Asia Minor, where small groups of undocumented migrants from Asian and African countries employ various types of vessels to cross the maritime border and slip into Europe clandestinely. Visitors to remote beaches on Lesbos can come upon dozens of abandoned boats and dinghies that migrants have used for unauthorized entry and left behind with belongings such as wet blankets, plastic water bottles and plastic boots.

Considerable numbers of undocumented migrants manage to arrive on Lesbos every year. Figures from the Lesbos police department show that the number of arrests after clandestine arrival grew constantly in recent years: for example, 13,252 irregular boat migrants were apprehended in 2008, and 8,893 were apprehended in Mytilene in 2009. The total number of undocumented migrants arriving on the island every year is likely even higher, since it includes those who have not been detected and arrested by the authorities.

Given that the influx of undocumented migrants started at the beginning of that decade at a much lower rate of about a thousand boat people arriving per year,[5] the regional administration is clearly under pressure to deal with constantly growing numbers of desperate, frozen, hungry, wet foreigners appearing on the island's beaches. The local authorities organize and manage reception of these boat migrants in a framework set by national budget possibilities and national asylum and migration law on one hand, and EU policies and approaches towards irregular immigration on the other.

But EU policy briefing and national regulations always leave room for varying modes of implementation under specific local, social and economic conditions. What really happens in the process of receiving undocumented migrants in the local context of a small island community is the focus of the following anthropological analysis. The next section investigates the ways and means of crossing a 'forbidden' maritime border in more detail, based on interviews and observations made during field research on Lesbos.[6]

Means and Ways of Illegal Border Crossing
in the North Aegean Sea

The maritime border between Lesbos and Turkey, which is about a hundred nautical miles (approximately 180 km) in length, cannot be guarded by fences and wire netting.[7] The sea works as both barrier and bridge, providing chances for small boats to cross the border clandestinely. The system of border patrol developed by the Greek port police in cooperation with the Greek army[8] is not effective enough to completely prevent clandestine border crossing. Despite efforts to prevent undocumented entry through improved border control, figures show that more than a thousand people a year manage to enter the island of Lesbos at points other than the authorized control post, having crossed the sea between Turkey and Lesbos in various types of boats and in different-sized groups. Participant observation on Lesbos and interviews with the port authorities in Mytilene provided data on the ways and means used to enter Greek waters.[9]

First, there are the small inflatable rubber dinghies usually used by tourists to paddle near the beach. Small groups of undocumented mi-

Figure 11.1. Remains of inflatable dinghies on a remote beach on Lesbos. (Photo: Jutta Lauth Bacas)

grants (usually four to six people) squeeze together to enter Greece clandestinely in these overloaded, barely seaworthy boats. They are of mixed composition: young men and women, families with small children, minors without family members, sick and elderly people. In interviews with the Greek authorities or journalists, they speak openly about the costs of this dangerous trip: the organizers of the passage (who probably operate on both sides of the Greek-Turkish border) usually charge about €1,000 per person. Before leaving Turkey, passengers are instructed on how to cross the sea channel and row towards one of the remote beaches of Lesbos (six to seven hours of rowing).

The migrants also carry instructions on how to react, should the Greek coastguard discover them on the open sea: to prevent being immediately sent back, they sometimes puncture the rubber dinghy with a knife, causing the inflatable boat to sink immediately. The undocumented boat migrants risk their lives in this way because by intentionally becoming shipwrecked, they trigger a Greek coastguard rescue operation (according to the International Law of the Sea), whereby every effort is made to save them, regardless of their lack of authorization to enter the country. Of course the whole procedure of an intentional shipwrecking and subsequent rescue is highly dangerous, especially in those frequent cases where undocumented migrants are not equipped with life jackets, and strong winds and heavy seas complicate the manoeuvres of the Greek coastguard.

Second, fibreglass or inflatable boats with outboard motors carry larger groups of about ten to fifteen persons. Because passage in a wooden or plastic boat with an outboard motor is thought to be quicker and safer, it is also more expensive; boat migrants say it costs more than €1,000 per person to be brought to the Greek shores of Lesbos by motorboat. In reality, crossing in this sort of boat is as dangerous as using a small inflatable one, because often the boats are not seaworthy and are overloaded with passengers. Under conditions of strong winds and rough seas, boat migrants who are unfamiliar with the dangers of the Mediterranean Sea put their lives at risk. Again and again accidents happen, and the Greek coastguard makes great efforts to save helpless shipwrecked foreigners. For example, on 23 August 2005, I witnessed a rescue operation off the north coast of Lesbos. Coastguard officers with patrol boats from Mytilene and the Molivos harbour spent many hours searching for approximately fifty shipwrecked migrants whose wooden boat had broken apart north of Molivos. The crew of the port police patrol boat managed to rescue forty-one migrants in a 26-hour period, but the others were never found and presumed drowned.[10] Dozens of cases of drowning fatalities on the maritime border between Greece and Turkey and are regularly documented every year by reports in the media.[11]

Figure 11.2. Inflatable dinghies kept in Mytilene harbour after confiscation by the Greek harbour police. (Photo: Jutta Lauth Bacas)

Not all boat migrants are forced to put their lives at risk. A sort of 'class system' is discernible in irregular border crossings on the Aegean. More affluent boat migrants can afford a 'luxury version' of maritime border crossing in modern, well-equipped high-tech speedboats whose heavy engines accelerate very fast to reach the Greek shores literally in fifteen minutes. Since the risk of being discovered and caught by the Greek coastguard is far lower, this kind of passage costs more than €2,000 per passenger.[12] Dozens of confiscated speedboats and brand-new inflatable dinghies with expensive high-power outboard motors, intended for smuggling undocumented migrants to Lesbos, are docked in Mytilene harbour as witness to successful counter-operations by the Greek coastguard.

Although the strait between Turkey and Lesbos is so narrow that the opposite coast is visible at night to the naked eye, navigation is a challenge for transit migrants from Central Africa or Asia. According to information given to the local press, in some cases undocumented migrants, upon entering Greek waters, have used mobile phones to launch 'Mayday' calls directly to the Mytilene harbour asking the Greek port authorities to start search-and-rescue operations. Local media also report cases of coastguard patrol boats, navy ships and Greek army helicopters launching rescue operations along the coastline following reports of survivors.[13]

The protection owed to shipwrecked foreign passengers is not always granted to undocumented migrants in boats still afloat. Foreign boats in the middle of the strait trying to proceed into Greek national waters are sometimes systematically discouraged or repelled by coastguard action. Local newspapers report often on cases of small boats being forced to return to the Turkish part of the channel.[14] To mention but one of many similar reports, on the same night that twenty-six immigrants managed to reach the island's shores, two other boats with nine persons on board were discovered by Greek patrol boats and forced to return to Turkish waters.[15] The Greek patrol boats' operations to prevent undocumented foreign vessels from entering Greek national waters are clearly legal acts in compliance with the Schengen Agreement, which obliges Greece to guard the Greek-Turkish border as one of the external borders of the EU. Since 2007, the guarding of this maritime border has been reinforced by FRONTEX (an acronym for the European Agency for the Management of Operational Cooperation at the External Borders of the Member States of the European Union) operations in which other European states support the local authorities in the border patrol.

Cases of 'prevention' of entry into national waters (in Greek, αποτροπή), documented by the Greek coastguard, sometimes merit mention in the local newspaper as 'mixed local news'. Mytilene inhabitants familiar with the local conditions understand from these items that the coastguard patrol and the foreign ship were so close that the patrol could clearly count the number of migrants on board. These and other boat people were not rescued but made to return. In this and other cases, proximity in maritime border encounters is not effected to save people's lives, but to threaten foreigners and discouraging them from entering the Greek part of the strait.

As I have shown, in spite of efforts to prevent undocumented entry with an elaborate system of border controls, the sea channel inevitably provides plenty of opportunities for unauthorized border crossing. The available data on apprehended migrants at the sea border indicate a constant increase in the maritime migration flow from Turkey to Lesbos (from 1,037 apprehensions in 2003 to 8,893 apprehensions in 2009, as stated earlier). Also worth mentioning is that parallel to the growing numbers of illegal border crossings, the amount of money transferred from undocumented migrants to smugglers and boat owners increased as well. In June 2002, the local newspaper *Aeolian News* (Αιολικά Νέα) reported that in one case of smuggling forty-three persons from the Turkish coast to Lesbos, the smuggling ring was said to have made a profit of $107,500.[16] According to my own research data on the Mytilene-Ayvalik-Dikkili triangle, the money circulating for the illegal smuggling of people in the period 2003 to 2005 amounted to approximately €5,000,000 (Lauth Bacas 2006: 103).

This chapter's analysis of unauthorized migration from Turkey across the Aegean Sea will next report on the treatment of those who manage to enter Greek national territory and become subjects of investigation and administrative apprehension.

Entering the Detention Centre

This section follows the structure of the administrative detention procedure. First it describes the process of entering the detention centre in the island's capital; then it analyses the relevant legal regulations and the procedure for leaving the camp. Based on data gained by participant observation in Mytilene, this presentation aims to give an overview of how the detention of unauthorized migrants at the Greek-Turkish maritime border works.[17] For reasons of analytical preciseness I must stress that the following description refers to the situation as it could be observed in the fieldwork period between 2004 and 2008. Changes regarding the reception of undocumented boat migrants on Lesbos that occurred after 2009 will be discussed in an epilogue.

Sometimes, local fishermen are the first to encounter boat migrants who manage to arrive on Greek shores after their difficult passage. But since lack of a common language usually limits communication considerably and locals are afraid of being accused of smuggling, they often keep away from the newcomers and let the port police patrolling the coastline step in. The first act of the Greek port police, upon encountering newly arrived boat people, is to arrest them (including babies and small children) for illegal entry into the country. Thus the migrants' first personal contacts in Europe occur between themselves and police officers – individuals who are in a hierarchical and antagonistic standing. Again, the means of communication between migrants without documents and representatives of the Greek state are limited. Interpreters who know non-European languages are often unavailable, so state representatives have to use their basic school English. They usually ask the newcomers to choose one member of their group as a translator to answer questions about the primary identification of the newly arrived. The port and police officers representing the Greek state perceive the entire group of exhausted, tired, hungry boat migrants as suspects – not as people in need, but as subjects breaking visa regulations and national laws. In line with this official viewpoint, all such newcomers are branded 'illegal' with regard to their entry and put in administrative detention (i.e., without a court ruling). The undocumented migrants, on the other hand, see their arrival in the provincial town of Mytilene as one of many stopovers on their long journey to Western European centres. Some of them seem to be well informed about what awaits them (a stay at the detention centre) and come equipped with the will to survive and move on later.

After the arrest, a file is opened with the personal data of the newly arrived persons. At that stage of the interaction, the police officers are interested only in the newcomers' basic personal data, not in the reasons or circumstances of their flight to Europe. Answers regarding their names, surnames, fathers' and mothers' names are added to official lists in Greek letters (of course transliteration problems abound). Police officers are well aware of the fact that the local authorities cannot confirm the data given during the interview (name, surname, age, nationality), as most boat migrants do not carry valid travel documents. 'We do not know who they are. We give them their identity', commented a local police officer.

The personal data and fingerprints taken during the first encounter with the Greek authorities in a peripheral harbour town are highly relevant to the future fate of any undocumented migrant in Greece and the Schengen Area as well. From that point on, the data typed in Greek files and documentation of the case are the only identity documents the immigrants can refer to in Greece and the European Union. They are held to be 'true' by all other institutions and persons involved with the reception of undocumented migrants. In other words, the Greek authorities reinvent or literally 'construct' people's identities in the paperwork they produce on their cases. The fingerprints are added to a large EU database for identifying asylum seekers and irregular border-crossers (called EURODAC, an acronym for *European Dactyloscopy*), through which the undocumented migrants' first place of entry into the EU territory can be traced later.

After this first interrogation, the group of newcomers is transferred to a closed detention centre, officially called a 'centre for the provisional stay of illegal migrants' (Κέντρο Προσωρινής Εγκατάστασης Λαθρομεταναστών). The one on the outskirts of the town of Mytilene was situated in an industrial area called Pagani (Παγανί), so locals referred to the centre as 'Pagani centre' in everyday discourse. For Greek NGOs, the word 'Pagani' has become synonymous with human rights violations and the systematic disregard of the needs of asylum seekers and refugees in Greece. The detention centre consisted of a two-storey factory building with six large holding compartments, locked and fenced by wire netting and guarded by police day and night. During the period of fieldwork in 2004–2008, civilians were not allowed to enter the Pagani centre (with some rare exceptions), and inmates were not permitted to move freely or

Figure 11.3. The Pagani holding centre with irregular migrants held in large compounds. (Photo: Jutta Lauth Bacas)

leave the centre, where they waited until administrative decisions on their future were taken.

The local administration provided catering services, lawyers and doctors were granted access to the camp and detainees were allowed to keep some pocket money (volunteers of the Greek Red Cross made purchases for them) and use their mobile phones. 'They make calls all day. They make calls to those back in Turkey or to people who stay in other camps or in Athens', I was told in an interview. Regular phone contacts, which serve to maintain ties with the homeland and with friends in other destination countries like Germany, Sweden or England, are said to be characteristic of undocumented migrants' life in transit (Papadopoulou 2005: 13).

But next to covering the basic needs of shelter and food, services provided for the detainees forced to stay at the centre were of a very poor quality in all the years of the Pagani centre's operation. The conditions for the arrested boat migrants had been so poor in its early years that local police officers organized a demonstration in August 2003 to protest against the situation inside the camp. The holding premises consisted of six large halls, which from the very beginning of the centre's operation were unsuitable for long-term detention. They were not divided into separate compounds, and the sleeping accommodations, which served about one hundred and fifty inhabitants per hall, did not provide any privacy. Sanitary conditions were absolutely poor (only two or three toilets and shower units per 100 persons) and were many times the target of criti-

Figure 11.4. Women and small children being held in detention for several weeks. (Photo: Jutta Lauth Bacas)

cal intervention the Athens-based branch of UNHCR, the UN Refugee Agency, which visited the camp regularly. The absence of competent interpreters meant that all the centre's personnel – social workers, doctors and the Greek guards – had extremely limited communication with the foreigners behind bars, and that the needs of specifically vulnerable groups were difficult to communicate and meet. The social setting in the holding premises of Pagani was clearly hierarchical. The foreign boat people were not treated as persons in need, but as 'illegals', giving rise to a hostile reinvention of the Other.

Instead of finding support and humanitarian aid, the boat people who arrived on Lesbos found themselves subjects of administrative detainment. Their expectations of a secure life in Europe clearly were not fulfilled. 'When can we finally leave for Athens?' a desperate Afghan mother asked me on the occasion of my visit to the women's compound. She had been detained at Pagani for twenty-two days, sharing one bed with her adolescent daughter and her son (Lauth Bacas 2008).

Meanwhile, the young police officers on duty at the detention centre perceived the undocumented migrants as suspects, rather than asylum seekers or potential refugees.[18] They approached the growing numbers of detainees with institutionalized disinterest, seeing it as part of their professional ethic not to get emotionally involved. Thus personal contacts and interaction between detainees and police personnel were kept to a minimum, for example, by communicating only with self-elected 'leaders' of groups of undocumented migrants. The general picture was that the newcomers were segregated and kept in custody in a transitional zone where they were made to wait for things to happen. This treatment defines a new set of boundaries inside Greek society that deny any regular status to newcomers on European soil.

Leaving the Detention Centre

During my anthropological fieldwork (in repeated visits to Mytilene between 2004 and 2008), detainment in the Pagani centre was limited to a period of six months, and in practice many boat migrants were released earlier.[19] During this detention period, the foreigners inside the camp had very little contact with local Greeks, aside from the police guards, local medical personnel, volunteers of the Greek Red Cross and a few Mytilene lawyers who sought professional access to the foreigners inside. Other official visitors included representatives of the Athens branch of UNHCR and of the Greek Council for Refugees, a non-governmental organization providing legal advice to asylum seekers and refugees. Although there was face-to-face interaction between local Greeks and foreigners in all those cases, relations with the Other were transient. Both sides knew the stay in the centre was provisional and the newcomers would have to leave the camp and the island of Lesbos in a few weeks.

Contacts with other locals rarely occurred, because except for the volunteers of the Greek Red Cross, they were not allowed to enter the camp. In discussions with people in Mytilene I found that some of them were aware of the problems in the Pagani centre. I was also told, and myself saw, that locals regularly donated clothes and blankets to the centre. But because of the camp's location on the outskirts of the city and the limited time undocumented migrants spent there, most of the locals paid little attention to the inadequacies of the reception structure. Also little remarked on was the fact that services provided to undocumented migrants created a source of income for certain members of the island community, with a share of government money going to a range of enterprises involved in maintaining the migrants living in the camp.

The boat migrants saw their stay at the Pagani holding centre as a provisional one, too. They knew that sooner or later they would be released. Indeed, after several weeks every detainee in the centre was handed a Greek document with information about his or her fate in Greece: the document was an official expulsion.[20] Signed by the Head of the Regional Police Department, it ordered the irregular immigrant to leave the country within four weeks at his or her own expense, and to a country of his or her own choice (!). Undocumented migrants from Asian and African countries were usually unable to read the Greek document or to appeal against the decision taken. But this was less important than a particular side effect of the expulsion order. According to Greek law, the authorities may permit a provisional stay whenever the immediate expulsion of an alien is not feasible (Kanellopoulos 2005: 37). As a practical consequence, the expulsion order handed to the undocumented migrant was combined with a provisional residence permit granted by the Greek Ministry of the Interior. This provisional stay was limited; similar to the expulsion order it ordered the undocumented migrant to leave the country within thirty days. But for four weeks he or she was granted a moratorium and allowed to move freely – and leave the island of Lesbos. Money and personal belongings were returned, and the undocumented migrant was released. 'They have lunch at the camp and then walk down to the harbour', explained the chief administrator of the camp.

It is important to note that in this situation, the legal expulsion of foreigners who came from countries like Iraq, Iran or Afghanistan was not followed by further state action. Irregular migrants arriving on Lesbos without a passport were not forcibly returned to Ayvalik or Dikkili (the opposite ports of entry in Turkey), regardless of the legal decision taken. Implementing the expulsion was not feasible for two reasons. First, undocumented migrants did not carry valid travel documents and the Turkish authorities did not accept their re-entry without the necessary documents. Second, an agreement between Greece and Turkey concerning readmission of third-country nationals who have entered either country unlawfully (signed in 2000 and reconfirmed in 2010) never came fully into effect (Baldwin-Edwards 2006: 120). The only border post functioning for purposes of readmission up to 2010 was situated in Northern Greece, in the Evros area. Forced returns from Mytilene to the opposite Turkish ports of Ayvalik or Dikkili were thus ruled out.

These problems with implementing the readmission agreement between Greece and Turkey meant that that after several weeks in administrative detention, all undocumented newcomers in Mytilene were de jure expelled and de facto released. The provisionally 'regularized' migrants usually set off for the town of Mytilene on foot.[21] In 2005, only 3 per cent of them chose to ask for political asylum on the island; all the rest decided to continue their journey to Athens.[22] At the harbour they were able, as holders of 'provisional residence permits', to buy third-class ferry tickets to Athens from the Lesbos Maritime Company, which was said to provide free transport for foreigners who were unable to pay their way to Athens. The aim of this procedure can be clearly understood as a way to export a possible social problem from the island to mainland Greece. After their release the migrants legally embarked on the afternoon ferry to Athens – under the eyes of the watching coastguards – and disembarked at Piraeus the next morning. Lesbos turned out to be just a transit point on the long trip to the West.

Social Profile of Undocumented Migrants to Lesbos

One of the main difficulties in the study of undocumented migration concerns numbers. The difficulty derives from the fact that irregular migration, due to its clandestine character, cannot easily be measured. Many reports on illegal migration use estimations or other indirect methods with little precision or reliability. Thus, these data sets offer only a rough indication of the number and profile of illegal immigrants. In the present case study on irregular boat migration to Lesbos, the chosen focus allows a more precise analysis of the number and the social profile of foreigners arriving without documents. Singling out one gate of entry gives access to local data, which provide evidence regarding the national identity of un-documented migrants arriving on the island. These data will be presented and analysed in the following section.

The first aspect to be discussed is the number of irregular arrivals on Lesbos in the period under investigation (2003–2009). The data provided by the regional police department refer to the annual number of undocu-mented migrants apprehended by both police and coastguard after clan-destine entry on the island. Since not all boat people arriving on Lesbos are seized and registered by the police, it must be assumed that besides the following official figures, there exist an additional number of unre-ported cases. Still, the official data clearly show the constant increase of undocumented arrivals and the consequent pressure on the local recep-tion structure.

Arrivals of Undocumented Migrants on Lesbos 2003–2009

	2003	2004	2005	2006	2007	2008	2009
Figures	1,037	1,453	1,696	1,766	6,147	13,252	8,896
Increase		+ 40%	+16%	+4%	+248%	+116%	–33%

Source: Lesbos Regional Police Department, information provided on 28 July 2010. For the period 2003–2005, also see Lauth Bacas (2006: 102).

Data from Lesbos show that 1,037 irregular migrants were arrested in 2003; in 2004, 2005 and 2006 their numbers grew constantly. From 2006 to 2007 a dramatic and unforeseen rise in the number of (registered) arrivals took place, bringing the population of boat migrants held in detention up to 6,147 persons. This increase of 248 per cent led to a complete overload of the holding centre, since the regional administration had not accord-ingly adjusted the accommodation possibilities – the numbers of beds, blankets, showers and toilets. The pressure on the local reception struc-ture increased even further in the following year 2008, when the number of undocumented boat migrants again nearly doubled to reach a total of 13,252 persons. This build-up resulted in about a thousand boat migrants per month being squeezed into detention facilities designed and equipped to hold a maximum of three hundred persons.[23]

Looking at the period from 2003 to 2009 in total, the main fact is a dra-matic rise in undocumented arrivals on the island of Lesbos, leading to a tenfold increase in the numbers of boat people in need of shelter and material support within half a decade. Comparing the year 2003, when 1,037 boat people arrived on Lesbos, with the year 2009, when their num-ber was 8,896 persons, one can realize the serious problems involved in their accommodation and proper reception. Only after 2008, when border

controls were tightened and the local coastguard received logistical rein-
forcement from FRONTEX, the EU agency for external border security, the
number of clandestine arrivals dropped. But although the figure in 2009
was reduced by a third in comparison to the year before, the total number
of boat people arriving on Lesbos in 2009 was still higher than the total in
2007, indicating that strict border control is no solution to irregular migration. The available data clearly show that in spite of the efforts of permanent border patrol, the island remains the main 'port of entry' for irregular
migrants arriving in the country by the maritime route.

The second aspect to be discussed is the national origin of undocumented migrants arriving on Lesbos. During the period under investigation, they came from more than twenty-one different countries of the Far
and Middle East, as well as from East African countries. The following
table on the national identity of migrants without documents presents the
findings in more detail.[24]

Nationality of Undocumented Migrants on Lesbos, 2005–2009

	2005	2006	2007	2008	2009
Afghanistan	54%	79%	77.3%	72.5%	60%
Pakistan	—	—	1.5%	0.5%	1%
Iraq	5% .	1.5%	2.5%	1.9%	0.7%
Iran	3%	5.9%	0.1%	0.3%	0.2%
Algeria	17%	1%	—	—	0.2%
Kurds	0.1%	0.9%	0.2%	0.1%	0.1%
Palestine	5%	3.2%	2.5%	0.1%	16%
Somalia	5.4%	4.9%	10%	16.5%	16.5%
Sudan	0.5%	—	0.3%	0.1%	0.1%
Eritrea	—	—	0.8%	2.5%	3.7%

Source: Lesbos Regional Police Department, information provided on 28 July 2010.
For the period 2003–2005, see also Lauth Bacas (2006: 102).

Certain patterns can be observed through analysis of the available data
on the national origin of undocumented migrants apprehended on Lesbos. As the second table above indicates, from 2005 to 2009 most boat
migrants apprehended on the island did not originate from neighbouring
Turkey, and even the Kurds formed a minority of less than 1 per cent of
the arriving boat people on Lesbos. Most of the newcomers had a much
longer journey to Europe, mainly from the Middle East (i.e., Afghanistan,
Palestine, Iraq and Iran) and from East Africa. Unauthorized migrants
from Afghanistan formed the largest group among those apprehended
in this period.

As early as 2005, boat migrants who declared Afghanistan their country of origin clearly formed a majority of 54 per cent of undocumented migrants arriving. In the following year, 2006, a majority of 79 per cent arrived from Afghanistan and another 5.9 per cent from Iran. In 2007 the number of those apprehended who declared Afghan origin was still high, and along with people from Iraq and Iran, a (small) number of Pakistanis arrived on the island, too, bringing the portion of boat migrants coming from those four countries in the Middle East to 82.4 per cent. In 2007, although migrant detainees on Lesbos originated from more than twenty countries, four out of every five had started from Afghanistan, Pakistan, Iraq or Iran. Obviously, for many irregular migrants from countries involved in armed conflicts, the island functions as a main 'port of entry' to Greece and the West in general. This might be related not just to military conflicts in their home countries, but also to ethnic networks involved in organizing the journey of young people from Turkey to Western Europe.[25] In 2008 and 2009, the percentage of the total of young Afghans dropped (although they remained the most populous group among the arrivals) only because of increased arrivals on the island by another group of desperate boat people: those from Somalia.

In the period under investigation, irregular migration from Somalia constantly increased (from 5.4 per cent in 2005 to 16.5 per cent in 2009), and undocumented migrants declaring Somalia as their home country formed the second largest group of arrivals in 2008 and 2009. Smaller numbers of migrants without documents arrived from other African countries like Sudan, Eritrea and Ethiopia (not mentioned in the table due to the small numbers, under 0.1% of arrivals), with the result that one of five boat people arriving on Lesbos in 2009 declared as their national origin the war-torn countries of Somalia, Sudan and Eritrea. In 2009, the number of Palestinians arriving on Lesbos suddenly jumped in comparison to previous years, probably in relation to the armed conflicts taking place in the Gaza strip.

As the available data on the national origin of undocumented migrants on Lesbos and their increase in certain years show, boat migrants' arrival on the island seems unsurprisingly to be linked to military conflicts in their countries of origin. Some of them might be eligible for refugee status, although only a very small number of the newly arrived handed in an asylum application in Mytilene (e.g., 73 of 8,898 undocumented migrants arriving in 2009, or 0.8 per cent). The topic of asylum and the problems connected to the asylum system in Greece will not be discussed further here. Nevertheless, it should be mentioned that one of the main problems of the local reception structure in the period under investigation is the lack of information provided to the newly arrived, combined with a lack of investigation mechanisms that help identify people seeking asylum at an early stage. As has been stressed elsewhere, as one of the new host countries for undocumented migrants, Greece is characterized by a lack of both material means and institutional framework to support the new-comers fleeing their countries (Skordas and Sitaropoulos 2004). Although the numbers of undocumented migrants and asylum applications in the country are constantly rising, Skordas and Sitaropoulos (2004) and others have criticized the Greek government for choosing an ambivalent position and thus appearing to wait for the undocumented migrants to one day leave the country and release the state bureaucracy from its social responsibility and the need for financial commitment.[26]

Proximity and Asymmetry in the Reception of Boat Migrants

This section discusses the social consequences of the frequent acts of ir-regular border crossing. Obviously, the strait between Lesbos and Turkey serves as a gateway to Europe regularly used by undocumented African and Asian boat people. Since many of them are immediately arrested and kept in detainment for several weeks or months, few islanders actually come into direct contact with the undocumented newcomers. Efforts are made to keep them as strangers in a transitional zone outside the island's capital.

An analysis of the social effects of irregular migration on the local com-munity should differentiate between different social groups making a liv-ing on Lesbos. Representatives of state institutions – police officers, coast-guards and employees of the regional administration – form a relevant social group in the local community that takes a specific professionalized approach vis-à-vis the unauthorized migrants. As was argued earlier, in the interaction between civil servants and boat migrants, proximity is managed through asymmetry and by establishing hierarchical control. Chances are that this institutionalized hierarchy gives rise to a hostile and xenophobic positioning of the Other, especially when boat migrants are not perceived as people seeking refuge but as suspects who are 'guilty' of illegal entry into state territory.

I emphasize that this social and legal construction and positioning of the Other is apparent not only locally, but on the national and European levels as well. In the framework of the European Pact on Immigration and Asylum, EU member states jointly decided in 2008 to tackle illegal immi-gration, with the result that state employees on Europe's periphery have little room for manoeuvre in their everyday interactions with irregular migrants. As fieldwork data clearly show, the institutionalized and hierarchical form of reception of undocumented boat migrants on a Greek border island relied not on the well-known hospitality of the Greeks, but on locking the newcomers in a segregated space.

The local media kept the townspeople of Mytilene well informed about the problems of immigrant reception and the unacceptable living conditions in the Pagani holding centre. Some of them might nevertheless have agreed, openly or silently, to the segregation of the undocumented migrants, an assent linked to their impression of a social threat to the local population in the form of outsiders carrying 'strange' objects like viruses or bacteria (bringing the danger of diseases) and maybe small amounts of drugs. This segment of locals perceived the arrival of undocumented migrants as an exception, despite its being a regular, daily phenomenon. With hundreds of irregular migrants arriving every week in 2008 and 2009, the newcomer was no longer conceptualized as a guest, with whom face-to-face interaction takes place according to culturally elaborated rules, but as a stranger, who has to be kept away from the personal sphere to minimize encounters and possible threats. In the case of undocumented migrants crossing the Greek-Turkish border irregularly, social developments in a tense border setting gave rise to some hostile positioning of the cultural meaning of the Other, as expressed by some of the locals.

Other inhabitants of the island took a differing viewpoint, expressing more sympathy for foreigners who had left home and country to flee armed conflicts or war. For example, the owner of a photocopy shop in Mytilene's commercial centre was very clear in his approach towards arriving boat migrants: 'They are poor guys, anyway. What can we do? We cannot shoot them on the sea border!'[27] This positive attitude is sometimes related to the lived memory of another period in the island's crisis-ridden history: 1922 and 1923, when numerous Greek refugees arrived on the shores of Lesbos (and many other Greek islands near the Turkish border) after their forced expulsion from Asia Minor and the population exchange between Greece and Turkey according to the Treaty of Lausanne (1923).

Even today, many children and grandchildren of the Greek boat migrants who fled Asia Minor in 1922 and 1923 still live on Lesbos, keeping memories and moving stories of persecution, flight and escape alive (Lauth Bacas 2003). These family histories cause parts of the island's population to perceive the present arrival of foreign boat migrants with a certain understanding and empathy. They regularly donate second-hand items to the camp and participate in all kinds of solidarity activities organized by charity groups on the island. These are important contributions by a local civil society on the island, but it lacks the influence to alter the institutional setting of boat migrants' reception, which is organized by establishing hierarchical control according to European concepts of migration management and the fight against illegal immigration.

In summary, irregular boat migration can be understood as a relevant phenomenon in a maritime borderland that has traditionally been a transitional zone, and as a hint that remote Greek islanders are becoming more 'European'. Lesbos, as a peripheral border island at Europe's south-eastern end, is becoming more and more integrated into the complex international migration processes and flows of undocumented migrants and asylum seekers that have affected Greece since the 1990s.[28] In the framework of the island's reception structure, foreigners arriving on remote shores are not perceived as people in need of support and humanitarian aid; instead, a hostile positioning is carried out with their arrest for illegal entry into the country. The conclusion is that Europe's south-eastern maritime borders, with intensified border patrolling (as described in Lauth Bacas 2005) and increased FRONTEX operations, exhibit parallel tendencies of intensified cultural boundary construction and sharpening segregation between 'us' and the 'Other' who arrives as an uninvited migrant from a non-European country.

Epilogue

As already mentioned, the reception structure for undocumented boat migrants on the Greek island of Lesbos has undergone several changes. This epilogue updates the information given and briefly relates the most significant changes on the local level after 2009.

The most important change regarding the detention centre in Mytilene occurred in October 2009, when living conditions in Pagani were extremely problematic due to the high number of undocumented migrants detained there (more than seven hundred people squeezed in rooms designed for only three hundred persons). Several NGOs, such as the Greek branch of UNHCR[29] and the German Pro Asyl, had published critical reports on serious omissions from their proper reception.[30] Following these reports and their widespread discussion in the local, national and international press, the then newly appointed Vice Minister of the Ministry of Citizen Protection Spyros Vougias visited the detention centre on 22 October 2009. It was the first visit of a high-ranking state representative since the opening of the centre at Mytilene.

Although he had already been informed by various written reports, the vice minister was deeply shocked on seeing with his own eyes the overcrowded holding halls, the babies and toddlers of boat migrants locked

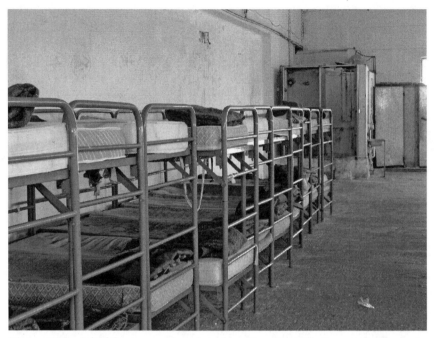

Figure 11.5. A holding compound and sanitary installation at the Pagani detention centre used by more than one hundred inhabitants. (Photo: Jutta Lauth Bacas)

behind bars, the filthy toilets and sanitary facilities. His comment – right on the spot, in the presence of press reporters – was that Pagani was worse than 'Dante's Inferno'.[31] He apologized to the detainees and took the decision to close down the Pagani detention centre the very same day.[32]

The closing of the 'centre for the provisional stay of illegal migrants' solved one problem but caused another: once the operation of the Pagani centre ceased as an organized site where shelter and food was provided to newly arrived undocumented migrants, no other place for their reception on Lesbos was available for months. The result was that the Pagani centre started operating again unofficially: the building site was opened again but not guarded by the police.[33] Undocumented migrants arriving in Mytilene had no other place. They used the worn-out beds and filthy blankets for a stopover of one night and the following day were sent on the regular ferry to the official reception centre on the neighbouring island of Chios. The need for a reception infrastructure was finally met by the Lesbos police department's decision to keep newly arrived boat migrants in holding premises within the police department in Mytilene. Future research has to document this development in more detail and analyse future developments in the relationship between proximity and asymmetry in the social interactions of locals and foreign boat migrants on a border island at Europe's south-easternmost fringe.

Notes

1. Press release in the local newspaper *Empros* (in Greek Εμπρός), 15 June 2007.
2. The Schengen Agreement, a treaty that came into effect after 1985, led to the removal of systematic border controls between participating EU countries and at the same time enhanced border controls at entry points to the Schengen Area. In 2010, the Schengen Area consisted of 25 EU member states, including Greece.
3. Fieldwork was conducted between 2004 and 2008 on Lesbos as well as in inner urban Athens, following the principle route of unauthorized entry from Turkey across the Aegean Sea to Central Greece. Research was supported by the Research Commission of the Academy of Athens (K.A.2000/591).
4. As Greek and Turkish national statistics show, Greek tourism to Turkey has been increasing steadily since 2000. See Lauth Bacas (2003: 249).
5. According to figures provided by the Lesbos Police department, the number of unauthorized arrivals in 2003 (when the documentation started) was 1,037 persons.
6. The fieldwork on which the present chapter is based took place during annual visits to Mytilini/Lesbos in the period 2004–2008. The following description refers to the situation as it was observed in the mentioned fieldwork period. The epilogue to this chapter discusses relevant changes after 2009.
7. In the growing literature on the anthropology of borders, the Mexican-U.S. border with its sophisticated surveillance installations has become a paradigm of border control against irregular migration (see Alvarez 1995). The sea route for irregular entry, increasingly chosen on Europe's Southern borders, is only recently investigated by social scientist (see Albahari in the present volume).
8. On border patrol and border control mechanisms in the North Aegean see also Lauth Bacas (2005) and Lauth Bacas (2010: 154–156).
9. Besides interviews with Greek coastguard officers and data on confiscated boats collected in Mytilini, participant observation was done by joining the night shift of Patrol Boat L.S. 602 on 1 September 2005.
10. Maritime Limnos Radio launched a 'men overboard' warning for the next twenty-four hours, asking ships in the vicinity to keep a sharp lookout. But the eight or nine missing persons were never found.
11. Monthly reports on deaths at EU borders, including Greece's, are prepared by the Platform for International Cooperation on Undocumented Migrants (PICUM). See http://www.picum.org. In 2009, 83 undocumented migrants were reported to have drowned at the maritime border between Turkey and Greece. In 2011, the UN Refugee Agency put the number of dead and missing on the Greek-Turkish maritime border at 51 persons. Retrieved 30 April 2013 from http://www.unhcr.org/pages/4a1d406060.html.
12. Data were provided orally by officers of Mytilini coastguard and also online by the Greek Ministry of the Merchant Marine (retrieved 30 April 2013 from http://www.yen.gr/wide/yen.chtm?prnbr=32029).
13. The local newspaper *Empros* (Εμπρός) reports frequently on such search-and-rescue operations in Mytilene. For example, see the report published on 3 June 2007.

14. For a critical discussion of maritime operations of the Hellenic Coast Guard see Lauth Bacas (2010: 156). Hess and Tsianos (2004) and Karakayali and Tsianos (2005) report on strategies and experiences of illegal border crossing based on anthropological research in the Ayvalik area.
15. Press report in the *Aeolian News* (Αιολικά Νέα) on 3 August 2004.
16. Press report in the *Aeolian News* (Αιολικά Νέα) on 22 July 2002.
17. As a rule, only lawyers and relatives of inmates are allowed to visit the Pagani Holding Centre. At the request of the Academy of Athens, I was permitted to visit the centre on 5 August 2004 and 13 September 2008.
18. Evi Voutira (2003) has analysed the etic and emic meaning of 'refugee' in Greek discourses.
19. Until August 2005, the average duration of detention was three months (Spathana 2003). In July 2009, a new presidential decree extended the legally allowed detention period to six months.
20. Foreign smugglers arrested by the Mytilini coastguard underwent a different procedure. They were accused of illegal trafficking in immigrants and a court case was opened. For example, the Mytilini court sentenced a Turkish human-smuggler to seven years in prison and a fine of €14,600, as the *Aeolian News* (Αιολικά Νέα) reported on 17 April 2004.
21. It is important to note that this type of provisional 'regularization' of migrants without documents who cross the Aegean differs from the regularization offered to undocumented economic migrants in Greece in 2001 and again in 2005. For the regularization of the latter, see Fakiolas (2003) and Cavounidis (2006).
22. Source: Lesbos Regional Police Department. For 2005, see also Lauth Bacas (2006: 102).
23. Source: Lesbos Regional Police Department, information provided on 28 July 2010. For the period 2003–2005, see also Lauth Bacas (2006: 102).
24. Source: Lesbos Regional Police Department, information provided on 28 July 2010. For the period 2003–2005, see also Lauth Bacas (2006: 111).
25. Ethnic networks are reported to play a major role in organizing irregular entry of Kurdish refugees into Greece by the land route in the Epiros area of Northern Greece. See Papadopoulou (2004).
26. Essed and Wesenbeeck (2004) discuss the link between the Declaration of Human Rights and social responsibility for those who flee home and country and become refugees in Europe.
27. Personal communication in Mytilene on 17 August 2009.
28. Anthias and Lazaridis (1999) and King, Lazaridis and Tsardanidis (2000) have presented research results on the new migration flows to the Southern Mediterranean countries of Spain, Italy and Greece since the 1990s.
29. Press release of UNHCR Greece No. 41/09 of 25 October 2009: Καταγγελίες για κακοποίηση στο κέντρο κράτησης αλλοδαπών Παγανής, Λέσβου - Η Ύπατη Αρμοστεία ζητά σε βάθος έρευνα. Retrieved 30 April 2013 from http://www.unhcr.gr/nea/deltiatypoy/2009/artikel/0270083455c7e4989c753b110fc79e93/kataggelies-gia-kak.html.
30. Press release of Pro Asyl of 24 July 2009: 'Dramatische Zuspitzung der Situation von Flüchtlingen in der Ägäis'. Retrieved 30 April 2013 from http://www.proasyl.de/en/news/news-english/news/dramatische_zuspitzung_der_situation_von_fluechtlingen_in_der_aegaeis/.
31. Press release of Pro Asyl of 23 October 2009: 'Tauwetter in Dantes Inferno?' Retrieved 30 April 2013 from http://www.proasyl.de/en/news/news-english/news/tauwetter_in_dantes_inferno/.
32. Ministry of Citizen Protection 22 October 2009: Δελτίο Τύπου με την επίσκεψη του Υφυπουργού Προστασίας του Πολίτη κ. Σ. Βούγια στον Ειδικό Χώρο Παραμονής Αλλοδαπών Παγανής στην Μυτιλήνη. Retrieved 30 April 2013 from http://www.yptp.gr/index.php?option=ozo_content&lang=&perform=view&id=3026&Itemid=405.

33. I visited the officially closed and 'opened', but not guarded, site of Pagani on 3 August 2010.

References

Alvarez, R. 1995. 'The Mexican-US Border: The Making of Anthropology of Borderlands', *Annual Review of Anthropology* 24: 447–70.

Anthias, F. and G. Lazaridis (eds). 1999. *Into the Margins: Migration and Exclusion in Southern Europe*. Aldershot: Ashgate.

Baldwin-Edwards, M. 2006. 'Migration between Greece and Turkey: From the 'Exchange of Population' to the Non-recognition of Borders', *South-East Europe Review* 3: 115–22.

Cavounidis, J. 2006. 'Labour Market Impact of Migration: Employment Structures and the Case of Greece', *International Migration Review* 40(3): 635–60.

Clogg, R. 1992. *A Concise History of Modern Greece*. Cambridge: Cambridge University Press.

Essed, P. and R. Wesenbeeck 2004. 'Contested Refugee Status. Human Rights, Ethics and Social Responsibilities', in P. Essed, G. Frerks and J. Schrijvers (eds), *Refugees and the Transformation of Societies*. Oxford and New York: Berghahn Books, pp. 53–68.

Fakiolas, R. 2003. 'Regularising Undocumented Immigrants in Greece: Procedures and Effects', *Journal of Ethnic and Migration Studies* 29: 535–61.

Hess, S. and V. Tsianos. 2004. 'Europeanizing Transnationalism! Konturen des "europäischen Grenzregimes'''. Retrieved 30 April 2013 from http://www.transitmigration.org/home archiv.html.

Kanellopoulos, C. (in cooperation with M. Gregou and A. Petralias). 2005. *Illegal Resident Third Country Nationals in Greece: State Approaches towards Them, Their Profile and Social Situation*. Athens: Centre of Planning and Economic Research.

Karakayali, S. and V. Tsianos. 2005. 'Border Regimes on the South-eastern Border of Europe'. Retrieved 30 April 2013 from www.meltingpot.org/articolo4894.html.

King, R., G. Lazaridis and C. Tsardanidis (eds). 2000. *Eldorado or Fortress? Migration in Southern Europe*. London: Macmillan.

Lauth Bacas, J. 2003. 'Greek Tourists in Turkey: An Anthropological Case Study', *Journal of Mediterranean Studies* 13(2): 239–58.

———. 2005. 'Marble Monuments and Symbolic Boundaries on Lesbos: A Case Study from the Greek-Turkish Border', in T.M. Wilson and H. Donnan (eds), *Culture and Power at the Edges of the State: National Support and Subversion in European Border Regions*. Berlin: LIT, pp. 55–80.

———. 2006. 'Maritime Borders and Undocumented Migration: The Maritime Road to Greece', in L. Stylianoudi (ed.), *Greek Society*. Yearbook of the Research Centre for Greek Society No. 6. Athens: Academy of Athens, pp. 95–139 (in Greek).

———. 2008. 'Impressions and Encounters at the Detention Centre Pagani on Lesbos', *When Escape Comes Up Against a Brick Wall: 11th European Conference on Asylum, Mytilene, 17. 9. bis 24. 9. 2008*. Düsseldorf: Evangelische Kirche im Rheinland, pp. 51–53.

———. 2010. 'No safe haven: The reception of irregular boat migrants in Greece', in: K. Roth and J. Lauth Bacas (eds), *Migration in, from, and to South Eastern Europe: Part 2 Ways and Means of Migrating*, Ethnologia Balkanica, vol. 14. Berlin: LIT, pp. 147–169.

Papadopoulou, A. 2004. 'Smuggling into Europe: Transit Migrants in Greece', *Journal of Refugee Studies* 17(2): 167–84.

———. 2005. *Exploring the Asylum-migration Nexus: A Case Study of Transit Migrants in Europe*. Global Migration Perspectives Series No. 23. Geneva: Global Commission on International Migration. Retrieved 30 April 2013 from http://www.iom.int/jahia/webdav/site/ myjahiasite/shared/shared/mainsite/policy_and_research/gcim/gmp/gmp23.pdf.

Skordas, A. and N. Sitaropoulos. 2004. 'Why Greece Is Not a Safe Host Country for Refugees', *International Journal of Refugee Law* 16 (1): 25–52.

Spathana, E. 2003. *Legal Advice to Refugees and Asylum Seekers in Greece.* Athens: Greek Council for Refugees (in Greek).

Tzimis, S. et al. 1996. *History of Lesbos,* 2nd, rev. ed. Mytilene: Association of Philologists (in
Greek).

Voutira, E. 2003. 'Refugees: Whose Term Is It Anyway? Emic and Etic Construction of "Refugees" in Modern Greece', in J. van Selm, K. Kamanga, J. Morisson, A. Nadig, S. Vrzina
and L. van Willigen (eds), *The Refugee Convention at Fifty: A View from Forced Migration
Studies.* New York: Lexington Books, pp. 65–80.

Contributors

Maurizio Albahari is assistant professor of anthropology and fellow at the Nanovic Institute for European Studies, University of Notre Dame (USA). Albahari received his PhD in anthropology from the University of California at Irvine (2006) and held research fellowships at the Center for Comparative Immigration Studies (University of California at San Diego) and at the Erasmus Institute (University of Notre Dame). He has authored several articles on the relationships between Euro-Mediterranean geopolitical borders and social boundaries of inclusion, and edited a migration-themed issue of *Italian Culture* (Vol. 28, 2010). His current research interests bridge epistemology, democracy and pluralism in urban Europe.

Laura Assmuth is professor of social policy at the University of Eastern Finland with specialization in border areas and migration. She holds a PhD in social anthropology (University of Helsinki). She has carried out ethnographic fieldwork in Southern Italy and Sardinia, and more recently in Estonia, Latvia, North-West Russia and Eastern Finland. She has directed several international research projects on cultural and social change in post-socialist Baltic countries, published for example in *Focaal: European Journal of Anthropology* (2003) and the edited volume *Culture and Power at the Edges of the State: National Support and Subversion in European Border Regions* (Lit Verlag, 2005).

Daphne Berdahl (1964–2007) was associate professor of anthropology and global studies at the University of Minnesota. She earned a PhD in anthropology from the University of Chicago. She worked on the relationship between mass consumption, globalization and changing understandings and practices of citizenship in post-Wall Germany and was the author of *Where the World Ended: Re-Unification and Identity in the German Borderland* (University of California Press, 1999) and co-editor (with M. Bunzl and M. Lampland) of *Altering States: Ethnographies of Transition in East Central*

Europe and the Former Soviet Union (University of Michigan Press, 2000). In 2007 she was awarded the John Simon Guggenheim Fellowship.

Lisa Dikomitis is research fellow at the Hull York Medical School. She gained her PhD in comparative sciences of cultures from Ghent University (Belgium). She is the author of *Cyprus and Its Places of Desire: Cultures of Displacement Among Greek and Turkish Cypriot Refugees* (IB Tauris, 2012) and co-editor of *When God Comes to Town: Religious Traditions in Urban Contexts* (Berghahn Books, 2009). She has published widely about Greek and Turkish Cypriot refugees. Currently, she is preparing a monograph based on her long-term fieldwork in a psychiatric hospital in Belgium.

William Kavanagh holds a doctorate in social anthropology from the University of Oxford and is lecturer in anthropology and sociology at CEU San Pablo University and the Madrid campuses of New York University and Suffolk University. His research focuses on borders, nationalism, and protected areas in central Spain, Galicia and northern Portugal and his publications include *Villagers of the Sierra de Gredos* (Berg Publishers, 1994) and the Disappearing World documentary film of the same title. Co-founder of the Mediterraneanist Network of EASA, he is on the executive committees of two Spanish anthropological associations and is a delegate on the World Council of Anthropological Associations.

Jutta Lauth Bacas holds a doctorate in social anthropology from the University of Zurich with a special focus on migration studies. She has held teaching positions at universities in both Switzerland and Germany and also worked as a researcher at the Academy of Athens, Greece. She has published widely on labour migration to Switzerland, on marriage migration, and on irregular migration to Greece, focusing on questions of migration pathways and on the analysis of cross-cultural contacts and identity formation. Co-founder of the Mediterraneanist Network of EASA, she is a member of the advisory board of InASEA and co-editor of issues of Ethnologia Balkanica and the Journal of Mediterranean Studies.

Birgit Müller (PhD Cambridge 1986) is senior researcher at LAIOS (Laboratoire de l'anthropologie des institutions et organisations sociales), CNRS, in Paris. Since 1990, her research has focused on questions of power, ideology and economic change in East Germany and the Czech Republic. She has written about the informal functioning of the planned economy, post-socialist labour struggles, grass-roots democratization and environmental mobilizations in post-socialist countries. Her current research explores global governmentality of food and agriculture at the FAO and local practices of food producers in Canada and Nicaragua, examining links between agricultural practice, political world views and structures of power.

Robert Parkin is departmental lecturer in social anthropology at the Institute of Social and Cultural Anthropology, University of Oxford, where among other things he runs a course on the anthropology of Europe, which he also offered to students at Vytautis Magnus University, Kaunas, Lithuania, in April 2013. He has written books and articles on kinship, religion and symbolism, Indian tribes and the history of French anthropology. His most recent field research has been on politics, identity and popular responses to the EU on the German-Polish border.

Mathijs Pelkmans is senior lecturer in anthropology at the London School of Economics. He holds a PhD from the University of Amsterdam and worked as a research fellow at the Max Planck Institute for Social Anthropology from 2003 to 2006. Over the past fifteen years he has carried out extensive fieldwork in Georgia and Kyrgyzstan. He is the author of *Defending the Border: Religion, Politics, and Modernity in the Georgian Borderlands* (Cornell University Press, 2006) and editor of *Conversion after Socialism* (Berghahn Books, 2009) and *Ethnographies of Doubt* (IB Tauris, in press).

Cosmin Radu is a PhD candidate in sociology at the University of Bristol, UK. He holds an MPhil in social anthropology from the University of Manchester and an MA in sociology and social anthropology from CEU Budapest. His interests include border crossings and dwellings, illegality and smuggling, spacetime, landscape and subjectivity. His recent publications in peer-reviewed journals include 'Beyond Border-"dwelling": Temporalising the Border-space through Events' (2010), *Anthropological Theory* 10(4), and 'Border Tricksters and the Predatory State: Contraband at the Romania-Serbia Border during the Yugoslavian Embargoes' (2009), *Focaal: Journal of Global and Historical Anthropology* 54.

Tatiana Zhurzhenko is currently a postdoctoral researcher at the Aleksanteri Institute, University of Helsinki. She studied political economy and social philosophy at V.N. Karazin Kharkiv National University (Ukraine), where she later worked as associate professor (1993–2010). From 2007 to 2011 she was an Elise Richter Research Fellow at the Department of Political Science, University of Vienna. Her research interests focus on transformation processes in post-Soviet societies, especially Ukraine. She has published numerous articles and books, including *Borderlands into Bordered Lands: Geopolitics of Identity in Post-Soviet Ukraine* (Ibidem 2010, co-winner of the 2010 AAUS Prize and winner of the 2012 Bronze Award of the Association for Borderlands Studies).

Index